Shooter's GUIDE TO SHOTGUN SPORTS FOR WOMEN

D1089359

▲ Credit: Collection of the author.

Shooter's Bible®
GUIDE TO
SHOTGUN SPORTS
FOR WOMEN

A Comprehensive Guide to the Art
and Science of Wing and Clay Shooting

Laurie Bogart Wiles
Introduction by John Wiles

SKYHORSE PUBLISHING

Skyhorse Publishing books may be purchased in bulk at special discounts for sales promotion, corporate gifts, fund-raising, or educational purposes. Special editions can also be created to specifications. For details, contact the Special Sales Department, Skyhorse Publishing, 307 West 36th Street, 11th Floor, New York, NY 10018 or info@skyhorsepublishing.com.

Skyhorse® and Skyhorse Publishing® are registered trademarks of Skyhorse Publishing, Inc.®, a Delaware corporation.

Visit our website at www.skyhorsepublishing.com.

10 9 8 7 6 5 4 3 2 1

Library of Congress Cataloging-in-Publication Data is available on file.

Cover design by Daniel Brount
Cover photo credit: Ryan Stalvey

Print ISBN: 978-1-5107-4503-2
Ebook ISBN: 978-1-5107-4504-9

Printed in China

To
KARL GRAFTON WILES

"And place your hands below your husband's foot:
In token of which duty, if he please,
My hand is ready; may it do him ease."
—WILLIAM SHAKESPEARE
Katherina's closing speech from *The Taming of the Shrew*

Books by the Author

CONTENTS

his book isn't about me, but you need to know a little something about me to understand whether I am qualified to help my wonderful wife, Laurie, in her endeavor. I have loved and been a part of the outdoors since I was just about old enough to walk. In the American South, where I was raised, Tennessee to be exact, bird hunting was a way of life. If you had bird dogs, they were pointers or setters. If you went bird hunting, you were hunting bobwhite quail. If you went grouse hunting, you said you were going grouse hunting, but if you were *bird hunting*, you were quail hunting, and quail were pretty much everywhere.

Sixty years ago, sprawling subdivisions, pesticides, too many vermin, and too many hunters had not yet come on the scene. It was the 1950s, a time for prosperity, family, church, friendships, and bird hunting. And my dad loved bird hunting. He loved dove shooting, too. We called it dove shooting because you weren't dove hunting, you were going to a place where you knew there were plenty of doves and you were going to be able to shoot a lot. If you were a very good shot, a box of twenty-five shells would get you your limit of twelve.

Bird hunters were a close-knit group. You went bird hunting with a friend, and your dogs and his dogs were in competition for which one had the best nose, best point, best retrieve, or the softest mouth when retrieving. A bird dog needed to do four things—point, back, retrieve, and load. Point the birds; stop and honor another dog who found the birds first; locate and retrieve downed birds; and jump in the back of the truck, usually into their own dog crates for travel to and from the fields. Bird hunting was classy stuff.

Dove shooting, on the other hand, was a social event. There might be ten or twelve hunters around a cut corn, wheat, milo, or sorghum field that was being frequented by large numbers of little rockets, called doves—mourning doves, to be exact. Doves fly in the morning and in the evening, and most Southern hunts back then were afternoon hunts. Usually we braved the hot afternoon sun, around one o'clock, to make sure we got a good spot on the field where we felt sure the doves would either approach toward or retreat from. If you were a good shot, and you limited out (got your limit) rather quickly because you found a good

spot, you went on back to the truck, and someone who had a worse spot in the field took your place.

Bragging rights were applied around the trucks when it was acknowledged that Old Tom, or George, or Bill, or whomever, had gotten his limit in fifteen minutes, or twenty, with fifteen shots, or seventeen, or less than a box of shells, and Old Tom, George, or Bill, usually quite humbly, mumbled, "It was nothing," or "I was just lucky." Eventually the social aspect of dove shooting evolved to a massive dove cleaning effort after the hunt, and the cleaned and washed birds were put on the grill, wrapped in bacon, or dipped in some sort of secret sauce, and then barbecued. All the participants shared stories, renewed friendships, laughed, ate doves prepared a variety of ways, and maybe drank a beer, but usually sweet tea, the essence of the South.

That love of shotguns, bird dogs, and dove shooting would be the basis for the following sixty years of my current seventy-year life. I had three world-class bird dogs whom I loved like children, and when they died, as bird dogs do, part of me died too. I buried the last one, blind and deaf but who could still find me by smell and love me in her heart, and that's when I said, "No more." The toll on me was too great, and the love too deep.

I have hunted quail all over the United States, and even in Mexico. I have shot doves in almost every state that offers a season on them, and that great love of dove shooting has taken me to Mexico, Colombia, Argentina, Bolivia, and Uruguay.

I moved to Maryland at age twenty-one and within a year had taken up goose hunting on Maryland's famed Eastern Shore. I loved Easton, Chestertown, and Centreville, and leased a farm for twelve years with a mile-and-a-quarter of waterfront on the Chester River. I got my professional guide's license and took people hunting for money. For quite a few years, I lived the waterfowl life most people can only dream about today and participated in hunts that would put the outdoor television shows of today to shame.

Waterfowl hunting took me to Canada, naturally, and then Mexico, and I have shot wild ducks and geese in Kansas, Arkansas, Mississippi, Missouri, North Carolina, South Carolina, Florida, Texas, and other states I don't even remember, plus Argentina, and driven ducks in Hungary, England, and France.

Quail hunting became more of a preserve sport after changes in farming practices and urban sprawl ruined most of the native quail coverts that were once so prevalent. Preserve hunting also allowed people to pheasant hunt over pointing dogs, and a lot of us liked it. I have hunted wild pheasants in just about every state that offers them and preserve pheasants in a lot more. I have shot driven pheasants in England, Scotland, Hungary, Slovakia, the Czech Republic, and France. I have checked a lot of boxes on my bucket list, including driven partridges in Spain, but there are still a few places I want to visit, shotgun in hand.

When I was young, my vision was terrible, and all I can say about that is thank God for glasses and contact lenses. I loved shooting and was a fair shot even as a young person, but my real skill in shooting grew out of the dove fields of Argentina.

Ah, Argentina, where the doves are considered pests: there are millions of them, and there is no limit. Shooting fifteen hundred shells a day, three days in a row, every three months for a couple of years, can make anyone an accomplished shot. With that kind of practice on doves or pigeons, you can keep your eye pretty well, even when age slows your reflexes and wears on your body.

At age sixty-five, I met the author of the book you are about to read. She was a published author, and we were brought together by an old mutual friend, Dez Young, who had a terrific run in outdoor television with his wingshooting shows, *Hunting with Hank* and *Dash in the Uplands*. Together our efforts produced a twenty-minute film based on a short story by Corey Ford, best known for his "Minutes of the Lower Forty" column in *Field & Stream* in the 1950s and 1960s. Written in 1965, "The Road to Tinkhamtown" is considered by many, me included, to be one of the greatest outdoor stories ever written. It is about a man's journey toward death and how his beloved hunting past becomes more and more his reality of the afterlife. You will want a Kleenex or two by you if you read it or watch our film (www.youtube.com/watch?v=G_PN6ZL0fMA).

While working together with Laurie, I realized that I had met one of the smartest, most interesting, most capable women I had ever known. She was the only woman who had hunted in places I had not—Scotland, at the time, and Patagonia. And, of course, I had lots of hunting stories from places she had never been. My view was, and still is today, that Laurie was wasting away in rural New Hampshire, while her calling and abilities as a writer, hostess, speaker, and entrepreneur were dying. And she was dying too, beaten down by northern New England's never-ending winters. At the first opportunity, I took her to Pinehurst, North Carolina, my home of eight years at the time. Pinehurst is an incredible piece of New England dropped south of the Mason-Dixon Line in the middle of North Carolina. I loved it, and she fell in love with it, too.

We had planned to marry the following summer, but the requirement for some additional heart stents for me moved the timetable up dramatically, and on February 6, 2013, before the preacher, Laurie's maid of honor, my best man, and the Living God, we were married. The rest, as they say, sort of, is an unfinished history of which I hope there many more chapters.

Laurie and I often discuss how, when you really, genuinely, care about someone, you are no longer just yourself but are as much a part of the other as that person is a part of you. Being a couple still implies two. Being husband and wife has the same effect. Being an item implies a oneness, but I find no life in the word. I do know, and Laurie would agree, that we are better together than we are apart. I respect her knowledge base, her thought process, her passion for the things she loves, her understanding. I love her very much, but I respect her more. We approach things from different perspectives, but in the end, our joint perspective is better than anything we could have designed or developed on our own. If this type of sharing, caring, and joint approach were more prevalent, I believe the divorce rate around the world would be much smaller. In a sea of six billion people, one is incredibly blessed to be able to find someone with whom to share your life.

Somehow, this was supposed to segue into women shooting, and I suppose it does because I actually have a shooting partner who is also my wife. Laurie wrote this book to take away the mysteries of shooting a shotgun, and to show any woman interested in learning that shotguns can truly broaden your horizon. It did so for me, and I am sure I would have enjoyed it twice as much before I met her, if I had had the lovely Laurie to go on shotgun adventures with me.

Besides being an entrepreneur, I had a long and successful career in the defense business and, for a decade before, and a decade after those twenty years, I had a wonderful career as a teacher of hormonal, thirteen-year-old middle schoolers. You've got to love children to be a teacher. Twenty years of teaching, I believe, qualifies me to talk about teaching shotgun shooting, because the key word is teaching.

But let's talk about *you* now. Either a) you're thinking about getting into shooting, and/or b) you're growing in the shooting sports.

Being the best shotgun shooter in the world does not necessarily qualify someone to teach someone else how to shoot correctly or well. If you are new to the sport and want to learn, *please, please, please* don't just go to the local club and ask the most recent club champion if he can help you get into the shotgun sports. Unless a person has spent a lot of hours understanding the mechanics of shooting a shotgun—focus, fit (length of pull, drop at comb, drop at heel, cast, cant), safety, eye dominance, eye protection, vision enhancement, ear protection, hands, feet, recoil, velocity, practice and where/what it really means, confidence, and a myriad of other things—all the novice is going to get is how Club Champion Bob shoots targets. This is worthless to the beginner at best and usually detrimental to the overall success of the novice at worst. A good teacher starts with a few basics and really helps the beginner become comfortable with those. Once the base is in place, then the building blocks of success and growth start to be cemented into place.

One of the greatest misconceptions in this country has always been that, if I am an American man, I know how to shoot a gun. No one takes up golf with any desire to become at least proficient without talking to a certified golf pro, learning about the game, trying different clubs, having their swing analyzed and, usually, getting a lesson. In golf, you hit a stationary target with speed and accuracy in order to get it to go to a particular place a distance in advance of where you are. In shooting, you send an oblong mass of lead pellets at 1,100- to 1,350-feet-per-second toward a moving object traveling thirty to fifty miles an hour in an arc that will cover less than one hundred yards and is traveling toward, away from, or across you at some angle and distance, and you are expected to deliver the shot at just the right time so that it intersects the flying object. If you learn the basics on both sports, you can have a lifetime of enjoyment. Mess up the start and the chances of your enjoying your new sport, and looking forward to repeated outings doing it, diminish greatly.

There are many qualified shooting instructors and coaches in this wonderful country of ours, as well as in the United Kingdom, who offer shooting lessons at local clubs for any level of shooter. Shotgun shooting needs to be a pleasant sport. Early in my shooting life I read that clay shooting was an incredibly stress-relieving sport. Seeing a target at which you are shooting turn into a cloud of tiny pieces of fragmented clay, called "smoking the target," literally makes you feel good about yourself, makes you happy, makes you powerful, gives you the feeling of control. Of course, you must hit the target to get those feelings, so success is an important part of the learning process.

If you go back a couple of paragraphs, you will see I mentioned the club champion as a 'he.' Shotgun shooting has been a male-dominated sport since its inception. There was only one Annie Oakley, and she was so unique as to be truly legendary, not only in her time, but for all time. This idea of men being the shotgun shooters, especially in a sporting, competitive, or hunting capacity, probably goes all the way back to the hunter-gatherer mentality of old. Men were expected to be the bread winners, the defenders, the fighters, and therefore, the weapons experts. A lot of perceptions have changed, but men and women still compete from different tee boxes in golf, and tournaments are geared for one or the other of the sexes.

In the shooting sports, men and women stand in the same shooting stands, at the same positions, shoot at the same targets, and are scored according to ability. Prizes are awarded for High Over All, High Gun, and Class Champions in both men's and women's divisions. Seeing a woman's name in the upper echelon of a shooting tournament does not bring raised eyebrows or strange stares. It brings acknowledgement that this person, who happens to be a woman, is a very good shooter. End of story.

I have been fortunate to work with several women's groups to help novices with basic groundwork in the shotgun sports and also to help intermediate shooters work on aspects of their game to bring a more consistent performance to their shooting. One of the great things I have enjoyed about teaching women to shoot shotguns is their eagerness to learn. They want knowledge; they want experience; and they want to succeed. Many young men who want to learn to shoot only want you to show them how to load the gun, tell them where the target is coming from, and get out of their way so they can show you how good they are. This belief that "I can shoot because I live in the USA and I am a man" is deeply imbedded in the male psyche. How do I know? Because I am one. It was only when I began to read about the requirements for getting a hunting license in the United Kingdom or the (then) Eastern Bloc countries did I realize that owning guns, shooting guns, going hunting, shooting clays, and being afield are all privileges in this country. Our right to freedom allows these things, and these privileges are something not to be taken lightly.

Most of us learned to shoot to be better game-shots. Today, the shotgun sports appeal to those who want to shoot recreationally as well as competitively. I myself shoot sporting clays with a group of us older gentlemen, and occasionally one or two women, on Saturdays at various ranges to simply enjoy our sport. We don't keep score, we share the bill, and we shoot as few or as many targets as we choose. It is simply a fun day at the range. And that's really what shotgun shooting should be all about.

Laurie and I share about one hundred years of outdoor experience between us. What I don't know about the shooting sports, she does, and vice versa. I genuinely hope the wonderful content in these pages moves you toward a better understanding of the shotgun sports and allows you to enter and enjoy a whole new world in the great outdoors.

—JOHN WILES
Pinehurst, North Carolina

▲ Victorian Shooting Party.

THE WOMAN WHO SHOOTS
Adapted from Anthony Trollope by the Author

mong those who shoot there are two classes of shotgunners who always like it, and these people are shooting sportsmen and shooting sportswomen. That it should be so is natural enough. In the life and habits of men and women there is much that is antagonistic to shooting, and they who suppress this antagonism do so because they are Nimrods at heart. But shooting under difficulties—shooting sportsmen and shooting sportswomen—leaves a strong impression on the casual observer of the sport; for such as one it seems that the hardest shooting is forthcoming exactly where no hard sport should be expected. On the present occasion I will, if you please, confine myself to the lady who shoots, and will begin with an assertion, which will not be contradicted, that the number of such ladies is very much on the increase.

Women who shoot, as a rule, shoot better than men. They, the women, have always been instructed, whereas men have usually come to the sport without any instruction. They go out to the shooting fields when they are all boys, and put themselves upon their fathers' guidance as they become hobbledehoys: and thus they obtain the knowledge of handling a shotgun, even when the shotgun kicks and shies; and, so progressing they achieve an amount of sportsmanship which answers the purposes of life. But they do not acquire the art of shooting with exactness, as women do, and rarely have such exactitude as a woman has with a shotgun. The consequences of this is that women miss less often than men, and the field is not often thrown into the horror which would arise were a lady known to tumble in a duck marsh or caught up in a gorse thicket walk-up grouse shooting.

I own that I like to see three or four ladies out in a field, and I like to the better if I am happy enough to count one or more of them among my own acquaintances. Their presence tends to take off from shooting the character of "shootingness"—of both fast shots and slow shots—which has become, not unnaturally, attached to it, and to bring it within the category of gentle sports. There used to prevail an idea that the sportsman was of necessity loud and rough, given to strong drinks, ill adapted for the poetries of life, and perhaps a little prone to make money out of his softer friend. It may now be said that this idea is going out of vogue, and that sportsmen are supposed to have that same feeling with regard to their guns and gun dogs—the same and no more—which ladies have for fashion, or soldiers for swords. Gun dogs are valued simply for the services they can render and are only valued highly when they are known to be good servants. That a man may hunt without drinking or swearing and may possess a dog or two without any propensity to sell it or them for double their value, is now beginning to be understood. The oftener that women are to be seen "out," the more will such be improved feelings prevail as to shooting, and the pleasanter will be the field to men who may nevertheless be good sportsmen.

There are two classes of women who shoot, or, rather, among many possible classifications, there are two to which I will now call attention. There is the lady who shoots and demands assistance; and there is the lady who shoots and demands none. Each always—I may say always—receives all the assistance that she may require; but the difference between the two, to the men who shoot with them, is very great. It will, of course, be understood that, as to both these samples of

female Nimrods, I speak of ladies who really shoot—not of those who grace the coverts and shooting fields with, and disappear under the auspices of, their papas or their loaders when the work begins.

The lady who shoots and demands assistance in truth becomes a nuisance before the shoot is over, let her beauty be ever so transcendent, her sportsmanship ever so perfect, and her battery of general feminine artillery ever so powerful. She is like the woman who is always wanting your place in a railway carriage—and demanding it, too, without the slightest idea of paying you for it with thanks; whose study it is to treat you as though she ignored your existence while she is appropriating your services. The shooting lady who demands assistance is very particular about her shots, requiring that aid shall be given to her with instant speed, but that the man who gives it to her shall never allow himself to be hurried as he renders it. And she soon becomes reproachful—oh, so soon! It is marvelous the manner in which a shooting sportswoman will become exacting, troublesome, and at last, imperious—deceived and spoilt by the attention which she receives. She teaches herself to think at last that a man is a brute who does not shoot as though he were shooting as her servant, and that it becomes her to assume indignation if every motion around her is not made with some reference to her safety, to her comfort, to her success. I have seen women look as Furies look, and heard them speak as Furies are supposed to speak, because men before them could not get out of their way at a moment's notice, or because some Labrador would still assert himself while he was flushing pheasants, and not sink into submission with dog-like obedience when he ranged too far for her liking.

I have now before my eyes one who was pretty, brave, and a good shooting sportswoman; but how men did hate her! When you were in a line with her there was no shaking her off. Indeed, you were like enough to be shaken off yourself, and to be rid of her after that manner. But while you were with her you never escaped her at a single shot, and always felt that you were held to trespassing against her in some manner. I shall never forget her voice—"Pray, take care of that shot!" And yet it was a pretty voice, and elsewhere she was not given to domineering more than is common to pretty women in general; but she had been taught badly from the beginning, and she was a pest.

It was the same at every gap. "Might I ask you not to come too near me?" And yet it was impossible to escape her. Men could not shoot wide of her, for she would not shoot wide of them. She had always some male escort with her, who did not shoot as she shot, and consequently, as she chose to have the advantage of an escort—of various escorts—she was always in the company of some who did not feel as much joy in the presence of a pretty young woman as men should do under all circumstance. "Might I ask you not to come too near me?" If she could only have heard the remarks to which this constant little request of hers gave rise. She is now the mother of children, and her hunting days are gone, and probably she never makes that little request. Doubtless that look, made up partly of offence and partly of female dignity, no longer clouds her brow. But I fancy that they who knew her of old in the driven bird field never approach her now without fancying that they hear those reproachful words and see that powerful look of injured feminine weakness.

But there is a shooting lady who shoots hard and never asks for assistance. Perhaps I may be allowed to explain to embryo Dianas—to the growing huntresses

of the present age, that she who shoots and makes no demands receives attention as close as is ever given to her more imperious sister. And how welcome it is! What a grace she lends to the day's sport! How pleasant it is to see her in her pride of pace, achieving her mastery over the difficulties in her way by her own wit—as all men, and all women also, must really do who intend to shoot; and doing it all without any sign that the difficulties are too great for her!

The lady who shoots like this is in truth seldom in the way. I have heard men declare that they would never wish to see a woman on the shooting-field because women are troublesome, and because they must be treated with attention let the press of the moment be ever so instant. From this I dissent altogether. The small amount of courtesy that is needed is more than atoned for by the grace of her presence, and in fact produces no more impediment in the shooting-field than in other scenes of life.

But in the shooting-field, as in other scenes, let assistance never be demanded by a woman. If the lady finds that she cannot keep a place in the first flight without such demands on the patience of those around her, let her acknowledge to herself that the attempt is not in her line, and that it should be abandoned. If it be the ambition of a shooting lady to shoot straight—and women have very much of this ambition—let her use her eyes but never her voice; and let her ever have a smile for those who help her in her little difficulties. Let her never ask any one "to pick up those spent cartridges," or look as though she expected the profane crowd to keep aloof from her. So shall she win the hearts of those around her, and go safely through moor and marsh, over ditch and dyke, and meet with a score of knights around her who will be willing and able to give her eager aid should the chance of any moment require it.

There are two accusations which the demurer portion of the world is apt to advance against shooting ladies—or, as I should better say, against shooting as an amusement for ladies. It leads to flirting, they say—to flirting of a sort which mothers would not approve; and it leads to fast habits. The first of these accusations is, I think, simply made in ignorance. As girls are brought up among us now-a-days, they may all flirt, if they have a mind to do so; and opportunities for flirting are much better and much more commodious in the ballroom, in the drawing-room, or in the park, than they are on the shooting field. Nor is the work in hand of a nature to create flirting tendencies—as, it must be admitted, is the nature of the work in hand when the floors are waxed, and the fiddles are going. And this error has sprung from, to form part of, another, which is wonderfully common among non-hunting folk. It is widely thought by many, who do not, as a rule, put themselves in opposition to the amusements of the world, that shooting in itself is a wicked thing; that shooting sportsmen are fast, given to unclean living, and bad ways of life; that they usually go to bed drunk, and that they go about the world roaring hunting cries, and disturbing the peace of the innocent generally. With such men, who could wish that wife, sister, or daughter should associate? But I venture to say that this opinion, which I believe to be common, is erroneous and that men who hunt are not more iniquitous than men who go out fishing, or play dominoes, or dig in their gardens. *Maxima debetur pureris reverentia*, and still more to damsels; but if boys and girls will never go where they will hear more to injure them than they will usually do amidst the ordinary conversation of a shooting field, the maxima reverentia will have been attained.

As to that other charge, let it be at once admitted that the young lady who has become a shooting sportswoman has made a fearful almost a fatal mistake. And so also has the young man who falls into the same error. I hardly know to which such phase of character may be most injurious. It is a pernicious vice, that of succumbing—and making yourself, as it were—her servant. I will not deny that I have known a lady to fall into this vice; but so also have I known ladies to marry their music-masters and to fall in love with their footmen. But not on that account are we to have no music masters and no footmen.

Let the shooting sportswoman, however, avoid any touch of this blemish, remember that no shooting sportsman ever likes a shooting sportswoman to know as much about the sport as he thinks he knows himself.

—Adapted by the Author from "The Lady Who Rides to Hounds," from *Hunting Sketches* by Anthony Trollope. Published in 1865 by Chapman and Hall, London

Part I

LET'S GET STARTED

compare a woman of average build to an average man. A woman's cheekbones are generally higher, the neck proportionately longer, shoulders are narrower, arms are shorter—and then there is the most significant measurement of all, our breasts. We, the gentler sex, tend to bruise more easily than men. So, that black-and-blue shoulder you got from shooting a gun that didn't fit you properly means you won't be wearing that little black strapless dress right away.

Then there's *sight*. A woman is twice as likely to encounter eye dominance problems than a man. This means that one eye dominates the other when you are fixated on a target. It's almost impossible to get off a sure shot when your mind is trying to figure out *how* you see the target in relationship to *where* you are pointing the gun. The professional instructors who have contributed to this book each address this important subject. Unless you identify and deal with your eye dominance problem, you can never be sure of whether you are shooting above, below, in front of, or behind the target.

▲ Photo courtesy of Griffin & Howe.

*L*adies, we're not built like men. We don't think like men. We don't respond to, move through, or process life like men. And we don't shoot like men. But the shooting sports make us equal.

The objective of wing and clay shooting is to effectively intercept a flying target with pellets that, at the pull of a trigger, have been discharged from a cartridge fired through the barrel of a shotgun. The mechanics and components of a shotgun, shotshell loads, and targets, inanimate or live, favor no one, man or woman. However, there are some subtle, and not so subtle, differences between the sexes.

First is *gun fit*. To shoot accurately, your shotgun must fit *you* properly. Your father's shotgun won't fit you and likely as not, neither will a gun off the rack at a sporting goods store. That's because certain allowances must be made for our feminine physique. Let's

Anyone who takes up the shotgun sports must devote the time and practice to acquire the necessary skills and knowledge. Correct shooting technique is essential to becoming an accurate and consistent shot. There is no such thing as being a "natural" when it comes to shooting. Fact is, it's not unusual to see a woman pick up a gun for the first time and hit a clay target. The reason is, she is not thinking about what she is doing because she doesn't really know what she's doing, so her inherent senses take over. Invariably, the more she shoots, the more she misses. That's because our beginner no longer is innocently using her senses to look at the target—now she's looking at the gun, shifting her focus away from the target, and thinking about what she ought to be doing. Over-thinking a target is the foil of many a seasoned shooter. Therefore, as a beginner, it is absolutely necessary that you start out properly—and the only way to do that is by taking lessons from a professional shooting instructor. Even seasoned shooters rely on regular instruction to keep their technique honed. Chapter 3, "Shotgun Technique," is devoted to this subject with the invaluable assistance of professional gun fitter and trapshooting instructor Jack Bart of Maryland; professional shooting instructors and founders of the O.S.P. Shooting School in Houston, the husband and wife team of Gil and Vicki Ash; and five-time World Skeet Champion and international shooting instructor John Shima, based out of San Antonio. Their expert advice raises this book to a level never before achieved by any book devoted to the shooting sportswoman and will guide you on your journey to enjoyment, confidence, and excellence in the field and on the course.

Before you even pick up a shotgun, you must know the rules of shotgun safety. This is not an option, and you must drill the important basics—such as never point the muzzle of a gun at anyone—until these rules becomes second nature to you. For this reason, chapter 1 of this *Shooter's Bible* opens with "Shotgun Safety and Responsibility," and is one of the most comprehensive reviews of the subject in any book today.

There are practical aspects to the shotgun sports, as well. Unlike many men, it is likely a woman who is new to the gun hasn't enjoyed the advantage of being taught from a young age by her father, not to mention her mother. The beginner shooting sportswoman enters the sport a clean slate, eager to learn, like clay in the hands of the sculptor who is her shooting instructor. You want to be a proficient shot, but as you advance, you will discover so much more. You will grow in self-esteem, improve your hand-eye coordination and overall agility, meet new and interesting people with whom you share a common interest, and most importantly, you'll spend time in the great outdoors.

A bruised shoulder, or bruised ego when you miss an "easy" target, is a small price to pay for a sport you can invest in your whole life long and consistently reap satisfying returns.

There are precious few stories of women who were given their first shotgun or rifle by their father and learned to hunt at his side, as I wrote thirty years ago in *Shooting Sports for Women*. No woman I know tells of sitting on her dad's knee in front of a blazing fire on a wintery night, seeing, through his eyes, woodcock spiral sky-bound on wind-snapping October days, or deer a-skitter in naked November woods come first snowfall. Such has been the domain of men. This has been the legacy an outdoorsman passes on to his son; the very ritual that he, in turn, received from his father before him. Women, in turn, have had their own special legacies, left to them by their mothers and grandmothers.

However, by becoming a competent and confident shooting sportswoman, you can bestow upon your

▲ Photo courtesy of Griffin & Howe.

daughter a mantle of memories that will adorn her the rest of her life, and a legacy to pass down to her own children. So many new possibilities await you that can enrich your and your family's lives in such wonderful ways!

Captain Charles Askins opened his book, *Wing and Trap Shooting* (The Macmillan Company, 1926) with this interesting anecdote:

> In wing-shooting, an object in motion must be struck by my missiles from an arm also in motion. The whole science of wing-shooting consists in delivering a charge of shot, not directly at the flying target, but to a point where the bird will be when the charge reaches it. A woman novelist states the matter very naively when telling her sister sportswomen how to shoot English sparrows with a .22-cal. rifle. According to the authoress, she early discovered that when attempting to hit the little birds while they were sitting, she missed because of their springing away with the flash of the gun, *but when she jumped them and shot where they would be when the bullet got there*, she killed them every time. Wing-shooting is as simple as that, merely shoot exactly where the bird will be when the shot gets there and success is certain, even with a rifle.

> Many of us have had more trouble to do this with a shotgun, however, than this feminine writer of fiction seems to have found with a rifle. If the birds invariably flew in the same direction with a motion as even as the flight of an arrow, at one unvarying rate of speed, and the gunner knew how to gauge the speed and angle to the fraction of an inch, possessing at the same time the mechanical regularity of a machine in every movement made, I see no reason why he should not be as successful as the lady.

Not long ago, while rummaging through some old papers, I came upon an ancient fax. It was from my longtime friend, Silvio Calabi, and was dated June 14, 1995. In those days, Silvio was editor of *Shooting Sportsman*, a magazine devoted to shotgun enthusiasts, and I was editor of the "Game & Gun Gazette" section. It seems he received an interesting phone call

from a reader concerning me and thought I should know about it.

"Good day," Silvio wrote in his fax. "I have to pass along a conversation I had late Monday on the phone. As verbatim as memory allows:

Caller: "Let me ask you something. Is 'Laurie Morrow' a real person?"

Silvio: "A real. . . ? Well, yeah. Of course. We don't make stuff up like that."

Caller: "Really? I gotta tell you, that's some of the very best gun writing I've ever read. I have some detailed knowledge on certain things Laurie's written about and I can tell you it's right on."

Silvio: "Well, she'll be pleased to hear that. . ."

Caller: "She? You mean Laurie Morrow's a *woman*?!"

Silvio: "Uh, yeah, boy is she ever a woman. I mean . . . she's a recognized Winchester collector, she's married to a gunsmith, and they have two gun-happy kids and they all live on Corey Ford's Lower Forty. . ."

Caller: "Wow!

Silvio ended, "And so on. Nauseated though you are by such droolings, I just had to let you know."

My friend and former editor took a giant leap of faith when he put me on the masthead of a magazine with a 99 percent male readership. A woman who shot was still something of a novelty; a woman who wrote about it was a rare bird indeed. What pleased me was not the reader's surprise that I, a woman, wrote about guns, but that I wrote about guns with authority.

How I Got Started

I took up the gun when I was eighteen, hunting ruffed grouse in rural northern New England, my home of forty years, and I pulled a trigger on my first bird, a red grouse, on a let leased by friends in Scotland. Sporting clays was a decade away from being introduced in America and no trap or skeet clubs existed in my remote neck of the woods. But we had a rusty, hand-pull clay target trap in the front field, used well but cautiously, because if you didn't properly latch the spring, it whipped back and bruised your hand something fierce.

I had no women friends who hunted, and yet I never set out alone. My hunting companions were of the canine variety. I always had gun dogs—over the years, three wonderful English Labrador retrievers, two black and a yellow; three springer spaniels; a beagle; a granddaughter of Tober, the last of the late, great writer Corey Ford's famous family of English setters; a mahogany Irish setter from a hunting line; a liver and white Llewellin setter; and, incredibly, a beautiful *black* "British" setter, as I called her, from the unanticipated mating of the Llewellin and the Irish; and an enthusiastic little short-legged dog who ran so fast he flushed more ground birds than any of the others—a Cavalier King Charles spaniel I adopted from my dear friend, Hollywood legend, Mickey Rooney. It was not until the early 1990s that my sons were old enough to hunt with me; as they entered their teens, and I was traveling the world writing about hunting, shooting, and fishing, I took them with me.

About that time, organized shooting for women began to open up. The first and original venture was the Women's Shooting Sports Foundation, founded by the finest shooting sportswoman I have ever known, Sue King of Houston, Texas, in association with the National Shooting Sports Foundation. This was followed several years later, in conjunction with the National Rifle Association, by Women on Target, also started by Sue, and I was pleased to be involved with both in the early days. Since then, numerous national, state, and local women's shooting organizations and clubs have formed in all shooting disciplines—rifle, shotgun, and handgun.

I have never been crossed, undermined, demeaned, or criticized in the field or on the clays course by any man; on the contrary, I've been welcomed and treated with respect. Generally speaking, such unanimity between men and women is the exception rather than the rule but, in my experience, if a fellow is a good sportsman, he's a gentleman, and that calls for a woman to behave like a lady. Perhaps I'm "old school," but as I said, the shooting sports make us equal.

Now, a good shot surely deserves praise. However, too often I have witnessed women whooping and hollering, jumping in the air to give a high five to their girlfriends, disrupting nearby shooters, and quite frankly, adversely affecting their own group's concentration. Frivolous behavior is reckless behavior when holding a gun, whether it's loaded or not, and that is unacceptable under any circumstances.

A woman who dresses inappropriately and comes to the field without hearing and eye protection deserves suspicion, even reproach. Wearing flip-flops, cut-off shorts, and a tight tee-shirt gives a poor impression and questions whether she knows anything about shooting at all.

Then there's the matter of competition. Competition is healthy—providing you are competing against yourself. In other words, you want to be the best you can be, and the measure of that is not how well you shoot against others but how well you are shooting against your own standard. Competing to be high gun, or the first to get a limit on birds, is not the goal to which any shooter should aspire. A shoot or hunt can be ruined by just one person who pushes in, admonishes a fellow shooter, or throws a tantrum for any reason whatsoever. Once you are branded as being a bad sport, it sticks to you like glue. Shooting is not about numbers. It's about the experience, the day, enjoying the camaraderie of others, and perhaps most important of all, the sense of personal enrichment and enjoyment the sport affords for the taking.

Therefore, gain knowledge. Practice to shoot consistently. Shoot conscientiously. Develop and hone your skills. Focus and be composed. Wear good manners as you would a custom-tailored outfit. Show respect for others, on and off the field, and you will earn their respect and, just as importantly, gain self-respect for yourself. Remember: the greatest compliment a shooting sportswoman or man can be paid is not, "You're a good shot," but rather, "You're a good sport." And that, my friend, is what matters most of all.

1. Shotgun Safety and Responsibility

This is the first *Shooter's Bible* in a long and illustrious line stretching back over eighty years to be written by a woman, for women. I, the author, do not take this privilege—or responsibility—lightly. I am beholden to my editor and longtime friend, Jay Cassell, for giving me this opportunity. For decades, his contribution to outdoor books and magazines is unequalled in the realm of outdoor literature. Had it not been for his modesty, his utter inability to self-promote, and his selfless generosity in spotlighting lesser writers over himself, then the rich accolades he so rightly deserves would be far more widely known.

Therefore, while this is, for all intents and purposes, a woman's book (I hope men will find it fulfilling, as well), there is no difference between the sexes when it comes to the finger that pulls the trigger. Each and every one of us must abide by the rules—and nowhere have these been stated more clearly, in my opinion, than on page 2 of the 81st edition of the *Shooter's Bible*, published in 1953 by Stoeger Arms Corporation.

The rules of gun safety are absolute. There's no wiggle room for interpretation. No one who handles a gun is exempt from knowing them; all must abide. Editor John Olson's advice is as appropriate today as seventy years ago, when he wrote:

From the desk of the editor. . .

I fear that in the shooting fraternity there are some who consider the problem of anti-firearms legislation a closed issue. It's true that we've won some early victories, but our antagonists, upon discovering the nature of the opposition, have simply resolved to re-double their efforts and re-map their strategy. Make no mistake—they haven't given up the fight; complacency on our part now will assuredly guarantee their eventual success.

In the coming months be more watchful than ever. Send those letters and wires to your legislators as soon as you learn of proposed legislation that is designed to restrict your ability to purchase, own, or use sporting firearms.

To prevent unfavorable publicity and to improve the image of the sportsman, the Shooter's Bible staff has proposed the following code for hunters and shooters:

1. Diligently practice the "10 Commandments" of Shooting Safety. (Teach these to your children and your shooting friends.)
2. Be particularly careful in your dealings with landowners. Be sure to ask permission before attempting to hunt on someone else's land. Be polite and courteous even when refused permission. Be especially careful to avoid damaging fences or equipment. Thank the landowner when you leave.
3. Do not display harvested game for the world to see! The sight of a bagged trophy may thrill you, but it frequently antagonizes non-hunters. Store game away, out of sight, especially when traveling public roads.
4. Be careful of your personal appearance! While it is often pleasantly relaxing to escape the daily razor while in the backwoods, a bearded, rough-clothed hunter is a decidedly unpleasant sight in public places. Don't look like a blood-thirsty game hog—strive to present the appearance of a gentleman sportsman. A neat, pleasing appearance will accomplish more than a thousand words. Urge your clubs to adopt a code of dress. [Author's note: The same applies to the lady sportswoman, with the exception of the beard and razor!]
5. Always carry your guns cased when not actually engaged in hunting or shooting. Do not make a public display of your firearms.

Before you pull a trigger, commit the unbreakable rules and regulations of gun safety to memory—and never forget them. Here are the "Ten Commandments of Gun Safety"—plus two, which I have added.

Twelve Rules of Shotgun Safety
Rule 1: Always keep the muzzle pointed in a safe direction.

▲ "Last known picture of Grandpa."

- Never point the muzzle of a shotgun at a person, even if you are sure the gun is unloaded and the safety is on.
- Only when you are ready to shoot should you prepare to shoulder your gun and point the muzzle at the target.
- Always be aware of where other people and gundogs are in proximity to you.
- Never assume that a person or gundog is out of range when you prepare to pull the trigger. A discharged cartridge travels a much greater distance than you may imagine.

▲ Clearly these women have no idea where the barrels of their guns are pointing. If both guns were loaded, and both were accidentally fired simultaneously—which you cannot rule out, since the woman on the left (and probably the other) has her finger on the trigger—then one would have her kneecap blown off and the other would likely never bear children.

- Never, ever look down the barrel of your shotgun at the muzzle unless you are absolutely certain it is fully unloaded, that there is no cartridge in the chamber, and the action is open.
- Always control the muzzle of your firearm. Know where your gun is pointing at all times.

Always be aware where you are pointing the barrels at all times, especially when you are loading or unloading a shotgun. You will sometimes rush and get excited as you are ready to take a shot and can easily get caught up in hitting the target.

Practice this exercise
First, be certain your gun is completely unloaded. If you have a double gun, you can perform this exercise with brass snap caps. Never use field blanks in any shotgun unless it is for the purpose of gundog training and field trials, and even then, be knowledgeable. Do not have any live cartridges near you when do this exercise.

1. Hold your gun in a safe carry position.

▲ Mrs. Gary Cooper, called "Rocky," was an expert skeet shooter. She is correctly carrying her Browning A5 with a Cutts compensator in one of the "safe positions." However, her husband, three-time Academy Award–winning actor Gary Cooper (*High Noon, Sergeant York*), is not. He could have blown off his hands had his Winchester Model 12 misfired.

▲ Here the Coopers are correctly carrying their guns.

2. Walk up to an imaginary position as you sight your target. Imagine you have a shooting partner on your left side and one on your right, a gundog is flushing a bird ahead, and you're not sure if there is someone ahead.

3. Stop, bring your gun down, see where the barrels are pointing, and assume the ready position.

4. Break open the gun with the muzzle perpendicular to your body and pointing downward. Pretend you are loading the gun.

5. Close your gun, aware where the muzzle is pointing. Assume the ready position, "look" at the target, and raise the gun in proper shooting technique. As you cheek the gun, pretend to pull the trigger.

6. Bring the gun down after you pretend-fire, keeping your eye on the muzzle and determine where to point it safely.

7. Open the gun, "unload" it, and assume the safe carry position.

Practice this exercise repeatedly until you feel your subconscious memory take over and the routine becomes instinctive. Always be conscious of where the muzzle of your gun is pointing at all times. Shooting situations always change, even on a trap or skeet field.

Cautions

Never dry-fire a double gun unless there is a snap cap in the barrel. A snap cap is a hollow brass "dummy" that is shaped like a cartridge. You can dry-fire a double gun (that is, safely pull the trigger when no live load is in the chamber) because a snap cap prevents the firing pins from otherwise breaking.

- No injury can occur in the event of an accidental discharge as long as the muzzle is pointing in a safe direction. A safe direction is a direction in which a cartridge cannot possibly strike anyone.
- Never place your finger on the trigger until you are ready to shoot. Place it alongside the trigger guard.
- Never rest the butt of your shotgun on the ground or on your foot with the barrel(s) pointing at your head, or anyone else's.

Rule 2: Always handle your gun as if it were loaded, even when you think it's not.

- Never assume a gun is unloaded—check for yourself!
- Firearms should be loaded only when you are in the field, on the target range, or shooting area, ready to shoot.
- When you are not shooting, keep the action open and your finger off the trigger. Be sure everyone in your group does the same.
- When not in use, firearms and cartridges should be secured in a safe place, separate from each other. It is your responsibility to prevent children and unauthorized adults from gaining access to firearms or ammunition.
- Unload your gun as soon as you are finished. A loaded gun has no place in or near a car, truck, or building. Unload your shotgun immediately when you have finished shooting, well before you bring it into a car, camp, or home. When you leave the field or range, put your unloaded gun in a gun sleeve or gun case.
- Whenever you handle a firearm or hand it to someone, always open the action immediately, and visually check the chamber, receiver, or magazine to be certain it does not contain any cartridges.
- Always keep the action of a shotgun open when not in use.
- Never cross a fence, climb a tree, or perform any awkward action with a loaded gun. While in the

field, there will be times when common sense and the basic rules of firearms safety will require you to unload your gun for maximum safety. Never pull or push a loaded firearm toward yourself or another person. When in doubt, unload your gun!

▲ Parker Stalvey "breaks open" her over/under whenever she's carrying her gun. Photo by Ryan Stalvey

Rule 3: Never rely on your gun safety. Never assume it is on.

- Treat every gun as though it can fire at any time. The "safety" on any gun is a mechanical device which, like any such device, can become inoperable at the worst possible time. You may think the safety may be "off" when it actually is "on." The safety serves as a supplement to safe shotgun handling, not a substitute for common sense. You should never handle a shotgun carelessly and assume that the gun won't fire just because the "safety is on."
- Never touch the trigger on a firearm until you are ready to shoot. Keep your fingers away from

the trigger while loading or unloading. Never pull the trigger on any firearm with the safety on the "safe" position or anywhere in between "safe" and "fire." It is possible that the gun can fire at any time, or even later when you release the safety, without you ever touching the trigger again.

- Never place the safety in between positions. Half-safe is unsafe. If your gun has a manual safety, take the gun off safety with a fluid movement of your thumb just as you are prepared to pull the trigger. Never take off the safety until you are absolutely ready to fire. If your gun has an automatic safety that comes off, safety the moment you close your gun after loading. Be sure you know how your safety works! Know your gun before you operate it—especially if it is a borrowed gun!
- Regardless of the position of the safety, any blow or jar strong enough to actuate the firing mechanism of a gun can cause it to fire. This can happen even if the trigger is not touched, such as when a gun is dropped.
- Never rest a loaded shotgun against any object because there is always the possibility that it will be jarred or slide from its position and fall with sufficient force to discharge. The only time you can be absolutely certain that a gun cannot fire is when the action is open and the chamber is empty.

Rule 4: Be sure of your target, what's around it, and what lies beyond.

- No one can call back a shot. Once a gun fires, you have given up all control over where the shot will go or what it will strike. Don't shoot unless you know exactly what your shot is going to strike.
- Be sure that your cartridge will not injure anyone or anything beyond your target.
- Firing at a movement or a noise without being absolutely certain of what you are shooting at constitutes disregard for the safety of others. No target is so important that you cannot take the time before you pull the trigger to be absolutely certain of your target and where your shot will

stop. Shotgun pellets can travel 500 yards, and shotgun slugs have a range of over half a mile.

- Always surrender (or forego) a shot if you are not sure of the target, the direction the target is going, and the location of every person and dog within, and beyond, range. No shot is worth taking if you have any doubt about these things.

Rule 5: Be sure you use the correct ammunition.

- You must assume the serious responsibility of using only the correct ammunition for your firearm. Read and heed all warnings, including those that appear in the gun's instruction manual and on the ammunition boxes.
- Never force a cartridge into the chamber.
- Never mix cartridges of different gauges and loads when stored away.
- Using improper or incorrect cartridges and loads can destroy a gun and cause serious personal injury. It only takes one cartridge of improper gauge to rupture or bulge your barrels—and only a second to check every shell before you load the shotgun. Be absolutely certain that the ammunition you are using matches the specifications that are contained within the gun's instruction manual and the gunmaker's markings on the shotgun, which you will see on the barrel and/or the water table of the action.
- Never put modern loads through a shotgun with Damascus barrels, even light loads, until you bring the gun to a shotgun expert for him to examine and make recommendations. A Damascus gun that has been proofed for modern loads still can be safely fired only with very specific loads. Although many double gun enthusiasts who shoot these beautiful older guns use handloads, a gun must be tested so the barrel pressure of the load when fired is not so strong as to burst the fine twists of Damascus steel.
- Firearms are designed, manufactured, and proof tested to standards based upon those of factory-loaded ammunition. Handloaded or reloaded ammunition deviating from pressures generated by factory loads or from component recommendations specified in reputable handloading manuals can be dangerous and can cause severe damage to shotguns and serious injury to the shooter. Do not use improper reloads or cartridges made of unknown components.
- Cartridges that have become very wet or have been submerged in water should be discarded in a safe manner. Do not spray oil or solvents on cartridges or place them in excessively lubricated firearms. Poor ignition, unsatisfactory performance, or damage to your firearm and harm to yourself or others could result from using such shells.
- Form the habit of examining every cartridge you put into your gun. Never use damaged or substandard ammunition—the money you save is not worth the risk of possible injury or a ruined gun.

Rule 6: If your gun fails to fire when the trigger is pulled, don't pull it again!

- Put the gun down! Handle with care! Watch where you point the muzzle and do not, under any circumstances, look down the muzzle of the barrel!
- Occasionally, a cartridge may not fire when the trigger is pulled. There are several reasons for this; just as you leave your doctor to diagnose your health problems, have a gunsmith diagnose your shotgun problems. If your gun doesn't fire or misfires, keep the muzzle pointed in a safe direction. Keep your face away from the breech. Then, carefully open the action, unload the firearm, and dispose of the cartridge in a safe way.
- Any time there is a cartridge in the chamber, your gun is loaded and ready to fire even if you've tried to shoot and it did not go off. It could go off at any time, so you must always remember Rule 1 and watch that muzzle!
- If a gun misfires, wait thirty seconds and manually extract the cartridge from the shotgun. If a cartridge gets stuck in a chamber, never try to pry it out. *Never use a penknife, metal cleaning rod, or a tool.* You can hit the primer and the cartridge will fire. This is not a problem you usually find in semiautomatic shotguns and

pump-action shotguns, where the barrels can be easily removed. In an over/under or side-by-side, break open the shotgun and carefully transport it to someone who knows how to dislodge the shotshell. It can be as easy as running a wooden dowel through the barrels (being sure the barrels are not pointing at your head); however, unless you are an expert shotgunner and have done this before, have someone who knows what he or she is doing take care of the problem.

Rule 7: Always dress appropriately to ensure your personal safety.

▲ Kate Trad is wearing protective shooting glasses, hearing protection, and a shooting vest with padded shoulder—all the right things to ensure your safety on the field.

- Wear eye and ear protection when shooting, appropriate outdoor clothing, and blaze orange where required.
- All shooters should wear protective shooting glasses and some form of hearing protectors while shooting. Exposure to shooting noise can damage hearing, and adequate vision protection is essential. Shooting glasses guard against twigs, falling shot, clay target chips, and the rare ruptured case or firearm malfunction.
- Wearing eye protection when disassembling and cleaning any gun will also help prevent the possibility of springs, spring tension parts, solvents, or other agents from contacting your eyes. There is a wide variety of eye and ear protectors available, from inexpensive to very expensive. No price is worth losing an eye or damaging your hearing. No target shooter or hunter should ever be without them.
- Dress appropriately. During fall and winter hunting seasons, wear sturdy, well-fitting boots and loose, moisture-wicking layers underneath outwear that protects you against the elements.

▲ Angela Thalgott dresses for the field fashionably and properly, wearing a wool tweed shooting suit, wool socks, leather boots, and gloves. Wool is the best cloth for field wear. It is water-resistant and wicks moisture.

- In warm weather, when you are shooting clay birds, wear a breathable shooting shirt with padded shoulder or lightweight shirt with a sleeveless shooting vest. Sneakers or other appropriate shoes with good support are a must.
- Blaze orange is mandatory for hunting in most, but not all, states, but generally not abroad. Unless specified otherwise, always wear a blaze orange hat, vest, or shirt when you go in the hunting field. It instantly identifies you to other hunters. Blaze orange is not worn for the clay target sports.
- Most rules of shooting safety are intended to protect you and others around you, but these rules are for your protection alone. Furthermore, having your hearing and eyes protected will make your shooting easier and will help improve your enjoyment of the shooting sports.
- Know the signs of hypothermia and how to prevent it. Wear warm clothing; bring extra clothing if it is raining, snowing, or you are going away for more than just the day.

▲ Proper footwear on the shooting field is a must, although the fellow in this photograph obviously would not agree. Not just for comfort, proper footwear supports the foot so that when you pivot into a shot your foot is secure. Sneakers or athletic shoes are common on the clay target shooting fields; however, you need a well-fitting, water-resistant boot with good treads for the field. Whether it's ankle-, calf-, or knee-high depends upon where you are going. If the fields are harvested and relatively open, an ankle-boot will do; if you are walking through wetlands or the woods, you'll at least want a calf-high boot, if not knee-high. If you do wear an ankle-boot and are going into the woods, wear bird-hunting pants or chaps over your jeans or wool pants to protect your legs from thorns and burrs. If you are hunting in parts of Texas or other areas known to have venomous snakes, then snake chaps are a must.

Rule 8: Never shoot a gun with an obstruction or bulge in the barrel.

- Mud, snow, excess lubricating oil, or grease in the bore can increase barrel pressure when a cartridge is fired. If a cartridge is fired in this instance, the barrel can bulge or even burst, causing injury to the shooter and possibly even those around her.
- If the barrel becomes obstructed with mud, snow, sand, or any other substance, the first thing you must do is carefully unload the gun, pointing the muzzle away from you and anyone else who may be around you. Once you are certain the gun is completely unloaded, including the magazine, you can run a bore brush through the barrels.
- Make it a habit to clean the bore and check for obstructions with a shotgun cleaning rod immediately before you shoot it. If the noise or recoil on firing seems weak or doesn't seem quite "right," cease firing immediately and be sure to check that no obstruction or improper size cartridge is lodged in the barrel(s).
- Placing a smaller gauge or caliber cartridge into a gun (such as a 20-gauge shell in a 12-gauge shotgun) can result in the smaller cartridge falling into the barrel and acting as a bore obstruction when a cartridge of proper size is fired. This can cause a barrel to burst. Avoid this type of accident by paying close attention to each cartridge you insert into your firearm. Don't mix different gauge cartridges, or same gauge but different loads, in your cartridge bag.

Rule 9: Never attempt to repair or modify your gun yourself. Leave it to a professional gunsmith.

- Firearms are complicated mechanisms that are designed to function properly in their original condition. Any alteration or change made to a firearm can render the gun dangerous unless undertaken by a professional gunsmith.
- Your gun is a mechanical device that will not last forever and is subject to wear. Just like a car, it should have a regular inspection by a professional gunsmith. He will clean and service your gun, and adjust it as needed.

- Meantime, you are responsible for regular maintenance. That means you should wipe your gun down when you come in from shooting, especially if the gun is wet from inclement weather or waterfowl hunting. Don't leave it until later. Carbon and plastic build up inside the barrels from cartridge wads.

Rule 10: Know the mechanical and handling characteristics of the shotgun you're planning to shoot before you take it to the field or shooting grounds.

- Shotgun configurations and models, even the design of actions that are unique to some gunmakers, operate differently from one another. An over/under, for example, does not operate like a pump-action, nor does a pump-action load or extract cartridges in the same manner as a

▲ If you are entering the sport, the most important decision you can make is selecting an instructor who is "right" for you. There needs to be a dynamic between you so that what you are being taught is thoroughly understandable and what you hear can be translated easily into what you do. Professional shooting instructor John Shima is pictured here coaching a student. Notice she is wearing proper ear and eye protection, a brimmed cap, and a shooting vest.

semiautomatic. A sidelever side-by-side shotgun and an underlever both open the action, but the parts are not the same design. Be familiar with the operation of the gun you're shooting!
- Take time to thoroughly read the instruction manual that comes with your new gun.
- If you have purchased or inherited a previously owned gun, the first thing you should do is to take it to a professional gunsmith and have it cleaned and serviced. He will show you how the gun operates. It is also interesting to look up the make, model, and year of manufacture of your gun online or in reference books and learn all you can.
- If you are a beginner, your shotgun instructor will go over the operation of the gun with you. You must never attempt to shoot a shotgun without proper instruction first.

Rule 11: Never shoot under the influence of alcohol or drugs.

- Alcohol and shooting don't mix. Never drink before or during a shoot or hunt. True, it's not uncommon for some to have a glass of beer or wine during a lunch break and in Scotland, a "wee half" of Scotch that's belted down just as the sun is rising "warms the blood" before you head out on the grouse moors.
- The fact is, anything that dulls your senses, causes dizziness, and compromises your judgement—whether it's alcohol, drugs, and even prescription medicines—makes you a potential menace in the field or on the course, and puts you—and more importantly, others—in danger. Likewise, if you have suffered a stroke, suffer from vertigo or chronic migraines, or have been hospitalized recently, discuss with your medical practitioner whether you should be shooting, and when and how you can resume.
- By the same token, if you have a sudden and temporary feeling of dizziness or lightheadedness, unsteadiness, loss of balance, feeling of floating, or a false sense of spinning, unload your gun immediately, get help, and quit shooting for the day—or days, depending upon how long these feelings last and are completely well. Causes may include a sudden drop in blood pressure,

an anxiety attack, anemia, hypoglycemia, an ear infection, dehydration, heat stroke, or simply "overdoing it."

Rule 12: Never shoot if you are uncertain of your shot or afraid to shoot.

- You can't take back a shot once it's fired. If you are unsure, don't shoot. If you're unsure of your gun, don't shoot. If you are suddenly afraid—and that can be for any number of reasons—don't shoot.
- Before you prepare to fire your shotgun, be absolutely sure of your target; be certain that nothing stands between you and your shot; and be aware of exactly where everyone in your group is standing—hunting buddies, team members, spectators; and if on a driven shoot, that includes the beaters, gun loaders, dog handlers, and dogs.

In conclusion, recreational shooting is among the safest of all sports, but only when a gun is in the hands of a responsible, rational, composed, qualified individual who thoroughly and properly knows how to handle her gun, and knows and abides by the rules of gun safety. No gun is foolproof and by the same token, no fool should ever handle a gun.

Beginners and young people must be closely supervised when handling firearms at all times until they are proven proficient by a shooting instructor or qualified shooter.

Never be timid when it comes to gun safety. If you observe anyone violating any safety precautions, you have an obligation to insist on safer handling practices. Always err on the side of caution.

Follow the rules of gun safety, develop safe shooting habits, and never forget: a gun is only safe when it is locked up or in safe hands. Firearms safety is *entirely* up to you. To access the National Shooting Sports Foundation's excellent safety advice, "Firearms Safety Depends on You," go online to www3.nssf.org/share/PDF/safety/FSDOY.pdf

Securing Your Guns at Home

Storing your guns at home in a safe and secure place is required of every gun owner. You may have a gun room, but unless your guns are kept in a locked gun vault, they are neither safe nor secure. You may have a burglar-proof home alarm system, if there is one, but that won't prevent a person, young or old, who is unfamiliar with guns from accessing them. The best solution is a gun safe. Gun safes come in all sizes, many variations, and a wide range of prices. Rather than buy the most expensive gun you can afford, buy one a little less expensive and take the extra money to buy a gun safe to put it in. That's an investment no money can buy.

- Never put a loaded gun away in your gun cabinet or safe.
- Store ammunition in a separate place from your gun, not with your gun in your gun safe.
- If you cannot afford a gun safe, set aside a closet you can secure with a heavy-duty lock. Keep the key or combination in a hidden place.
- Never leave a gun under the bed, under the cushions of a sofa, or as a wall-hanger.
- The National Shooting Sports Foundation's "Firearms Responsibility in the Home" is available online at www3.nssf.org/share/PDF/safety/FRITH.pdf

About 1.4 million firearms were stolen in the United States during household burglaries and other property crimes over the six-year period from 2005 through 2010, according to a report released by the US Department of Justice's Bureau of Justice Statistics (BJS). This number represents an estimated average of 232,400 firearms stolen each year—about 172,000 stolen during burglaries and 60,300 stolen during other property crimes. These estimates are based on data from the annual National Crime Victimization Survey (NCVS), which has collected information from victims of crime since 1973. Of the guns stolen each year during burglaries and other property crimes, at least 80 percent, or an annual average of 186,800 firearms, had not been recovered up to six months after being stolen.

From 2005 through 2010, firearms were stolen in about 4 percent of the 2.4 million household burglaries and in less than 1 percent of the 13.6 million other property crimes involving a completed theft that occurred during the period. Longer trends from 1994 to 2010 show a 49 percent decline in the total number of victimizations involving the theft of at least one firearm, from about 283,600 victimizations in 1994 to about 145,300 in 2010. Handguns were the most commonly stolen firearm from 2005 through 2010. At least one handgun was stolen in 63 percent of household burglaries and 68 percent of other property crimes involving firearm theft. More than one gun was stolen in 39 percent of burglaries and 15 percent of other property crimes involving gun theft. Household burglaries involving stolen firearms were more likely to be reported to police (86 percent) than burglaries involving the theft of other items (62 percent) of comparable value ($500–$999). When a handgun was stolen, about 90 percent of burglaries were reported to the police.

From 2005 through 2010, household property crimes involving only stolen firearms resulted in a total loss of about $27 million per year. The average financial loss when only one gun was stolen was between $400 and $500 per incident. Other findings showed:

- About three out of four household property crimes involving stolen firearms occurred in households headed by white non-Hispanic persons.
- From 2005 through 2010, the majority of household burglaries (56 percent) or other property crimes (59 percent) involving stolen firearms occurred in the American South.
- Households in rural areas experienced a disproportionate percentage of burglaries involving stolen firearms (34 percent), compared

GUN SAFES

Gun safes are made by a number of companies, in many sizes, capacities, styles, types, and colors. Among the many are:

Cabela's Outfitter E-Lock 25-Gun Safe by Liberty Safe holds up to twenty-five long guns and features a SecuRam electronic lock, protected by a drill-proof, triple-hard plate and military-style locking bars. The two-piece roll-form, 12-gauge steel body is enforced with three layers of fire protection in the ceiling and door jambs. Rated 68,000-BTU fire resistance. Weight: 490 lbs. 30 inches x 25 inches x 60.5 inches.

Cabela's Classic Series E-Lock 48-Gun by Liberty Safe holds up to forty-eight long guns plus an interior door panel for additional handgun and accessory storage. This vault features a SecuRam top-lit, electronic lock, heavy-duty, four-inch locking bars, and a three-point chrome handle for ultimate security. Constructed from 12-gauge steel body with black marble powder-coat finish, this vault's eleven layers of fireboard and Palusol heat-expanding door seal provide sixty minutes of fire protection at 1,200°F. Weight: 760 lbs. 60.5 inches x 42 inches x 25 inches.

ProVault 12-Gun Safe by Liberty is robotically welded, CNC-machined steel two-piece construction that virtually eliminates prying on all sides. Ten military-style locking bars and an electronic lock reinforces the safe's security and the one-inch-thick, Palusol door seal expands when exposed to heat. Multiple fireboard layers result in a thirty-minute fire rating at 1,200°F. Tough external hinges allow the door to open 180 degrees for easy access to firearms. Shelving allows storage of handguns and other small valuables. Weight: 247 lbs. 59 inches x 18 inches x 16 inches.

The Hornady 98190 Rapid Safe AR Gun Locker is ideal for storing long guns under a bed. Heavy-duty and tamperproof, it measures 42 inches x 15.25 inches x 6.75 inches.

The Black Label Mark V Blackout safe has a CMS Adjustable Interior and DPX door system that provide versatile storage for guns of all lengths. Its tactical black finish contributes to a 1400° F/sixty-minute fire protection rating.

The ultralight SecureIt Agile Model 52 Plus gun safe system is made with military-grade craftsmanship and CradleGrid Technology for secure, organized, and adaptable storage for six shotguns. At only 105 lbs., it is an ideal choice for apartments and basements.

to the overall percentage of US households located in rural areas (17 percent).

CREDIT: *Firearms Stolen during Household Burglaries and Other Property Crimes, 2005–2010* (NCJ 239436), written by BJS statistician Lynn Langton. The report, related documents, and additional information about the Bureau of Justice Statistics' statistical publications and programs can be found on www.bjs.gov.

Children and Guns

▲ Although she is not old enough to take lessons, shooting instructor John Shima paves the way by showing a little girl where to point the muzzle of the gun safely and that yes, she can touch a gun—but only under adult supervision. Photo courtesy of John Shima.

Guns must be kept from children and children must be kept from guns. Never assume when you tell a young child to stay away from a gun that you will be obeyed. Telling isn't enough. Children by nature are curious. When they are told not to do something, it's almost like a dare.

"Why not?" they ask. Young children simply do not have the maturity or understanding to be introduced to guns at this young age.

But as a child approaches her teenage years, her curiosity and naïve interest in guns cannot be dismissed with "when you're old enough" or "just leave it alone." If you shoot, it's likely your child will want to learn to shoot, too. If you have a gun at home, my feeling is that you have a responsibility to teach gun safety to your child who is aged twelve and over. Even

after your child shows an understanding of gun safety, he or she should never be allowed to handle a gun without adult supervision. You should never allow your child access to your gun safe by giving her the lock combination or key.

You may say, "But I trust my child. She'd never do anything I tell her not to do," and I hope that's true. But our children are overburdened by too many social influences, tethered to cellphones, stressed out over peer pressure. If the gun safe hasn't been locked, if you've set aside a gun to be cleaned after coming in from the field with the intention of cleaning it later— there are all kinds of scenarios that can play out when you assume your child, *any* child, will not be curious or tempted to reach for a gun. What may seem like an innocent bit of fun can end in tragedy if you have failed to teach, and strictly enforce, gun safety in the home.

Take time to sit down and explain to your child that when you feel she is ready and when she has shown the maturity and presence of mind to be responsible to handle a gun, then you will enroll her in a firearms safety course, and if she passes and earns her orange hunter's safety card, you will arrange for her to take lessons with a professional shooting instructor. Then, when you take them to shoot sporting clays or go on a bird hunt, not only will you have started your child on the right foot, but you will begin to share time and experiences together, weave memories, and prepare the sporting legacy you will eventually leave them. Equally important, having earned the privilege of handling a sporting firearm, they will have first proved to you—and themselves—that he or she is growing into a mature and responsible person. And that's something to be proud of, my friend.

Go online with your child and view together this excellent video, produced by the National Shooting Sports Foundation, called "Parents Talking with Their Kids About Gun Safety": www.youtube.com/watch?v=M86QxNZF3AE. This video, which is less than six minutes long, may be the best investment of time you and your family can spend together. Afterwards, discuss what you have viewed. You may be surprised at what your child has to say.

Project ChildSafe
Gun Safety Checklist for Families with Children under the Age of Eighteen

- Have you sat down with your children to discuss guns?
- Have you enrolled your child who is twelve years old or older in a gun safety course?
- Are your guns kept in a locked vault, gun safe, or closet rigged with a combination lock and heavy-duty chain that is bolted to the door and a wall stud? Is the key or combination kept in a secret place?
- Are your guns unloaded when stored in your gun safe?
- Have you stored your shotgun cartridges in a place away from your gun safe?
- Do you have gun sleeves or gun cases in which to put your gun when you get it out of the gun safe to take to the range or field?

The National Shooting Sports Foundation provides further information online in "Parent's Guide to Recreational Shooting for Children" at www3.nssf.org/share/PDF/safety/ParentsGuide.pdf.

Project ChildSafe is the largest, most comprehensive firearm safety education program in the United States. It was developed by the National Shooting Sports Foundation (NSSF), the trade association for the firearms industry, and is committed to promoting genuine firearm safety through the distribution of safety education messages and free firearm safety kits. The kits include a cable-style gun-locking device and a brochure (also available in Spanish) that discusses safe handling and secure storage guidelines to help deter access by unauthorized individuals.

Project ChildSafe is a real firearm safety solution that helps make communities safer. Since 1999, more than fifteen thousand law enforcement agencies have partnered with the program to distribute more than 37 million firearm safety kits to gun owners in all fifty states and five US territories. Through vital partnerships with elected officials, community leaders, state agencies, businesses, the firearms industry and other stakeholders, Project ChildSafe has helped raise awareness about the safe and responsible ownership of firearms and the importance of storing firearms securely when not in use to help prevent accidents, theft and accidental discharge. For a free ChildSafe kit, go online to www.projectchildsafe.org/safety/find-a-safety-kit.

▲ Safe firearm handling can lead to shared family activities. Ryan Stalvey and his daughters, Ella (left) and Parker, shoot together every fall. Photo by Nicole Stalvey.

Vehicles and Shotguns

As a gun owner, it is your responsibility to protect your guns and keep them out of the wrong hands. Whether you're going to the gun club or a preserve for a few hours or heading off on a hunting trip, there are times you will have to leave your shotgun in your vehicle.

▲ Project ChildSafe lock. Photo courtesy of NSSF.

Even a brief break at a rest stop or stopping for lunch creates a situation that deserves careful consideration—the last thing you want is to have your shotgun stolen and potentially misused by a criminal. In some states, you could even be subject under the law to serious penalties and fines for failure to properly secure a firearm.

Tragically, thefts of firearms from vehicles are on the rise. In September 2019, Tallahassee officials announced the number one problem in the surge of violent crime was guns stolen from unlocked vehicles. In the two previous months, fifty-three guns were reported stolen, increasingly from teen violence, loitering, and drug-related incidents. Thieves commonly steal cars and trucks even when they don't obviously contain firearms—a reminder that vehicle door locks are not totally secure. As a responsible gun owner concerned about your firearms falling into the wrong hands, it's best to always remember this rule: *Your firearm must be under your control at all times; when that's not possible, your shotgun should be locked and secured to your vehicle and out of sight.* Locking the doors on your vehicle does not constitute secure firearm storage. Cars and trucks are not gun safes. The trunk of your car or your truck console, even if lockable, can be broken into easily.

Safety Precautions in and around Vehicles

- It can't be repeated enough: you must always control the muzzle direction of your shotgun—and that goes for when you are taking your shotgun out of, or returning it to, your vehicle. Likewise, never *assume* your shotgun is unloaded—*be absolutely sure it's unloaded.*
- Never load your shotgun while you are in your vehicle. Always unload your shotgun before you get into your vehicle.
- Never leave firearms in or around your vehicle where they are accessible to children or pets—even if all you're doing is something as innocent as putting on your shooting vest. Accidents *always* happen in a split second.
- Keep your shotgun out of sight to avoid tempting thieves—and also conceal your ammunition and hunting accoutrements.

▲ Fast Box Model 40 gun safe system by SecureIt.

The Fast Box Model 40 gun safe system by SecureIt is a heavy-duty vehicle gun vault that weighs only forty pounds. It has pre-drilled holes so you can mount the box in trucks, SUVs, and large vehicles. It holds shotguns up to thirty-nine inches.

▲ Boss StrongBox Pull Out Drawer.

The BOSS StrongBox 7126-7640 Pull Out Drawer is a single, high-security Medeco lock drawer system constructed of cold-rolled steel and powder coated in wrinkled black. Made in America. www.bossstrongbox.com/vehicle-gun-storage

2. The Fundamental Shotgun

A shotgun is a smoothbore, short-range, shoulder-mounted firearm with one or two barrels; its length is no less than eighteen inches in length by law and generally no more than thirty-four inches. Also known as a "scattergun" and historically a fowling piece used to shoot birds, the modern shotgun is designed to discharge a cartridge, or shotshell, which is a shot charge that is contained within a water-impervious plastic hull (far less common are paper hulls, such as Federal Gold Medal Grand Paper shotshells).

When the shotgun trigger is pulled, the hammer is released, which forces the firing pin to strike the primer of the cartridge. The ignition from the primer lights the powder. The powder causes a controlled explosion; the gases formed from the explosion propel the wad with the shot charge down the barrel and toward the target. When the shell is fired, it results in an explosion. The explosion is contained in the chamber, which is the thickest part of the barrel. The subsequent force that propels the shell backwards is the recoil. The momentum of the explosion propels the shot charge down the barrel, which is the only opening for the explosion to discharge.

Shotgun Cartridges

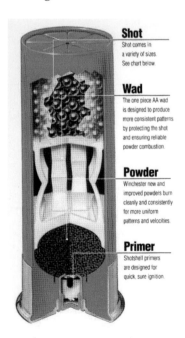

Shot
Shot comes in a variety of sizes. See chart below.

Wad
The one piece AA wad is designed to produce more consistent patterns by protecting the shot and ensuring reliable powder combustion.

Powder
Winchester new and improved powders burn cleanly and consistently for more uniform patterns and velocities.

Primer
Shotshell primers are designed for quick, sure ignition.

▲ Parts of a shotgun cartridge.

Also known as shotshells or shells, shotgun cartridges contain a plastic wad (some cartridges have felt or fiber wads) designed to hold the pellets together and to keep them from becoming deformed as they travel down the barrels. Once the wad holding the shot exits the barrel, the wad falls away from the shot charge as the shot charge travels toward the target. The shot charge is compact when it leaves the muzzle and the further it travels, the more the pattern, or spread of the pellets, elongates and widens, sort of in a funnel-shape.

A cartridge can contain anywhere between nine and five hundred pellets depending upon the cartridge size, but it only takes four or five pellets to effectively strike a target. Unlike a rifle, a shotgun does not rely upon the speed of the charge or projectile it fires. On the contrary, any increase in muzzle velocity would be lost within a few yards of the charge leaving the barrels due to the disproportionately increased air resistance that the shot pellets would encounter. For this reason, the optimum effective range of a shotgun is between twenty and forty yards, depending upon the gauge, load, and choke of the gun. The gun you shoot and the target at which you shoot, whether it is a clay bird or game bird, determine the load required to effectively hit the target.

There are three basic shotgun configurations: break-open, semiautomatic, and pump-action.

Shotgun Configurations

A break-open shotgun is a gun that opens where the barrels join the receiver. The majority of break-open shotguns have two barrels. (One-barrel break-open, single-shot shotguns are generally used for trap and skeet shooting.) This configuration is sometimes referred to as a hinge gun because it opens on a hinge. The maximum capacity of any two-barrel break-open shotgun is two cartridges, as only one cartridge can be loaded in each chamber at a time. There are two types of break-open guns: the side-by-side and the over/under.

▲ Break-open gun.

The side-by-side is a double-barreled shotgun with the two barrels, each identical in shape, size, and length. The barrels are connected to one another by soldering them together, to a rib, thereby creating a horizontal "sight plane" as you look down the barrels. This configuration is sometimes referred to as a "horizontal gun." There are two types of side-by-side shotgun receivers: the boxlock and the sidelock. A sidelock has many more working parts than a boxlock and is the action on most fine custom guns. The origin of the hammer shotgun dates to the early nineteenth century in France and Belgium; however the hammerless action was Anson and Deeley's boxlock patent of 1875 in England and in America, Daniel Myron Lefever's automatic hammerless shotgun patent of 1883.

An over/under is also a double-barreled, break-open shotgun, but in this configuration, the barrels are set one on top of the other. For this reason, it is sometimes referred to as a "stacked gun." The over/under was introduced by the London gunmaker, Boss, in 1909, but it did not achieve rising popularity until 1985, when sporting clays became popular in this country with the formation of the United States Sporting Clays Association (USSCA) in Houston, Texas.

A semiautomatic shotgun, or autoloader, is a single-barrel gun that fires a cartridge every time the trigger is pulled without needing to chamber another round. Types of semiautomatic shotguns are gas, blowback, and recoil-operated. Normally you can have three shells in the magazine and one in the chamber; however US federal law for most hunting requires that the magazine be plugged to only hold two shells, limiting the overall capacity to three.

▲ Cosmi 12-gauge semiautomatic shotgun.

A pump-action shotgun is a single-barrel gun that loads when the hand moves the fore-end back and forth to eject a spent shell and immediately load a fresh cartridge into the chamber. It is also known as a slide-action shotgun. First patented in England in 1854, the hand cycles the action using a back and forth motion, which lifts the shells loaded into a tubular magazine model to the level of the barrel. After the trigger is pulled, the round is fired, the bolt is unlocked, moves to the rear and extracts and ejects the empty shell from the chamber, cocks the hammer, and repeats the operating cycle.

▲ Boxlock receiver.

▲ Two Winchester Model 12 pump-action shotguns. Photo: Rock Island Auction Company, Rock Island, Illinois.

▲ Actress Jane Russell with a Winchester Model 12 pump gun.

There are two other types of single-barrel actions that you sometimes, but seldom, come across and these are the **bolt action** and the **lever action**. By and large, these are rifle actions. In the bolt action, the bolt is manually unlocked from the receiver to load and eject a cartridge. In the lever action, a lever is located under the trigger guard and pushed forward, then back, to eject and load the cartridge. Neither of these actions is used for clay target or game bird shooting.

▲ Bolt action.

Parts of a Shotgun

A shotgun is made up of three basic parts: the gunstock, the action, and the barrels.

The gunstock of a shotgun is made up of two parts: the buttstock and the fore-end. Most gunstocks are made of walnut, a dense, fine-grained wood, and sometimes maple, which is also strong and durable. Some guns have synthetic stocks, which are made of composite materials such as Kevlar or fiberglass whose durable, waterproof qualities are favored by waterfowl hunters. Synthetic stocks are offered in black, moss green, and a variety of camouflage patterns, depending upon the maker, which is an advantage in the duck blind, where a hunter must be visually concealed as waterfowl come in close enough for a shot.

The buttstock, or butt, is the predominant part of a gunstock that you raise up, or mount, to your shoulder. Correctly done, this puts your eye in alignment with the barrel and the object you are pointing at in the distance. The working mechanism, or receiver, is hung in the buttstock. The buttstock also serves as a recoil absorber, reducing the impact of the gun against your shoulder when you fire a shot. The fore-end, or forestock, is the part of the gunstock under the barrel(s) that you cradle with your non-shooting hand. A shotgun cannot operate without a gunstock.

The grip is the portion of the gunstock directly behind the trigger guard. There are three types of shotgun grips. The straight-hand, or "English-style," grip is designed for driven shooting, a sport we discuss further on, where birds fly overhead. A pistol-grip gunstock tends to give you better control of the shotgun, because it works more in unison with your front hand. Clay shooters favor the pistol grip because it aligns the hand with the stock. The pommel, or "Prince of Wales grip," falls between the straight grip and the pistol grip, sort of a marriage between the two, and allows you greater control of the gun on field shots, where you need a better reaction to what is happening. The British favor the Prince of Wales grip for rough shooting and the straight grip for driven shooting.

The butt is the back end of the gun you hold against your shoulder. It is usually covered with a metal, horn, plastic, leather, or rubber buttplate, which is also called buttpad or recoil pad. Its purpose is to cushion the shoulder from the rearward force of recoil when a shotgun is fired. On fine guns, custom guns, and many older British and Continental guns, the wooden butt is often finished off with a woodworking technique called checkering, a cross-hatch pattern of fine lines that prevents the butt from slipping on the shoulder. Fore-ends and the wrist of the gunstock are usually checkered for the same reason. Checkering affords a slip-resistant grip for your hand. Besides, it is a beautiful way of finishing off a gunstock. There are a number of checkering patterns, from plain to elegant, that can be specified on custom gunstocks. Many gunstock makers can checker a gunstock, and often an expensive custom or deluxe shotgun is placed in the skilled hands of a gunstock checkerer, whose specialty is checkering gunstocks.

Shotgun Barrels

A gun barrel is a steel tube through which a cartridge is fired. A barrel has four parts:

> The chamber is at the breech end of the barrel. The cartridge is inserted manually into the chamber or receiver of a gun. A side-by-side or over/under has two barrels and therefore can only be loaded with one cartridge in each barrel at any time. The magazine of self-loading shotguns (pump-action, bolt-action, lever-action, and semiautomatic) can be loaded with multiple rounds at one time. However, you never load more than two cartridges when you are shooting the clay target games and three maximum for ducks or other federally controlled game birds.

The forcing cone is like a funnel that tapers the interior of the barrel to the bore diameter. The forcing cone allows the fired cartridge to make a smooth transition to the choke at the muzzle. The bore is the section of the barrel between the forcing cone and the choke. The choke is the constriction of the barrel at the muzzle. Choke determines the spread of the shot pellets.

The metals and alloys used to make gun barrels are steel, an alloy of iron mixed with other elements, mainly carbon, since pure iron is too soft; stainless steel; and aluminum, all of which are capable of withstanding fifty thousand pounds of pressure per square inch. Most shotgun barrels are made from AISI

(American Iron and Steel Institute) 4140 chromium-molybdenum alloy, known as ordnance steel. Before this, most shotgun barrels were made of Whitworth steel, also known as fluid-compressed steel, a method patented by British mechanical engineer Joseph Whitworth in 1874 and used well into the 1930s in the manufacture of rifle and shotgun barrels by most gun-makers, including London gunmaker Purdey & Sons and, in America, by Parker, L.C. Smith, and Lefever. Before then, gun barrels were made from Damascus steel. Named after the ancient city of Damascus in Syria, the process dates to 300 A.D., when it was used in the manufacture of swords and knives. The process involves wrapping twists of forged steel around a tube and then soldering them together. Damascus barrels cannot withstand the pressure of modern, smokeless powder loads, as the pressure can cause the barrels to rupture. Before you shoot an older gun, first have it inspected by a professional gunsmith to determine if it's safe to shoot—and even then, *only shoot with black powder loads.*

▲ Extractors and Ejectors.

Extractors and Ejectors

In a fixed-breech gun, which would either be a side-by-side or an over/under shotgun, once the shell is fired the hull needs to be extracted from the gun so you can replace it with a live cartridge. Up until the early twentieth century, when the gun was opened, two levers, located under the rim of the hull, moved the hull out of the chamber to about a half-inch of clearance, allowing the gunner to remove the hulls with his fingers. This lifting of the hulls, so the gunner could extract them, gave rise to the word "extractor." These made it easy to unload and reload the shotgun. In the early twentieth century, gunmakers added a spring to the extractors so when the gun was opened, the extractors could now eject the empty hull without the gunner having to handle it. The spring-powered extractors that ejected the hull from the gun became known as ejectors, which would land the spent cartridge on the ground unless intercepted by hand. Ejectors are common today on over/unders, but not so much on side-by-side shotguns.

Shot Sizes

Shotgun pellets, or *shot*, are the most common projectiles fired from shotguns. Shotgun pellets were traditionally made of lead but have also been manufactured from bismuth, steel, tungsten–iron, tungsten–nickel–iron and tungsten polymer. Shot sizes for soft metals such as lead are measured on a different scale than shot sizes for harder metals such as steel.

LEAD SHOT SIZES

Shot Number	Diameter (in)	Diameter (mm)	Pellets in a 1 oz. load
12	.05	1.3	2300
9	.079	2.01	585
8.5	.085	2.16	470
8	.089	2.26	410
7.5	.094	2.39	350
6	.109	2.77	225
5	.120	3.05	170
4	.129	3.28	135
2	.148	3.76	90
BB	.18	4.57	50
4 Buck	.24	6.10	21
3 Buck	.25	6.35	19
2 Buck	.27	6.86	15
1 Buck	.30	7.62	11
0 Buck	.32	8.13	9
00 Buck	.33	8.38	8
000 Buck	.36	9.14	6.2

STEEL SHOT SIZES

Shot Number	Diameter (in)	Diameter (mm)	Pellets in a 1oz load
7	.10	2.54	422
6	.11	2.79	317
5	.12	3.81	244
4	.13	3.56	191
3	.14	3.30	154
2	.15	3.05	125
1	.16	2.79	103
BB	.18	4.57	72
BBB	.19	4.83	61
T	.20	5.08	53
F	.22	5.59	40

Chokes

Choke is the degree of constriction at the muzzle of a barrel. There are seven basic chokes: Cylinder (C); Skeet (S); Improved Cylinder (IC); Modified, or half-choke (M); Improved Modified, or three-quarter (IM); Full (F); and Extra Full (XF).

Type	Gauge	Cylinder	Skeet	IS	IC	LM	M	IM	LF	Full	XF	Turkey
10-ga. Standard	10	0.775	–	–	0.768	–	0.758	–	–	0.740	–	0.730
12-ga. Fixed	12	0.729	0.719	–	0.716	–	0.705	0.695	–	0.685	–	–
Beretta/Benelli Mobil	12	0.726	0.721	0.716	0.711	0.706	0.701	0.696	0.691	0.686	0.681	–
Beretta Optima Plus	12	0.732	0.727	0.722	0.717	0.712	0.707	0.702	0.697	0.692	0.687	–
Benelli Crio	12	0.727	0.722	0.717	0.712	0.707	0.702	0.697	0.692	0.687	0.682	–
Benelli Super Sport	12	0.727	0.722	0.717	0.712	0.707	0.702	0.697	0.692	0.687	0.682	–
Beretta Optima	12	0.732	0.727	0.722	0.717	0.712	0.707	0.702	0.697	0.692	0.687	–
Bettinsoli	12	0.729	0.724	0.719	0.714	0.709	0.704	0.699	0.694	0.689	0.684	–
Blaser	12	0.732	0.727	0.722	0.717	0.712	0.707	0.702	0.697	0.692	0.687	–
Browning Invector	12	0.727	0.722	0.717	0.712	0.707	0.702	0.697	0.692	0.687	0.682	0.670
Invector Plus	12	0.740	0.735	0.730	0.725	0.720	0.715	0.710	0.705	0.700	0.695	0.697
Krieghoff	12	0.733	0.728	0.723	0.718	0.713	0.708	0.702	0.698	0.693	0.688	–
Lanber	12	0.727	0.722	0.717	0.712	0.707	0.702	0.697	0.692	0.687	0.682	–
Remington	12	0.727	0.722	0.717	0.712	0.707	0.702	0.697	0.692	0.687	0.682	–
SKB	12	0.735	0.730	0.725	0.720	0.715	0.710	0.705	0.700	0.695	0.690	–
Winchester Invector	12	0.735	0.730	0.725	0.720	0.715	0.710	0.705	0.700	0.695	0.690	–
Beretta/Benelli Mobil	20	0.627	0.623	0.620	0.616	0.613	0.609	0.606	0.602	0.599	0.595	–
Browning Invector	20	0.618	0.614	0.611	0.607	0.604	0.600	0.597	0.593	0.590	0.586	–
Invector Plus	20	0.630	0.626	0.623	0.619	0.616	0.612	0.609	0.605	0.602	0.598	–
16-ga. Fixed	16	0.673	0.665	–	0.661	–	0.657	–	–	0.624	–	–
20-ga. Fixed	20	0.625	0.621	–	0.603	–	0.595	0.590	–	0.585	–	–
28-ga.Fixed	28	0.551	0.551	–	0.543	–	0.539	–	–	0.527	–	–
.410 Fixed	.410	0.409	0.404	–	0.404	–	0.402	–	–	0.398	–	–

IS = Improved Skeet, IC = Improved Cylinder, LM = Light Modified, M = Modified, IM = Improved Modified, LF = Light Full, XF = Extra-Full

Cylinder

Cylinder is the bore of a barrel without any constriction at the muzzle. Basically, the barrel is a straight tube when it has no choke. Cylinder is best for shooting targets at short range where the widest possible spread is most efficient, at basically twenty yards or less. Grouse hunting, woodcock, and quail are all good examples of use of the cylinder choke.

Skeet

The skeet choke was designed for optimum pattern at twenty-one to twenty-five yards. The game of skeet is shot at eight distinct stations. Seven of those stations are exactly twenty-one yards from the center of the station to the center of the field where the target crosses a specific line.

Improved Cylinder

Improved Cylinder features a slight constriction at the muzzle. This narrows the spread of pellets once the cartridge is fired and on its trajectory path to produce a slightly tighter, more consistent pattern than Skeet. IC chokes are good for any game bird shot in the twenty- to thirty-yard range, such as doves, pigeons, pheasants, chukar partridges, and ducks over decoys.

Modified

Modified is a general-purpose choke that has even more constriction at the muzzle and a tighter pattern than IC that is extremely effective up to forty yards. In a side-by-side, the left barrel of an upland game gun is often choked Modified if the right barrel is Improved Cylinder, so when the birds are going away, you shoot the first barrel because the birds are closer; you shoot the second barrel because the birds are further away. In driven shooting, and because on side-by-side you usually have two triggers, the opposite is best, and easily achieved, when you shoot the tighter barrel first at birds that are coming at you and the more open barrel on your next shot because now the birds are closer. When you're shooting a side-by-side, this approach is the same no matter what the chokes are.

Improved Modified

More often seen on British and Continental guns, Improved Modified is effective within forty-five yards on driven birds. As a shooter becomes more proficient, shooting at targets at greater distances is a natural progression in their skill set. Many driven shooting aficionados consistently shoot birds at forty to sixty yards, requiring ever-tighter chokes.

Full

For a long time, Full was the maximum constriction and tightest of all chokes. Primarily used for distance shooting at birds such as ducks, geese, sandhill cranes, and pheasants at distances in excess of forty-five yards, the birds require a larger number of pellets. You need to have enough pellets to kill the bird cleanly, and Full choke gives you that density of pattern at distance. The shot size depends upon the bird you're hunting. For ducks or pheasants, you use size 5 or 6; for geese or cranes, you use size 2 or BB.

Extra Full

Extra Full chokes came into vogue with the advent of turkey hunting. Turkeys are big, wary birds that are shot on the ground. The most effective way to kill a turkey is to shoot it in the head, but getting it close to concealment is often difficult. Heavy loads with large shot and dense patterns are required to kill a turkey cleanly at any distance—but especially at distances greater than thirty yards. Thus, the XF choke came into being to deliver this very dense pattern at distances up to fifty yards. Generally, four to six pellets with enough size and speed are required to cleanly kill a game bird. The choice of choke and shot size are critical to an effective kill.

3. Shotgun Technique

The Right Shooting Instructor for You

In selecting a shooting instructor, it's important you work with someone you can easily communicate with, who responds to your questions in a way you clearly understand, and from whom you can comfortably take counsel as she directs your progress. The National Skeet Shooting Association and National Sporting Clays Association offer the following excellent advice.

Choosing the right shooting instructor or coach is more art than science, as the instructor's personality and teaching style are almost as relevant as his or her qualifications. But there are some guidelines that can help steer you in the right direction and ensure that your choice is as objective as possible.

First, consider your purpose and your current level of experience. This will help determine which level instructor you should engage, as each not only has a different amount of training and expertise, but also has the expectation of teaching students at a corresponding stage. Here's what to expect from each level of instructor.

If you are a new shooter, a Level I instructor is the logical choice. Think of Level I as the entry-level stage where you should learn the basics of the game and shotgunning. This instructor will cover such topics as gun handling and safety, gun loading, eye dominance, leads, follow-through, how the game is played, and what you should know before shooting your first round of skeet. If you've shot skeet casually a few times but have never had formal training, you would likely start with a Level I instructor. You might choose a Level I if you are going to a corporate Skeet shoot and first want to become comfortable with gun handling. Even if you're an experienced hunter but haven't shot skeet, a Level I instructor would be a reasonable choice to teach you the game and help you make the transition to Skeet.

Level II instructors are for intermediate-level shooters, B Class and below. If you have already learned the basics from a Level I instructor or have been shooting Skeet for a few years, you are ready to move to this level. Shooters are ready for Level II instruction when they need an extra boost to take their shooting performance to the next level. These instructors will help you break down your shooting into finer elements that can be tweaked and corrected. They will help you see what

you're doing right and wrong, reinforcing positive traits and correcting those that need improvement.

Level III instructors have a great deal of experience and training, and they work with shooters from beginners through A and AA class. They are prepared to improve your techniques, correct target difficulties, and improve your shoot-off performance.

Master Level instructors have undergone a great deal of training, have spent many hours working as an instructor, and are very experienced diagnosticians. They work with the highest level of shooters, AA to AAA. They are generally full-time instructors who can assess, improve, and correct problems in all areas, including attitude and mental aspects.

Some Level III and Master Level instructors start with beginning shooters who want to learn the game from the most highly trained instructor and continue to train with the same person for a period of years. If you are serious about learning and improving your game and intend to engage an instructor on an extended basis, that can be a good approach.

Once you've considered your purpose and experience and determined the level of instructor you should hire, the choice becomes more subjective. Here are some pointers to consider:

- Does your local club have an instructor on staff or on call, or does it have visiting instructors who offer clinics periodically?
- Do you want private lessons or a clinic? Even if you feel intimidated by learning with other shooters in a clinic, don't discount this option, if it's available. You'd be surprised how much you can learn by watching the instruction of other shooters while you're waiting for your turn to shoot.
- Visit the websites of any instructors you're considering. You can learn a lot about how they do business and perhaps how they instruct. Have they made videos or written blogs or other instructional materials? While those aren't necessary qualifications, if the material is there, you should review it.
- Ask other shooters for recommendations. Inquire about instructors' teaching style and personality.
- Ask the instructor for references and follow through with contacting them. If the instructor is

insulted by this request, find someone else. Ask the references both what they like and what they don't like about how the instructor teaches.

- Remember that just as our personalities and learning styles are distinctive, so are the instructors. A good choice for your friend may not be a good choice for you, and vice versa. That's why it's just as important to know what someone else does not like about an instructor; that "offensive" trait may suit you just fine.
- Talk in advance to any instructor with whom you're considering booking lessons. This will help you decide if they are a good fit in personality.
- Tell the prospective instructor exactly what your level of experience and expertise are. Just as you are looking for a particular level of instructor, he/she may be looking for a particular level of student. For example, a Level I instructor may not accept students who are Master or AAA class, and it certainly isn't beneficial to work with an instructor who is expecting to teach you the basics if you're far beyond that. If you're participating in a clinic, the instructor will try to group shooters of similar experience together. Shooters tend to overstate their experience, perhaps from embarrassment at admitting they are new to the sport or haven't taken it seriously before. To get the most from your clinics or lessons, be as clear as possible about your current expertise.

Gun Fit

You need a professional instructor, a shotgun that fits you, and a positive attitude if you want to enjoy the sports. But first you need to understand gun fit—what it does, and just why it is so important. Proper gun fit is achieved when a gunstock is tailored to you, so the barrel alignment and line of sight are the same. A properly fitted gun benefits the shooter in two ways. First, it allows you to focus your full concentration on the target. A gun that fits properly also builds confidence. The shooter knows that the gun will hit what she is focused on. Second, there is less felt recoil. Felt recoil means just that—how much you feel the gun kick back, or recoil, into your shoulder when the gun is fired. When a gun fits properly, the recoil is absorbed equally among the hands, the shoulder, and the body.

▲ The entire philosophy of proper gun fit is the gun shoots where you are looking. Notice how Carole Lombard looks over the barrels at her target.

The entire philosophy of proper gun fit is the gun shoots where you are looking. Where you are looking and the point-of-impact must be the same if you are to hit the target accurately and consistently.

Your shooting instructor, or a professional stock fitter or stockmaker, can check this out for you. Under no circumstance should you purchase a gun, new or previously owned, unless the gun either fits you or can be adjusted by a professional stockmaker to fit you. Never, under any circumstances, should you assume that you, your friend, or your husband can "whittle a little here and there" to make a stock fit. Even the replacement of a buttplate for a buttpad is the work of a professional gunsmith because it can change the length-of-pull, the cant, and the cast. Cutting down or extending a stock is absolutely left to the professionals. And if you think you can pare down a fore-end, forget it. The delicate inlaid metal of a fore-end is made precisely to fit the wood and is the part of a shotgun that is the most difficult, and oftentimes most fragile, to work on.

A shotgun moves with the moving target. Gun fit, therefore, is as critical in clay target shooting as it is in wingshooting. In fact, it's probably more critical in target shooting. Bird flight is more consistent and even predictable than clay target flight. Birds are either accelerating or flying the same speed. Targets from the moment they leave the trap are decelerating. Traps can be set to throw the clays so that the clay turns in the air, follows the lay of the land, is visually deceptive. A good clay-setter can fool most shooters. In sporting clays, a shooter may ask for a "looker," which allows you to see the trajectory of the target before you "call for a target" to shoot. Clay target shooting often involves a lot more of what is referred to as "technical targets." This is very different from wingshooting.

Proper gun fit likewise can make all the difference in wingshooting between a clean kill, crippling a bird, or a sheer miss. There is little control over the shots presented in bird-hunting situations. On flushed targets, until the bird rises, you are never certain from where it is coming or where it is going. The time you have to get into the ready position, mount the gun, and pull the trigger is measured in milliseconds. It doesn't matter what you are shooting, it's what your mind is calculating every time. During the wisp of time you have to make your shot, you have to observe the speed, angle, and distance of the bird in order to determine the all-important lead, focus on the bird, and swing through the bird to intercept its flight pattern with the dispersing shot pellets from your cartridge. If that bird is weaving here and there, like the wily king of upland birds, the ruffed grouse, then it is your subconscious that will command your trigger finger. However, because a properly fitted shotgun is an extenuation of your sight line and hands, you should be able to focus entirely on the bird and virtually forget the gun. If you have to think about the gun, if you see the barrel of the gun in any way, you will lose your concentration on the target and you might as well forfeit the shot. In wingshooting, failure to concentrate invariably results in a miss.

A properly fitted shotgun will feel as natural to you as if it were an extenuation of your own hands. You will have a reliable sight line and you don't need to, or should, see the rib of the barrels. This is what enables you to track the target effectively. Always focus on the target, never focus on the gun. When a shotgun fits you properly, you will have no reason to look at the barrels, jostle the buttstock into your shoulder until it is comfortable, bend your head down into the stock for it to meet your cheek, or wonder where the barrels are pointing.

When a gun fits you, you will bring the stock up until it touches your cheek. The barrels will follow your eyes as you point. And you will swing through the moving target.

There are several aspects of gunstock fit that must be considered for a gun to fit you properly. This is a subject I deal with extensively, and also with the help of experts—so be prepared to hear about it repeatedly because yes, it's that important to your becoming an efficient shooting sportswoman. And if you don't shoot efficiently and effectively, how can you enjoy the sport?

There are several measurements that must be accurately taken when you are properly fitted for a gun. Some gun fitters will use a "try gun," which is a stock that is sectioned into moveable pieces and adjusted with screws and bolts, so each aspect conforms with your measurements. While most gun fitters have a try gun, they only use it for clients who are ordering custom stocks.

Most important of all measurements is the length-of-pull (the measurement from the trigger to the butt of the stock). Most factory-made guns, apart from those specifically made for women, have a length-of-pull of fourteen and a half inches, more or less. A wood gunstock can be shortened or lengthened with a spacer or extender at the buttpad. This is a job for a professional gunsmith. A length-of-pull that is too long or too short for you will affect the way you shoot. If you are being struck in the face, thumb, or knuckle, your gun fit is wrong, and if your gun fit is wrong it stands to reason that your gun mount is too, because you've been forced to compensate for a gun that does not fit you properly.

Gun fit also depends upon the gun configuration. The length-of-pull shooting a side-by-side is sometimes longer than an over/under and the two barrels alongside one another in a side-by-side provide a wider sight plane that requires a different cast to the stock than the narrower sight plane of an over/under gun.

Drop at heel is the vertical distance taken from the top of the rib of the barrels to the top of the butt, or heel, of the shotgun. Drop at comb is the vertical distance tween the top of the rib and the front of the comb, directly over the grip. A 1⅝-inch drop at the comb and a 2½-inch drop at the heel is generally correct for 95 percent of male shooters. But that's not true for women.

What the gun is intended for can play a significant part in gun measurements. Take trap and skeet, for example. A straighter stock is usually preferred for trap and skeet guns, both at the comb and the heel. A clay target is small and generally shot when rising, and a straighter stock is less apt to shoot under the target, even when the shooter is holding dead-on when the shot is fired. Drop at heel puts the heel of the butt in the proper place in the shoulder in relation to the neck, slope of shoulders, and arm length. The measurement is taken from the shooter's earlobe to the top of her shoulder. The elevation of your shot is determined by the drop at comb and the position of the pupil of your eye as you look over the rib. If there is too much drop at comb, you will stare at the back of the receiver instead of across or alongside the barrels. This will cause the gun to shoot low. Too little drop and you will shoot too high.

Pitch is the degree of the angle of the butt in relation to the rib. When the pitch is correct, the entire butt of the gunstock will contact you fully in the soft part of the shoulder. Properly mounted, this reduces recoil and keeps the gun stable. Pitch also determines whether you shoot high or low. If the gun has too much pitch, you get "muzzle jump," which means the barrel lifts up at the muzzle, which increases recoil at the toe of the gun. This means the gun doesn't have enough "positive pitch." If there is too much pitch, the gun will jump up and you'll feel more recoil at the heel. Upland bird hunters generally want a gun with a down-pitch of about two or three inches, as most shots are taken at relatively close range—twenty yards and less. The duck hunter usually shoots a gun with more of a positive pitch because she is generally pass shooting.

Drop corrects the elevation as you look over the barrels. Cast corrects windage—that is, whether you are shooting to the left or right of the target. A person needs cast at the face and at the toe of the gun. Cast at the face is related to facial structure, specifically the width of the face in relation to the set of the eyes. Cast at the toe relates to the natural pocket in the shoulder and the way the gun is canted. Average cast measures are a quarter inch at the heel and one-eighth inch at the toe. Correct cast is especially important for

women. Usually we need a little more cast at the toe. Correct cast means that when you look down the rib and pull the trigger, assuming your gun fits you properly, you will not get slammed in the breast and you will feel little or no recoil. Sometimes you can correct cast by having a professional gunsmithing bend the stock, a steam process.

If the comb is too thick, a right-hand stock will shoot to the left. If it is too thin, it will shoot to the right. Cast-off is the stock adjustment for a right-handed shooter; cast-on is the stock adjustment for a left-handed shooter. Get the picture? Now you see why being measured for a shotgun is so important. It's like wearing a 42DD bra when your actual size is 38C, or vice versa. When something doesn't fit right, you don't realize the full benefit of what it's supposed to do. The height and angle of the comb also affects your line of sight.

Gun fit is more critical in wingshooting than in any other shooting discipline. It can make the difference between a clean kill and a sheer miss. This is due to several factors. First, there is little control over the shots presented in bird situations. Until the bird rises, you are never certain where it is coming from or where it is going. Second, the time you have to get into the ready position, mount the gun, and pull the trigger, can be measured in seconds. During this sliver of time, you must observe the speed and flight path of the bird in order to determine your shot. A shotgun is an extenuation of the shooter's sight line and hands. When the gun fits the shooter naturally, she should be able to focus on the target and not on the gun. If she must think about the gun, she will lose concentration on the target. In wingshooting, failure to concentrate on the target invariably results in a missed shot.

If the stock is too long or too short, the shooter will nudge it into the soft part of her shoulder, hoping the butt will settle into the "right" place—which it never will. This will force her to try to compensate for the stock. She will either lean backward or too far forward, in which case she will shoot above or below the target because the barrels will fail to be in alignment with the flight path of the bird. The shooter will become aware of the barrels, not the bird, and attempt to aim instead of point at the target. This is a guarantee that her shot

▲ Bring the stock up until it touches your cheek. The barrels will follow your eyes as you point. And you will swing through the moving target—as long as your gun fits you properly. Pictured: British sportswoman Claire Zambuni.

will not connect with the target. By trying to accommodate the gun, the shooter fails to properly track the bird and therefore loses the optimum window of firing. If, by chance, her shot makes contact with the target, then chalk it off to luck—because that is the only thing working for her when she shoulders an ill-fitting gun and attempts to hit the target.

A properly fitted gun will feel as natural to the shooter as if it were an extension of her own arm and hands, and it affords a dependable sight line across the rib of the barrels as she points and swings through the target. That's the secret of successful shooting—always focus on your target, never on the gun. If a gun fits well, you have no reason to look at it, no need to jostle it into position, and no necessity to wonder where the barrels are pointing. When a gun fits you and becomes instinctively familiar to you, you will naturally bring it up to your shoulder, point, follow, and swing through the moving target with your hands

and eyes. Anything that takes away from your visual concentration on the target will diminish your chance of a clean shot.

When you mount a shotgun correctly, it is brought to the shoulder in a fluid and seemingly effortless motion. The butt of the stock settles snugly into the soft part of the shoulder. The shooter's head remains high and steady as the stock comes up and touches her cheek—at which point, the safety is released, the trigger is pulled, and the cartridge is discharged.

Nineteenth-century British gunmaker and firearms inventor W.W. Greener maintained that guns made to fit the physique of the average man will fit 80 percent of all shooting sportsmen. A number of shotgun manufacturers have been producing women-specific shotguns under the same assumption, that "one gun size fits all." I wonder whether this is a marketing stratagem in response to outdoor industry surveys that suggest a growing market niche among women who

▲ Factory-made guns are designed to fit 80 percent of all shooting sportsmen. However, that does not apply to women.

▲ Think of gun fit like a custom-tailored suit of clothing. It fits in all the right places.

shoot. No matter, let's take this notion and consider how it applies to women's clothing:

First, let's count the number of dress sizes between 0 and 24. There are thirteen. The same range for men is nine jacket sizes between 30 and 48. In theory, that means shotguns made to fit the physique of the average woman will fit 55 percent of all shooting sportswomen. Add to this the vast variety of bra sizes, because chest and breast measurement has a great deal to do with gun stock fit for a woman, and the nuances of fit multiplies exponentially.

Now let's go a step further. You've bought a dress off the rack, and though it fits, a nip here and a tuck there will make it fit perfectly. What seems to be an imperceptible measurement, even a quarter inch, makes a difference. Shave a quarter inch off the comb of a shotgun and it will make a dramatic effect on how the gun fits you when you bring the stock up to your face and "cheek" the gun. We'll talk about this more when we discuss shotgun technique. The bottom line is, even if you are of average build, gun fit is as unique and individual to you as the color of your eyes. The length of your neck, the length of your arm,

the slope of your shoulder, even your facial structure determines gun fit. You can get an idea of whether a gun fits you properly by performing the following exercise.

First and always, be sure your gun is unloaded. Then, stand a safe distance back from a full-length mirror. Bring the gun up to your cheek, look over the barrels, and point at the reflection of your right eye in the mirror (if you are left-handed, point at your left eye). Hold this position. If the gun fits, you will see the pupil of your eye peeking over the rib. The rib will have the appearance of being an eighth-inch high, more or less. To be exact, the rib should cross the bottom third of your pupil and you will shoot 60/40, meaning 60 percent of the patterning of your cartridge will be above the target and 40 percent will be below. This, or even 70/30, is favorable for a rising shot on an upland bird or a trap target or quartering target, depending if it is coming at you or going away from you.

If the pupil is cut in half, you are shooting the gun dead-on at 50 percent above the target and 50 percent below. This is good for pass shooting. Pass shooting is firing at birds that are flying from one place to another. There's really no attempt to decoy them—you simply shoot at the ones that fly within range. Pass shooting is typically thought of when you are shooting doves, pigeons, and ducks. Swing through, sustained lead, and pull-away is where you are going to practice your technique for pass shooting, because the technique is going to work no matter the distance of the target as long as it is in range. If you see no rib or, quite the opposite, too much rib, then you need to take your gun to a professional gun fitter.

Your shooting instructor, or a professional stock fitter or stockmaker can check this out for you. Under no circumstance should you purchase a shotgun, new or previously owned, unless the gun either fits you or is close enough so that it can be adjusted by a professional stockmaker. People often make the mistake of falling in love with a shotgun that needs an inch trimmed off the butt of the shotgun. That is a very risky thing to do. For one reason, it will alter the balance of the gun. For another, it could affect the recoil. In fact, every stock measurement—drop at toe, drop at heel, cast, cant, etc.—likely will have to be adjusted.

What's more, never, under any circumstances, should you assume you, your friend, or your husband "who's very clever with his hands" can make a stock fit.

Frequently you hear a shotgunner say, "I own ten guns and I only shoot one well." Likely as not, that one gun is the only one that fits her properly. Sometimes you'll hear someone say, "My gun isn't shooting as well as it used to." Chances it's not the gun, it's the shooter. A gun that fit you in your twenties may not fit you as well in your sixties. You may have a fluctuation in weight or have sustained injuries, your muscles are not as elastic, you may have even lost an inch in height—these things will all impact the way your stock fits and will need adjustment. Your professional gun fitter will solve your problem but be aware, when he gives you an estimate the cost of his services, that expense must warrant the value of the gun to you. Remember, a gun is only as valuable as its value to you. A five-hundred-dollar gun that was your mother's may mean more to you sentimentally than a new five-thousand-dollar gun you just bought.

When a gun fits properly, the weight of the gun feels evenly distributed between the hands. A stock that is too long will force the shooter's fore-end

hand to slide back toward the hinge-pin, creating a "muzzle flip," or a seesaw motion when the gun is mounted. It will also put the butt of the stock lower on the shoulder and the gun will shoot high. A stock that is too short for a shooter feels "whippy" and it can be difficult to maintain a flat, level swing and consistent mount. Do not confuse this with a short-barreled gun. It seems generational, but I have observed that barrel length seems to be favored at different times, in different places. For example, before World War II, a twenty-six-inch-barreled gun was long considered the preference of upland bird hunters in America and walk-up shooting in Great Britain, the reason being the shorter barrels allowed the gun to come up more quickly. This changed sometime in the 1970s, maybe earlier, when the twenty-eight-inch barrel came into vogue, affording a longer sight plane, and some feel, a smoother follow-through. The twenty-nine-inch barrel was sometimes seen on the Guild guns of Belgium and France before the war, and thirty-inch, even thirty-two-inch, barrels are preferred by most waterfowlers. Even a thirty-two-inch "fowling piece," the forefather of the shotgun, would be considered short by seventeenth-century standards, when the barrels were generally six feet long! Remember, when a gun doesn't fit right, it doesn't feel right. And if it hits you in the wrong place in your shoulder, if the recoil is too pronounced, you will anticipate discomfort and flinch whenever you pull the trigger.

However, for a gun to fit perfectly, you have to have a custom stock measured and made expressly for you. No matter how you slice it, this is a very costly proposition. There is no point choosing a relatively plain, semi-inletted blank, because it's the cost of commissioning a custom stockmaker that's the lion's share of the bill, so go into this knowing that a blank of 3X or 4X American or Turkish walnut is the least expensive part of the deal. There are fewer and fewer professional custom gunstock makers today and even fewer who fall into the category of master. This time-honored craft is a combination of skill acquired as an apprentice and artistry that is cultivated over years of experience. "Custom" means your measurements are applied to a roughly shaped single blank of hardwood that you have either acquired from your stockmaker or acquired from a source he personally recommended. There are several companies that sell gunstock blanks online. Having had years of experience working with gunstock blanks, and selecting them for clients, I am of the old school in that I prefer to see and handle a blank myself. You may order a blank online and, when it's delivered, the grain and color are so beautiful that it takes your breath away; however, if the grain does not run through the wrist in a very specific manner, the wrist being the weakest part of the stock, you run the risk of the gun, at some point, breaking. The wrist is vulnerable when the grain is irregular or flows in a direction contrary to the shape of the wrist.

As the shotgun moves with the moving target, you probably are seeing lead in quarter-inch increments, which further explains why gun fit is so critical. In fact, it's probably more critical in clay target shooting. Bird flight is more consistent and even predictable than clay target flight. Birds are either accelerating or flying the same speed. Targets are decelerating from the moment they leave the trap. This is one of the tricks that clay target setters use in determining when a target can be thrown, lose speed, turn, and begin to fall just as the shooter would take the shot. Clay target shooting often involves a lot more of what is referred to as "technical targets." Just remember, gun fit doesn't matter unless you mount properly and consistently.

Let me repeat: First, a properly fitted shotgun should feel as natural to you as if it were an extenuation of your own hands; second, you will have a reliable sight line; third, you can track the target effectively because you will not see, or be aware of, the rib down the barrels as you focus on the target, and finally, when a gun fits you, the stock comes up easily until it touches your cheek, and the barrels follow your eyes as you point as you swing through the moving target. When a shotgun does not fit you properly, you will see the barrels, jostle the buttstock into your shoulder until it is comfortable, bend your head down into the stock for it to meet your cheek, and whip the barrels around as you consciously attempt to point at the target.

Okay, now let's see what expert Jack Bart has to say.

Advice from a Professional Gun Fitter

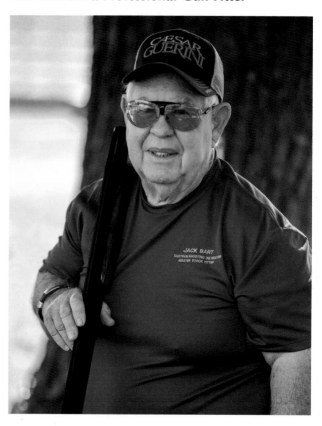

Jack Bart is a double-certified NSCA and NSSA shooting instructor and master gun fitter. In addition to instructing shooters for over five decades, he has shot competitively in all disciplines of the shotgun sports, earning numerous awards on the state and national level, and was invited to the Olympic team trapshooting tryouts for the 1972 summer Olympic games in Munich, Germany. His instructional DVD, *3-Shot Trapshooting*, is a must for any trapshooter. Tap into Jack's encyclopedic knowledge of shotguns by contacting him at Bart Brothers, LLC, www.onlinebarts. com. If he and his two brothers, Wayne and Roy—who share over fifty years of combined experience as shotgun dealers—do not have the right gun for you in stock, they can find it. What's more, Bart Brothers offers the Syren line of shotguns created especially for women.

The Shotgun Stock Fitting Process by Jack Bart

Let's see if we can take some of the mystery out of this before we start.

Shotgun shooting is like driving a car. You watch the road, not the car. You steer. Your hand-to-eye coordination controls the car. When you get in the car, you must get ready to drive comfortably and efficiently. Your seat must be adjusted forward or back so you can reach the pedals and the steering wheel. It must be adjusted high or low so you can comfortably see over the steering wheel. Adjust the rear-view mirror, buckle up, and you're ready to drive. After that is done, the next time you get in, everything is already adjusted. You just drive. If the car seat isn't adjusted to fit you properly, you can still drive. You just won't be an efficient driver.

Now that all the adjustments have been made, it doesn't mean you're a good driver. That takes instruction and practice. The shotgun is like the car. If the gun isn't adjusted to fit you properly, you can still shoot. You just won't be an efficient shotgunner.

The trick here isn't entirely in the fitting. It's how you mount your gun. Once the gun is adjusted to a proper gun mount, it doesn't change. It's the gun mount that requires consistency. A stock-fitting session is really a lesson in proper gun mount. You'll be shown how to place your hands, face, and shoulder in the proper place on the stock. We check the length of the stock, and if necessary, we make it shorter or longer to move your face/cheek forward or back. We look at your cheek on the top of the stock and adjust the stock up or down and left or right so you can properly see over the gun. We check the back of the stock to see if it makes proper contact with your shoulder/body. And all this is done after we've established your dominate eye. You can't fit a gun to a poor gun mount. I can't say this enough.

First, we must establish eye dominance. What is it? Eye dominance is the superiority of one eye whose visual function predominates over the other eye. It is that eye which is relied upon more than the other in binocular vision. This is called the dominant eye. It is not necessarily the eye with the best acuity. Why do we need to know this? In shotgun shooting, both eyes should always be open. The dominant eye should be the one that's looking over the barrel or rib of the gun. This means if you're a right-handed shooter (gun on the right shoulder), your right eye needs to be centered over the barrel, and looking over, and down the barrel. But, that doesn't mean you are right-eye dominant. If you are, that would be nice.

With both eyes open, point to an object across the room. Close one eye. If you're pointing at it, that's your dominant eye. If you're not, switch eyes. If it doesn't work with either eye, you don't exactly have an absolute dominant eye. *We need to fix it.* We're looking for the ideal situation: Right-handed shooter, absolutely right-eye dominant. Left-hand shooter, absolutely left-eye dominant.

Unfortunately, that's not always the case. The term used is "cross dominance." If you are right-handed, and not right-eyed; or left-handed, and not left-eyed, then you are among the 40 percent of men and 80 percent of women who have an eye dominance problem when it comes to shotgunning. Plan A: switch sides. If you're right-handed and left eye dominant, shoot from the left side. That would be the ideal situation, but if someone has been shooting for years, not knowing about the eye dominance, it's very difficult to switch. There's a Plan B, to close the off-eye. That's not so good either. You're trying to analyze a moving object with no eye. Your brain doesn't like that very much. Seeing with one eye takes away almost 70 percent of your visual acuity.

If a woman is a new shooter, it's fairly easy for her if she is right-handed to shoot from the left or if she's a lefty, to shoot right. Then we're back to the ideal situation. But what about other women?

Two different ways seem to work best. One, keep both eyes open and close the off eye just before you shoot. Or the other and most popular way is to adhere an "impeder" on your shooting glasses. (Remember, eye and ear protection are required to shoot on all shooting ranges. In fact, the rule of thumb is you should use wear shooting glasses and hearing protection every time you shoot.)

An impeder can be anything. It's usually a small translucent dot, about a half-inch or so in diameter, the kind you can buy most places that carry office supplies. The size is not critical. In fact, I'd make it as small as possible. It doesn't have to be fancy. A piece of Scotch tape, a dab of Chapstick, anything that will impede the off-eye (the dominant eye) from seeing the front of the barrel, or muzzle, when the gun is mounted properly. The dot is placed on the glasses and positioned so it blocks the off eye from picking up the front of the gun when it's mounted properly. This allows the shooter to keep both eyes open, see around the dot, and not be able to see the front of the gun as the shot is taken.

Now, for the first time, the shotgun comes in to play. *Always make sure the gun is safe and unloaded.* The gun fitter is a professional and he will be certain your gun is unloaded—but remember, it's your gun, and your responsibility, to make sure your gun is safe and unloaded at all times except when you are preparing to shoot. During this process, and often throughout the fitting process, these important safety rules cannot be broken because you and the fitter will be pointing the gun at each other. This is a controlled environment. The gun fitter will need to look back at you down the gun to see if what you are doing is correct. In turn, he will point the gun at you in order to demonstrate the proper technique.

All right, let's continue with the gun fitting procedure. The gun mount is the most important part of a fitting. You can't fit a gun to a poor gun mount. I keep saying that over, and over. Because that's what this is all about. The gun mount is how and where you hold the gun on your body when you shoot.

Let's look at a gun stock and review the terms used to describe the parts of it that relate to a

▲ Always break open your gun when you're not getting ready to shoot.

proper gun mount. The line of sight is an imaginary line extending along the top of the barrel or rib to the back end of the stock. The comb is the top of the stock, front to back. It's where you place your cheek when you shoot the shotgun. It controls the point of impact, both up and down, and left and right. I believe it's the most important part of stock fit. Now, take your shotgun and see how these measurements fit you.

When you shoulder your shotgun, note the distance from the line of sight to the comb. Drop at the face is the place on top of the comb, about two inches from the front of the comb, where you place your cheek when you shoot. Drop at the heel is the top of the stock at the back end. Notice it's lower than the drop at the face. That's so when your cheek is on the gun the back end, or butt, of the gun is lower so it's is on your shoulder. Your shoulder is lower than your eye, so the stock has to be lower to land there. Pitch is an angle at the back of the stock in relation to the line of sight. This part of the stock is cut on an angle. That angle is to make the butt fit properly in the soft part of the shoulder—the pectoral muscle for men, and breasts for women. The angle of pitch is greater for women. The grip is where you hold the gun with your back hand. Wrap your hand around it like a baseball bat with your index finger forward to reach the trigger. Length-of-pull is the measurement from the center of the trigger to the center of the back of the stock.

Learning the proper gun mount is really what a gun fitting is all about. As you're learning the mount, the fitter will be adjusting the various parts of the gun. When the gun mount session is finished, the gun will have been adjusted to fit. This will be geared to a right-hand shooter, gun on the right shoulder, dominant eye either natural or taken care of. Everything is opposite for a lefty. It's a combination of stance, posture, stock position on the body, face/cheek, and shoulder. The gun fitter will show you how to begin. These instructions are for the right-hand shooter. Do the opposite if you are a left-hand shooter.

1. Have the gun in your hands. Check to be sure it's safe and unloaded. *Never* depend upon a gun being safe if the safety is on.
2. Hold the gun on your right side, pistol grip in your right hand, and fore-end in your left hand.
3. Place the back of the gunstock under your armpit with your front hand, straight ahead of you and in front of your feet and under your nose.
4. Now, for your feet. Stand like you're going to run a race. You know, "On your mark, get set, GO!" Pick an object directly in front of you. That's going to be your finish line. Start with your feet side by side, about your shoulders' width apart or even a little less. Take a half-step forward with your left foot. Now you're "on your mark."
5. For "get set," you want to bow slightly, do not shift your hips forward, lean at the waist with your head slightly beyond your toes, derriere back, nose forward and pointed about 45 degrees toward the ground. This shifts your weight to the front foot and allows you to move horizontally or perpendicularly to the ground.
6. Now, from the side: Your feet are apart, about shoulders' width, and your shoulders are slightly forward. Your nose and head are tilted down slightly so when you're looking straight ahead, the iris of your eye is just under the upper part of your eye socket, which is called the *sclera*. It's a big help in keeping your eye down the center of the gun. The back of the gun is a little below the top of the shoulder, and 70 percent of your weight is on your front foot. The length-of-pull may need to be shortened or lengthened to allow the shooter to be comfortable in this position.
7. View from the front: Eyes are level in the center of the sclera. If your eyes are not level, the brain takes 25 percent longer to analyze the target. That's a big deal. Bend your elbows at about 45 degrees. Your front hand is directly in front of your nose (your correct foot position helps this), the iris of your eye as above, which puts it just on top of the line of sight. I once heard this compared to a

"marble on a table," and I think that's a good analogy. Now you're not aiming/looking down the gun. You're looking at the target. It is not unusual for a woman to correctly cheek a gun, to make the comb higher so she can see over the gun properly.

As we discussed, the very first thing you must establish is eye dominance. As I mentioned, 80 percent of women are cross-dominant, that is, right-hand shooters who have a dominant left eye and vice versa, which means there is a real good chance in a lady, if she is right-handed, that her left eye is dominant.

Once we've established eye dominance, the most important sentence I use is, *you cannot fit a gun to a poor gun mount*. If you're not holding the gun properly, you won't be able to see the target across or alongside the barrels, and your shot charge will not intersect the path of the flying target. The key is this: when you are looking at a target, the gun points where your eyes are looking, without you looking at the gun. I can't reiterate this enough. Proper gun mount is the key.

Once the gun's mounted properly, we start from there with the fitting process. Now, this is important: I would say that 70 percent of the time, you don't have to do anything to the gun with proper gun mount. So, once you have the proper gun mount and the eyes are correct, then we start the fitting process as far as we have to do anything to the gun. In the case of ladies, it's not uncommon to talk about the various parts of the gun that relate to gun mount. The most important is the length-of-pull. With the proper mount, it should put you about 1½ inches with your face on the gun properly and 1½ inches from your front knuckle to your nose. And that measurement is what you go by to make the stock longer or shorter. That means every quarter inch you lengthen or shorten the stock will move your face one inch forward or back.

Now we have established that your head is in the correct position when you properly mount your gun. The eyes are taken care of with the head in proper position on stock. The length of the stock has been measured so you have the two-finger space between knuckle and nose. Now, you want to be able to look across or alongside the gun so that the sight is just below your eyeball. Remember: The eyeball is supposed to look like a marble on a table, so when the person is looking down the rib, the gun fitter (once he has established the gun is unloaded) is at the muzzle of the gun looking back at the shooter. What I do is use my cellphone to take a picture of exactly what I'm seeing so she can see what I'm looking for. That relationship to the rib will make the gun shoot where you look, and that has to take care of both left-and-right and up-and-down positions. Now, the up-and-down part is measured as the height of the stock in relation to the rib. The terminology for this is "drop at the comb," meaning the part of the stock on which you physically put your cheekbone.

Now that we've established up-and-down, we have to establish left-and-right, and what that controls is the cast. The cast of the stock is an angle left to right, in the case of the right-handed shooter, to the right of the centerline that runs down the rib to the end of the gunstock. For the right-handed shooter, then, in most instances, the cast will be off to the right. For a lady, the cast at the top of the stock to the heel at the bottom, the cast is somewhat twisted at the bottom of the stock. This is true for a lady more generally than for a gentleman because of a lady's anatomy. The stock should not push on the breast. Correct cast allows the gun to be held in the proper position, so it doesn't interfere with the breast.

Now we have established up-and-down with the eyeball and left-and-right by twisting the stock toward the back, so you are looking straight down the gun when you put the face on it. You have properly mounted the gun with butt of the gun on the proper place of your shoulder. Make sure the gun's unloaded when you do this simple exercise: turn the gun upside and standing at the muzzle, look at the pointing part of the stock. You'll see the stock is twisted off to one side.

My next step as a gun fitter is to make sure the back of the stock is on an angle that totally makes contact with your body when you mount the gun properly. Generally, that angle of the butt is shorter at the bottom and a little longer at the top and that's called pitch. We want that to make total contact with the body. That controls the fluid movement and also felt recoil. Here's an example I often use. Think of a refrigerator. It stands on four feet, which means the weight of the refrigerator is spread over its four feet, at four points. If you take two of the feet off of the refrigerator it shifts its weight, changes the balance, and there is less pressure on the floor where the feet remain. Recoil, too, is divided equally over a butt with proper pitch. The result is there is less recoil when the recoil is spread equally over the entire area of the butt of the gun.

The only other thing you run into when you fit a gun to a shooter is reach. It exists, but not much and not often. This is the distance from your hand where you grip the stock to the first pad of your index finger, not wrapped around, just parallel to the trigger. That's a measurement you can't do much about unless you have a custom stock built. However, most people get away with it whether it's perfect or not.

One last thing with regard to ladies is the comb. Manufacturers lower the recoil pad on a gun made specifically for women because a woman generally has a longer neck than a man. Lowering the recoil pad on the stock moves the gun up closer to the face, so the lady doesn't have to bend over to get her face on the stock. Guns made specifically for women appear to have an abbreviated version of a Monte Carlo comb. This higher style of comb looks to be about a quarter inch, give or take, higher than a recoil pad. Don't mistake this for the stock being higher. It's not higher, it's the same height with the drop at the comb, which is an imaginary line from the rib to back of gun, usually 1½ inches, on average. So, when you see that Monte Carlo "hump" on as the comb of a stock, it has not been raised higher; it has simply lowered the recoil pad. Thus

if the recoil pad needs to be lowered, you are not changing the height of the stock elevation to the rib. If you lower the recoil pad, that will make stock thick from top to bottom, and a standard recoil pad is generally not long enough to cover the wooden butt of the stock. So, manufacturers of guns specifically made for women make the comb long and then cut a little bit off the top. That makes the butt the same height to take a recoil pad.

▲ Open your gun completely before you load the shells.

▲ Now, as you close the gun, lift up the forend, snap it shut—it doesn't take much, but it has to be fully shut.

▲ Good job. Now the gun is closed.

▲ Keep your feet shoulder-width apart, with the left foot forward if you are right handed.

▲ Put your gun down and hold in the ready position. Look for the target.

▲ Relax! No need to get tense.

▲ Bring the stock up to your cheek.

▲ Cheeking the gun.

▲ Lean into the shot.

▲ That's it. Touch your cheek and lean into the shot.

▲ Remember, as you bring the gun up you are looking at the target, not the barrels.

▲ You're going to look over the barrels, not at them.

▲ Look for the target before you bring up the gun.

▲ Look for your target.

▲ Look over the barrels.

▲ Okay, look for the target.

▲ That's better! Remember, your only opponent is the clay target.

▲ Point your gun where you will meet the target, but follow the target with your eyes.

▲ Bring up the gun as you see the target approaching.

▲ Don't hunch over the gun; instead, bring the gun up.

▲ Keep bringing the stock up so it just touches your cheek.

▲ That's it. Bring the gun up and cheek the stock. Keep your eyes on the target.

▲ This too is a safe way to carry your gun. Be sure it's always open.

▲ You can hold your gun open on your shoulder like this when you're not shooting.

Practicing Correct Gun Mount

Once you have a properly fitted gun, it is important that you practice correct gun mount every day. This can be done at home. First, be sure your gun is not loaded. (You should never leave a loaded gun at home, anywhere, anytime.) Pick an object about ten or twelve feet away. Mount the gun and point at the object. Check that you have assumed the proper shooting position.

1. Has the gun come up to touch your cheek? Yes!
2. Is the butt snuggly in your shoulder? Yes!
3. Are you seeing the gun barrels? If the answer is "yes," then you have mounted the gun incorrectly.
4. Do this again and again until you get it right!

Ten minutes of daily practice will help you immeasurably when you're on the shooting field.

So, to review. A women's specific shotgun with a modified Monte Carlo stock is designed to adapt to a standard recoil pad. It will put your face on the stock closer to the cheekbone and will spread the recoil over the surface of the butt to reduce felt recoil if the gun is mounted properly.

Cast is particularly important to a lady because of her build. Cast is the imaginary line that comes off the top of the gun and goes all the way back to the recoil pad of the gun. The measurement is taken at the beginning of the comb, and at anywhere along the line of the stock. The drop at comb, where your face is, to the drop at heel allows the gun to drop to your shoulder. You need some space from your eye to your shoulder when you are in the proper gun mount position, as the stock itself must go to your shoulder a couple of inches lower than the line coming off the rib.

This chart compares standard women's gun fit measurements with standard men's gun fit measurements. These are general industry approximations of the average women's and men's measurements. The women's average measurements are approximately those of the Syren ELOS Sporting Shotgun, which is made expressly for women.

Measurement (in inches)	Women	Men
Drop at comb	1.375	1.5
Drop at Monte Carlo	1.6	1.8
Drop at heel	2.25	2.25
Comb to grip	4.75	6.00
Length-of-pull	13.75	14.75
Cast at heel	0.125	0.120
Cast at toe	0.375	0.250

How You See the Target

Much of the discussion in this chapter deals with eye dominance, and how you are taught to shoot. You just heard from Jack Bart. The experts profiled in this book each have their own trademark way of teaching—all professional instructors do. And each also addresses eye dominance problems, especially for us women. The reason is simple: if you cannot see the target accurately, then you can never shoot a target with certainty. That's why I've asked the instructors in this book to weigh in on this critical subject. I'm not being repetitive; I'm just providing you with all the information I can so you can determine for yourself just how you see a target and why you should seek the help of a qualified instructor. The number one reason women are frustrated when they begin shooting is because they do not understand how they see; it is also the reason why many women don't persevere and cut short what could be a terrific outlet for them as a gratifying leisure sport. I know. I have a serious eye dominance problem. Had I not become an outdoor writer, I doubt I ever would have persevered.

Many young people first learn to shoot with a BB gun or a .22-caliber rifle. They are encouraged to close one eye, line up the front and back sights on the target, and squeeze the trigger when the target is lined up. You are shooting at a stationary target, and you line up the sights at the precise place you want the bullet to arrive. Maybe you were taught this way, too. If so, you will have to unlearn what you were taught when you take up shotgunning.

Shooting a shotgun is just the opposite. You have no sights to look through. You focus your eyes on the target, not on the gun. The rib or top of the barrel is only seen obliquely in your peripheral vision. The object is not stationary, it is always moving. And you don't squeeze the trigger, you pull the trigger.

Some people shoot with one eye closed because of eye dominance problems. Almost everyone has a dominant eye. For most people, either the right eye is dominant, or the left eye is dominant. If you are right-handed and right-eye dominant, no problem. If you are left-handed and left-eye dominant, no problem. Problems only occur when your dominant eye is the opposite of your dominant hand. If you are either left- or right-eye dominant, when you shoulder a shotgun with both eyes open and focus on the bird, you will see the whole side of the shotgun rather than have a clear line of sight over the barrels to the target, and therefore the lead picture will be totally askew. Those afflicted with this malady may smudge the lens of their shooting glasses with lipstick, obliterate the center of vision with a self-adhesive dot, or some other occlusion to obscure the dominant eye from seeing clearly. Sometimes—in fact, many times—this works; however, there are also some people who consciously strive to move their head so their dominant eye can see better, thus lifting their head from the gunstock, or changing their facial position so their check is not correctly on the stock. This is bad.

A simple cure, but one that can be accomplished only through much practice, is to keep both eyes open as the gun comes to the shoulder and close the dominant eye as the shotgun comes in line with the bird. The eye, now aligned correctly with the shotgun barrel, will take over the focus on the head of the bird, and the mind—incredible organ that it is—will bring the shot and target together correctly. Once you practice closing the dominant eye enough times, this becomes second nature.

There are, among shooters and their instructors, different philosophies and observations concerning one- or two-eyed shooters. (By this I mean whether you shoot with one eye closed or both eyes open.) This is related to just two things: eye dominance, and how you are taught to shoot.

The ultimate goal is to make a clean shot—one that centers the bird in the pattern. Whether you can do this naturally or whether you have to practice closing

an eye or smudging the lens on the dominant eye side, the result needs to be the same: a good, clean, shot.

In *Wing and Trap Shooting*, originally published in 1911, Major Askins addressed this vital subject. His advice is as pertinent today as it was a century ago.

Aiming the Gun by Major Charles Askins (PD)

Wingshooting really dates from the invention of percussion caps in a practical form, about 1830, and the present style of shotgun shooting is of very modern origin.

Naturally, the rifle method of aiming had its influence for a good many years, a full half-century, in fact, long after the invention of breech-loading guns. The old manner of shooting a shotgun was to close one eye and squint low over the breech, theoretically never pulling the trigger until the front bead was accurately aligned upon the target. Many an old veteran still speaks learnedly of "drawing a bead" on the game. The author's wing-shooting career has been connected with the breechloader only, yet in his first lessons, given by his father, the necessity of closing one eye if any accuracy of aim were to be attained was strongly emphasized.

In truth the primer of gun-firing was to learn to close one eye instantly and invariably, preparatory to aiming, and the second principle was not to shut them both before pulling the trigger. If in those days any man had discovered that he could kill game by simply pointing his gun without closing his eye or seeing a sight, he would never have had courage enough openly to advocate such a system of gun aiming.

Doubtless the coming of nitro powder has had much to do with the development of our present slap-bang fashion of shotgun shooting, yet due credit should be given to Doctor [William Frank] Carver who is properly entitled to be called the father of modern wingshooting. Probably no less wonderful shot than he could have had influence enough to have changed a style of shotgun aiming that was once universal.

The "one eye" method of sighting a shotgun is not altogether obsolete yet. Many a veteran sportsman has shot long and successfully in this way and will not change; neither is there good reason why he should, for it is hard to teach an old dog new tricks, nor does he learn them quite as he knew the old. Nevertheless, it is true that few or no expert shots ever close an eye in aiming today, though some of them in effect sight exactly the same as though they did. The writer has followed the Carver scheme of gun pointing more years than he can remember, and among all his friends who shoot well, especially in the uplands, there are none who have any other method of aiming.

Many who point a gun without regard to sight or rib do it unconsciously. As an example, a shooting companion of mine who found difficulty in connecting with crossing birds concluded that a patent sight with three beads would assist him greatly. With a bird passing to the left he would use the right bead, and he figured to a mathematical nicety just how far ahead that would throw his charge. After a shot of the kind that usually troubled him, which he missed exactly as before, I asked him where he had held that off bead. He admitted blankly that he never had seen it, and neither could he remember ever seeing one of those three beads afterward when making a quick shot, though they were big enough to cover a balloon. He soon threw the patent sight aside as being theoretically fine but practically worthless.

One-Eye Sighting

One-eye sighting is distinctly slow and is not adapted to killing game that in the nature of its flight is either imperfectly outlined or rapidly gets beyond range. One-eye aiming implies that the instant the gun comes to the shoulder there shall be a pause in its movement while the eye adjusts itself to the sight, or, as it is called, finds it. This focusing the eye upon the sight necessarily dims the vision of the target, for there is no such thing as the human eye focusing perfectly both upon the gun sight and the game. Notwithstanding this, the target can be seen, even though it appears shadowy, and the sight placed upon it very accurately; indeed, if the game were not moving, or the shot was directed straight at it, it could be placed with greater precision than in any other way. But it occurs not infrequently that after you have paused to find the sight, the opportunity is gone; either the game cannot be seen again or not quickly enough to cover it before it escapes.

What is required in wingshooting is that we cover the target with the utmost dispatch and pull on the instant—not a hundredth of a second sooner or later. While I am opposed on principle to the novice learning to sight a shotgun with one eye shut or both eyes open, in fact, to sighting the arm at all, believing that so taught he can never become a first rate performer on all sorts of game, yet I have seen so much excellent work in wildfowl shooting by men who closed one eye or who focused on the sight that I hesitate to say it is not an effective style of firing at ducks or any bird of large size that is habitually outlined against the

▲ One-eye sighting with the dominant eye closed. Photo by John Wiles.

sky. In shooting of this kind, the game is often seen while approaching and allowance can be made for the time required to focus on the sights; neither is it requisite that the gun be handled with such rapidity as in ordinary upland work.

Success with wildfowl is more due to correct estimates of distance and speed of flight than to manner of aiming, and since there is never any question of being able to see the bird, even with half an eye, it is probable that any system of sighting or pointing the gun can be made about equally effective.

Binocular Shooting—Two-Eye Aiming

Two-eye aiming, or binocular shooting, has all the advantages of closing one eye even for rifle firing while a distinctly clearer view of the target is obtained, and distances can be estimated more positively. All of us who were taught to close one eye can well remember that the instant we blinded the left eye to find the sight, the bird at once appeared to be a great deal farther away. I can recall that more than once when a boy I had shut the left eye and then decided that the quail was out of range, after which I opened both eyes and found it still well within reach.

It is no doubt true that with only one eye a gunner could finally learn to judge distances as

▲ Binocular shooting—both eyes aiming. Photo by John Wiles.

well as though he had the use of both, but when from birth he uses both eyes to see and estimate distances a million times to where he does once with an eye shut, it reasonably follows that he will do better work in the style in which he has been trained, even though that training were not with a gun. Therefore, we can take it as a simple statement of fact that with both eyes open, we can most accurately estimate the distance that game is from us, the speed of its flight, and the lead necessary in order to kill. Moreover, we can secure equally fine sight with both eyes open provided one eye alone governs the line of sight or is focused upon the sights. This eye is then said to be the master eye for the reason that the brain pays attention only to what this eye is doing. The other eye sees just the same, but of its vision the brain fails to keep any record.

Ordinarily it is supposed that the master eye has the stronger vision, which entitles it to govern, but this does not follow by any means. In shooting from the right shoulder, the right eye controls, not because its strength is greater, but for the simple reason that the grain has been trained to register only what this eye sees. It may be the stronger eye, or it may not, nor would this make much difference unless its vision were extremely defective while that of the other was normal. Ninety-nine times in a hundred one eye governs the line of sight entirely because it has been trained to do this and for no other reason.

The usual manner of testing the eyes for shooting is to hold up an object a proper distance from them and align it with a point beyond while keeping both eyes open. Now close the left eye and if the alignment doesn't change, the right eye governs, but if on shutting the left eye the line of aim swings to the left, the wrong optic has been in control, and the student will have to begin training the right eye to assume the mastery or learn to shoot from the left shoulder. Either can be done, but it is much simpler and easier as a rule to put the brain to making its records from the proper eye. It might be noted, in passing, that in ease of an experienced shot no eye tests are necessary, for the one with which he has been accustomed to sighting is certain to govern.

The style of aiming with both eyes open may be exactly the same as with one closed; that is, the gun is brought up and there is a slight pause long enough for the eye to find the front sight which is then placed upon the point of aim. The focusing of the eye upon the front sight, however, will probably not be so sharp as with the left eye shut, with the consequence that the vision of the game will be less dimmed. The man accustomed to aiming with one eye closed may find it best to teach himself to shoot with both eyes open while still focusing upon the sight after his acquired fashion. However, this is not the favorite or most effective mode of two-eye aiming.

Gun pointing has been miscalled "instinctive shooting," though in reality there is nothing instinctive about it. There can be nothing instinctive in doing a thing that we have learned to accomplish through repeating a performance thousands of times. It is merely perfecting an art that we have been acquiring from babyhood, that of being able to point the finger or something else directly at an object toward which we are looking fixedly. We might as well say that we write instinctively because we give no thought to what the next stroke will be. In civilized human beings, training takes the place of instinct, which is a very important factor, though it must be admitted that every man has inherited tendencies.

The advantages of pointing a shotgun in place of getting the eye close down to the barrels and aligning rib and sight are these: Point your finger at an object quickly, without any effort to sight or closing any eye, and you will find that while it is directed precisely, yet nevertheless you are glancing some distance above the finger. Now close one eye and you will note at once a tendency to drop the head and sight the finger. The same optical principle applies to pointing and sighting a gun; under the former system you naturally keep the barrels well down out of the line of vision, but at the same time direct them at an object with exactly the same precision as in the other way.

Moreover, in pointing a gun by means of a thorough training of the hands, you are in a measure independent of fit of gunstock. Indeed, in my own experience and that of others, any gun can be shot accurately so long as the drop of stock is not so great as to bring the barrels within the line of sight, or where they will interfere with a clear view of the target. Correct alignment is not nearly so dependent upon drop of stock as it is upon the position of the two hands grasping grip and fore-end.

For instance, if you are accustomed to a gun that is grasped nearly in the line of fire, and you then attempt to shoot with one having a deep fore-end which places the left hand low, or a piece with grip set low behind the frame, you will at once note a feeling of uncertainty as to where you are pointing. I should therefore conclude that an accustomed grip and fore-stock were of as much importance as drop at comb and grip. Additionally, it should be noted that if the hands are to do the pointing unassisted by sights, they should grasp the piece well apart, that is with the left hand extended as far as possible without strain, and the places where they grip the arm should never vary an iota.

In gun pointing, the sight should never be seen, nor rib, nor barrel, neither should they be even thought of, for if the eye is permitted to interfere with the calculations of the brain, two bosses of equal authority are installed, with the obvious result that nothing will be accomplished. In this style of aiming, the gun should be swung methodically, with mechanical uniformity of movement, and the trigger pressed the moment you feel that the aim is correct. No mystery need be made of this feeling of being right, for it is merely the signal of the brain to the nerves that the work has been well accomplished.

In some descriptions of wingshooting, as quail or ruffed grouse in the woods, the gun is discharged within three-quarters of a second after the brain has realized that the bird is on the wing; during this length of time the shooter takes position, brings his gun to his shoulder, selects the point of aim, directs his piece there, and presses the trigger. No "second sight" can be obtained under such circumstances, whatever error the eye may detect at the instant of firing, and accuracy is absolutely dependent upon the mechanical training of the hands which direct the gun. By putting the eye and mind upon the gunsights these can be noted very clearly but while doing this the bird is lost."

John Shima: Advice from a World-Class Shooting Instructor

▲ World Skeet Champion and Instructor.

John Shima is a former five-time World Skeet Champion and was high average in 12-gauge for two consecutive years. He is the leading authority on detection of visual deceptions and prescribing appropriate visual training to unleash the power of reality for clay target shooters. I first met John over twenty years ago at a Ducks Unlimited sporting clays tournament on Lanai in the Hawaiian Islands. From the moment he saw me shoot, he recognized my dominant eye problem and I recognized in him a lifelong friend. Many times since then John has instructed me, and his expertise and insight into how we see a target has provided me with the understanding I have needed to personally identify my problem, surmount it, and successfully deal with how I shoot.

John mentions his late father, Dr. Arthur T. Shima, a pioneer in anesthesiology who practiced in West Suburban Hospital in Oak Park, Illinois. John has two older siblings, both extremely successful in their respective fields. John could have grown up in their shadow, and having dyslexia would have been an acceptable reason for his difficulties reading. But Dr. Shima could see only his youngest child's strength. John could not see words on a page and connect their

meaning, but he could see targets flying through the air and connect his shots.

Dr. Shima learned how to fly a plane and bought one specifically so he could fly John to tournaments around the country. Every weekend they flew to a tournament, and that paternal devotion paved the way for John's tremendous accomplishments in the world of skeet. There is no doubt John could have continued, won more championships, and broken his own records—but that wasn't in John's plan. Five world championships were plenty, he reckoned. Like his father, John's plan was to help people. And he has helped thousands of us, the men and women he has instructed and helped to understand how to become a better shot. That John's area of expertise is how the eye sees, and how the brain interprets that information, has proven to be the consequence of his own personal struggles—and thank goodness, because we, his students, are the beneficiaries. Helen Keller wrote, "Life is either a daring adventure or nothing at all." Dr. Shima was a great man of medicine. But he was an even greater father. He set his son on a road to adventure and personal success. Doing nothing at all was never a consideration. John turned his disability into a daring adventure and lives his life to the fullest.

That is what the shooting sports can do for you.

Visual Training by John Shima

When I was a child I struggled to read and write. It was as if the words were playing tricks on my eyes. I felt smart outside of school but accepted that my brain was wired to see things differently than my classmates in school. Fortunately, my father was an avid skeet shooter. As compensation for my struggling through school each week, my father would take me to the gun club on weekends. At age nine, I began entering skeet shoots. By the age of fifteen, I realized that, although my brain was not wired for reading and writing, it was wired for seeing moving targets and shooting skeet better than most adults.

I earned a degree in psychology at Trinity University and was on the college skeet team that was coached by the venerable Col. Tom Hanzel. I have been teaching skeet shooting since 1977. Whenever I observed a shooter doing, saying, or thinking something that created a mechanical or mental fault, I always asked myself, "Why?"

A few years into my career as a shooting instructor, I realized my true gift. Almost intuitively, I discovered that I could watch someone shoot and not only see where he or she missed the target but know why they missed the target. I could imagine what they were seeing and what they were thinking between the moments they thought to call for the target and when the shot stream passed the target. This epiphany changed my approach to teaching from a focus on how to shoot at targets to an emphasis on how different people perceived the virtual relationship between the gun barrel and moving target, and what the relationship was in actual reality. I call this "the moment of truth."

Psychology helped me appreciate the amazing capacity of the human eyes and brain. Humans are capable of finding different ways to see things and integrating them so the mind can interpret the visual input. This phenomenon underlies the idiom "Beauty is in the eye of the beholder." I understood this phrase to mean that an individual's perspective of an object or event is their unique visual perception, and their "perceived sight picture" was merely the outcome of various neurological, psychological, and physiological factors related to their personal circumstances and life experiences. The more I learned about vision, the more I became convinced that the way we look determines what we see.

In the 1985 comedy *Spies Like Us*, Austin Millbarge said, "We mock what we don't understand." This phrase resonated with me because many clay target shooters and coaches do not understand my teaching philosophy, diagnostic abilities, and visual training drills. Moreover, these critics clearly don't understand why and how I utilize the eye patch to help skeet shooters train their eyes to correctly see targets and perceive lead at various skeet stations.

I know that when I introduce eye-patching aids, I am literally altering the shooter's perception of reality. I seriously appreciate the

eye patch can precipitate psychological consequences. Therefore, my use of eye patching is not a gimmick or parlor trick. My purpose for introducing eye-patching techniques to clay target shooters is to unleash the power of visual reality so all shooters can look at moving targets and see actual lead instead of an optical illusion.

The idea of using an eye patch or eye dot (occluder) is not new. Optometrists commonly used eye patches on children to treat strabismus, or lazy eye. In the 1950s and 1960s, most skeet shooters with an eye dominance problem just closed or squinted the non-shooting eye. Ed Scherer, an accomplished shooter and shooting coach in the 1970s and 1980s, interviewed several all-American skeet shooters and national champions for an article on the topic. His data revealed that almost all the competitors he interviewed shot skeet with both eyes open, just like hunters, trap, and sporting clays shooters, so he came to the apparently logical conclusion that individuals must shoot skeet with both eyes open to be champions in the sport.

There is an underlying fallacy to Ed's well-meaning conclusion; individuals with binocular visual problems were incapable of realizing their true potential as skeet shooters if they felt compelled to compete with both eyes open the way the champions did. At that time our sport truly favored the natural two-eyed shooters with a dominant shooting eye. Furthermore, Ed didn't consider things like age of the shooter, how many years they had shot, and how shooters

▲ Everyone sees targets differently. Here we see three right-handed shooters. Each will see the target differently—the man, the woman, and the man who is seated in order to shoot. However, each share the basics: (1) they are looking over the barrels at the target, not at the gun; (2) they are leaning toward the target, weight and torso forward; (3) the elbow is held at a 45-degree position to the body; and most important of all (4) the gun each is shooting fits.

practiced using their eyes correctly. Please don't misquote me. I believe Ed Scherer did a great job and was a pioneer in teaching skeet. He should be recognized as one of the leaders in elevating the game of skeet to where it is today. Regrettably, the traditional methods for teaching the mechanical and mental aspects of skeet shooting did NOT take visual deception into consideration.

Why We Miss Targets

Anyone who has watched a magician perform "magic" understands the concept of optical illusion. It is the art of misdirection that deceives the eyes of the viewer by producing a false or misleading perception of reality. Intelligent viewers know they were deceived; they are merely perplexed by how the visual deception occurred. Although shooters may believe that some clay targets attempt to trick them during a round of skeet, intellectually they know that is not possible. I came to the conclusion that most shooters miss targets because they were shooting at an optical illusion rather than the actual target.

▲ The Shima Shooting Method emphasizes the importance of discovering visual deceptions, enabling visual reality and training visual discipline.

During the past three decades of coaching skeet and sporting clay shooters, I have made it my life work to solve the riddle of visual deception for my clients. My ability to understand and interpret the factors underlying visual problems is often intuitive. I have developed training aids that change the way the shooter looks at the target to enable him or her to see the actual sight picture (visual reality).

The Shima Shooting Method emphasizes the importance of discovering visual deceptions, enabling visual reality and training visual discipline. To accomplish these goals, two essential items in my bag are moleskin strips and black rectangular vinyl eye patches. These are not "gimmicks" or quick fixes for shooters; they are diagnostic and training aids that, when used properly, eventually allow me to ascertain the shooter's visual deceptions and enable shooters to see real sight pictures and train their shooting eye to develop the visual discipline necessary to overcome optical illusions.

Experts report that the human eye can only focus on one thing at a time. Shooting skeet targets requires the eyes to center the primary focus over a moving barrel at a faster moving target while the gun "points" somewhere ahead of the target. The human eye cannot simultaneously center primary (hard) focus on the barrel of the gun and the moving target twenty yards in the distance. Physiologically, with both eyes open and shooting at a target closer than twenty yards, the right and left eyes see two different images. This phenomenon is called depth perception, which is essential to shooting moving targets beyond twenty yards but creates optical illusions for many two-eyed shooters at twenty yards or closer. This visual phenomenon explains why a right-shouldered shooter that is shooting with both eyes open may need to see a huge lead picture on a high house 4 but almost no lead on a low house 4. The discrepancy between visual reality, as defined by the laws of physics, and virtual reality, as created by an optical illusion, is inherent in human binocular vision.

The concept is that optical illusions are the cause of the majority of missed targets during a round of skeet. This, and other neurological, psychological, and physiological factors, are the basis for the Shima Shooting Method. In my teaching, I emphasize the importance of discovering visual deceptions, enabling visual reality, and training visual discipline for skeet and sporting clays shooters at all levels of the sport. Now let's examine visual deception in greater detail.

Visual Discipline: Looking Beyond the Gun

Experienced shotgun shooters know that we look at a moving target while pointing the gun somewhere ahead of it. I find that most inexperienced

▲ Experienced shotgun shooters know that we look at a moving target while pointing the gun somewhere ahead of it.

shooters attempt to aim the gun somewhere ahead of the target. In fact, one old-time shooter would tell his friends to "shoot at the phantom target" in front of the real target.

I encourage my clients to shoot sustained lead because it keeps the gun out of the way so they can watch the target continuously. I introduced many of my clients to shooting the "heads up" method so they could look over the gun. Either the shooter placed his or her chin next to the stock instead of their cheekbone or I "raised the comb" with strips of moleskin to create a 70/30 point of impact. The purpose was to position the shooter's eyes parallel to the flight path of the target, which enabled them to look beyond the gun so they could see the targets clearly.

When the target is closer than twenty yards, most shooters with a dominant shooting eye can shoot with both eyes open if they really stare at the target. I describe this as similar to a temporary hypnotic trance. However, visual deceptions creep into the game of many two-eyed shooters when they lose the ability to continuously hard focus with their shooting eye due to mental and/or visual fatigue, and the non-shooting eye affects their visual perception.

However, I am a one-eyed skeet shooter. I shoot with both eyes open, without a patch, when I am doing trick shooting demonstrations or shooting sporting clays because I need the depth of field of two-eyed shooting in order to shoot from the hip and to judge angle and distance for some sporting clays shots. When I was young, I shot skeet with both eyes open. Around the age of thirty-five

I noticed the lead pictures were occasionally changing while I was shooting, so I intuitively closed my left eye. When I looked at the targets with one eye, I perceived them to be much larger and slower. Although I didn't feel as if I was "seeing" the targets as quickly, I was able to run 100x100s again, so I wasn't concerned.

When I shoot skeet with both eyes open, even with a patch in place, I can shoot straights but I have a surreal experience, as if I am standing behind myself, watching myself shoot at the targets while I see the breaks from behind.

Eye patches, whether frosted or solid, are not magic. I utilize both types for specific reasons but introduce an eye patch judiciously because it can dramatically alter a shooter's perception of reality. Since the frosted patch allows the same amount of light to come through to the non-shooting eye, the brain thinks it can still see through the frosted patch and tries to see the old way, which causes the shooting eye to de-focus.

In my experience the quickest way to "train the brain" to see a new lead picture clearly and allow my client to shoot visually, instead of viscerally, is by completely blocking the visual signal the brain wants to see with the non-shooting eye when the gun is fired. The solid patch not only blocks the visual image but also blocks the light input as well, so the brain more readily "switches focus" over to the shooting eye.

Sometimes the eye patch will cause a shooter to experience dizziness, headaches, or nausea. According to Dr. Wayne Martin, these reactions are due to the statokinetic reflex (the cause of motion sickness) that senses angular acceleration of the head and awareness of any induced head, eye, and body movements and is responsible for balance and maintaining equilibrium.

For some shooters, the eye patch initially creates serious difficulty seeing the target, especially on baseline targets (H1 and L7). Assuming they are shooting with their dominant eye, the only reason the non-shooting eye is putting up such a fuss is that the shooter was using their non-shooting eye to look at these targets more than they thought.

Other times a right-shouldered shooter will see the H1 target come out, but when they pull the trigger, they don't see the target break. Even though their shooting (right) eye saw the correct lead and broke the target, the non-shooting (left) eye, which is connected to where the emotions live (right brain), didn't see the target break. So, the shooter actually saw the target break, their brain just didn't perceive the break because the left eye was covered with a patch.

Components of Visual Discipline

If I have convinced you that the way you look determines what you see, then the key to shooting well is to train your shooting eye to see real targets instead of virtual targets. As with any training modality, discipline is the key to success. I believe there are three components to achieving visual discipline for skeet shooters: where you look, how you look, and what you see.

Where You Look: Your pre-shot routine should establish the proper eye hold and gun hold for each target on the station prior to stepping on the pad. The conscious mind (thinking) reminds you to set your eye(s) up on the target path and out to where the target is first visible. This look point determines the position of the gun hold, which is slightly below and farther out from the eye hold.

How You Look: Awareness is a natural state of calm with a sense of alertness. There is no anticipation of when the target will appear, expectation of where the target will go, or intention to break it. Trance is an altered state of consciousness (in the flow) that enables the adaptive unconscious to automatically activate a visio-motor response to the appearance of peripheral movement. The shooter merely settles the shooting eye on the target path, soft focuses to activate peripheral vision, and allows the natural ability of the visual system to function normally.

What You See: The peripheral movement of the eye will capture the flash of the target as it emerges from the window. As the target reaches the seeing point the pursuit movement will rapidly converge and center focus on the actual target while the barrel of the gun moves ahead of the target in the periphery of the visual field. The visual shooter will fire in the break zone when the picture looks right and he or she will see the target break. The visceral shooter will fire when the picture feels right and usually sees the target break if the shooting eye maintains continuous focus on the target. The break zone is determined by muscle memory.

The critical period of time in the execution of each shot at a clay target is from the time the shooter calls for the target until he or she sees the target break. This moment occurs "in the blink of an eye," and I call it the moment of truth. The manner in which the shooter uses his or her eyes during "the moment of truth" determines whether the target the shooter sees is real or whether it is an optical illusion. If the shooter centers his or her focus intently on the target and allows the adaptive unconscious to point the gun, the target will look larger, the details will be clearer, and it will seem to move slower, just before it breaks!

Training is necessary to establish muscle memory (conditioned response) and maintain visual discipline so the adaptive unconscious can function normally during the moment of truth and complete the shot successfully. A properly positioned solid eye patch will usually accelerate the training of the shooting eye. The goal of visual training is to develop visual consistency—a consistent visual image for each target as it enters the peripheral visual field. This familiar image (stimuli) empowers the adaptive unconscious to activate an appropriate neuromuscular response.

Attempts by the shooter to change visual focus, compensate for an improper setup by anticipating the target, or make adjustments to the sight picture during the moment of truth will activate visual deceptions that result in weak breaks or completely missed targets.

The Power of Reality

The lack of visual discipline usually results from carelessness during pre-shot routine, distracted thinking on the pad, or mental/visual fatigue. These behaviors embolden the conscious mind and create emotional distractions such as: anticipation, expectation, or misguided intention (outcome).

A shooter's anticipation of the target, expectation of the target's flight path, or intention to break the target all result in irregular pursuit movement of his or her shooting eye. This oscillation of visual focus is the primary cause for streaking. The shooter initially sees the target, then it suddenly jumps ahead while the eye attempts to catch up. Streaking often results in flinching, pushing, or poking the gun and loss of balance.

Leaving on the call causes the peripheral vision to acquire the barrel of the gun (the larger, closer object) instead of the target. It is also the most common cause for a poor eye shift when shooting the second target of a pair because the shooter moves the gun in anticipation of where the second target will be before centering focus of the shooting eye on the second target.

Moving the gun up quickly to engage the slow incoming target usually results in trapping the target with the barrel. It creates the perception of pulling the target slowly to the break zone and results in missing behind the target due to slow gun speed. Trapping also occurs on out-goers if the shooter fails to move the gun on the flash of the target.

Developing a consistent and precise pre-shot routine that supports visual discipline, along with proper mechanics, is the key to eliminating visual deceptions and unleashing the power of reality for skeet shooters. I developed the Shima Shooting Method to teach skeet and sporting clays shooters how to look at targets correctly by using visual discipline to train their shooting eye to see reality instead of optical illusions.

Shooting the OSP Way with Gil and Vicki Ash

▲ Houston-based Vicki and Gil Ash are NSCA Level III, full-time professional shooting instructors with over forty years of teaching experience. They have published sixteen books and produced six instructional DVDs.

How It All Began by Gil Ash

Vicki and I were married in August of 1975 in Houston, Texas, and our shooting journey began with dove hunting and deer hunting with a few quail mixed in for diversity. Truth be known, we had a shotgun wedding but not necessarily what you might be thinking of as a shotgun wedding. I came from a family of modest means and when I began my hunting career, my father's boss bought me a Remington 1100 16-gauge with a twenty-eight-inch vent rib barrel, which I mostly used to shoot doves. This gun was the gun I grew up shooting, and I could shoot it really well. When I was introduced to skeet in 1974, I fell pretty hard in love with skeet and realized that I would have to reload my own ammo in order to afford to shoot more. In that day and time, 16-gauge reloading components were non-existent, so I reluctantly took my favorite shotgun, the cherished gun I grew up with, down to a gun shop and traded it for the same model in 20-gauge. I felt that because 20-gauge reloading components were easily available, I could double the amount of shooting I could do just by reloading my own ammo.

Enter Vicki Watson on the Scene

When Vicki told her father that she was dating someone who shot shotguns, and that she wanted to buy a shotgun so she could shoot with him, her dad jumped at the chance of having his daughter actually become interested in shooting a shotgun. It was as if suddenly he had the son that he never had in his daughter! Even though Vicki and I had only been dating for a few weeks when all this happened, little did we know how big of a change this shotgun would have on our lives. As luck would have it, Vicki's dad had some leases west of Houston that happened to have some doves, and he invited Vicki and her "friend" out on a Sunday afternoon for a dove hunt. We were near a pond and it was a little windy and I had missed a few doves that afternoon when I exclaimed, "I think if I had had my old 16-gauge I would have gotten some of those birds I missed."

So here is where it gets really good—so get the tissues out. The following Tuesday, Vicki went to the gun shop where I had traded in my 16-gauge for the 20-gauge, and she bought that gun back for me as a Christmas present. Think of that! After only dating for a few weeks—and this was in September! Well, as you might imagine, she did blow my socks off and the following August—August 2, 1975, to be exact—we were married. So, you see, we did have a shotgun wedding, though not exactly like you might have imagined.

That was forty-seven years ago. It is only fitting that our lives eventually evolved around shotguns and wing and clay shooting. Little did we know how much we would be involved in shotgunning and the sport of sporting clays specifically. We both shot skeet until this "new game" came to Houston in April of 1983 called "sporting clays." After reading about sporting clays in the paper in an article written by a soon-to-be very close friend, Bob Brister, I set out one Saturday morning to find the new range with this new game called sporting clays. On my first round I missed the last target due to my semiauto shotgun not cycling correctly. In my first tournament, I shot a perfect score, and was hooked, as it turns out, for life, and soon Vicki was, too.

Vicki and I were among a group of Texans who traveled to different out-of-state tournaments, and everywhere we went, we either won or placed in the top five of the competition. Eventually the phone began to ring and shooters at different clubs across the country were calling and asking how much we would charge to come to their club and teach them how to shoot sporting clays. In the beginning Vicki and I would take turns going on the weekend, but then the demand increased so much that we began to travel together. About that time, photography began to go through the digital conversion, and being a professional photographer, nothing about the early stages of digital photography appealed to me, even though I have a bachelor's degree in photography and business from East Texas State University. It was as if God had put us in the right place at the right time. I sold my photography business, and Vicki and I began to teach sporting clays together as America's first professional married shooting coaches at gun clubs across the country.

My competitive career was cut short when I injured my left shoulder and could not shoot for eighteen months. I could not leave the game I so loved, so I began to study coaching and motivation. Vicki went on to be a multi-time All-American and National Women's Champion. Meantime, Brian, our son, began competing and became an All-American Sub-Junior Champion in his teens.

As Vicki and I began to travel more and more, our reputation grew, and to this day we as a couple are arguably the most experienced shooting coaches in this country, if not the world. Together we have been coaching since 1992, have traveled to shooting facilities across North America, and have coached wingshooting in South America and Europe. We each have in excess of sixty thousand hours of platform time and each of us have taught in excess of thirty thousand students—that's sixty thousand total!

We also are published authors of sixteen books, six shooting DVDs, and countless articles written for magazines across the hunting and outdoor world. We were the shooting editors for *Sporting Clays* magazine and are the shotgunning editors for *Safari* magazine, the publication of Safari Club International, as well as contributing editors for *Clay Target Nation*, and are contributors to other publications besides. There have been many articles written about our unique and scientific approach to teaching wing and clay shooting. We have developed a one-of-a-kind membership website, the OSP Knowledge Vault, which contains over five thousand videos, sixteen books, more than two hundred fifty one-hour podcasts, and four thousand pages of written materials. All this material is keyword searchable at www.OSPschool. com. New videos, articles, blogs, and shooting tips are added on a weekly basis as the OSP Knowledge Vault continues to expand as the world's largest single-source library of clay and wingshooting information. Our impressive multimedia library is the result of thousands of hours studying with neurologists, sports vision experts, psychologists, as well as other coaches in other arenas to try to understand how the brain functions and how to mold what the brain perceives when shooting a moving target with a shotgun. The OSP Knowledge Vault features animations illustrating where the gun and the eyes are relative to the target on the different shots in sporting clays and in the field on various game birds. The brain cannot do anything unless it first has a picture. Called "perceptual cognitive learning," this relatively new science has been developed by sports vision scientists and is being used today to help good athletes become great.

In 2014, our son, Brian, joined OSP to work with us and push the envelope in developing a shooter's skill potential and shooting technique. The legacy continues!

OSP School: Optimum Shotgun Performance Instruction

▲ This photo sequence of OSP shooting instructor Vicki Ash shows classic, correct gun mount that needs no verbal explanation. Study how Vicki mounts, shoulders, and points the gun and, most important, how she looks over the barrels. Vicki is shooting a custom Krieghoff shotgun with extremely long barrels—thirty-two inches, which is her barrel length of choice. As you can see, Vicki is a trim, petite woman—which goes to show you that barrel length is not dependent upon build or height, in Vicki's case, but in her ability to point the gun. The gun weighs eight pounds—not a problem for a woman who has developed her muscle strength over years of shooting. Photo credit: Gil Ash.

Life Begins at the End of Your Comfort Zone

THE ABSOLUTE FIRST THING you must do is to be honest with yourself about how quickly you want to get good at shooting a shotgun. The first time anyone has shouldered a shotgun and looked down the barrel can be one of the most visually confusing experiences of her life. It takes a lot of time and effort, especially in the beginning, and there is no "magic bullet." You can only get out of learning how to shoot correctly what you put into it and nothing more! It's confusing, difficult, and frustrating all at the same time—but oh! what rewarding results you will see once you have persevered through the beginning stages of learning and seeing just how to hit a moving target with a shotgun.

What we have learned from almost three decades of professionally coaching over many shooters on three continents is you must work at being a proficient wing or clay shooter.

Looking Down the Barrel

In all other target shooting sports, looking down the barrel is an accepted part of success because the targets are not moving. (Note: This means looking *over* or *across* the rib of a shotgun barrel, *not* looking down the muzzle of a shotgun.) When the target is moving, everything changes because you must look at the target where it is and shoot where it will be. What this looks like is as varied as women's shoes, or purses, or lipstick colors—oh, well, you get the point. The reason that the sight picture is so varied is because it occurs in the periphery and everything in your periphery is a perception due to the information from the periphery being 300 milliseconds behind real time, but we will refer to this later.

Physical Strength Left Arm/Shoulder

Men carry weight in their arms and shoulders and women carry weight on their hip, which leads to a weakness in the muscle in the front part of their shoulder just outside of the bra strap. Well, here is the good news and the bad news. You do have this muscle, but in almost 95 percent of women it does not get much exercise. Therefore, although you have the muscle it is not very strong. This muscle is the muscle that you will be using to lift, shoulder, and swing the shotgun, so you're going to have to build up this muscle to the point that you feel like you can lift the front of a Volkswagen off the ground!

Gun Fit Must Have Gun Mount

Once you are knocking around the herds of wing and clay shooters out there, you will inevitably hear about gun fit and how important it is, which will lead you on a journey going from gun shop to gun shop mounting different shotguns, looking for one that fits you. You might as well be looking for the Holy Grail. The chances of you picking up a gun off the rack and having it fit is a pipe dream even though there are shotguns out there that are "made for women." One dimension will not fit all the different sizes and shapes of women! To think that one gunstock dimension would fit all men is a pipe dream—and all the adjustments for men are based on height and facial shape. To think that one stock dimension will suffice for all sizes and shapes of women is even more unrealistic. After all, you not only have to have your gun adjusted for your height, weight, and neck length, but the adjustment on your bra strap is right in your shoulder pocket; and then there is bra cup size, whether the woman shooter is wearing a sports bra or underwire bra (yes, that matters), bra size . . . well you get the picture. Don't misunderstand, men are certainly appreciative of the differences between men and women, and vice versa. But there are a lot of things that are stacked against you, the female shooter, from the beginning that must be sorted out.

We met a woman who was six feet tall and had a long neck. She had a beautiful custom-fitted over/under shotgun that was fitted by three gun fitters at the factory. They all came up with the same dimensions. Well, long story short, she was left-handed with a custom stock with an adjustable comb with one of those roll-over cheekpieces that adjusted so that her eye was three-quarters of an inch over the top of the rib. She was struggling when Vicki was teaching her on her first day of instruction, so we took the spacers from under the comb. I asked her if she had any discomfort while or after shooting, to which she replied her neck had begun to hurt after shooting four boxes. I touched the base of her neck on her left side and she cringed. Her stock was one- and three-quarters inch too short, which was causing her to pull her head back on the stock to keep her nose from being hit with her thumb knuckle when she pulled the trigger. We put her original stock back on the gun and added two inches to the stock and it fit as though it had been made for her. You guessed it—no pain and soon she was shooting lights out.

Gun fit will change three times over the first two thousand to five thousand rounds you fire through your shotgun. Yep, it's going to change, and you are going to have to accept it. As your proficiency improves, your gun mount will become more consistent along with your move to the target, and as your form and technique evolve, adjustments can be made in your gun fit that will make everything you do when shooting easier. The perceptions you see when pulling the trigger will begin to make more sense and when that happens, the brain begins to subconsciously learn how you interpret the visual data from your retinas. That's when things really take off.

Sight Picture Animation and the "3-Bullet Drill"

If you want to see what we are talking about, then consider subscribing in the OSP Knowledge Vault. Begin by looking at the Shot Simulator and view the sporting clays animations with voice-over instructions. We aren't trying to coax you into becoming a subscriber, but the tools we have developed were developed for shooters just like you. You will be able see what goes where and what the difference is between the left-to-right and right-to-left sight picture in our videos.

Why is this so important? Because there are only two sight pictures, and there is a real difference between them. The sooner you force your brain to deal with what these two different pictures look like and their differences, the quicker everything will begin to make sense to you. In the OSP Vault we discuss the "3-Bullet Drill." If you watch the video, then do this drill every day till your arms fall off. Remember, you are not only learning to move and mount the gun, but you are building up your muscles so when you are at the range you will not get tired as easily as you did before. This, of course, will lead to more shooting and longer times at the range—not to mention more enjoyment.

Body Posture

Women are taught to always stand up straight and walk with shoulders back and chest out, but when shooting a shotgun at a moving target, it is just the opposite. The body posture is *shoulders forward and chest in with the spine curved slightly forward* so the gun can be mounted to the shoulder and cheek at the same time. With the stance

this way, the body position is ready to accept the gun when mounted. This makes the shoulder flat and puts the face in front of shoulder pocket so the gun can fit the face and shoulder, and recoil can come straight back. When the recoil comes straight back there will be less felt recoil. By the way, use light loads. For example, if you are shooting a 12-gauge shotgun, use 7/8-ounce loads that are going 1,150–1,200 feet-per-second. There will be much less recoil. When beginning to learn the timing of the shot, and the move and mount, then everything comes together like you want, every time! Remember, it is all about repetition, and this takes time. In our experience, it is an exceptional person who commits at the very beginning to doing the work necessary to go past being a novice. Once you do, that's when you begin enjoying the fun of wing and clay shooting, because the hard work is behind you.

If a shooter takes her gun every day and does the Flashlight Drill and the 3-Bullet Drill we show on our website, then you'd be amazed how quickly things begin to fall into place. Just carry your unloaded shotgun around the house in a safe carry position. Eventually you will get the feel of where the gun is pointed and how to handle the gun both in tight quarters and in open spaces. Remember, repetition creates skill. Opening and closing the unloaded gun properly will help you become comfortable handling it, too. The more comfortable you are with your shotgun, the less you will have to think about it on the shooting field. Once you are comfortable with your gun, you will focus on the target instead of the gun, which is what you want. The more consistent and confident you become, the better your shots at moving targets.

Consistency and Repetition Build Skill

How often you go shoot at your local gun club or sporting course will determine how quickly you become a proficient shooting sportswoman. How much practice you do at home to improve your mount and build strength will determine how long you can comfortably shoot at the range or in a lesson.

A Lightweight 20-Gauge Over/Under Kicks More than a 12-Gauge

One of the first mistakes we see fathers, husbands, and boyfriends make is to buy their girl a lightweight 20-gauge shotgun so she can carry it around easily. What you need to understand is that a light 20- kicks more than a 12-gauge! This mistake has turned many ladies away from shooting and often has made them wonder just what their man was doing when he says he is going shooting! Few women have the strength to handle this kick when they are first introduced to shotgunning. But if there is enough determination, and if a woman follows a few simple rules, she will have the strength in little or no time and be on her way to having fun with her husband or male friend or relation.

We recommend you invest in a good 12-gauge shotgun that is pretty, but be sure she only shoots seven-eighth-ounce loads going 1150–1200 feet-per-second. The gun will have little or no recoil and be just as effective as a heavier load. The gun is the cheapest part of the journey. Guys, just remember, for a lady it is important that the gun is pretty. You want her to have a gun she loves, right?

Conversely, if you have the money, buy her a 28-gauge over/under. The shotgun itself and 28-gauge cartridges are generally more expensive than the universally popular 12-gauge, but do you want her to shoot with you or not? Without exception, in our forty-three years shooting, twenty-seven as professional coaches, everyone who has followed our advice about the best "first gun" for a woman will agree that a 28-gauge is the best choice.

SHOTGUNNING EXCERCISES

The First Month
First week, two to five times a day:
Mark the break-point at chin height level on a full-length mirror with a round Band-Aid, colored, self-adhesive dot, or another decal.

- Assume the proper posture and stance.
- Focus on the dot and mount gun to the dot. Check alignment of your shooting eye. It should be centered along the rib. Note where your cheek is resting on the comb of the gunstock when the eye is aligned with the center of rib. Remember where the comb touches your cheek, as this, through repetition, will become your anchor point.
- Repeat, repeat, repeat, till the gun hits the same place on your shoulder and face every time your shooting eye is aligned with, and flat on, the rib and the gun is pointed at the dot. Again, repeat, repeat, repeat, as many times as you can. This will be the last time you will look at the gun when you are mounting it, so get a good look at it because you aren't going to get to look at it anymore!

When you do this mounting drill till your arms fall off, two things will be accomplished. First, you will be able to move and mount the gun and second, you will be building up the muscles that you will need to move and mount the gun, and you'll need these muscles for the next two drills we'll discuss, at the range when you take your first lesson.

In the beginning, you will feel yourself leaning back to hold the gun up. However, as you build up the muscles in your arms and shoulders, you will be able to keep your weight on your front foot, which is essential to have the correct posture for shooting a shotgun. Shooters who make the time to build the skill of mounting the gun with the correct posture and develop an anchor point learn correct shooting technique as much as three times faster. On the other hand, shooters who do not build the skill of mounting the gun with good shooting posture learn around four times slower. Remember, the brain sees skill as a sequence of events. Through repetition, the sequence will occur synchronously and without conscious thought! It is the unconscious mind that keeps most beginning wing and clay shooters from avidly pursuing improvement with a shotgun. Until everything you do with your body and the gun become second-nature, muscle memory, or your unconscious mind, whatever you wish to call it, then you will not experience much, if any, consistency or improvement in your skill with a shotgun.

The OSP Flashlight Drill and the 3-Bullet Drill

▲ Gil and Vicki Ash with their son, Brian, who is also an OSP shooting instructor.

Once the mount is consistently coming to your face and shoulder the same way, each and every time, it's time to graduate to the OSP Flashlight Drill and the 3-Bullet Drill. We show you how to do these simple exercises online. Just search "OSP Flashlight Drill" and "OSP 3-Bullet Drill" for our videos.

Each Day, Thirty Times in Slow Motion

The OSP Flashlight Drill is a very easy drill to do and will make all the difference in you being able to focus on the target and not have to think where the gun is. Do it every day for twenty-one days and it's done, but no one wants to do it. They would instead be happy with having that gun mounted and not be able to see the target till after it passes by the gun, making you have to hurry to get in front of the target. Panic in the streets! Even if you have the gun in a soft mount—get your eyes away from the barrel and pull your nose back away from the barrel so you can see the target and begin your move "away"

from the target when you see it. Nose needs to stay on the target!

The 3-Bullet Drill also takes twenty-one days for it to make sense to the brain. I cannot stress enough how doing these two simple drills can make such a big difference in your shooting. Before you call "pull," make sure you tell the brain what the sight picture is—either to the right of the gun or left of the gun. When I got my students to be stubborn with those two pictures they were amazed with the results.

Ten corner . . . rest ten times in the corner . . . rest ten times in the corner rest . . . Once you have done this enough so that you can keep the light in the corner as you mount the gun, your shoulder muscles should be getting stronger so you can do the drill more without resting. Now we will be adding the movement of the gun and following of the target by doing ten left-to-right . . . ten right-to-left repetitions. Start with five and build up your way to ten in each of the three positions. Now add the OSP 3-Bullet Drill thirty to fifty times per day. Start with five times on each side and leave the gun mounted for about twenty to thirty seconds so the brain can understand how you want it to see the image of the gun.

Here is the puzzling part of the picture and it is really confusing. The first time you look over the rib of the barrel of a shotgun with both eyes, if you are focused on the target, you see two barrels and if you are focused on the front bead, you will see two targets! The 3-Bullet Drill will help you to show your brain when it sees two barrels, which is the barrel image you want it to use when you are taking the shot. Once it understands which of the barrels you want it to use, and it gets the success when using it, then it will begin to suppress or suspend from your awareness the other image, much like your brain had done with the dashboard of your car. It is aware of everything that is there, but until it becomes critical for you to get from point A to point B, you are not aware of it. Let the gas gauge get low or the water gauge get too high and boom—you will be aware of it! It is only through repetition and practice that you can make clear to your brain which image you want it to use, and after that repetition and predicting what it will look like when you take the shot before you close the gun and call "pull" will aid your brain to give you what you want. Then you can begin to build a library of sight pictures, which is necessary for you to continue to improve and become more consistent in your shooting.

4. Sportswomen and Sportsmen

▲ Ernest Hemingway was a consummate, experienced, and highly proficient sportsman. Here he is instructing his wife, Martha Gelhorn, in the pheasant field. In the end, "Papa" took his own life purposely at the muzzle-end of a shotgun for reasons that remain his. Although it must have made sense to him at the time, his choice was unfortunate, probably unnecessary, for his departure left generations of readers who hung on his every written word with the unresolved question: Why?

Field Etiquette

Now let's discuss another type of responsibility: shooting etiquette in the field and on the course. Good manners are the rule, not the exception. It's a subject that's taken for granted and too often dismissed, but being respectful of your fellow shooters and being responsible for your behavior at all times are also unbreakable rules of shotgun safety.

Not that long ago, a British magazine published a piece about a woman who attended a driven bird shoot and flew into a rage when a gentleman shooter mistook her for the tea lady and asked her to get him a cup of coffee, cream, no sugar.

"Miscreant pig!" she shouted and stormed off the field.

Had the woman dressed properly for the field and not like a tea lady, this unfortunate situation might have been avoided. As it was, she behaved like a shrew not a shooting sportswoman, and her behavior sullied the rest of the day for the other shooters. What's more, when a person has flown into a temper, she should immediately be invited off the field.

Remember, the first impression you make in any social situation is the image people remember and will convey to others. Happily, poor behavior is the exception, not the rule. Unfortunately, there are women who are loud, behave badly, make a point to act superior to men, disrupt the shooting if they miss a shot (and act equally disruptive when they make a good shot), flirt, drink alcoholic beverages during a shoot, and drink too much after shooting is over for the day. These women tarnish the image most respectable shooting sportswomen strive to maintain. If you encounter a woman who exhibits this behavior, quietly ask her to cease and if she refuses, discreetly ask the director of the shoot to invite her off the field. She doesn't belong there.

▲ How to be a good sportswoman? Dress appropriately, behave like a lady, and respect others.

Remember these three things: dress appropriately, behave like a lady, and follow the unspoken rules of field etiquette. As a safe and considerate shooter, you are worthy of being called a shooting sportswoman.

Here are some additional tips on etiquette (and safety):

1. A hair trigger is a trigger of a firearm set for release at the slightest pressure. How about

a hair-trigger temper? That means someone whose behavior is liable to change suddenly and violently. If you find yourself with, or near, anyone with a gun—on the field, at the range, or on the course—who exhibits a hair-trigger temper, walk away immediately. Don't attempt to placate that person, even if she is familiar to you. Conversely, never give anyone cause to fly into a temper.

2. Whether icy cold or boiling hot, any degree of temper has no place when you are holding a gun at the range, in the field or forest, on the marsh, or in the blind. Stand clear of anyone who exhibits a temper while holding a gun. There is no place for a person like that in your shooting squad or with your hunting group. In fact, a person with an uncontrollable temper has no right handling a gun.

3. Make sure everyone in your shooting party understands each shooter's zone of fire before taking positions or pegs or heading out to the field. This especially applies at driven shoots and shooting preserves, or wherever there is a line of "guns" (shooters). Keep your place in the line. If the line is moving forward, never get ahead of or behind the line. Under no circumstance should you shoot across another gun. Discuss and plan a drive with your hunting party before you begin your drive and enter the woods. Know where the others start, their path, and agree upon the rendezvous place and time you will meet.

4. Accidents occur when a hunter mistakes a movement in the woods, or sees a flash of white, or believes she hears a flutter of wings, and doesn't take that extra split second to be sure it is not another hunter or a dog. You must always identify your target without a doubt and if you hesitate or are unsure, simply forfeit the shot. The uncertainty is just not worth it.

5. If you are hunting over bird dogs, watch where they are ranging, never shoot low, never shoot over a dog.

6. Never hunt over a gun dog without first getting the dog owner's consent.

Husbands and Wives Who Shoot Together

Going to the local gun club so your husband can teach you how to shoot is generally not a good idea. Just because he is a good shot doesn't make him a good teacher. Inevitably, you may both end up frustrated. And that romantic dinner you were planning? Well. . .

A Wife's Perspective

My husband wasn't behaving like himself tonight. We had made plans to meet after work at a nice restaurant for a romantic dinner. I was a little late, and he appeared upset but said nothing.

I asked him how his day went, and he said, "Fine." He didn't ask me about mine. I told him that new tie I got him for our anniversary really looked great.

He said, "Thanks."

The conversation just wasn't flowing. Then I asked him whether we were going to go shooting at the gun club again this weekend and he summoned the waiter, somewhat urgently, and ordered another Scotch on the rocks.

He didn't say a word throughout dinner. After we paid the bill, I suggested we go somewhere quiet so we could talk. He said, "Sure," and we walked through the park, but he didn't say much. Finally, I asked him what was wrong.

He said, "Nothing."

I asked him if I had done something wrong.

He said, "No. Don't worry about it."

When we got home, I put my arms around him and told him that I loved him.

He said, "I love you, too," and gave me a little kiss.

I was hoping for a whole lot more. Instead, he turned on the TV and watched a football game. I didn't even bother to take out that new lacey negligee I bought especially for tonight. So, I decided to go to bed. In my flannel pajamas.

About a half-hour later, he came to bed, but he was still distant. His thoughts were somewhere else. After he fell asleep, I cried. I don't know what to do. I can't explain his behavior. I'm almost sure that his thoughts are with someone else. My life is a disaster.

A Husband's Perspective

A twenty-five-yard, right-to-left crosser . . . Who the hell misses a twenty-five-yard right-to-left crosser? And she wants to go to the gun club this weekend and humiliate me again?

A Husband and Wife Talk Wingshooting

"Tell me," I asked my husband one gentle winter's evening, "what do you think about wingshooting? I mean, what do you really think about when you think about wingshooting?"

He looked over at me from his chair in front of the fireplace and laughed, "What do you mean?"

"What do you mean what do I mean?" I replied. (We talk like that quite a bit in our marriage.)

Then he said, "I will admit it. There is a romance to bird hunting that is often overlooked. There, I said it."

I was a little taken aback. I thought he'd talk about his hunting past, or his shotguns, or his father, who taught him how to hunt when Johnny was just a tot. So, I asked, "What in the world are you talking about?" And here's what he said:

"Okay, think about this. There is a beauty about being in nature. There is a beauty about bird dogs, and retrievers, and spaniels that flush birds, and the skills they possess innately. There is a joy in lacing up old boots, putting on clothes that have a faint outdoor, wet leaves, oak and pine forest smell to them. There is beauty in a finely crafted shotgun—a wonderful English or American side-by-side that fills your hand as you carry it, and hundreds of stories of days that lie before you, already within it. There is magic in sunrise, or sunset, or lunch by the brook, or in the quiet shade overlooking the land you have walked, will walk, and the thought of flushes of fast-flying birds, fine shots, great points and retrieves—all priceless memories to add to your collection. There is a magnificence to bird hunting that you will learn, and love, and enjoy all your life—if you choose to."

It was my turn to pause and be silent and ponder. My husband did not simply answer my question; his response came from a place in his very soul, deep from heart. And then I spoke the words that filled mine: "I love you, Johnny."

Profile of a Sporting Couple: Carole Lombard and Clark Gable

▲ Carole Lombard and Clark Gable.

You know Gable. He was that tough-skinned, soft-hearted, smart-mouthed, sweet-talking guy who always got the gal in the movies. Opportunity and adventure followed him like a lost puppy. For almost four decades, Clark Gable was Hollywood's most popular leading man and the only actor whose sixty films made the top ten at the box office every time. Judy Garland represented millions of swooning females when she sang, "You Made Me Love You ('Dear Mr. Gable')" in the MGM motion picture *Broadway Melody of 1938*. And as Rhett Butler in *Gone With the Wind*, his greatest role, he played poker with his Confederate jailers, and won; soldiered with the Union Army, and won; fought Ashley Wilkes for Scarlett O'Hara and eventually won, but lost the Academy Award for Best Actor, which he should have won. He was the King of Hollywood.

"The King of Hollywood is pure bullshit," Gable replied in an interview. I eat and sleep and go to the bathroom just like everyone else. There's no special light that shines inside me and makes me a star. I'm just a lucky slob from Ohio."

He never pretended to be anything else. As one of Hollywood's highest paid actors, Clark now had the means to live the life he loved most, hunting and fishing. During breaks, he'd head north to Lake

Manitoba's Delta Marsh with his 12-gauge Remington semiautomatic to hunt with *Sports Afield* editor Jimmy Robinson at his famous Duck Lodge, where local Métis, Canada's earliest multiancestral indigenous peoples, were their guides. He hunted pheasant in the Dakotas with Ernest Hemingway and Gary Cooper, shot white-wing doves in Mexico, and timed his trips to Oregon's Rogue River to coincide with the height of the steelhead run in mid-May. Always the first to rise at hunting camp, he'd stoke the fire, heat up the cast iron frying pan, and make a mess of bacon and a big stack of flapjacks for everyone in camp.

"My favorite gun for hunting is a Browning over-and-under 20-gauge shotgun, and my second choice is a Parker double-barreled 20-gauge," he explained in an interview. "I recently returned home for a trip hunting quail and duck and found my 20-gauge Browning eminently satisfactory."

In 1932, Gable had starred opposite Carole Lombard, then twenty-four, in the romantic drama *No Man of Her Own*. Though their chemistry on screen sizzled, off screen they behaved with professional propriety, since Carole was married to actor Dick Powell, and Clark to heiress Ria Franklin. "Clark and I did all kinds of hot love scenes . . . and I never got any kind of tremble out of him at all," Carole later told their friend, director Garson Kanin. Four years later, they encountered one another at Hollywood's glamorous Mayfair Ball and stole away together before the evening ended, ditching Carole's escort, actor Caesar Romero. From that moment on, Carole and Clark were inseparable.

On March 29, 1939, during a break in filming *Gone With the Wind*, Clark and Carole Lombard secretly eloped. The first two weeks were spent camping and fishing in Baja California and Mexico to accommodate Clark's notion of a honeymoon and two weeks would follow in New York to satisfy Carole. But when she discovered the blissful seclusion of camping, and joy in catching your own dinner and cooking it over an open fire, she asked her new husband, "Do we really have to go to New York?" The outdoor life set the bar for the rest of the marriage.

They went fishing and hunting wherever their station wagon could take them (and the studio bosses couldn't reach them). Clark taught Carole how to shoot a shotgun and hunt pheasants and ducks. She quickly became a keen and capable shooting sportswoman and put away her dancing shoes for a pair of hip waders. She grew to love watching the sun rise from the duck blind as much as he. A rare home movie shows the Gables at duck camp, Carole hoisting a string of dead ducks over her shoulder while Clark dances around her like Puck from Shakespeare's *A Midsummer Night's Dream*.

He called her "Ma" and she called him "Pa" or "Pappy," and sometimes, "the old man." To her, he was the evening star; to him, she was the rising sun. They didn't need anyone else. Although Carole and Clark were touted as "Hollywood's golden couple," their love was real. Esther Williams described them as "soulmates who made life delicious and made life delicious for everyone around them."

▲ Carole Lombard and Clark Gable duck hunting.

"Here is a girl who talks in slangy lingo, who is frankly thrilled by sapphire jewelry, perfumes, new hairdresses, and sleeping raw, and who is ready at a moment's notice to go more places than any other woman I've ever met," Clark once said. "And you wonder why I love her. But you can trust this little screwball with your life, or your hopes, or your weaknesses, and she wouldn't even know how to think about letting you down. She's more fun than anybody, but she'll take a poke at you if you have it coming and make you like it. If that adds up to love, then I love her. You know, I think the only religion is a good man in love with a good woman."

The Gables also loved dogs. "You can get a world of pleasure out of owning and training a hunting dog," Clark once commented. "A good one can be bought for around twenty dollars, and you can get books out of the library and do the training yourself. Studying up should be part of the fun. There is always something new to be learned about an animal. From the time I was six, I have had some kind of mutt at my heels. The first dog I owned was a beagle-mongrel who helped me hunt rabbits. One day he disappeared. I've never been able to ask my father what became of him. Of the five dogs we have now—two German short-hair pointers, two dachsies, and our Labrador retriever here—two were trained by me in the initial stages." They would add a couple of setters, an English and an Irish, to their canine family.

"Getting fun out of a sport is very simple. Start in easy and don't overdo. When I hunt my dogs, I never take them out all day long the first day—only for a couple of hours, so they can get used to the country without getting sore feet. Next day, I take them out a little longer. I don't overdo my hunting, either, or my fishing. When I come to an inviting grassy bank, if I feel like it, I lie down and go to sleep for a while. That's part of the fun.

"When you're doing something for pleasure, don't be too serious about it. When Mrs. G. first went along with me on hunting trips, I bought her small-sized men's clothes, since I couldn't find hunting-wear for women. They were hot and coarse and heavy, but she had so much fun discovering the outdoors that she didn't mind them.

"Companionship plays a big part in having fun. At first, Mrs. G. was merely being a good sport when she went along with me on hunting trips. Now she enjoys camping as much as I do. And she's handy around a camp, whether it's our cabin up near Bakersfield or a tent down in Mexico, where we frequently hunt.

"I knew Mrs. G. was going to make the grade the first time I took her duck hunting in Lower California. It was actually a part of our honeymoon; we were having a vacation together, the idea being to devote part of it to my hunting and the rest to a visit to New York. But it didn't quite work out that way. We never made it to New York, just spent all our time hunting and fishing in Mexico.

"Now, there is nothing fancy about a Gable camp; no hot water in the morning, no sheets, nothing beyond the bare essentials. Food has only to be filling, and it is best prepared in one big frying pan and over an open fire: eggs, ham, beans, spuds, trout, quail, or whatever luck provides. It isn't necessary to have long vacations to enjoy the outdoors. An occasional weekend in the open is the ideal tonic for anyone who feels dragged out, and usually there are interesting places to be found a few miles from home where a healthy sport can be the source of a lot of fun. And finally, it doesn't matter what sport you pick, just so it is a means of getting away from it all."

"I'll work a few more years, and then I want a family. I'll let Pa be the star, and I'll stay home, darn the socks and look after the kids," Carole said. "Clark isn't the happy-go-lucky, carefree man the public sees. He's not had a very happy life and is inclined to be depressed and worried. I want to make it up to him if I can. I don't give a damn about me. I want to take care of my Pappy; give him everything he wants. You know, we never do anything much, but we have a lot of laughs and Pa is relaxed and happy."

▲ The Gables at their Encino, California, ranch.

On December 7, 1941, Pearl Harbor was bombed by the Japanese and the United States entered World War II. Carole was asked in an interview what she'd do if she caught a Japanese parachutist landing on her ranch and she replied, "Let 'em come! Pappy and I haven't been banging away at ducks and skeets all these years for nothing. We've put the ranch on a wartime basis, sold a couple of horses, and are growing vegetables instead of alfalfa."

One month later, Carole traveled to her native Indiana to sell war bonds, the first actor to join the patriotic drive to finance the war. "Let's give a rousing cheer that can be heard in Berlin and Tokyo!" she cried out to the crowds that gathered to see her.

Clark hadn't wanted her to go, and he couldn't accompany her because he was working on a movie. Anxious to return home, when her tour was over, she flipped a coin with her mother, who was traveling with her, to decide whether they should take the train or fly. Carole won the toss and mother and daughter boarded TWA Flight No. 3 instead. Sixty miles out of Los Angeles, the plane crashed in Mount Potosi. All twenty on board perished. The date was January 16, 1942.

Clark rushed to the crash site, so high in the mountains it was almost inaccessible, but there was nothing to be done.

"Did you ever see anyone more beautiful? There was never a person in this world who was so generous, so full of fun. God damn it, why Ma?" he wept. His spirit and heart broken, he withdrew to the ranch and stayed there in seclusion for ten months.

"It was a perfect thing. I never expect to find it again," he mourned. "Sometimes I wonder how she'd take things the way they are today, and I always come up with the same answer—with a laugh. She'd get through it better than me."

Clark had to find another way to live. "I don't want to sell war bonds, I don't want to make speeches, and I don't want to entertain. I want to be sent where the going is rough. I'm going to enlist in the Air Corps but not until I get my head together and sort things out. I don't expect to come back and I don't want to come back." At forty-one, well past the draft age, he nonetheless joined up.

He gave up hunting and fishing. He couldn't, not without Carole.

On November 16, 1960, Clark died of a heart attack—three months before his only son, by his fifth wife, Kay Williams, was born. Clark Gable was fifty-nine years old.

Shortly before his death, Clark said, "On my tombstone they should write, 'He was lucky, and he knew it.'" Any two people who find a love like that is lucky, believe you me.

A Husband and Wife Discuss the Mental Game

"When I started my shooting career more than fifty years ago," John Wiles reminisced, "I met a wise, old sage on the skeet field who said, 'John, shooting is ten percent equipment and ninety percent mental.' No truer words in the shooting world were ever spoken."

The "mental game" has been an important subject between instructor and student and a subject of lively discussion between many a shooter on the skeet, trap, and sporting clays fields. As a long-time student of shotgunning, I can honestly say there is a huge gap that only narrows with experience and time between *understanding* the concept of the mental game and *applying* the concept when you shoot.

"Johnny," I asked my husband, "What *is* the mental game, in your opinion?"

"Many sportsmen, especially American sportsmen," he replied, "spend an inordinate amount of time considering makes and models of shotguns, gauges, barrel length, type of action, chokes, bead colors, styles of recoil pads, trigger widths, the grade and beauty of wood, and so on."

"What does buying the right gun have to do with the mental game?"

"Much like pretty fishing lures are designed to catch fishermen, the same can be said of pretty shotguns."

"Honey, fishing lures catch fish, not fishermen."

He grinned. "That's true, but it's also true that a worm on a string tied to a stick can catch a fish just as well as a Royal Coachman tied to a 5-weight line on an eight-foot graphite rod that costs hundreds of dollars. Part of the delight of fishing is going to a fishing store or opening a fishing catalogue and choosing lines, tippets, hooks, reels, and all sorts of rods from a very vast selection of flies that are designed to land you a fish. That's the way it is with shotguns. You can shoot your grandfather's old single-barrel shotgun that wouldn't bring two bills in the local hardware store and take a bird just as well as a fully engraved English 'best' gun with a highly figured walnut stock that costs as much as a luxury car. Every shotgun is designed to do just one thing: expel a quantity of pellets toward an object with the idea of intersecting a target and stopping its flight. It is the mind that controls this activity."

"But honey, I have always maintained that the more highly engraved a gun, the straighter the shot."

"Yes, dear. You would. But seriously, the mental game is more art than science in shooting. If you believe a certain gun enables you to shoot better, it will. If you believe you shoot a gun with twenty-seven-inch barrels better than one with twenty-eight-inch barrels, it will. That's your mind at work.

"And because I shoot my custom stocked W. C. Scott better than any other gun I own, it's all in my head, right?"

"That's right."

"One thing I've noticed when shooting sporting clays is some shooters get very competitive and shoot well at the beginning, while others who shoot tentatively at the beginning finish up strong."

"Everyone is nervous when they shoot in a tournament or on a squad, expert or beginner alike. Honey, if your readers learn anything else, I hope they come away with this: nobody cares about your shooting except you. They are concerned about their own performance. The number one mental game to overcome is your own fear. Forget the other people. It is simply you and the target. And every fiber of your concentration needs to be focused on that target. Until you get past that point, shooting is not going to be the recreational sport you hoped it would be."

"That's where the mental game fits in, right?"

Johnny thought about this for a moment. "Yes," he continued, "but you always want to go back to the basics. The mental game cannot kick in until you are on top of your shooting technique. One problem you have, and that we've worked on together, is your eye dominance problem."

"I know," I replied. "It's a really big problem for me and I've tried every trick in the book, like smearing my glasses lens with lipstick. I've discussed the problem with each of the many instructors I've had. Even now, it is still a personal hurdle that I am constantly trying to overcome."

"Number one, the greatest disservice that was done to you with a few of your instructor's attempts was to teach you 'tricks.' The more you concentrate on the tricks, the less you concentrate on the target."

"Like smearing lipstick on a lens?"

"No, not necessarily. That's the way some instructors try to get you to focus on your non-dominant eye. But there are others who say, keep both eyes open."

"Or close one as you track the bird then open both. But that's a rhythm that takes a lot of getting used to before it comes naturally."

"That's right. And it's personal to each shooter as to which method works best. That, too, is part of the mental game. Number two, eye dominance issues can be overcome if the shooter really wants to focus the target. Normally in eye dominance issues, the instructor first asks the student to mount the gun and close one eye to confirm the problem. This is what has happened with you."

"Always, and even now, where I point with both eyes open is not where my finger points with my dominant eye closed. But it's more than that, Johnny. Yes, shooting is a mind game. I understand this. To me, it's the game I play to focus my mind on the target, and to ignore the gun as I bring it up to my shoulder, like the gun isn't even there. I get it and since I married a man who's such a terrific shooting instructor . . ."

"Me?"

I gave my husband one of my 'looks' and a kiss, besides. "Of course, you. I have to say, I'm shooting better now than I ever have done before. But I have to say, I have always shot better on wild birds than on the sporting clays course. Why is that?"

"Your focus is more intense on live birds than an inanimate object, a clay target. Shooting wild game is serious business, a life and death situation. You are a serious sportsman if you are shooting wild game. Shooting clays is a leisure sport."

"Yes, I understand that completely. When I go into the woods or am on a driven or walk-up shoot, I feel—I don't really know how to explain it. I guess it's almost a spiritual experience for me. The outdoors, the camaraderie of fellow shooters, the crisp autumn air, the dogs—wingshooting lends itself to a special experience that has become so much a part of my life, just as it has been for yours for what? Sixty years? And who I am in the field is not who I am in my day-to-day life. Does that make any sense?"

"Absolutely. We as hunters/shooters have a moral responsibility to do our best to deliver the cleanest and quickest lethal dose of pellets at the bird we take. That's why shooting a shotgun well is so important."

"Okay, so where does the mental game come in? Help me in this kind of situation because I do enjoy sporting clays, I really do, but I am more comfortable when it's just you and me."

"The solution is to get out of the uncomfortable situation. I have suggested to many beginners, or even people who really want to 'practice,' to go to the range by themselves. Get your spouse or a friend to be your trapper and pull targets for you, like we do. Go out there determined to focus on the target and ignore everything else around you. Here's a summary of the mental game, at least to me:

"Up until the moment your eyes focus on the target, a lot of things can be going on. What you want to have happen is, the moment you focus only on the target, you go on autopilot. Your mind has taken over. In my case, I don't see the shotgun. I generally don't even hear the shot. My entire being is focused on the object I am trying to hit. "

Some Wives and Husbands Who Shoot Together

▲ Kate Trad took up hunting and shooting with her husband, Joe, after they had raised their family. Intent on sharing quality time with Joe, early on Kate showed a natural proclivity for shotgunning and, to her own amazement, discovered a real love for the excitement, challenge, and pure joy of being outdoors that shooting provides. Since then, they have traveled the world, hunting in South Africa, the United Kingdom, in Argentina and Bolivia, and throughout the United States—together and with friends. As Kate and Joe will tell you, shooting has added a new dimension to their forty-year marriage. Kate's guns are custom-fitted—a necessity when accuracy in the field is so vitally important.

▲ Betsy and Wayne Holden have been shooting together for more than three decades. Their travels have taken them to France, Spain, the United Kingdom—indeed, all over the world and throughout the United States— and up until recently, they owned a private duck hunting club on the Atlantic flyway. Betsy is a consistent, accurate shot who credits her success and pleasure as a shooting sportswoman to her custom-fitted shotguns.

▲ Tomas and Clarita Frontera own and operate Frontera Wingshooting in Argentina, where they have welcomed international guests since 2002 at their dove hunting lodges La Zenaida and El Paraiso north of Córdoba, pigeon hunting further north at Montaraz, and duck hunting in Veracruz. This warm and wonderful couple have a shared love for the outdoors and wild places, which is the foundation of their business, and have passed it on to their four young children.

▲ All-round sportswoman Marguerite Harris, a champion clay target shooter, and her husband, Mark Harris, a retired professional champion polo player, have traveled the world, but it is their home shooting grounds in Jamaica that have provided them, their family, and friends with their most exciting and memorable sporting experiences in the course of forty years of marriage.

◀ Dieter and Betty Kreighoff.

◀ Claire Zambuni and her husband, Patrick, have immersed themselves in the sporting life. Claire, founding director of Zambuni Public Relations in London, is one of the United Kingdom's most prominent sportswomen, representing her high-profile clientele in the country sports while enjoying wingshooting, hunting, and fishing together with Patrick, throughout in the UK, around the world, and at their home in the Pyrenees.

Part II

CLAY BIRDS AND GAME BIRDS

▲ Academy Award–winning actress Greer Garson (*Mrs. Miniver, The Forsythe Sage, Random Harvest*) was an avid shotgunner.

5. Clay Target Games

he shotgun target sports consist of over twenty different forms of regulated competition. Known as disciplines, these are generally grouped under the three primary target games of trap, skeet, and sporting clays. With the exception of helice, which uses plastic discs, the targets used in clays shooting are usually in the shape of an inverted saucer, made from a mixture of pitch and pulverized limestone rock, which is robust enough to withstand being thrown from traps at very high speeds but at the same time, easily broken when hit, even by just a few lead or steel pellets from a cartridge. The targets are usually fluorescent orange or black, sometimes white or yellow, as long as they can be seen clearly against outdoor backgrounds and varying light conditions. The two primary methods of projecting clay targets are airborne and ground (rolling). These are thrown from fully automatic, spring-loaded flywheel or rotating launchers that can hold up to six hundred targets and throw singles or pairs at distances up to one hundred meters.

Targets are manufactured by weight and dimensions to exact specifications that must conform to international standards. Standard, the most common target, must weigh 105 grams and have a diameter of 110 mm overall and height of 25–26 mm for international competitions and, for American competitions, must weigh approximately 3.5 ounces, and measure 4.3 inches in diameter and 1.10 inches to 1.14 inches in height.

Traps

On sporting clays courses, targets are generally thrown from fully automatic, spring-loaded, flywheel or rotational traps, in singles or in pairs, at high speeds and distances of up to one hundred meters. And yet, type of traps vary, from the very simple hand-cocked, hand-loaded, and hand-released types to state-of-the-art, fully automatic competition traps that can hold up to six hundred targets in their own magazine, and are electrically or pneumatically operated. Targets in automatic traps are released by remote control, either by pressing a button or by an acoustic system activated by the shooter's voice. Target speeds and trajectories can be easily modified and varied to suit the level of shooting, from easy to difficult, and variety of presentations.

TYPES OF CLAY TARGETS

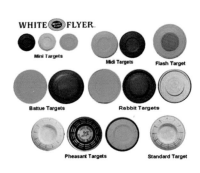

▲ Types of clay targets. Illustration courtesy of White Flyer.

MIDI: Same saucer shape as the standard, but only 90 mm in diameter. These targets are faster than the standard types when thrown at the same rate of speed.

MINI: This small, fast-flying target is only 60 mm in diameter and 20 mm thick.

BATTUE: This very thin target measures 108–110 mm in diameter, flies fast and falls off suddenly, simulating a duck landing.

RABBIT: Though a standard 108–110 mm in diameter, this thicker, flatter, wheel-shaped target mimics a rabbit as it "runs" on the ground.

Shotguns for Shooting Clay Targets

Side-by-side, over/under, semiautomatics, and pump shotguns are all used for clay shooting; however you can only have two shells in the gun for each presentation (trap you can only have one, unless you're shooting doubles).

The side-by-side was the original and, for decades, the only double-barreled shotgun configuration for both live bird and clay bird shooting. Because the barrels of a side-by-side are next to one another, they create a horizontal plane that's twice as wide as a single-barreled shotgun or over/under. This proved to be more difficult to aim for some shooters, especially those new to the sport, since the two horizontal barrels do not provide the same instinctive feedback as the single visible barrel of a semiautomatic or over/under.

Today, as a result, modern production of side-by-side firearms is very limited and older guns are not usually rated for steel shot, which means they cannot be shot at many shooting ranges.

Though first developed in the early 1900s, affordable over/under shotguns did not come into general circulation until the 1990s. This configuration quickly gained in popularity over the side-by-side shotgun with the innovation of the ventilated rib, which dispels the heat waves that rise from the top barrel when a shot is fired and provides a reliable sighting plane on an over/under or single-barreled gun. Longer barrels started to become more popular, especially in handicap trap, where the shots are much longer and more precise and require a dense pattern to hold up at fifty and sixty yards. Trap guns are generally heavier and normally have 30-, 32-, and even 34-inch barrels with tight choking and are stocked to shoot slightly above the point of aim. Skeet guns are usually lighter and faster handling, with barrel lengths of 26 or 28 inches and with fairly open chokes. Sporting models most often come with an interchangeable choke facility and barrel lengths of 28, 30, and 32 inches, depending upon the shooter's preference.

An over/under is available in three trigger options: a double trigger, in which one trigger shoots the top barrel and the other, the lower barrel; a single, non-selective trigger, in which the bottom barrel is fired first; and a single-select, or single selective trigger (SST), which allows the shooter to select which barrel she wishes to shoot first, thereby affording more control over the gun.

Trapshooting

The first important thing for the beginner to have is a gun of proper fit. A mistake often made by the novice is to try some gun, which, as a rule, is not suited to his or her particular makeup. If a lady, the borrowed gun is almost certain to be too long in the stock and, as a rule, too heavy. The result is that it is held in an awkward manner, the recoil received from the shot frightens the shooter, and she loses all of her enthusiasm then and there. Have anyone who knows how to "fit" you with a proper gun teach you the way to stand and hold.

When you have learned that you must "lead" your quartering targets, then "line up" your gun properly and shoot as quickly as you can. When you have learned to "concentrate" on each and every target, forgetting the ones you missed, and look forward with grim determination to smash the next one, then you have the makings of a shooter.

Do not try to shoot too much to begin with. Twenty-five or fifty shots is enough, at least until your shoulder becomes accustomed to the recoil. Shooting when you are tired may cause you to flinch, a habit which has spoiled many a good shot. While a properly fitted shotgun and concentration are great factors, you must not get the idea that you can learn the game right away. Just because you were fortunate enough to get that last string of ten or fifteen straight does not spell that you are a great master of the game. The longer you stay at the game, you will make the wonderful discovery that the "bad half hours" slip in very frequently. The missing of one or more targets in an event, every so often, is what makes trapshooting so interesting and one of the most difficult games to master. If you could get so proficient that you could break them all, all the time, you would soon lose all interest in the sport; but the fact a host of top-notch shooters who have shot thousands of targets frequently have their "bad-hours" demonstrates that breaking targets thrown from a trap, with a shotgun, is a study which requires a great deal of practice and patience and no small amount of skill.

—Annie Oakley (1860–1926) on trapshooting for women, 1916

▲ Photo courtesy of Griffin and Howe.

big money purses. But, along with any blood sport, there comes change, especially a high-profile one where lots of money was wagered and a great deal was made of killing and wounding pigeons. After a long series of changes, pigeons were replaced with clay discs that could be thrown spinning from machines out to eighty yards or so. New rules and regulations were written, and the Amateur Trapshooting Association (ATA) was organized.

Modern-day trap is shot with a 12-gauge gun. There are three standard competitive set-ups: sixteen-yard singles, sixteen-yard doubles (two targets released simultaneously), and handicap, which is shot at the twenty- to twenty-seven-yard line. In sixteen-yard singles and doubles, the target starts a minimum of sixteen yards from the shooter, going away at forty miles per hour. In trap, as in skeet and sporting clays, there are five shooters in a squad. The exception is international trap, which has six shooters in a squad.

In American trap, targets are thrown either as singles or doubles from a trap exactly sixteen yards in front of the shooter and are going away from the firing point at varying speeds, angles, and elevations. The shooter must locate the target with her eyes and move the gun to the target.

There are five members to a squad. Each squad member shoots a target in rotation until all five shooters have fired at five targets. The squad then rotates to the next station and continues until all five shooters have shot five targets at each station. Four rounds of this shooting, often done on four different, side-by-side trap fields, constitute a competition of one hundred targets.

Trap shooting originated in the United States in 1825 and six years later, the first recorded match was held in Cincinnati, Ohio. Americans led the way in developing artificial targets for trap competition—first glass balls containing feathers, then clay targets. Among the greatest of the nineteenth-century trapshooters were Adam Bogardus, Ira Paine, and Annie Oakley. In a one-day exhibition, Colonel Adam Bogardus once broke 5,681 glass balls before missing, while Oakley once shot 4,772 of 5,000 glass balls released from fifteen-yard traps.

Trap grew from live pigeon shooting. Traps started out rather simply. Birds were trapped under a hat, later a box, eventually evolving into multiple traps with electronic releases and rules and regulations for fields, boxes, the size and shape of the ring, and on and on. Eventually the sport became very grand indeed, growing into a competitive sport that draws

Skeet

Trap, sporting clays, and FITASC (an international form of sporting clays) originated in Europe, but skeet is a purely American clay target game.

Skeet shooting was invented in 1920 by two ardent grouse hunters, Charles Davis and William Harnden

Foster, a celebrated wildlife artist and author of *New England Grouse Hunting,* as a means of preparing for grouse season in New England, which opens October 1 and ends December 31. First called "Round the Clock," the squad of five shooters circled the trap like the hands of a clock, in a complete circle of shooting stations set at a distance of twenty-one yards from the center stake, and the trap was set to throw clays that simulated the flight pattern of a grouse rising from the ground. The original game was modified by Foster in 1923 to address safety issues and the field was reduced to half the size, with one trap positioned at 3 o'clock and another at 9 o'clock.

A writer and wildlife artist, Foster introduced the game in the February 1926 issue of *National Sportsman,* offering a prize of one hundred dollars to anyone who could come up with a name for the new sport. The winning entry of "skeet" was suggested by Gertrude Hurlbutt, which she derived from *skyte,* the Norwegian word for 'shoot.'

The first National Skeet Championship was held in 1926. Shortly thereafter, the National Skeet Shooting Association was formed, and the field was regulated to allow targets to be thrown at the same time, in different presentations, for a total of twenty-five targets. The game gained instant popularity, and in 1928 the

National Skeet Shooting Association was founded. During World War II, skeet was used by the American military to teach gunners the principle of leading and timing on a flying target.

In a skeet field, shooting positions 1 through 7 are spread around a half-circle and the final station, 8, is in the center, midpoint between 1 and 7. There are two traps, one that throws the targets high ("high house") and the other, which throws the targets low ("low house.") At station 1, one target is thrown from the high house and one from the low house. Single targets and double targets, one from each trap simultaneously, were thrown to increase the fun and the difficulty of the shooting. Skeet fields are the same dimensions no matter where you go to shoot, which makes for fun as there are many fields around the United States.

Not only are the targets faster in international skeet, but there is a zero- to three-second delay from the moment the shooter calls for the target until the target appears, during which time she must hold the gun below her armpit before she raises the gun for her shot. International skeet is a tough game, and shooting one hundred straight is a rare and remarkable achievement. American skeet permits the shooter to pre-mount her gun and shooters who achieve one hundred straight in any major competition is not unusual. Also, American skeet has a four-gun format for tournament play. A shooter can compete in a 12-gauge, 20-gauge, 28-gauge, and .410-caliber competition.

Popularly, skeet guns all had twenty-six-inch barrels since back in the day, shorter barrels were considered quick and fast-handling for upland bird shooting. Since skeet was designed to imitate the flight and speed of wild birds on the wing at twenty-one yards away, the same gun served the same purpose on the skeet field. But as the game progressed, people got much better at shooting trap, and though the targets didn't change, you changed your positions and it became much more of a mathematical game.

Sporting Clays

The over/under shotgun became the darling of the sporting clays crowd when this relatively new sport was introduced to American shooters by the late, great Bob Brister, shooting editor of *Field & Stream* magazine, in his feature article in the July 1980 issue.

Although already established in England, sporting clays took off like lightning and on September 27, 1980, the first sporting clays shoot in the United States was held in Connecticut at Remington's Lordship Gun Club, with ninety registered shooters. Sporting clays was also designed to simulate shooting wild game birds. Targets are thrown in a great variety of trajectories, angles, speeds, elevations, and distances, and the discipline was originally devised to simulate live quarry shooting, hence some of the names commonly used on sporting stands: springing teal, driven pheasant, bolting rabbit, crossing pigeon, dropping duck, and so on. No two sporting clays courses are the same, which makes it different from trap or skeet, where the fields are regulated in dimension and layout.

Disciplines in this group include English or American sporting, international (FITASC) sporting, super sporting sportrap, and Compak sporting. As much as American sporting clays is the most popular form of clay shooting in the United States, English sporting is the most popular form of clay shooting in the UK. In both, a course or competition will feature a given number of stands, each of which has a predetermined number of targets, all traveling along the same path and speed, either as singles or doubles.

Each stand will feature a different type of target, such as a crosser, driven, quartering, and so on. International (FITASC) sporting gives a much greater variety of targets in terms of trajectory and speed and is shot by squads of six competitors in rounds of twenty-five targets at a time. Super sporting is a hybrid of the two preceding varieties. There are also other formats such as Compak sporting and sportrap, in which five cages are surrounded by a number of traps, and shooters fire specific combinations or singles from each stand according to a program displayed in front of the cage.

A sporting clays course usually consists of ten to fourteen stations with at least two traps at each station. Some ingenious courses with deep pockets now have four traps for each station, allowing an almost infinite

▲ Marguerite Harris.

variety of singles, following pairs, or simultaneous pairs. All courses are designed to offer either fifty or one hundred targets. One hundred targets is a normal sporting clays competition.

Each station is usually marked with the number of targets and the order they are to be presented. As an example, station 1 would have a card stapled to the stand that would say "One, from Trap A, following pair, Trap A first, and One Simo Pair" (where both targets are thrown at the same time). If you shot this configuration ten times, one time at each station, you would have shot fifty targets. Double it, and you will have shot one hundred targets. If you are shooting more than ten stations, you can vary the sequence to throw more following pairs or more simo pairs (also called true pairs), and even multiple singles. The object is to have shot fifty or one hundred targets when you're done.

In early clay target games, traps were a single arm that usually threw one target. The machine was cocked by an individual and released by that individual who sat on a seat at the back of a trap. Later, with the invention of the electric trap, targets could be thrown from a distance away from the trap by a scorer who was standing near the shooters. This eliminated the need for one person pulling and one person scoring. It also reduced injuries to the trapper.

As is normal with trap and skeet, a sporting clays squad is five people. Each person will shoot the menu—that's the number of clay pigeons at that station—one shooter at a time. If you are scoring the targets, often one of your fellow shooters will push the buttons for trap 1, trap 2, or the simo button, while another shooter scores the targets. Shooters rotate the pulling and scoring responsibilities. The score is normally kept on a single scorecard where the names of the shooters are listed and an individual scores an X for targets hit and a 0 for targets missed. Scores are totaled at the end of the round to show who was the best shot in that round. In competitive sporting clays, each competitor gets her own scorecard and there is a puller/scorer at each station. That person both pulls the targets and marks the score for each competitor, then signs the card at the end of the station to show that he has verified the score is correct.

The gun and load you use to shoot clays, while generally determined by the game you are shooting,

are, with the exception of tournament and regulation shooting, your choice. There are, of course, recommendations. For example, the National Sporting Clays Association (NSCA) rule book suggests 12-gauge lead shot up to 1 1/8-ounce loads with a shot size of 7½ and 9 and, for steel shot, a shot size of up to 6. When shooting FITASC, the maximum load permitted is one ounce, and spreader shells are not allowed. Reloads are fine for the leisure clay target shooter, but not permitted in regulation play.

A game bird does not drop straight down from a high tower at fifty yards. However, at some innovative sporting clays tournaments today you might see that very target. You might see a target launched from a trap that bounces off a trampoline into the air at some direction that is inconsistent on every throw. You might see a target that skips across the top of the water, a target you would never see in the wild, much less shoot at. So, while sporting clays started as a clay sport to improve your field shooting, it has morphed into a competitive format all its own. This does not mean that all sporting clays targets are technical, overly difficult, or unhittable. A really good sporting clays course will offer a variety of clay target presentations for every level of shooter.

I believe your first and last station on any sporting clays course should be set up for the recreational shooter. Those can be changed for tournament shooters, but your average shooter wants to start on station 1 with success and end the course with success. Just like golf, it is good to begin and end on a high note. That is what will bring the shooters back to try again.

In the course itself, there should be some moderately difficult targets that challenge a shooter, whether with speed, simultaneous pairs, or distance. There should be some targets that move, usually in an arc, about the time the shooter wants to fire. These types of targets make you shoot outside your comfort zone. While not necessarily representative of game birds, they do cause you to really focus on the target and understand the importance of having a gun that is going to hit what your eyes are focused on.

The goal of target shooting is to make you a better shooter. If competition does that for you, great. But many recreational shooters simply like shooting with their friends. Score is not the object. Becoming better is the object. Helping one another is the object. Enjoying yourself and the outdoors are the objects. The point is, don't get caught up in the competitive world if that's not what you want. Shooting can be fun even if you don't compete. Your real competition is yourself. By constantly and consistently working to improve your shooting, you are competing and improving your own abilities.

Big competitive shoots offer more than just competition. Usually, at the big competitions, there are a number of exhibitors, each with their own booth. On display will be everything sporting—guns and gear, sporting clothes and boots, eye and ear protection, even bird dogs. Sporting magazine publishers are there as well as representatives of international sporting destinations and sporting properties that are for sale. Best of all are the people who frequent these gatherings, because you're among other shooting enthusiasts, all of whom have enjoyed similar experiences in the realm of shooting and have their own stories to tell.

Olympic Shooting

In 1978, the US Olympic Committee selected the NRA as the sole national governing body for Olympic-style shooting in the United States. The NRA's International Shooting Sports division has been designated to fulfill this responsibility from its headquarters office at the Colorado Springs Olympic & Paralympic Training Center. However, organizations such as the Amateur Trapshooting Association (ATA), the Pacific International Trapshooting Association (PITA), and the National Skeet Shooting Association (NSSA) actively govern and develop American-style trap and skeet shooting in this country.

Universal Trench or Flurry

Trench is a variation on the theme of trapshooting, sometimes known as five trap. Five traps are installed in a trench in front of the shooting stands, all set at different angles, elevations, and speeds, and upon the call of "Pull!" by the shooter any one of the five machines, selected at random, will be released. Horizontal angles can vary from 0 to 45 degrees either side of the center line and target distance is between sixty and seventy meters. Elevations can vary, as in other trap disciplines (except DTL, i.e., down-the-line), between 1.5 and 3.5 meters above ground level.

Helice (also known as ZZ or Electrocibles)

Helice (ha-*lees*) shooting originated in Belgium in the early 1960s as the simulated version of live pigeon trapshooting. On a helice course, or ring, the shooter stands about thirty yards from the shooting line, at the edge of the circle. The ZZ targets are randomly released from five mechanical traps positioned in a semicircle in front of the shooting post. Each trap has an oscillating motor that throws the targets in a random, unpredictable order and spins the ZZ birds at a speed of five thousand revolutions per minute. Shotguns 12-gauge and smaller may be used with a maximum load of one ounce, 7½ factory-loaded shells.

The ZZ target is also called an electrocible. It is made up of two parts: a round, detachable white plastic center piece called a witness cap and a two-winged, blaze orange or red plastic propeller, called wings. If the shooter hits the target, the witness cap is knocked off its wings. However, the cap must land within a boundary fence twenty-one meters from the shooting post to score. A perfect score is thirty. Although thousands of dollars can be made on the tournament circuit, it can be an expensive sport because generally, a round of thirty ZZ birds costs ninety dollars or more, plus shells. The United States Helice Association is the governing body of the sport in the United States (www.ushelice.com). The FITASC World Cup and World Championships are held annually.

Live Pigeon Trap
A Bird of a Different Feather

The late Cyril S. Adams, in his highly acclaimed book *Live Pigeon Trap Shooting*, explains shooting technique as it applies to this rarefied sport, which originated in England in the late eighteenth century. The crowning competitions of international live pigeon trapshooting were held in Monte Carlo from 1872 until 1960, notably among them the Prix de Larvotto and Prix Gaston Rambaud.

Mr. Adams makes the point that there is no scientific way to shoot a target, and that the right technique "is a contentious subject between strong-willed and determined individuals."

Every person sees and perceives objects in an array of time and space snapshots that are very different. Rudy Etchen, a phenomenal shot, could see the dimples of a flying clay target and judge how fast it was spinning. Olympic trap gold medalists will often smoke a target before an observer can focus his eyes on the clay. Many live pigeon trapshooters can see the bird's head—and some say they can clearly see its eye. Some shooters swing a gun slowly and will see a foot or more of lead, while others swing so quickly that they see only a small fraction of that. We all have certain genetic limitations that cannot be overcome by analytical thinking and constant training.

As a wingshooter, do not beat yourself up when you miss a bird. Just keep practicing. And clay target shooting and helice is the opportunity you have to practice regularly and often.

"One of the great characteristics of these sports is that you can experiment with any part, see the results, repeat the results, and then decide if you want to adopt the change as a benefit or discard it as a detriment," Mr. Adams observes. For this reason, many wingshooters practice on target clays as a means of honing their skills in the field.

It is interesting to note that historically, at the peak of live pigeon trapshooting around 1890, virtually every gun configuration was a side-by-side. Today, over 90 percent are over/unders, and only 3 percent are side-by-sides. The remaining 7 percent are semiautomatics.

Over-under trap guns are well-suited for this type of shooting because they are heavy, and easy

▲ Pigeon shooting tournament in Monte Carlo.

to customize for pigeon shooting; their narrow sighting plane makes it fast to develop a lateral relationship with the target, there can be a different choke in each barrel, and when using a pre-mounted gun there is good visibility on each side of the gun using a high rib. There is a huge selection of models available and they are (often) inexpensive. In this, as in trap and skeet, and unlike game bird hunting and sporting clays, the gun is pre-mounted.

If a shooter has a thick chest or short arms, he will tend to use shorter barrels along with a shorter stock. If he is lightly built or has long arms and/or neck, he will tend to use longer barrels with a longer stock. Short barrels and long stock or the other way around produce a poorly balanced gun. Short barrels give the impression of pointing quickly but in reality, they are just not pointing accurately. Long barrels allow the shooter to point the gun with great accuracy and they seldom lie. Today, a large variety of weights can be added at various locations on a gun to give a shooter the balance he desires.

To secure every possible mechanical advantage, your gun must fit perfectly and shoot exactly where you look. These are two different issues and must be addressed in that order. Gun fit means that when you mount the gun your eye is centered on the rib, the butt is fully engaged by your shoulder and firmly against it, your trigger finger has only the last joint in contact, you have a firm, comfortable grip on the wrist of the stock, the base of your right thumb does not interfere

▲ Cyril S. Adams.

with the nose of the comb or your own nose, your neck is relaxed and not pushing down or over on the comb, and the barrels are not canted. When these requirements are met, the gun fits and it can easily be properly mounted every time. In addition, a well-fitted gun will help in reducing muzzle jump, a critical factor in (this type of) shooting.

The perfect position of your head on the comb is a subject for some experimentation. Some shooters prefer to push their cheek firmly into the comb while others hold their head lightly on the wood. As a shooter learns to be relaxed and calm, his stance will usually become more upright. The straighter stance requires more drop at the heel.

The "relaxed, slightly forward stance with the left arm (of a right-handed shooter) somewhat bent is normal for most shooters," Mr. Adams explains, and this position, leaning into the shot, is as appropriate in shooting game birds as it is any of the clay target games. However, he also recognizes the "upright stance" with the right-handed shooter fully extending his left arm. While this slows the shooter's swing to the right, it affords a smooth move to the target.

Stance also affects stock dimensions. The more the shooter leans forward, the lower the butt will be on his shoulder and his eye will be higher above the rib, causing the point-of-impact to be higher.

The position of the shooting (right) arm also affects the stock dimensions. As the elbow rises, the muscle that forms the point of the shoulder pushes the comb of the stock into the cheek, reducing the amount of cast required.

Be aware that both gun fit and point-of-impact will change over time as you grow older, or as you lose or gain weight and develop joint and/or muscle impairments. When making changes or adjustments to your gun (or cartridges or stance), make only one at a time. Thoroughly try and evaluate the single change before making another—or you will not be able to tell which one did what.

Most shooters can accept a small variation in the length-of-pull without difficulty. Slightly long stocks swing smoothly but are slow on right-hand birds (for right-handed shooters). Slightly short stocks move more quickly but with jerky motions. On this subject, on a day when you feel you are jerking your gun around, you can smooth it out by moving your forward hand an inch or two toward the muzzle, thus making the stock feel longer. On the contrary, should you feel you are moving the gun too slowly, you can speed up your swing by moving your forward hand back on the fore-end an inch or two.

The Right Load for Trap, Skeet, and Sporting Clays

Contributed by Ron Reiber of Hodgdon Powder Co. with permission. This article originally appeared in the December 2014 issue of Inside SSSF.

Ask five shooters what the right load for clay target shooting is, and you will get five different answers. We are not talking about the components that go into the individual load, rather, how much shot, size of shot, and velocity of shot is necessary to "always" break the clay target.

The truth is that more velocity and more shot are not the answers to the best loads. High velocity means many, many deformed shots at the bottom of the shot column as the shot starts down the barrel. The higher the velocity, the more deformed pellets. Those deformed pellets do not "buck" the air well, and become flyers that skew off in various directions, or slow down rapidly, lengthening the shot string. That means less shot on the clay target.

From years working in the ballistics laboratory and viewing shot strings on camera, I have come to see ideal patterns form in the velocity range of 1150 fps to 1200 fps. No matter if it is $1\frac{1}{8}$ ounces, 1 ounce, or $\frac{7}{8}$ ounce, patterns are best in this range.

How much shot is enough? It depends on the target, but it is a proven fact that no more than 24 grams or $\frac{7}{8}$ ounce shot is necessary to cleanly break the most difficult trap targets thrown in competition, that being international trap competition. That game started with 1⅛ ounces of shot and went to 1 ounce because scores were too high. Scores went up, so they decided to again drop the amount of shot to lessen scores. They went to 24 grams (approximately ⅞ ounce), and scores rose again!

What does that teach us? The lesser amount of shot is still more than adequate, but recoil has been significantly reduced, and we are better able to keep our heads on the stock, and thus produce better scores.

Now apply that concept to using the 1150 fps to 1200 fps velocity range to load our clay target loads, and we have produced the perfect reload with a shot string of optimum dimension. I tell shooters this is a 99 percent head game, and we need to believe in our gun, load, and ability to place the shot in the right spot! My motto regarding the load is, "It's not how much you throw, but what you throw and how you throw it."

If I were to start over shooting each of the clay target games mentioned above, I would not be loading 1⅛-ounce loads, rather for comfort and keeping my head down for correct follow-through, I would load either 1 ounce or ⅞ ounce, depending on what my gun patterned the best with the components I had available. The diameters of these patterns are the same as with 1⅛ ounces but have shorter shot strings due to less shot set-back and less deformation, thereby having just as many pellets contacting the target as the heavier load. Why take the recoil when it is not necessary, and why not save the money on expensive lead shot, when less will do the same?

Load one hundred rounds of 1⅛ ounces, one hundred of 1 ounce, and one hundred of ⅞ ounce at the same velocity level, pattern them, and shoot a couple rounds of trap, skeet, or sporting clays. Then see if your scores are not equal to or better than those shot with the heavier loads. Watch how they compare in how the targets break. I believe your scores will be better because you were more easily able to "stay in the gun," especially for doubles. Less recoil and fatigue do not become a factor toward the end of the one hundred rounds.

One of the greatest sporting clays shooters of all time, George Digweed, shot at ten crossing targets at one hundred yards with standard 1 ounce, size 7½, and broke seven of the ten. He performed this phenomenal feat at the American Shooting Centers in Houston, Texas, and it was witnessed by many. Case closed.

6. Wingshooting

Women don't hunt game to feed their families these days. My mother's idea of hunting was hunting for bargains at Saks Fifth Avenue. My grandmother, like her mother before her, would have hunted had she not left Italy and moved to Brooklyn after she married my grandfather. She said her mother, who was six feet tall, always went hunting. It gets a little hazy going back from my great-great-grandmother, but I know for a fact that my great-grandmother on my father's side threatened her husband with a 12-gauge Parker when he won—and lost—all their money on a horse race in Saratoga Springs. And at least one great-grandmother, many greats ago, defended her children and home from the British with a muzzle-loading shotgun during the American Revolutionary War.

Before the grocery store, before fast-food joints, shooting wild game put meat on the family dinner table. Usually the husband went into the woods, sometimes the wife, as late as the early twentieth century. Why bother with that pheasant you shot when you can go to the grocery store and get a plucked, cleaned, roasted chicken?

Because eating what you shoot is an important part of the creed of a responsible wingshooter.

Hunters should, and do, take pride in eating what they shoot. Once you have earned your hunter's safety card and have become a confident outdoorswoman, you can go into the woods to hunt your dinner. And that's what this chapter is all about: hunting wild game birds.

Richard Blome's seventeenth century term for wingshooting, "shooting flying," became known as "wingshooting" in Victorian England, which referred to both upland and lowland birds. Upland birds, an American term, refers to wild game birds that live "up land" on elevated ground above, or some distance from, the sea. Their natural habitat is woodlands, harvestable fields, and hills (in the United Kingdom, moors). These birds—among them, bobwhite quail and ruffed grouse (also called pa'rtridge by old-time New Englanders) are non-migratory birds. These birds cluster in small groups, called coverts. Coverts can be home to quail and grouse for generations. A covert is hallowed ground to the consummate upland bird hunter. The location of the Old Churchyard Covert, for example, or the Beaver Pond Covert is a sacred place to the dedicated grouse hunter, the location of which he would never dare disclose to anyone, at any price.

Lowland shooting, also an American term, refers to waterfowl hunting, or waterfowling. Ducks, geese, and other wild game birds whose natural habitat is rivers, lakes, marshlands, and the sea are waterfowl, or wildfowl. Waterfowl are migratory birds; they fly south in the winter and north in the spring, usually returning to the same home habitat after the seasonal journey.

The geese you see year-in and year-out on the golf course, however, are the exception. These are resident birds that have grown accustomed to the neighborhood and simply won't leave. There's a classic story about the great American comedian W. C. Fields, who was seen in his pajamas running down the sloping lawn behind his Beverly Hills mansion waving a golf club at a flock of geese shouting, "Crap green, dammit!"

The tradition of waterfowl hunting started in 1937, when hunters initiated conservation measures to stave off the marked decrease in duck and goose populations from over-hunting and market hunters, who hunted wildfowl with no limit and sold the birds to restaurants and markets.

Not so the wing shot. We can be in peak physical condition. We shoot a gun that fits, we've practiced our shooting technique and we look for the target, not at the gun. We've got it down-pat, right? No—and we never will. You see, there's an extra element in wingshooting that goes beyond any of the clay target sport, a different goal, a singular attitude, and a knowledge of, and communication with, Nature and God's lesser creatures. We enter the woods as a challenger would enter the boxing ring: we are the opponents in Nature's woodland arena, and the wild birds are on their home turf. It is up to us to know their ways and become familiar with their habitat. If you do not, you are unprepared. And if you are unprepared, do not go into the woods until you are.

How do you prepare to enter a grouse wood or quail field? You must listen. You must look and be aware of everything and everyone around you. You must instantly recognize and know all you can about the game bird you are hunting. Your footfall must be light and sure, your senses alert, and your eyes must scope out the foreground while maintaining a clear view of your periphery. Only experience will hone your shooting skills and even then, you may return home with an empty game bag. There are always reasons, of course:

"It was too windy—the bird got caught up in a gust."

"The sun got in my eyes."

"The woods were too dark."

"It was too warm, the birds just sat."

"It was too cold, the birds got skittish and took off a mile away."

"A tree got in the way."

"I couldn't find the trigger."

"I forgot to load the gun."

"I couldn't find the safety."

"I didn't have any luck."

What does wingshooting mean to a wingshooter? The very definition of the word defies all reason; nonetheless, we return to the woods, the fields, and the marshes again and again, like a lover's call to a yearning heart.

▲ Illustration by Currier & Ives.

Shotguns for Upland and Lowland Game

The shotgun you choose to shoot clays with is up to you. The shotgun you choose to shoot game birds with is up to the bird.

Over/unders, semiautomatics, and pump guns are all seen in the field, but the side-by-side is the favored gun of the wingshooting traditionalist, and the old argument is that if God wanted us to shoot an over/under, he would have placed our eyes one on top of the other rather than side-by-side. However, the wider sight plane across the barrels of a side-by-side is preferred by many a wingshooter when leading a bird.

The side-by-side was the original and only breech-loading double gun for almost a century. Among the early classic American gunmakers were Parker Brothers, L. C. Smith, A. H. Fox, and Lefever. Though identified with English gunmakers, Americans were responsible for many innovations—the most important of which was the invention of the first breech-loading shotgun, in 1880, by American gunmaker D. M. Lefever and his patented internal cocking rod system. Likewise, L. C. Smith's innovative rotary lock bolt system made for a stronger, more reliable gun.

If you are a traditionalist at heart and want to own a *new* classic, American-made, side-by-side, the place to go is Connecticut Shotgun Manufacturing Company (www.connecticutshotgun.co). Tony Galazan, the visionary gunmaker and force behind CSMC, brought back the Winchester 21, one the finest American side-by-sides ever made, and A. H. Fox, among others, which you will find in the shotgun section of this book.

There's something wonderful about older guns that have been cared for and are in good shooting condition. The action takes on a luster like the patina on fine silver. However, as sound and well-cared for as an older gun may appear, all pre-World War II guns should be inspected by a professional gunsmith before they're fired. Guns made in the first third of the twentieth century or earlier may have 2½-inch chambers and therefore will need 2½-inch cartridges. RST Classic Shotshell Co., Inc. offers a 2½-inch Bismuth cartridge and a Fibre Wad Nice Shot, 7/8 ounce, in 16-gauge, and a one-ounce, 2½-inch shell in 12-gauge that is available in Bismuth, Nice Shot, Lite Copper Plated lead and for high pheasants, and RST makes a Lite shell that's good for walk-up (www.rstshells.com).

Never shoot a modern load through a gun with Damascus barrels. Early guns with fluid steel barrels may have 2½-inch chambers and therefore will specifically need 2½-inch cartridges from shotgun cartridge manufacturing companies, such as RST, which makes 2½-inch shells. Metallurgy back then was not what it is today, so always be cautious and never shoot a high-pressure load, even with 2¾-inch chambers in a pre-war (before WWII) gun. Your older gun, if re-proofed for modern loads, will have a marking on the barrels.

If you are unsure, leave nothing to chance. Again, consult a professional gunsmith first.

The 16-gauge, once so popular and long considered the gun of choice for old-time upland bird hunters, is now the least common gauge and it can be difficult to get loads. The 20-gauge surpassed the 16-gauge as sporting clays catapulted in popularity. The 28-gauge and .410-caliber are effective in expert hands, with the right load. No gauge has ever displaced the 12-gauge in popularity, which universally remains the all-around gauge for clay target, waterfowl, and high or distant pheasant. Twelve-gauge guns tend to be heavy, so look for a field gun that weighs under 7¼ pounds.

The semiautomatic and the old reliable, much-less-expensive pump shotgun are likely the guns you'll find in the duck blind. Both can hold either three or four shells in the magazine and one in the chamber, but legally the gun has to be "plugged" with a wooden or plastic plug to prevent the magazine from holding more than two shells, plus one in the chamber, when you're hunting waterfowl. Benelli (www.benelli.com), the Italian gun manufacturer, changed up the game in semiautomatics with its innovative Inertia-Driven System with rotating locking bolt action, introduced in the model M2 and followed by the Black Eagle and Vinci series. Almost indestructible, these guns are impervious to water and the harsh environment you encounter in a duck blind and adverse weather conditions in the field.

If, for example, you are hunting Canada geese and other larger waterfowl, you may shoot a 12-gauge semiautomatic choked Improved Modified or Full with 32-inch barrels using a heavy shot, such as 1¼-ounce, No. 2s. But that's too much gun and load for bobwhite quail. A 20- or 28-gauge over/under is the popular gun for quail and other small upland birds, and an expert wing shot might even choose a .410-caliber with a ½-ounce, No 6 or 7½ load. It's the size of the bird and the distance at which you are shooting that determine the gun, choke, and load, taking into consideration that the bigger pellets retain their energy and are shot at targets that are further away.

Range

Successfully connecting your shot with the bird depends both upon the accuracy of your shot and the spread of pellets that effectively intercept the target. Unlike rifle shooting, where range depends in part upon the velocity of the bullet, a shotgun does not depend upon the speed of a shotshell. On the contrary, any increase in muzzle velocity in a shotgun would be lost within a few yards of the charge leaving the barrels due to the disproportionately increased air resistance the shot encounters. For this reason, the optimum effective range of a shotgun is generally between twenty and forty yards, depending upon the gauge, load, and choke of the gun.

Many bird hunters shoot sporting clays in the off-season as a way of getting ready for hunting season. When you're hunting ruffed grouse, woodcock, or any wild bird, you're always on the alert, never sure of when one will burst out of a cluster of young birch trees or rise up from a marshy patch in the woods, only to fly away like a kamikaze pilot with vertigo. That silence-splitting beating of wings can stop the heart of even the most seasoned wingshooter. And you wonder how you missed that wily, cunning, clever, devious, trickiest thing in feathers! Just a stroke of bad luck, perhaps . . . The heart of the matter is why we hunt. It doesn't matter that you didn't get the bird; you got something far more precious: sharing a moment with one of God's lesser creatures.

▲ The Blue Sky Rule, "Only shoot a bird when it is surrounded by blue sky," means the bird you aim to shoot must be completely surrounded by sky. When you have a clear view of everything surrounding the target, you run no risk of hitting a person or a dog that might otherwise be concealed by trees or on the near side of a hill.

When you are shooting clays and miss, you can usually see whether you shot above, below, or behind. You don't necessarily have that luxury when your target is a bird. There is little control over the shots presented in wild bird situations. Until the bird rises, you are never certain where it is coming from or where it is going. In the sliver of time you have to take a secure stance and mount the gun, you have to concentrate on the speed and flight path of the bird in order to determine your shot. Because a properly fitted shotgun is an accurate extenuation of your sight lie and hands, you can put your entire focus on the bird with no thought to the gun. If you have to think about the gun, you're not concentrating on the target. And if you are not concentrating on the bird, you will miss. All this in perhaps five seconds.

Before you go hunting:

1. *Know your birds*. Visually be able to identify the game bird you are hunting—at least as close as shooting-range.
2. *Study flight patterns* and *speed*. Every species varies. Go online and access some of the many shooting videos available.
3. *Know which gun, gauge, cartridge,* and *load* is correct to affect a clean kill that follows the laws and rules where you are hunting.
4. Know the daily and seasonal limit of birds you can legally shoot.
5. Be sure your hunting license is current and covers the game you are shooting, that you are in possession of a current federal bird banding permit if you are hunting migratory birds, and have been assigned a H.I.P. registration number.
6. Know which species are *not* huntable. For example, plover were once fair game; however, the breed became a protected species under the Endangered Species Act on January 10, 1986, and, if harmed or if its habitat is disturbed, the perpetrator will be subjected to penalties as provided by this Act. In North America, this includes American golden plover, black-bellied plover, mountain plover, Pacific golden plover, piping plover, semipalmated plover, snowy plover, and Wilson's plover. By the way, more than one plover is called a *wing* of plovers.

Speed of Game Birds

In *Speed of Game Birds* (1911), Major Charles A. Askins wrote, "No amount of mechanical ability to handle a gun, such skill as might be acquired in trap-shooting, will ever make a crack field shot out of a man who cannot estimate distances accurately, or who would not know where to hold if he did. In treating the subject of speed of mark, distance of target, and amount of lead, the writer feels constrained to admit that no theoretical knowledge can take the place of experience."

The distance game birds fly in feet-per-second determines the amount of lead when you take your shot.

TABLE OF FLIGHTS
Configured by Major Charles Askins

BIRDS	Feet per second	Average
Quail	65 to 85	75
Prairie Chicken	65 to 85	75
Ruffed Grouse	60 to 90	75
Dove	70 to 100	85
Jacksnipe	50 to 70	65
Curlew	45 to 65	55
Plover	50 to 80	Various
Mallard	55 to 90	75
Black Duck	55 to 90	75
Spoonbill	55 to 85	75
Pintail	60 to 100	80
Wood Duck	70 to 90	80
Wigeon	80 to 100	90
Gadwall	80 to 100	90
Redhead	110 to 130	120
Blue-Winged Teal	120 to 140	130
Green-Winged Teal	100 to 130	115
Cinnamon Teal	100 to 130	115
Canvasback	130 to 160	145
Canada Goose	130 to 160	145
Brant	Various	100

This table, developed a century ago by Major Charles Askins, is as accurate today as it was then. It estimates timed speed of flight of America's most common game birds, taken when they are in full plumage and ability, after they have acquired momentum after flying some distance. As Major Askins observed, "It may be noted that birds of the order of quail and grouse are much more uniform in rate of progress than wildfowl. Nature did not give the grouse family such wing powers as the migratory birds, the one style of flying they have developed giving a very regular velocity."

The greater the strength of wing of a species of game bird, the greater speed it is capable of. Likewise, wind and atmosphere affect all birds' flight speed, and the height at which they fly, but as with quail and grouse, it is unlikely these birds will accelerate to simply "get out of the way" of your gun barrels. Not so the "duck tribe," as Askins refers to all ducks. They "sprint or loiter," he says, but my own experience is that ducks take off as a flock; the moment their leaders are suspicious of danger, they give the command to fly and off they go with a flurry of wings. Of course, there's the old-timer who is long in the tooth that may fly slower than a youngster; likewise, a heavy bird as opposed to a lightweight. Or, as Askins points out,

Give a blue-winged teal a forty-mile breeze behind him, have the little rascal dropping down with it, and he comes on so fast as to be simply unhittable. Some have claimed a speed for him of 150 miles an hour or 220 feet a second. The canvasback, redhead, and bluebill have a way of driving before a gale, too. Much of the fascination of wingshooting comes from the fact that shots will always be afforded quite beyond the skill of mortal man.

On the contrary, many wildfowl are jumped, killed when hovering over decoys, or shot while unsuspicious of danger and moving slowly. Moreover, many birds like snipe, quail, and grouse are generally killed before they have attained full speed, perhaps 90 percent of such birds falling before they have reached normal flight velocity. Generally speaking, upland birds are not shot while passing the gun at right angles, but are going straight away, quartering, or twisting. It follows that in the fields, our gravest shooting problems are other than reckoning speed of flight but on judging distance to hold ahead by the lengths of the bird.

▲ Calculating lead ahead of the bird is based on the speed, distance, and angle of the bird.

Shot Size	Max Range (Yds)	Normal Use
BB	60	Waterfowl, Fox, Coyote, Other Large Fur-Bearers
2	55	Waterfowl, Small to Medium Fur-Bearers, Turkey (when regulations allow)
4	50	Turkey, Pheasant, Squirrel, Rabbit, etc.
5	47	Turkey, Pheasant, Squirrel, Rabbit, etc.
6	45	Grouse, Dove, Partridge, Close-Range Pheasant
7-½	42	Clay Pigeons, Woodcock, Dove, Snipe, Rail, Rabbit, Quail, Grouse
8	40	Clay Pigeons, Woodcock, Dove, Snipe, Rail, Rabbit
9	37	Clay Pigeons, Quail Snipe, Woodcock

▲ Shot sizes—yardage—game.

Pellet Energy

Minimum pellet energy is one foot-pound on doves, woodcock, chukars, Hungarian partridge, grouse, and quail shot with 20- and 28-gauge guns, with 130 to 230 pellet strikes in a thirty-inch circle. A light, small gauge gun is easier to carry than a heavy 12-gauge, and since you are not shooting many shells, there's little or no recoil fatigue that results in a throbbing shoulder if you're shooting an unfamiliar gun that doesn't fit properly. A 2¾ inch, 20-gauge shell will do nicely for most upland game birds, such as Winchester AA Heavy Target Load. A 2¾-inch, 20-gauge one-ounce 7½ shot, it is a high-quality, efficient cartridge with a 350-pellet count at 1200 fps (feet per second) muzzle velocity that's effective at thirty to thirty-five yards. In a 6½-pound shotgun, you'll feel 18.7 foot-pounds of recoil. Federal Wing-Shok Quail Forever 2 3/5 inches, 20-gauge, one-ounce No. 8 is comparable, but has 410 pellets in a cartridge. Winchester AA costs about ten dollars for a box of twenty-five whereas Federal's Wing-Shok costs about twenty-three dollars a box. You can shoot lead on all upland birds except when you are in a wetland area, shooting, say, woodcock, and such areas that are subject to non-toxic laws.

Wingshooting Technique

Lead

How much lead do you give a wild bird in flight? How do you determine distance, speed, and angle of flight with sufficient accuracy to connect your shot, all within the breath of a few seconds? Most upland birds are effectively shot at thirty yards or less. In all likelihood, you should be able to hit a target at such a close distance, right? Not so if the target is a winged rocket. Even the most seasoned wingshooter will attest that putting a bead on that feathered missile as it weaves through a copse of pines is one of the challenges of being an upland hunter. However, you will reap nothing but frustration if you do not lead the bird.

"Given the velocity of our projectile, the speed, distance, and angle on which our mark is traveling, it should be easy to work out the exact spot at which the aim must be taken in order to connect with the target," Major Askins explains. "But all our theories will be much modified and nullified by the different styles of shooting that men and women have acquired. Indeed, so many factors have a bearing that it is rare for theory and practice to agree, and it is seldom that two skilled shots can be found who will not have divergent views about where to hold."

While the three methods of leading a bird are all good, it must be remembered that shooters perceive lead in two very different ways: at the bird or at the gun. If you were to ask the late, great exhibition shooter Tom Knapp how far he would lead a dove in Argentina, he might say something like eight feet. For someone who sees lead at the gun, meaning an eight-foot lead at the bird would be a one-inch lead at the gun muzzle, to tell them to lead a bird eight feet would make no sense whatsoever. This perception of lead is important for a teacher/instructor working with a student. You cannot help the student if you do not understand what the student "sees." One of the basic questions in discussing lead with a new shooter is "How far were you in front of that bird?" If the student says, "About a pick-up truck's length in front," you know they are seeing lead at the target. If the student says, "About a half-inch or so," you know they are seeing lead at the gun. This understanding really helps the progression of a new shooter.

Say you are in the blind, anticipating a flock of mallards to come to your calls and decoys. A duck comes in about fifty yards distant and you hold ten lengths, or ten feet, ahead. Your point of aim is in front of the bird and you cover the distance with your gun muzzle, calculating both horizontal and vertical distances in order to get ahead of the bird.

The *swing-through method* requires that you start the gun behind the bird, accelerate through the bird, and pull the trigger as the gun passes the bird's head. There's probably some scientific study that could show how this works, because now your gun speed is faster than the target and the shot is going toward the intersect point of the bird.

The *sustained lead method* requires that you focus on the head of the bird, bring the gun up in front of the bird and in your peripheral vision, see some sort of gap between the head of the bird and the barrel. This is very subconscious because looking at the barrel will cause you to slow the gun down. In sustained lead, since you started in front of the bird, there is a "feel" for how far the gun should be in front of the bird. When the mind says the lead is correct, the shot is taken.

The *pull-away method* has the shooter bring the gun to the head of the bird, move at the same speed as the bird, and then accelerate the gun away from the bird, pulling the trigger when the mind says the lead is correct.

The methodology doesn't change with bird species. One of the most famous swing-through methods was taught to young people shooting driven pheasants. They were told, "Butt-Belly-Beak-Bang," which is no more than starting at the back of the bird, moving through to the head, and pulling the trigger. That's swing-through. The same sustained lead that is often taught on skeet ranges is the same sustained lead you would use in the dove field. And the pull-away method, which most shooters I know use on long crossing birds, works on any long crossing bird regardless of what species it is. The reasons this works is because your mind is calculating the lead based on the speed, distance, and angle of the bird. As Askins says, "The manner of swinging is something everyone will have to decide for himself." It all goes back to how you perceive lead.

Footwork

Proper footwork is the first element of proper shooting technique. When your feet are properly placed, you will be able to pivot while keeping your shoulders square with the target and maintaining an even distribution of your weight between both feet. Keep your feet about the same width as your shoulders. A right-handed shooter puts her foot slightly forward of the right foot, pointing the toe away, in the anticipated direction of the target or bird. Of course, this is more difficult if you are hunting birds. You cannot always predict where the birds are coming from or when. Proper footwork, as much as possible, will allow you to follow the flight path of the bird.

From the moment you begin to swing your shotgun on the target, you gain muzzle speed. If your feet are not in or near the proper position, you will bind your movement, your shoulders will drop, and you will not be able to swing through the target. Keeping your shoulders square with the target is so important. If you have to take a step into the shot, the muzzle speed will slow, and you will shoot behind the target.

1. Start with your feet. The toe of your off foot (back) comes to the arch of your shooting foot (front) as the bird rises; pivot your body so your shoulders are square with the flight path of the target. The muzzle of the gun and your torso should be pointing in the same direction as your shooting foot. Keep your weight

slightly forward, your hands and eyes always fixed on the target. Hold the barrel muzzle just below your line of sight, at chin level. This allows you to track the bird the moment you pick your shot.

2. As the bird rises, pivot slightly on the shooting foot and anchor your off-foot for balance. This will allow you full control of your body. You can pivot 180 degrees in this position without having to reposition your feet. If you spread your feet wider apart, you will restrict your ability to pivot. As the bird rises, push your gun forward and point at the bird. Your weight should be equal between both feet. As the bird continues to rise, track the bird with your eyes. Never look at your gun, do not juggle the barrels, do not try to reposition your gun. Forget the gun. Just keep your eyes on the target. Period. Do not bend at the waist. Bring the gun up to your cheek. The forefinger of your forehand is naturally pointing the gun as you hold the fore-end in your non-shooting hand. Continue to pivot as you track the bird. Your shoulders and hips are square with the flight path of the bird. Your focus is entirely on the bird. Your subconscious is calculating your lead.

3. Continue to lean into the shot. Maintain your weight forward. Keep your head steady as you touch your cheek with the comb of the stock. Do not bring your head down to the stock. Remember, if your head is moving, your eyes are, too, and if you have lost focus on the target and hit it, then believe me, your shot was pure luck. There is little luck in the shooting sports. It is a very calculated sport and you can take nothing whatsoever for granted.

4. Moving and mounting the gun is one, smooth, almost ballet-like action. Some shooters mount the gun in anticipation of a bird, or as they catch their first glimpse of a single, pair, or a flock rising. If you do, you have to pick your shot with the barrels in the way and you must attempt to "catch up" to the bird by tracking it with the barrels. That's a violation

of everything gun fit and proper shooting technique dictates. If you mount the gun then look for the target, you have to find the bird a second time before you can track its flight path. That's two separate steps, and twice the chances you'll miss your shot.

The Ready, or Alert, Position

Each presentation begins with the ready, or "alert," position. You must come to the ready position before you mount the gun. This means your feet are in the proper position and your shoulders and hips squarely face the rising bird. The butt of the gun is tucked slightly under your arm. The muzzles are under the line of sight. Hunting over a good gun dog can buy you time to get into the ready position when you are in the field; of course, on the clays field, you're "alert" before you call "pull." A wingshooter has little control over the hunting environment but she should always have control over her shot.

1. The shooter prepares to take the ready, or "alert," position. She holds the stock firmly, but not in a stranglehold, with the shooting hand. Her trigger finger rests alongside the trigger guard, not on the trigger, and her thumb is behind the safety, ready to push it forward if it is a manual safety. If the gun has an automatic safety, the safety is off once the gun is loaded.

2. The fingers of the pointing hand are spread out and do not come over the top of the barrels, so you do not impede your sight line across the rib. Maintain a firm but relaxed hold on the gun.

3. The proper way to pull a trigger is to bend the fleshy tip of your index finger at the first joint. If you wrap your finger around the trigger, you will pull it with your knuckle, and this will jerk the trigger and throw off your shot.

Presentations

There are three presentations in shotgunning: The straight, going-away shot; the right-to-left crossing shot; and the left-to-right crossing shot. The technique you use to shoot the straight, going-away shot and the right-to-left crossing shot are similar. In all cases, these rules apply:

1. Pick your shot.
2. Raise the gun as you pick your shot. Your forehand is cradling the fore-end of the gun and you are tracking the bird with your eyes only.
3. Your weight is on your forward foot.
4. Your eyes remain on the target as you bring the gun up to touch your cheek.

The Straight, Going-Away Shot

The focus in this shot is on the center of the target. As you focus, bring the gun to the shoulder in a smooth movement, slightly below the target. The mind will tell you when the barrel is in alignment with the target and it is then that you pull the trigger. Neither bird nor clay can outrun the shot. As a rule, you do not have to hurry this shot. Being focused and smooth almost always results in a hit.

Right-to-Left Crossing Shot

Identify your target, track the bird with your pointing hand as you begin your mount. Legs are straight, slightly bent at the knee. Your weight is spread equally between both feet. You are holding the gun in the ready position, with the muzzle below your line of sight. You are not looking at the barrels. You are looking at the target. Push the safety off as you continue to bring the gun up. Raise the gun until the comb touches your cheek. Do not move your head. Keep your shoulders square with the rising bird. Do not take your eyes off the target. Lean into the shot; your weight moves forward as your back foot anchors you and keeps you steady. Your lead hand is pointing the bird. Push the gun forward. As you track the bird with your eyes, your subconscious mind will calculate lead and tell you when the target will intercept as the target flies into the trajectory of shot pellets once the gun is fired. Your weight is on the forward foot, you lift the heel slightly, your back foot is your fulcrum, so you are now in a position to pivot with your shoulders square to the target, and you pull the trigger.

Left-to-Right Crossing Shot

This is the most difficult shot for the right-handed shooter and an easier shot for the left-handed shooter. When a shotgun is mounted correctly, the appearance is one seemingly effortless motion—gun to cheek, shoulder to gun. The butt of the stock settles snugly into the soft part of the shoulder. The shooter's head remains high and steady as the stock comes up and touches the cheek. The trigger is pulled, and the cartridge is discharged. As you swing you pick up muzzle speed. Even after you fire, keep swinging. This is where and why footwork is so important. When your feet are in the proper position, you can pivot 180 degrees.

Principles of Wingshooting

If you do not concentrate on the target, you will miss, and if you don't concentrate on the target and connect, then chalk that up to luck. Concentration is the most powerful and important part of the mental game of shooting. You need to screen out everything around you except the target and maintain a clear picture of the target and its flight pattern. To improve concentration, try this exercise. Using your finger, not your unloaded gun, pull a clay and point to the leading edge of the target. When you track a bird with your eyes, you need to focus on the beak. Concentrate on where the bird is going, not where it has been, and, so important, always keep your head steady. If your head is moving, your eyes are, too.

Timing is dictated by the speed of the bird and your ability to pivot and move the gun into the line of flight. The target never stops, and neither should you.

Always assume a safe carry position when you are entering the field. Your gun must be fully unloaded. The safety must be on. Always be aware at all times of where others on the field are standing and where they are going.

When you are hunting or shooting with one or more people, it is critical to first establish a safe shooting zone. This should be established before you enter the field, guns unloaded. If a guide, outfitter, or gamekeeper is directing the drive, he or she will point out, or escort you to, your position, or "peg." In driven shooting, you remain at your peg until told otherwise or have moved on to another drive. Whether simulated pheasant or live birds, you will set a visual boundary with the shooter on either side of you. This will determine the targets that you take, and the ones that are hers. Sometimes a target will fly right down the middle between you. Whoever takes that shot must be certain it doesn't cross the other shooter's path. Sometimes the shooter alongside of you will be on higher or lower ground. Be certain you do not shoot over her head. If you can, even with the wave of a hand, communicate regularly with your neighbor. Be aware, too, at all times, where your loader, guides, gundogs, and dog handlers are.

Everyone in the shooting party or team should be clear about what's expected of them. Whether you are crossing a cornfield in a line, walking on either side of hedgerow, sitting in a duck blind or among a row of blinds, or in the woods, you always must know where everyone is. Even a few moments of uncertainty can trigger an unsafe shot. If there's any change in the designated drive, have a signal or call that everyone's familiar with so you can regroup and make a new strategy. The key is, always communicate, always stay within calling range.

In a shooting party, the hunter on the left should point her gun to the left or straight ahead, never to the right. The hunter on the right should point her gun to her right or ahead of her, never to the left, and only straight ahead and within, say, a 45-degree arc to the left and right of center point if she has someone on both sides. Be aware of your safe carry positions. Never carry a break-open gun closed over your shoulder with the muzzle pointing behind you. Never shoot across or behind your hunting partner.

Never run ahead of the line. If you do, you may fall in the line of fire, force your partner to sacrifice a shot, and put yourself and others in danger. Conversely, make certain you do not lag behind your shooting partner. You are not shooting within your safety zone if you do. If a crossover shot comes your way and you take it, you will be shooting behind your partner. I have heard one too many stories of situations just like this, with fatal results. Yes, in wingshooting, a gun is a tool to a means, that means being shooting a bird that you and others will feast upon for supper. That said, a cartridge knows no difference between a game bird and a human being. If you ever have any doubt whatsoever, no matter how slim, then surrender your shot completely—do not take it. It's simply not worth the possible consequences.

BASIC SURVIVAL KIT

▲ Illustration from a vintage Winchester Repeating Arms Company poster.

You want to be safe in the woods, on the water, and in the hunting field. Therefore, every outdoorswoman should always carry a basic survival kit. You may be far from help and need to be prepared for any emergency. Items can include:

- Pocketknife
- Compass
- Whistle, preferably sturdy plastic that can be heard at distances
- Matches in a waterproof container
- Backup fire-making device, such as a butane lighter
- Fire starter, such as fine steel wool, candles, paraffin-coated cord, fat wood
- Antibacterial soap
- Water purification tablets (available at any drugstore)
- Non-drowsy medication you may need, such as aspirin. Likewise, be sure you carry

your regular medication with you, on your person. If more than one medication, carry a small, pocketsize pillbox.

- First-aid kit with bandages (large and small), gauze and bandage tape, antibiotic ointment, iodine, tourniquet, scissors, tweezers, splint material
- A water bag or lightweight water vessel, as well as a collapsible cup or other drinking container. Keep a five-gallon water container in your car as a reserve freshwater source.
- Nylon cord or rope
- Topographical map of the area
- If you are waterfowl hunting, tide tables, times, forecasts, and charts
- If you wear corrective lenses, an extra pair of glasses
- Extra lenses in various colors for your shooting glasses so you can adjust them to the amount of light where you're shooting
- Hearing protection and an extra package of foam hearing plugs. Carry an extra set of batteries with you if your ear protectors are battery operated.

- Space blanket
- Hand towel
- An emergency rain poncho, or heavy grade lawn and leaf garbage bag you can cut a hole in for your head. This also serves as something to sit on if the ground is wet.
- Instant energy food like protein bars, chocolate bars, and jerky
- Cellphone fully charged (even though you may not have reception where you are going)
- Last but not least, sanitary napkins or tampons. You can use a sanitary napkin, by the way, as you would a gauze bandage and to stem a bleed.

Before you go hunting, be sure you know the location of the nearest ranger station, gas station, hospital—the closest place you can get help in an emergency. If you plan on hunting birds in the Back of Beyond, it would be wise to take a first-aid course before you set out.

7. Upland Birds

Depending upon the species, habitat for upland birds is woodlands, fields, prairies, mountains, valleys, or deserts.

Dove

▲ Mourning dove (and the similar Eurasian collared dove). Check state hunting laws. For example, hunting mourning doves in New York is illegal, while other states, such as Idaho, have a daily bag limit of fourteen, possession limit of forty-five, require a migratory bird (HIP) permit, and a shotgun capable of carrying no more than three shells and a shot size no larger than 0.2 inches (T).

- common ground dove
- Inca dove
- mourning dove
- white-tipped dove
- white-winged dove

Region: Predominantly in the American South. Not all states have a dove season.
Method: Pass-shooting as they fly to and from the roost or descend into agricultural fields
Gauge and Load: 12- or 20-gauge; No. 7½ shot
Dogs: Pointing or flushing
Two or more is a bevy, cote, dole, or dule of doves.

Grouse/Galliformes

▲ Ruffed grouse. Print by John James Audubon.

- blue grouse
- capercaillie (more than one bird is called a tok of capercaillie)
- hazel grouse
- prairie chicken (greater and lesser)
- rock grouse
- rock ptarmigan
- Ruffed grouse ("King of the Woods," "pa'tridge")
- sage grouse (also known as greater sage grouse or sagehen)
- sharp-tailed grouse
- sooty grouse
- spruce grouse
- tundra grouse
- white grouse
- willow ptarmigan (also known as red grouse)
- white-tailed ptarmigan

Region: Woodlands, grasslands, from the sub-arctic to high plains desert.
Gauge and Load: The "classic" New England grouse gun is a 16-gauge, side-by-side choked IC/M. Some grouse hunters prefer a 12-gauge, others a 20-gauge. A 28-gauge is enough gun in the hands of a hunter who knows how to use it. Common shot size is No. 6.
Dogs: Flushing or pointing
A pair is a brace of grouse. More than three are a covey, drumming, or pack.

The Ruffed Grouse, King of Upland Game Birds

"Pa'tridge," Yankees call these glorious, wily, wildest of wild game birds. But whenever I think of grouse, the first grouse that comes to mind is . . .

"The One That Got Away"

October first in New England is Opening Day, as hallowed to every devout grouse hunter as Christmas—apart from the veneration due that holiest day of the Christian calendar. The late, great writer Corey Ford wrote:

"October brings golden days and frosty nights. Now sumac and maple leaves turn red, the beechnut burrs split open, and gunners with pointers and setters and close-working spaniels search the oak ridges and abandoned apple-orchards for the explosive ruffed grouse, king of our upland game-birds. Deep in alder thickets and swamps the shy woodcock pauses overnight on its southward flight, and ducks and geese start their fall migration under the Hunter's Moon. Along stone-walls and hedgerows, the yellow husks of the bittersweet berries burst open, revealing their bright red hearts and offering a tempting food for pa'tridge and migrating birds."

In the thirty-five years he, and I, called northern rural New England home (although at separate times), Corey missed opening day twice, while serving in World War II, and I just once . . . *or did I . . . ?*

Morning dawned to sun-drenched skies and the telltale snap of chill in the air and leaves approaching the peak of color heralded opening day. My grouse gun, a 16-gauge Ithaca Flues side-by-side with 28-inch barrels, bored improved cylinder and modified, stood in the gun cabinet, along with a half-dozen unopened boxes of Remington 7½, one-ounce shells.

The old farm clock struck nine. "Sorry, Frosty," I apologized to the English setter slumbering at my feet. "Not this year." She looked up forlornly and thumped her tail. The stylish orange-flecked white belton I adopted was the granddaughter of Cider, who Ford immortalized in his writings.

We should be heading down to the Old Church Covert about now, then over to the Old Orchard Covert, and end up at the Sheep Pen Covert at the end of the road to Tinkhamtown, where we'd lunch on sandwiches by the bridge, like Corey always did. But not this opening day.

Deer hunting demands you rise before the sun, but grouse sleep in and rarely fly before the morning dew has evaporated. Opening day had fallen on a Wednesday and our regular hunting group—eight longtime friends, their wives, and children—would not arrive until the weekend. I was enormously pregnant and weary. My second child was due to be born in twelve days. Auntie Gin had taken Tommy, my three-year-old son, so I could rest and have a day to myself. I took my well-thumbed copy of Daphne Du Maurier's *Rebecca*, sprawled out on the living room sofa, and before I read a single page, I nodded off.

I was caught in that blissful place between awake and asleep when suddenly I was awoken by a terrible crash and the sound of shattering of glass. Frosty was at the end of the living room by the French door that led to the summer room—quivering on point. Cautiously I tiptoed over and looked through the glass.

I could not believe my eyes.

Sitting on my new chintz-covered sofa, wearing the abject expression of disdain of a wine expert offered a glass of red poured from a box, was the plumpest, grandest, most exquisite grouse I had ever seen. The bird was stunned but, amazingly, unscathed. Not a feather was out of place! I opened the door a crack. A mullioned windowpane was shattered. Blue sky reflected off the wall of windows and the disoriented grouse flew right through, landing on the sofa.

The arrogant bird cocked her head as if to say, "What are *you* doing here?" How terribly funny! Every opening day I go out to hunt grouse and usually return home with an empty game bag and here's the mother of all grouse sitting on my new sofa! I gently closed the door. There was only one thing to do. I must call Archie. If anyone had been more stupefied, misguided, or taken as a fool by a grouse, it was Archie. For years he had tried to outwit that wily bird. His escapades of "the one that got away" were hunting group legend. I couldn't wait to tell him a grouse was sitting on my sofa.

I rang his office in Boston. "Archie, you won't believe it!" I cried into the hall phone. "There's a grouse sitting on my sofa!"

"What?"

"A grouse! The biggest, fattest grouse you ever saw!"

"Where?"

"In the summer room. On the sofa . . ."

"All right," he said excitedly. Ann and I can't get up till tomorrow. So, here's what you've got to do. Stay calm."

"Then," he continued, "open the door slowly. You don't want to spook her. She may be pregnant. And if she *is* pregnant, she may attack you."

I thought Archie was kidding. He was not. After I hung up the phone, I laughed so hard I thought I would go into labor.

Tom, who had been out working on the other side of our farm, suddenly came running into the house carrying a long-handled fishing net.

"Archie just phoned!" he cried out. "At first I thought he meant you when he said 'pregnant.' Then I realized he was talking about a pregnant *grouse*."

Frosty had remained outside the summer room door, staunchly on point.

"Stand aside," Tom whispered. Guardedly, he went into the room, scooped up the bird, carried her outside, and off she flew. As she did, I caught a glint in her beady black eye, as if to say, "Yes! I am the one who got away!"

I hadn't missed opening day after all.

Partridge

▲ Grey partridge.

- Altai snowcock
- Caucasian snowcock
- chukar
- Daurian partridge
- francolin
- grey partridge
- Himalayan snowcock
- mountain (chukar) partridge

Region: The largest populations of partridges are in the cultivated fields of the midwestern grain belt and the cool, dry grasslands in the foothills and valleys of the western Mountains.

Gauge and Load: 12-gauge with No. 7½ shot

Dogs: Pointing breeds

More than one is a covey of partridges.

Pheasant

▲ The Japanese pheasant and ring-necked pheasant.

These large, lovely birds hail from China and only arrived on American shores (the Pacific Northwest, see page 98) in the late 1800s. Mature males are showy, colorful, and have long tail feathers while the considerably smaller female is plain and brown. They flourish in agricultural, grain-rich regions of the American West and Midwest and are common preserve birds.

Gauge and Load: 12-gauge with No. 6 shot.
Dogs: Flushing breeds for field shooting; flushing and pointing breeds for preserve shooting.
A brood, bouquet, covey, nest, nye, nide, or nest refer to more than one.

Pheasants, America's Naturalized Game Bird
How Pheasants Came to America

What you are about to read is true, though the conversation is constructed. Judge and Mrs. Owen Nickerson Denny brought the first pheasants to America from China, to their home state of Oregon. In 1861, they imported sixty pheasants and did the same again the following year. Judge Denny then was United States Consul General in Shanghai. He and Mrs. Denny were among the original pioneers to come by wagon train to settle in Oregon. In 1896, the Dennys traveled to Pinehurst, North Carolina, the first resort village in America, and as a gift to their host, Pinehurst's founder and owner, James Tufts, they brought pheasants. These were the first pheasants to cross the Mississippi River and be introduced to the East.

▲ Judge Owen Nickerson Denny.

"My wife and I returned home, to Oregon, on March 13, 1881 after five years acting as

United States Consul in Amoy, China," Judge Owen Nickerson Denny explained. "Among the Oriental treasures we brought back on the steamship *Otago* were five dozen Chinese ring-necked pheasants, a dozen or so Mongolian sand grouse, and several Chefoo partridges."

"Male pheasants have gold, emerald, and sapphire plumages that shimmer like jewels from Ali Baba's cave," Gertrude Jane Hall Denny, the judge's wife of thirty years, continued. "Iridescent, blue-green neck feathers surround a pearl-white collar. Their eye wattles are ruby red and their variegated tails are banded with black chevrons. The females are plain-featured, their feathers a mottled mix of earthy browns—alas, Mother Nature can be so cruel!"

"Pheasant are docile in China because they are not hunted, but I believed that once we released them in the great country of Oregon, if they freely propagated in time, they could furnish fine sport," the Judge allowed.

"And delicious eating!" his wife chimed in.

"Aboard the *Osago*, Captain Royal took pains to ensure the birds' survival," Judge Denny continued, "and they remained quiet and unfrightened in the ship's dark hold the whole of the voyage. But the rattling and noise of the train from Port Townsend scared them, and they beat and bruised themselves on the bars of their cages. Few of the pheasant and none of the grouse or partridge survived. We were deeply disappointed.

"We entrusted the survivors to our friend, Mr. A. H. Morgan, who released them on Sauvie Island, in the Columbia River. At first, we held out no hope for their survival, let alone their ability to adapt and establish a breeding population. Then, in 1882, we decided to make a second attempt. In 1888, the United States Agriculture Department issued a report confirming the pheasants that were released had 'wintered well and have been increasing ever since.'"

"Within a year, ring-necked pheasants populated every county and, knowing no boundaries, immigrated into neighboring states and out to the Dakotas. They even crossed the Strait of Juan de Fuca and colonized Vancouver Island!" the judge beamed proudly. "I knew a period of time was essential to successful propagation, so I solicited my political friends to pass state legislation banning hunting in Oregon until the population was sufficiently established. The first pheasant season was fall of 1892 and fifty thousand birds were reported taken by sportsmen opening day. Now they are estimated to be in the millions! More than nineteen states now boast sizeable pheasant populations."

"The pheasants' American cousins today outnumber their Chinese ancestors. Some call them 'Denny pheasants,'" Mrs. Denny smiled.

"Well, just days after arriving home from China, the judge received a message from the Emperor of Korea, inviting him to Seoul as his foreign advisor and director of foreign affairs. Of course, we accepted. My husband was so highly regarded that in 1885, he was proclaimed Foreign King of the royal court. Those were fairy tale years, full of beauty and magic. We would have stayed forever had it not been for the judge's health. We returned home in 1892, ten years to the day we had first left Oregon.

"Our dear mutual friend, the Reverend Dr. Edward Everett Hale, wrote about a charming new village in the healthful piney forests of North Carolina and encouraged us to come, certain the judge's health would be restored here."

"We had sent word ahead, of course, that we were bringing you a rather unusual gift!" Judge Denny added.

"Yes!" Mrs. Denny interjected with enthusiasm. "Six dozen Chinese ringed-neck pheasant, a pair of golden pheasants, and a gloriously colored Lady Amherst cock pheasant—the first pheasants in all the South!"

Pigeon

▲ Pigeon shooting by Currier & Ives.

- band-tailed pigeons
- red-billed pigeon
- rock pigeon (rock dove)
- white-crowned pigeon

More than one is referred to as a *dropping* or *flight* of pigeons.

Quail

▲ Bobwhite Quail by Lynn Bogue Hunt.

- black-throated bobwhite quail (Yucatan bobwhite)
- bobwhite quail (affectionately known as "Mister Bob")
- California quail

- Gambel's quail
- Japanese quail
- Montezuma quail (Mearns')
- mountain quail
- northern bobwhite quail
- scaled quail (blue)
- valley quail (California)

Gauge and Load: 16-, 20-, and 28-gauge; No.'s 9 and 7½ loads.
Dogs: Flushing and pointing breeds
A covey or bevy or quail is two or more birds.

Snipe and Woodcock

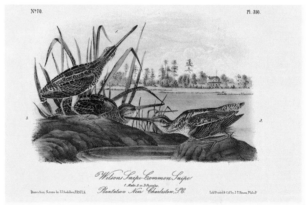

▲ Snipe, by John James Audubon.

▲ Woodcock, by Lynn Bogue Hunt.

The woodcock (affectionately called "timberdoodle" in the North) and snipe are migratory upland birds that are distinctive in that their bills are almost as long as their bodies. A forest mate to the grouse, this much-smaller bird can be hunted with a small gauge gun and No. 9 shot, but if you think (or pray that) your dog may flush a woodcock while you are hunting grouse, and you are shooting a 12- or even a 16-gauge gun, let the woodcock get out further or you may end up with a handful of feathers. More than one is called a walk or wisp of snipe. A fall of woodcock refers to more than one bird.

Hunting Bobwhite Quail
By John Wiles

▲ Hunting Bobwhite Quail, by A. B. Frost.

A boy growing up in the South was fortunate if he had a father who hunted. I was such a boy. My father loved dove shooting and quail hunting. The early, warm days of September were spent in cut cornfields trying to shoot a limit of doves. I served as Dad's retriever until I was old enough, at age twelve, to shoot at a few birds myself. We always had bird dogs, either pointers or setters. Dad preferred pointers because they didn't get burrs in their fur that he would have to comb or cut out. Pointers were all business, and setters were more loving. When it came to quail hunting, Dad was all business, but I liked the relationship of the English setter.

Quail hunting in the South fifty years ago was open to everyone. Quail were abundant. They were found in every hedgerow, swamp, farm-land, you name it. There were big bobwhite, too, not to be confused with smaller bobwhite introduced into the United States from Mexico. When Southerners talk about bird hunting, they mean quail hunting. When they talk about bird dogs, they are talking about dogs that point quail.

Quail are covey birds. You don't find one by himself usually. You find them in family groups—six, eight, ten, twenty, up to a hundred. They are "patternable," too. You usually find them at the edge of heavy cover in the mornings, feeding in the fields around lunch, going to water or wet areas later in the afternoon, and back along heavy cover just before dark. They like to roost at night in briars, thick tangled brush, where they can get next to one another, usually in some sort of circle, butt-to-butt, side-to-side, so that if a predator approaches, they can flush in all directions, confusing their would-be captor, and giving all a chance to get away.

A good bird dog gives the hunter a great and unfair advantage. Any hunter who steps into a covey of quail not knowing that he is about to do so is usually immobilized by the noise and fluttering to the point he doesn't even get a shot off. A good bird dog changes the game dramatically. He uses his nose to scent the birds and will point them, which means stop and stand still, oftentimes with one foreleg up and tail straight up in the air at a distance of fifteen to fifty feet from the birds, depending upon the quality of his nose. The hunter now knows the birds are somewhere close to the front of the dog and has time to prepare for the sudden explosion of birds and get off a well-placed shot or two. Advantage: man and dog.

Quail are tasty little creatures. Because they spend most of their lives walking, they are mostly white meat, and some of the tastiest game birds that anyone can eat. Fried quail, like fried chicken in the South, was a delicacy growing up. If you shot a limit, usually eight quail, they would be prepared together and referred to as having a "mess" of quail, meaning a lot. Fried quail with gravy and biscuits remains a Southern treat.

Quail season usually began around Thanksgiving and ran until the end of January. Those were the days of wild quail. Sadly, there are few places in the United States anymore where you can find wild bobwhites. Most quail hunting these days is done on shooting preserves where the quail are either raised on the preserve and released at an early age to become as wild as possible, or brought in from a game farm, where they are housed and then released the day of the hunt. Pen-raised or preserve quail do not have the fire in their bellies like the wild ones, which, when flushed, can disappear in a second and fly behind a sapling. Preserve birds tend to be bigger, slower, and fly in a straighter line. However, the work of the bird dogs is still the same and still beautiful.

"Gentleman Bob" is a small-gauge quarry. Twenty-gauges are the order of the day, but the 28-gauge and even the .410-caliber are used to shoot quail over pointing dogs on most preserves. It doesn't take many shots to get a quail down, and a good bird dog will do four things: point, back, retrieve, and load. To back means the dog will point when it sees another dog pointing ahead of it. To load means he will jump in the truck and go to the kennel. Retrieving is self-explanatory.

The small-gauge gun is usually choked cylinder and/or improved cylinder. Single-barreled guns, like pumps and semiautomatics, are usually choked improved cylinder. This is a great choke for a bird twenty to twenty-five yards from you. A more open choke, such as cylinder, is often the choice for the first shot of an over/under or side-by-side since the birds may be close, ten to twenty yards, when they get up in front of the dogs.

Light loads are the order of the day. Seven-eighths-ounce loads for 20-gauge, three-quarter-ounce loads for 28-gauge, and even half-ounce

loads in the .410-caliber, in either 6s or 7½s, are enough for a true shot.

One of the requirements for upland game hunting, which includes quail, pheasants, and grouse, is that the hunter wears some measure of blaze orange. This is the law. The amount of blaze required differs from state-to-state, and if the reader is going to hunt birds, check the legal requirements. Usually an orange vest or even an orange ballcap may suffice. You do not wear camouflage. The blaze orange is so that other hunters can see you, and you can see them. The old tradition of men wearing coats and ties, and women wearing long skirts, has waned into the past, but there are some who continue to carry on the tradition, a graceful tradition redolent of graceful times. These few people understand the joy of hunting is a privilege, not necessarily a right.

Quail hunting, in the South especially, has long been considered a gentleman's sport. Some hunters ride horses or ride in mule-drawn wagons; some ride in ATVs equipped with dog boxes and gun scabbards. Many people still just follow the bird dog on foot. Even today, all you really need to go quail hunting is a good dog, a fine gun, and a place to hunt. Regardless of where you hunt quail, they're always testy targets and tasty eating.

▲ The genteel sport of shooting bobwhite quail is a time-honored tradition of the American South that was—and in some places, still is—hunted on horseback or by hunters carried to the field in mule-drawn carriages. The English pointer is the classic field dog to seek out "Gentleman Bob."

8. Lowland Birds

Lowland birds, or waterfowl, are ducks, geese, and swans. Waterfowl habitat is wetlands, potholes, lakes, rivers, and oceans.

▲ Duck shooting from a blind, by A. B. Frost.

One or more is called a flock, flush, paddling, raft, or team of ducks.

Types of Lowland Birds

Diving Ducks ("Divers") and Mergansers
- Barrow's goldeneye
- black scoter
- bufflehead
- canvas back
- common eider
- common goldeneye
- common merganser
- greater scaup
- harlequin duck
- hooded merganser
- king eider
- lesser scaup
- masked duck
- redhead
- red-breasted merganser
- ring-necked duck
- ruddy duck
- spectacled eider
- Steller's eider
- surf scoter
- tufted duck
- white-winged scoter

Puddle Ducks (Dabbling Ducks)

▲ Gadwall Duck, by Robert Havell after John James Audubon.

- American black duck
- American wigeon
- black-bellied whistling-duck
- blue-winged teal (teal in numbers are a spring of teals)
- cinnamon teal
- Eurasian wigeon
- gadwall
- green-winged teal
- fulvous whistling-duck
- mallard (a sord of mallards is two or more)
- Mexican duck
- mottled duck
- northern pintail
- northern shoveler
- white-cheeked pintail
- wigeon (a raft of wigeons refers to more than one)
- wood duck

Sea Ducks

▲ Long-tailed duck, courtesy of Biodiversity Heritage Library.

- common eider
- common (black) scoter
- harlequin duck
- king eider
- oldsquaw (now called the long-tailed duck)
- surf scoter
- white-winged scoter

Whistling-Ducks

▲ Yellow-Breasted Rail, by John James Audubon.

- black-bellied whistling-duck
- fulvous whistling-duck
- West Indian whistling-duck
- yellow rail

Geese and Cranes

▲ Canada Goose, by John James Audubon.

- barnacle goose
- blue goose
- brant
- cackling goose
- Canada goose
- emperor goose
- greater snow goose
- greater white-fronted goose (also known as the specklebelly)
- lesser snow goose
- pink-footed goose
- Ross's goose
- sandhill crane
- snow goose
- white-fronted goose

More than one is a flight, gaggle, skein (in flight), or wedge of geese.

Rails, Gallinules, and Coots

▲ American Coot, by John James Audubon.

- American coot
- black rail
- clapper rail
- common gallinule
- king rail
- lapwing (more than one is a deceit of lapwings)
- moorhen
- purple gallinule
- sora
- Virginia rail
- water rail
- yellow rail

Swans

▲ Trumpeter Swan, by John James Audubon.

- mute swan
- trumpeter swan
- tundra swan (whistling swan)

Waterfowl Terms
A group of birds that has gathered together
congregation of birds
dissimulation of birds
flight of birds
flock of birds
volery of birds

Waterfowl / Wildfowl
plump of waterfowl

Ducks
brace of ducks
flock of ducks
flush of ducks
paddling of ducks
raft of ducks
team of ducks
deceit of lapwings
raft of wigeons
sord of mallards
spring of teal
wing of plovers

Geese
gaggle of geese
skein of geese
wedge of geese

Introduction to Waterfowl Hunting

▲ Duck hunter in the blind.

Of the types of hunting in the United States that are most favored, two stand out. One is deer hunting; the other is duck hunting. These two represent classic American hunting. Hunting ducks and geese fall under the category of wingshooting.

Duck hunting is a beautiful sport. You get to see the sun rise, participate in the hunt by calling the birds, and watch the whole panorama unfold in front of you. Of course, you get to shoot, and many times you get to watch a good water dog work. There are many enjoyable aspects to waterfowl hunting and probably this is why it is so popular.

Waterfowl Migration Flyways

Pacific
Central
Mississippi
Atlantic

▲ Waterfowl migration flyways.

There are four major flyways in the United States: the Atlantic, Mississippi, Central, and the Pacific. All four offer their own varieties of ducks; there are some that overlap, of course; for example, mallards are the predominant species in almost all the flyways. However, you will find a lot of pintails in the Pacific flyway, more teal varieties in the central flyway, a predominance of mallards in the Mississippi flyway, and more diving ducks, like canvasbacks and American black ducks, which often flock with mallards, in the Atlantic flyway.

▲ Labrador retriever, by Maud Earl (1864–1943).

▲ Flat-coated retriever, by Maud Earl (1864–1943)

How to Hunt Ducks

The best way to hunt ducks is to find a place where the ducks want to be and set up decoys there. It is much easier to get ducks to come to a place they are used to visiting than to try to get them to come to a place

they have never been before. Once you have your rig, which is how many decoys you are going to put out, in whatever pattern you're going to put them, you can also call the ducks. In fact, the duck call has become a fine art form around the country. Duck calls are meant to imitate either the female or male (mallard, primarily), and the duck caller learns to "speak duck." The better the caller is at imitating the sounds a duck makes and using those calls at the correct time, the better the chances of having a successful day.

Calling ducks, and geese for that matter, has become such an art form that there are competitions around the country, regionally and nationally. To be recognized as a world champion caller can mark the long-term success of an individual in the call-making business.

An even greater art form that has evolved over the past hundred years or so is the art of making decoys. Decoys have been made from different materials over the years, but the epitome of decoy making is the wooden decoy. Not many people hunt over wooden decoys anymore, but the wooden ones were hand-shaped, hand-carved, and hand-painted; different types of weights were used to make the decoy stable and float correctly in the water like a real duck. Some decoys made at the turn of the twentieth century are worth thousands of dollars, depending upon their condition and who made them.

▲ A few of the many decoys from John Wiles's private collection. Attractive and functional, the value of the most collectible can easily reach five figures.

Wooden decoys gave way to plastic decoys, probably in the sixties. Plastic decoys are easy to manufacture and sufficed for the time being to look like ducks. As more people used plastic decoys, the ducks became more aware of what these looked like and there was the continuum of change to improve the decoys to continue to fool the ducks. This has led to mechanical decoys with wings that flap or spin to look like a duck flying. What the hunter is trying to do is to fool the ducks with some new and innovative method. Today, decoys can be made with the same coloration, the same reflection, and many positions that you would find on real ducks.

Oftentimes multiple species of ducks or geese will be in the same area, so a decoy spread—the rig—will contain goose decoys and different varieties of duck decoys. This actually serves two purposes: goose decoys are larger and therefore easier for the ducks to see at a distance. Geese tend to be wary birds, so if the ducks see geese resting on the water, it acts as a confidence decoy for the ducks.

▲ Photo courtesy of USFWS Midwest Region.

▲ The workshop of the Ward brothers, Lemuel (1897–1984) and Steven (1895–1976), the most famous decoy carvers of all, who lived and worked on Maryland's legendary Eastern Shore. Photo courtesy Preservation Maryland.

You get up early because ducks, especially wood ducks, are early risers and on the wing at first light. Another reason is because ducks tend to feed on the full moon, so you either plan your duck hunts around the dark moon phase or you're there early to catch the ducks coming back to their resting areas in the early morning.

Geese tend to fly in small family groups or very large colonies ("a gaggle of geese"). Both ducks and geese are social species and prefer to rest together and eat together. That's why decoys work: because the small group wants to be with the large group.

Most waterfowl tend to fly in the morning to a feeding area, having spent the night on the water, whether it's a pond, lake, or the bay. In the morning at some point—and a lot of this depends upon the weather—once they go to where they feed and have fed, they probably will go back to their resting area, rest awhile, and then in the afternoon they will feed again and go to the rest area for the night. When the weather's warm and there's no storm and it's pleasant, they may feed only once a day. If the weather is warm, and it's pleasant and it's a full moon, they're only going to feed at night. If the weather's cold and it's windy and icy, they may feed more than twice a day. They will feed and then will look for other groups that are feeding and travel from group to group, looking for an easy meal, returning to the rest areas once again at night.

Waterfowl hunters generally shoot a 12-gauge at ducks, and most people shoot semiautomatics. Semiautomatics are plugged to only allow three shells, which is the law, and the thought process is that you can either get off three shots at a group of ducks or you can get off two good shots and use the third shot to cleanly kill a cripple. The difference between wood stocks and synthetic stocks is that synthetic stocks are impervious to saltwater and the elements, whereas wood stocks will swell and get banged around in a boat or in the blind. However, it is not true that wood stocks absorb water and get heavier.

Synthetic stocks are usually black or camouflage, which is desirable in waterfowl hunting. Also, lead shot is banned for waterfowl hunting. You must use steel or non-toxic shot, such as Bismuth or Tungsten Matrix. Duck hunting is always in the fall and winter months, and the migratory seasons are federally posted, whereas the upland birds, with exception of doves and woodcock, are posted by state.

Ducks are generally hunted before the sun rises, in cold climes, and where the winds let loose and howl over the remote places. When they fly depends upon the species of duck. They are either returning from or going to the feeding area. Wood ducks fly early. Mallards and most puddle ducks fly a little after dawn. In the United Kingdom, you hunt ducks at night—which is against the law in the United States. No matter what, you want to be sure you're dressed for the weather and the prospect of what the day may bring.

▲ Most duck hunters shoot 12-gauge semiautomatic shotguns.

Dress in layers that are designed for heat retention and repelling water. The clothing you wear needs be camouflaged so you are "at one" with the marsh. Because of the placement of their eyes, even from high above a duck can see white, bright, and surprisingly vivid color. For that reason, duck hunters will often wear a balaclava hat to mask their head and the lower half of their face, which also serves to keep your head warm; a face mask; or black or camouflage face paint. My husband, Johnny, a consummate waterfowl hunter, grew a beard for that reason. A brimmed hat or cap keeps your face covered, but I prefer one with a short brim that doesn't get in the way when I'm looking skyward. A knitted hat with a short visor is a good choice for cold weather. Remember, you will be wearing eye protection and dark lenses will help mask your upturned face from those cunning ducks and geese. Best not to wear bright yellow, orange,

or light blue lenses in your shooting glasses, even if the light warrants it, since waterfowl will spot those vivid colors.

▲ Dress in layers when you go duck hunting. This woman will be warm—but the ducks might veer away from her. Why? Ducks will see the white trim around her hood. And while red lipstick may attract men, it won't attract ducks.

You wear hip boots in shallow water and waders where the water is deep. Waders, especially polyurethane waders, which are padded and warm, are good when you are sitting in a duck blind because they keep your derrière dry, too. If you wear waders, you must be sure to wear a wader belt. Some years back, I was hunting ducks in Mexico on a huge, remote lake in the back of beyond when one of my hunting partners hit a duck far out, maybe fifty yards from the blind. The bird boys and a retriever had parked the truck a half-mile away from the blind. Despite our entreaties, he decided to wade out after the fallen duck before it drifted out to the middle of this big lake. For as much as there is terrain above water there surely is under water. He went out quite far and encountered a deep crevice through which a very fast current was flowing. Because he was not wearing a wader belt with his chest waders, when he lost his footing, and went under, the water filled his waders and next thing we knew, he had flipped over, with his head under water and his feet above. By the grace of God, we were able to pull him in, using a shotgun to extend our reach. One minute later and he would have been a dead man.

Many waders have the boot built into the wader and others do not. There are two types of boots, felt bottom and ridged bottom rubber. Felt-bottom boots are for fly fishermen. The felt helps prevent you from slipping.

You need wool, neoprene, or moisture-wicking socks that are warm and fit easily in the foot of your waders without cramping your feet. Always keep an extra pair with you, just in case. If you are wearing polyurethane chest waders, a good set of moisture-wicking thermal long johns (a long-sleeve turtleneck top and bottoms, in black, dark green, or camouflage) works well and is non-binding. If it is cold, add a layer with a pair of fleece-lined stretch pants or leggings over. Many hunters wear blue jeans under their waders, which is fine if you're wearing lightweight waders but can be restrictive under the heavier-weight polyurethane waders.

▲ Waders and boots for a duck blind out in the water, or hip boots for shallow water, are mandatory gear for the duck hunter—as consummate, all-'round sportswoman Carole Lombard knew.

Hip boots have a strap that runs from the top of the boot along your outer thigh and hooks over your belt to stay up. If it's early in the season and warm, and you're in shallow water, this, or lightweight waders, is a good choice. You always want to dress for the weather but on the other hand, you always want to be prepared. If you're wearing a lightweight shirt, have a turtleneck and a wool shirt handy should the wind come up and the sun disappear behind the clouds.

Never wear bulky gloves. You need to curl your trigger finger around the trigger without forcing bulky fingers through the trigger guard and running the risk of setting off the gun. Wear gloves or mittens that you can peel back to expose your fingers or a pair of fingerless gloves. You can wear a pair of thin, stretchy, fingerless gloves that you can slip into a pair of waterproof mittens for warmth as you wait.

Hearing Protection When in the Duck Blind or Field

▲ Even if you aren't shooting, you need hearing protection.

Finally, electronic hearing protection, whether earplugs or muffs, enhance the heart-stopping sound of whistling wings as ducks are decoying and cancel loud noises over eighty decibels, such as a shotgun report. When the shotgun of your hunting buddy sitting next to you "speaks," it's deafening. No roast duck dinner is worth damage to an unprotected eardrum. An old-timer may tell you he never used hearing protection—after you ask him the question two or three times at increasing volumes.

Ear plugs are commonly dismissed by hunters, believing they get in the way of their hearing and it's true—those little yellow or orange silicone foam plugs you stuff in your ears, which are meant to dull the shock of a gun report, mute everything else, as well. However, the greater truth is, you need to protect your hearing. No gun is safe to shoot without hearing protection. If someone tells you they're used to hunting without some sort of ear protection, chances are they have "hunters ear" and already have lost some hearing—and once it's lost, you can never get it back, or fully delight in the rustling of autumn leaves, the whispering of wings, or the jolly cackle of pheasant when you miss a shot.

Hearing can be damaged with the blast of a single shot. Noise-induced hearing loss can occur at eighty-five decibels (dB) of sound. At this level of sound, the fine hairs in your ears that stimulate auditory nerve fibers are permanently destroyed.

Decibel (dB) Comparisons	
Sound Source	**Noise Level**
power lawnmower	96 dB
farm tractor, garbage truck, or outboard motor	100 dB
thunderclap or chainsaw	120 dB
a standard velocity bullet from a .22-caliber rifle	140 dB
report from a 26-inch or 28-inch barrel, .410-caliber shotgun	150 dB
report from a 28-inch barrel, 20-gauge shotgun	152.50 dB
report from a 26-inch barrel, 12-gauge shotgun	156 dB
big-bore rifles and pistols	175 dB

(Gun data collected by Dr. Krammer, Ph.D., of Ball State University, Indiana)

HEARING PROTECTION

It is extremely important to wear hearing protection when shooting and most especially in the duck blind where shoots are in close proximity to one another. A study of 3,753 hunters and shooters conducted by the University of Wisconsin in 2000 revealed that 38 percent of the target shooters and 95 percent of the hunters reported never wearing hearing protection while shooting, thereby increasing their risk of hearing loss 7 percent every five years.

EXPENSIVE

◄ ESP Digital Model.

Hi-tech developments cancel out loud, harmful noises without dulling normal hearing. Custom-fit digital hearing protection is expensive—but what price can you put on your hearing? E.S.P. Custom-fit, waterproof Dynamic Premium Digital Model has six auto environmental controls, custom tuning, and is available in an assortment of colors. $2,500. www.espamerica.com

MODERATELY EXPENSIVE

◄ Walker's Razor XV 3.0 Headset.

Walker's Razor XV 3.0 Headset is a non-intrusive, neck-worn design with flat, no-tangle cables. The Bluetooth version (BWP-BTN-BT) controls the headset with a control app downloaded from Google Play to your smartphone. Standard digital, $139.99. Bluetooth, $179.99. www.walkersgameear.com

LEAST EXPENSIVE

◄ Caldwell Range Muff.

Ear muffs are popular on the clays course and in the field. There's a wide range of manufacturers and prices run the gamut. Caldwell, a leader in shooting equipment of all kinds, makes ear muffs for adults and children. www.caldwellshooting.com

Waterfowl Hunting by John Wiles

1. John has identified where his dog handler and her dog are standing before he loads his gun.

2. He points to an incoming flock of ducks.

3. The flock has separated. He focuses on one bird from the flock that is approaching.

4. He maintains his focus entirely on the bird he has picked, ignoring a second, even larger flock that is following close on the heels of the first. He is not looking at the gun. He is focused only on the duck he picked that is approaching.

5. This is how John views the bird. Notice he is looking over the barrel and preparing to lead the duck as it flies within range. He sees the bird in his peripheral vision, and he prepares for an oncoming left-to-right crossing shot.

6. This is an incredible photograph. John has pulled the trigger. You can see the elliptical pattern of the shot pellets as it travels ahead of the duck John has picked out. You can see the two ducks flying into the tightest pattern of pellets. It only takes a few pellets to fell a bird with the correct shot charge. John takes a double—two ducks—effectively hitting the duck that slightly leads the pair with his first barrel and the higher single duck with his second.

7. He does not stop the gun. He continues to swing through the target. This is important. If you stop the gun, it is likely you will

shoot behind the target. The second flock, hearing the shot, flies higher . . . but no worries. John has fired both barrels.

8. The dog retrieves the first of the two ducks, then goes back for the second.

Waterfowl hunters are as passionate about their sport as any quail hunter, or pheasant hunter, or any other hunter, for that matter, is about his game of choice. Waterfowl hunting falls into two categories: goose hunters and duck hunters. My great love of waterfowl hunting began when I moved from Tennessee to Maryland. The famed Maryland Eastern Shore was exactly an hour and fifteen minutes from my house across the Bay Bridge to Kent Island. Kent Island marked the entrance into the Eastern Shore from Baltimore, Maryland. I scheduled a few hunts with reputable outfitters, mostly who were goose guides using "pit blinds." Pit blinds are large, symmetrical, rectangular holes dug in a field, large enough for four to six people to sit in, and then stand up to shoot with their head, shoulders, and half of their waist above ground. Some people love it. I wasn't one of them. You couldn't see anything because the blinds were all covered so the geese couldn't see you. Only the guide was able to watch the spectacle that truly is "decoying geese."

After a couple of miserable hunts that did produce bag limits, but no joy in hunting, I found through a friend a large farm located on the banks of the Chester River. For the next fifteen years, I was privileged to participate in some of the finest goose hunting that has ever been on the Eastern Shore.

Goose hunting really is a sport of kings. The gentleman who taught me about goose hunting was named Calvin "Pop Pop" Richardson. He had lived on his farm all his adult life and he knew every inch of it, especially the mile and a quarter of waterfront on the river. Pop Pop taught me how to call geese by mouth. "Mouth-callers" are an unusual lot, as most guides use mechanical calls. Mouth-callers use their voice, and if one were to do some calling like this in the mall, they would no doubt be arrested. Mimicking a goose is not easy, but Pop Pop gave me the secret to becoming a very proficient caller. He told me, "Johnny, go down and get in the blind along the shore at night. Sit there and listen to the geese. They will trade up and down the shoreline all night and also probably rest somewhere close by. You will hear them talking to one another. Learn to say what they say, and you will be able to call geese." He was right.

Not only did he teach me how to call geese, he taught me about the tides, and how to sit the decoys on high tides and low tides. He taught me about decoy arrangements, the "J" hook, the pipe stem—all very famous patterns used both for geese and also for ducks. He taught me about winds, the best winds to hunt particular blinds, since you always wanted the wind at your back so that the geese are decoying into you, the front of the blind. Choosing the right blind and the right set of decoys on the right wind makes the opportunity for success much, much greater.

When Pop Pop hunted, long before I got there, baiting was an illegal but common practice. Many of the farms along the river put out corn to attract ducks. Geese tended to rest in the river and fly inland to feed on the harvested corn fields prevalent in that area. Pop Pop also hunted over wooden decoys, most of which are now considered expensive collectibles and antiques, but in his day, in the 1930s and 1940s, putting out twelve decoys and a five-gallon bucket of corn was a good combination for success. By the time I got around to goose hunting, we literally used hundreds of decoys, both full-bodied and silhouette decoys. Full-bodied goose decoys look like a goose. You can use them in the field or in the water. When used in the water, they are referred to as "floaters." Floaters have a string attached to their keel at the front of the decoy, and a lead weight attached to the other end of the string, thus anchoring them in a particular spot. The silhouettes were first used in the field and primarily because you could make several out of one sheet of thin plywood and paint it like a goose. We would attach a metal stake to the bottom of the goose so you could easily push it into the ground.

When you have quite a few of these—say twenty to one hundred—you can carry them to the field an armload at a time, and you simply arrange them in a variety of directions a foot or two apart. As the geese approached, it appeared that the flock was moving because the silhouettes gave the impression of one goose disappearing and another appearing, having changed position.

These were also effective sets on the water. What we did was to create what became known as "V boards." The truth is, they were actually "Y boards" with one silhouette goose decoy on a two-by-two in the middle of three. It looks like a three-pronged wooden fork with the silhouettes slipped on the end of the prongs.

Each prong bends back to an angle that sets the silhouettes up like a threesome feeding together.

▲ Mojo Outdoors Spinning Wing Motion Duck Decoy.

▲ "V" board decoys.

Again, you can carry quite a few V-boards out into the water each time you go and set up several hundred decoys in this manner.

As the geese became more knowledgeable to blinds and decoys, the decoy manufacturers were constantly improving the shape, the colors, and the materials used to attract both ducks and geese. Later in my hunting experience on the Eastern Shore, we often hunted large cornfields from hedgerow blinds with "stuffer decoys." Stuffers are real geese that have been mounted, usually on fairly small wooden boards about the color of dirt, that can be set about as a family flock of decoys would be when feeding.

There are very few sights in nature that are more beautiful than geese decoying. Often coming from considerable heights, these large birds cup their winds and drag their feet to lower their altitude and cut their air speed. If necessary, they will turn ninety degrees in the air or more and simply drop like a stone. Then they open those big wings and continue their flight down toward the water. They appear slow when they're flying, but they're actually going quite fast. The sight of a half-dozen or a hundred geese coming to your decoys is quite breathtaking. I don't think I ever got tired of seeing that spectacle, and if I had, it would have told me it was time to find a new sport.

Early in our goose hunting, lead shot was the order of the day. We shot heavy loads because geese are big birds. Mostly we shot 12-gauge, copper-plated, No. 2 shot. This shot penetrates better than plain lead, and two or three of these large pellets will put a big bird on the water. Later in my history on the Eastern Shore, if you shot a 12-gauge you were required to shoot steel shot; however, if you shot a smaller gauge—say, 20-gauge—you could still shoot lead. We all bought 20-gauge Remington 1100, three-inch magnum shotguns, three-inch 20-gauge copper-plated No. 2 shells, and continued to shoot geese with the same devastating results as before. Those who shot steel, especially in the early days, did not have the success that we did.

While most of us like the beauty of a fine-grained walnut stock, the practicality of being around saltwater, water in general, sand, dirt and other natural elements that can affect the finish of a shotgun has moved most goose hunters toward synthetic stocks, either in black or camo patterns, since they are impervious to the elements. There aren't a great many quality over/unders that come in camo patterns, and a hunter is much more likely to find pump shotguns and semiautomatic shotguns with synthetic and camo stocks available. One of the things that people like about pump shotguns is their reliability, especially in cold, wet conditions that can affect the cycling of a semiautomatic shotgun. Pump shotguns are very, very reliable. Modern-day semiautomatic shotguns are pretty close to being infallible as well. The problem with pump guns is the felt recoil, since basically you are shooting a fixed-breech firearm. Semiautomatics tend to bleed some of the gases from the discharge to make the action work, thus reducing felt recoil. Other automatics use a spring-operated system to achieve the same thing. Modern-day shotguns now also have elaborate recoil systems and recoil pads to further reduce felt recoil.

The gentleman sportsman or sportswoman can still shoot with an over/under or wonderful side-by-side. You must use non-toxic (lead-free) shot, such as bismuth, tungsten matrix, or steel. Most people are reticent to shoot steel through their double gun. I don't blame them. Also, as stated earlier, since you are often goose hunting in damp, dirty, sandy conditions, you probably don't want to take your expensive heirloom on a waterfowl hunt.

Another factor is the number of shells. With double guns, you are limited to two shots. Pumps and semiautomatics can hold four and sometimes five shells, but by federal law, you are limited to three and have to plug the gun so that only three shells—two in the magazine and one in the chamber—are in the gun.

What's the advantage, you might ask? Geese or ducks come in. You get off two shots; maybe you kill one cleanly and you wound another. As an ethical hunter, your job is to dispatch the wounded bird as quickly and efficiently as possible. That third shot makes that happen.

Goose hunting is available in many states, usually along the prevalent flyways. There's the Atlantic, the Mississippi, the Central, and the Pacific, but it is also available in countries around the world.

Everyone knows Canada has great duck and goose hunting, but Mexico also has great duck and goose hunting. Some areas of Europe have marvelous goose hunting for species we don't find here in the United States. South America, for a long period, has had excellent goose hunting for geese found only in that part of the world. New Zealand has great goose hunting. Africa has some wonderful duck and goose hunting—again, offering species not found in North or South America or Europe, for that matter. Duck and goose hunting can quite literally take you all over the world.

Hunting Ducks

While for me Canada goose hunting is the most beautiful waterfowl sport I have ever experienced, I can also say duck hunting ranks right up there with great waterfowl enjoyment. While I learned about geese on Maryland's Eastern Shore, I learned a lot about duck hunting when I moved to Arkansas. It is amazing to me how few people—and I was actually one of them —even know where Arkansas is among the states.

Arkansas is just north and east of Texas, east of Oklahoma, south of Missouri, west of Tennessee and Mississippi, and north of Louisiana, with the eastern border being the Mississippi River. Add to that the fact that Arkansas is one of the great rice-producing areas of this country, and you have a perfect storm for duck hunting in the center of the United States.

Arkansas is known for flooded timber hunting. Ducks often feed at night or even during the day and return to flooded, shady areas where they can loaf, sometimes find white oak acorns, and rest, but they enjoy the woods—the woods that are called the flooded timbers. When the Mississippi River rises it can flood thousands of acres that adjoin it. Those flooded areas can be hard on farming but create a smorgasbord of food sources for the ducks. In dry years, outfitters often divert water from the river, or farm ponds, or deep-dug wells to rice and corn fields specifically designed to hold water during the winter months to attract the mighty mallard. Mallard is the duck of choice

and referred to as the "king of ducks" in the old duck clubs of the American South. Most other ducks, no matter what the species, are referred to as "trash ducks," meaning they are not mallards. A whole industry has been spawned over the years around duck hunting, with Stuttgart, Arkansas, really the center of that industry. There even are famous places in Arkansas that almost any diehard waterfowler knows. Places like Stuttgart, Bayou Meto, and Red River are noted for the duck hunting and there are some famous lodges and "honey holes" (places you almost always find ducks) like Peckerwood Lake, where Nash Buckingham, the famous outdoor writer, hunted in the early 1900s. Many places were developed just for duck hunters.

In the world of duck hunting, there are two types of ducks: puddle ducks, also called dabbling ducks, and divers. Puddle ducks or dabblers, of which mallards are the number one species, tend to tip up, which means they simply put their heads in the water, tilt forward and, using their feet to paddle and keep them inverted, feed in very shallow water, usually on grain. Flooded rice fields and flooded cornfields are the perfect dining room table for all puddle ducks. Other puddle duck varieties are pintails, all the teal species, wood ducks, black ducks, gadwalls, and the American wigeon, also called a baldpate.

▲ "Wild Duck Shooting" by Currier & Ives, 1852.

Sometimes, even in areas noted for puddle duck hunting, you will find diving ducks. Diving ducks actually dive below the surface of the water to feed on submersed aquatic vegetation or sedentary invertebrates. The ducks that feed on the former are still quite good to eat. Ducks that feed on the latter have a very strong fishy taste. One of the most famous of all the diving ducks is the canvasback. Again, it was known primarily as the duck of choice on the East Coast. It's a big duck and was considered a choice duck back during the market hunting days. Besides canvasbacks, there are varieties of scaup, referred to as blackheads or bluebills, redheads, and mergansers.

Duck hunting, like goose hunting, requires the use of decoys—oftentimes, the more decoys, the better. Ducks are looking primarily for places to rest. Seeing a large number of their brethren in a protected cove, in a large area in a flooded timber makes them confident and more easily decoyed. For duck hunting, calling is also an art form. There are many duck-call makers, and some have become famous for winning duck calling championships. Every year, the town of Stuttgart is closed off for Wings Over the Prairies, a long weekend celebration of ducks, duck hunting, and all things related—art, calls, clothing, outfitters, dogs, guns, and the like.

Duck hunting in Arkansas is primarily done either in the flooded timber or over flooded rice- and corn-fields. Again, large number of decoys attract passing ducks and the long-range calling gets the ducks' attention. By changing the calling from a "hail call," which means, "hey, look over here," to greeting calls, soft hen calls, feeding calls, and confidence calls, ducks are lured into shooting range with a language all their own. Duck hunting is one of the most popular hunting sports in the United States, probably, only behind deer hunting as the hunters' choice.

Duck hunting and goose hunting are also popular outside the United States. Canada, of course, is probably number one since all the ducks and geese pass through Canada on their way to the states. Additionally, many of the ducks and geese in the central, mountain, and Pacific flyways funnel into Mexico and, until recent years, Mexico was a real haven for duck hunters, especially in January and February. One of the big differences between hunting in North America and Mexico is that the laws of Canada and the United States prevent baiting. Baiting is the illegal use of grain to attract ducks or geese to a place to be hunted. An example would be that you have a nice farm pond near a river but there are no grain crops growing on your farm. You go down to your pond and spread corn or wheat or rice along the edge of the pond. A few wood ducks find the grain; they tell other wood ducks; the wood ducks tell the mallards, and before long, you have a pond full of ducks feeding on your grain. At this point, nothing is wrong. It only becomes wrong if you go down to the pond, throw out a few decoys, and start shooting the ducks. The ducks would not have been there had you not fed them. That's the gist of baiting.

In Mexico, however, baiting is legal. The only good news about that is that a lot of people bait, so that if you shoot ducks in one place, they will go to some other place where no one is shooting and dine there. This baiting trick is also used in some South American countries. Again, the advantage for hunters is that it gets ducks into a particular place. Without baiting, in a place such as Argentina, where the majority of the ducks live and feed along the Parana River, hunters would probably shoot very few ducks, and no one in Argentina hunts ducks except Americans, Spaniards, and other foreign nationals.

Driven Ducks

In both Western and Eastern Europe, the art of driven ducks has become a sport in and of itself. Like driven pheasants, where the pheasants are raised in a particular area and fed from the time they are young birds, so too are mallards raised and fed on estate ponds. By the time hunting season rolls around, the ducks are mature and capable of flying distances. Driven duck hunting as a sport has the hunters oftentimes away from the pond area and in a line to intersect the ducks as they fly from one area to another. Beaters,

usually with dogs, approach a pond and flush the ducks off the pond. The ducks take flight and wing their way toward some pond anywhere from a quarter-mile or further, where they are used to feeding and resting as well. The hunters are put on ground between these two points.

▲ Claire Zambuni with a handsome brace of mallards after a driven shoot at Chateau de Villette, France.

Once mallards have been shot at a few times, they know the game. They are not going to leave the areas where they are fed but they are going to know where the hunters are, and they are going to fly higher and higher to avoid being shot. This is where the mastery of shooting high birds, practically a religious order in places like England, comes into play. Hunters in places such as England, Scotland, or Wales can consistently make shots on ducks fifty, sixty, or seventy yards high. This is a feat not duplicated by most American duck hunters. We want our ducks close: twenty yards, over decoys. The Europeans want their ducks high, fast, and on the wind. The challenge for them is hitting the most difficult target and the sport is only killing a few, not a limit, nor a lot.

Because shooting high birds—whether pheasants or ducks—is a sport in and of itself, the guns for duck hunting are not unlike the guns for high pheasants. Duck hunters shoot thirty-, thirty-two-, or even thirty-four-inch barreled over/unders or side-by-sides. In the United States, primarily because we are required to use steel or some other non-toxic shot, we tend to shoot semiautomatic shotguns, shoot our ducks over decoys, and use the third shot to help dispatch cripples. Europeans tend to shoot side-by-sides or over/under guns primarily because it is the quality of the shot that they seek.

They do not, however, shoot three-inch cartridges. They shoot 2¾-inch shells, sometimes even 2½-inch shells, loaded with one to 1¼ ounces of nickel-plated lead shot, usually No. 5s. By correctly matching their loads to their chokes, they can produce effective killing patterns at these distances. In some of the European countries (Sweden comes to mind), ducks and geese are hunted in the more traditional way—over decoys and from blinds. This is also a practice in some parts of the United Kingdom. Hunting waterfowl in Europe differs from the United States in that there are no set limits in Europe. European hunters' limits are based on ethics rather than law.

Speaking of ethics as opposed to law, Europe allows shooting at night, both for waterfowl and even some big game, like wild boar. Waterfowl is shot at night primarily on the full moon. I know this because I have participated in nighttime shooting. It is a waterfowl experience like no other. Shooting at silhouettes against a moonlit sky is something this American never really got a grasp of. My English counterparts knocked down two ducks at a time with two shots. I could barely find the ducks in the moon and was very fortunate if I was able to get one! It is, however, an experience I will cherish as it must have been something in which the early duck hunters here in the United States also participated. I remember Pop Pop Richardson telling me, "Oh, we used to shoot them at night on the full moon! It made for a great hunt!"

There are only a couple of criteria for what to wear duck and goose hunting and that's that the clothing keeps you warm and dry in keeping with the temperature and weather conditions of the day you're hunting. In the United States, camouflage, dark greens, and browns—the earthy tones—are worn because ducks and geese are not color blind. They can see colors. They see movement more than they see anything else, but the clothes you wear should allow you to blend into nature and not stand out.

Part III

WINGSHOOTING DESTINATIONS

9. Wingshooting in the United States

etting off for distant shores on a shooting excursion can take you far beyond the sport. There's the prospect of adventure, new wonders to behold. You are the foreigner in a foreign land. There you experience the local people's language, see how they live their lives, prepare their cuisine, savor their wines, sing their songs, and dance their dances.

What happens, however, when you venture into the back of beyond to hunt? There are no creature comforts in the wilderness except for those you provide for yourself, or conditions except those which Mother Nature imposes. Whether you harvest a bird depends upon skill and luck, mostly luck, and if all goes well, you will have fresh meat to cook on the open campfire for your dinner. You are a foreigner in the lands of God's lesser creatures.

There's a marvelous paragraph that the greatest mystery writer of all, Agatha Christie, wrote in her novel, *And Then There Were None*. Justice Wargrave reflects on his invitation from an old friend to visit her on Indian Island and ". . .cast back in his mind to remember when exactly he had last seen Lady Constance Culmington. It must be seven—no, eight years ago. She had then been going to Italy, to bask in the sun and be at one with Nature and the Contadini. Later, he had heard, she had proceeded to Syria where she proposed to bask in yet stronger sun and live at one with Nature and the Bedouin."

I just love the phrase, "being at one." Whether in the wilds of New England or in search of new experiences at an unfamiliar sporting destination, I, too, try "being at one" with my surroundings—wherever my journey may take me. You can find outfitters for every state on BestWingshooting.com or in the appendix on page 191.

Regional Specialties

Never have there been more quality opportunities for wingshooting in the United State than now. Bird hunting runs from northern Maine to southern Florida, from the East Coast to the West, and everywhere in between. If you divide the country into quadrants, New England and the mid-Atlantic states comprise the Northeast, the South Atlantic and East South Central are the South, the East North Central and West North Central are the Central region, and the Mountain and Pacific is the West.

▲ Photo courtesy of Winchester.

New England, for example, has a legendary sporting heritage for hunting wild game birds, specifically grouse and woodcock. Not many people know that northern Maine, New Hampshire, and Vermont have incredible wilderness areas. Maine boasts a commercial logging area of over one million acres in its northern territory. This is home to some of the best grouse hunting you can find in the United States. Colloquially referred to as "partridges," grouse populations are cyclical, and when the cycles are high, you can walk the logging roads to find them picking up gravel and sunning themselves. Likewise, Maine's many inland rivers and its 3,478-mile-long coastline, which is longer than California's, has an unparalleled waterfowl history. With the right guide or outfitter, in the right place, at the right time, its sea duck and goose hunting opportunities are among the greatest in the world. The Atlantic flyway runs from Maine all the way down to Florida. One of the species that's seldom hunted anymore is the brant, though good numbers can be found off the coasts of New York and New Jersey. Sea duck hunting has grown in popularity over the past several years and some species, such as the long-tailed duck and eider, are considered trophy ducks.

As you move south along the coast you come to perhaps the most famous duck hunting region in the East—the Eastern Shore of Maryland, the Chester River, and Chesapeake Bay—and nowhere more famous than Easton, Maryland, where the great waterfowl hunting traditions are preserved and continued to this day.

When you enter the southeastern quadrant of the United States, you step into the "good old boy" network of quail hunting and dove shooting. This is the land where Opening Day of mourning dove season, in the first week of September, marks the beginning of a lengthy hunting season which, depending on the game animal or species of bird, goes through March. This is an important social time—a time when families and friends gather for an afternoon's sport on a corn, wheat, millet, or other grain field that attracts dove. The sultry summer air resounds with cries of "Good shot!" and "One coming to you!" and "Bird over-head!" There's a lot of laughter and, on a good day, lots of good shooting.

Quail hunting is the South's traditional hunting heritage. There's nothing more beautiful than a well-trained, stylish, energetic hunting dog scenting a quail and coming to a hard point. Alas, the days of the great wild coveys of wild quail are gone; even one wild covey is hard to come by anymore. But the traditions continue with top-quality shooting preserves that not only offer quail hunting, but pheasants and chukars as well. Duck and goose hunting camps along the southern coast, and even inland to some extent, still tell great stories of days gone by. North Carolina, the first southern state to attract Northern quail hunters in the winter, also has rich waterfowl hunting traditions on the Outer Banks and Mattamuskeet, home, in the heyday, to some of the great duck hunting clubs. The area remains one of the few (if not only) places with a limited season on whistling (or tundra) swans, which require a special permit by lottery drawing. The limit is one, and with the right outfitter, you will see great flocks of hundreds of swans.

Heading as far south as you can go is, of course, Florida, which has a lot of quail. The problem is, there are also a lot of snakes. Quail are ground-nesters and snakes eat quail eggs. For that reason, among others, wild quail have become sparse—not just in Florida, but in all the Southern states. Georgia has most famously tried to maintain wild quail in the hunting traditions of the late 1800s, with mule drawn wagons, people on horseback, and wide-ranging dogs. Even so, though the wild coveys are carefully monitored, preserves supplement the population with birds grown and released very early in the quail cycle, in early spring.

The state of Tennessee is unusual because the east is in the mountains and the western border is on the Mississippi, so you can grouse hunt and quail hunt in eastern Tennessee and duck hunt in western Tennessee on the Central flyway. Arkansas has been known as the "duck hunting capital of the South" for a long time. Places like Stuttgart, Arkansas, have been a mecca for duck hunters because of the region's endless rice fields. Over the years, Arkansas has seen an influx of specklebellies and snow geese, many of which pass through and travel on to winter in the south of Texas, and even Mexico.

The Midwest is known as the pheasant capital of the United States. North and South Dakota, Iowa, Nebraska, and Idaho have been meccas for pheasant hunters since the late nineteenth century, when pheasants were first brought to America (see page 97, "Pheasants, America's Naturalized Game Bird"). Also, quality duck and goose hunting on the Central flyway, which divides the country from the Canadian border to the Gulf Coast, offers tremendous opportunities, famously in Michigan, Wisconsin, Missouri, and Illinois—anywhere there's lots of water and farmland crops.

▲ Megan Watts, a member of the Syren ProStaff, hunting with a Syren Tempio Sporting semiautomatic 12-gauge.

The Southwest—specifically, Texas—has the highest number of wingshooters in the country. They turn our for dove shooting, quail hunting, and waterfowl along the coast butting up to Louisiana. West of Texas you'll find running quail, such as Mearns', scaled, and Gambel's, which are hunted over big-ranging pointers in wide-open country. And though it can get pretty hot, except for January and February, there are great outdoor traditions to be had in Arizona, New Mexico, Utah, and in Nevada, where duck hunting is a well-kept secret.

Moving on to the Western states . . . There's Montana, most famously known for big game hunting, but it likewise has abundant mountain, sage, and sharp-tailed grouse, partridge, and duck hunting. Idaho, too, has great duck and pheasant hunting, and such great flights of pigeons during the summer harvest that they blacken the sky.

Inasmuch as hunting as a sport has changed over the past century, so has the nature of the wingshooter. On one hand, there are true wild bird hunters—men and women who seek out the wild places in the back of beyond, despite inclement weather, with hopes of coming upon a spiraling woodcock or brace of rocketing grouse. That's their passion and their reason to hunt birds. Then there's the wingshooter who wants a hunting experience in a more controlled environment, where opportunities to shoot are assured and after the hunt a good meal awaits you in a lodge with a blazing fire in the fireplace. Although these may be two different individuals, their passions are the same: the love of the outdoors, the camaraderie of friends, the joy of hunting over a confidential gun dog, a gun that shoots straight, and the wonderment and freedom that comes from having land to hunt upon, and game to hunt, here in the United States of America.

Hunting Licenses

Just as a driver's license is required by state law to drive a vehicle, a hunting license is required by state law to hunt game. To obtain a hunting license, you must be sixteen years old or older. Here's what you need to do:

- Go online to your state wildlife agency and review your state's requirements.
- Find and complete a hunter education course.

- Purchase a hunting license and any additional stamps or permits that may be required.

Your local gun club, outdoor or gun store, and/or state wildlife agency will have information on hunter education courses. You are required to take, and pass, a hunter education course and earn your hunter safety (orange) card before you will be able to buy a hunting license.

Some states offer an "apprentice hunting license." If your state is one of these, you may be allowed to head afield with an experienced, licensed hunter before taking a hunter education course. If a person under the age of sixteen has completed a hunter's safety program successfully, she will be issued a "certificate of competency" but must be accompanied by a properly licensed adult when hunting.

You can buy your hunting license at most outdoor or gun stores, and online with your state agency. You will have many options to choose from on the application: you will be charged a Wildlife Habitat Fee of $2.50, which is required; determine whether you want a combination fishing and hunting license or a hunting license only. If you are over a certain age (generally around sixty-five), you will be eligible for a senior license in your state of residence, which costs considerably less money; in some states, such as Georgia and New Hampshire, senior licenses are free. There are additional charges for hunting pheasant and turkey.

If you plan to hunt in another state, you will be required to purchase a nonresident hunting license (the same applies to fishing). Some states offer privilege licenses at special rates to residents of nearby states. For example, in North Carolina, there are short-term (ten days) and annual licenses available to residents of Georgia, South Carolina, Tennessee, and Virginia.

If you plan to hunt ducks, geese, woodcock, snipe, coot, and other migratory birds, you must have a H.I.P (national Migratory Bird Harvest Information Program) permit number. There is no charge for a H.I.P. number. Call the new toll-free H.I.P. phone line, (1-800) 207-6183, and be sure to write the number you are assigned on the back of your license.

Additionally, you are required to purchase a Federal Duck Stamp if you are going to hunt migratory birds. Go online to www.fws.gov/birds/get-involved/duck-stamp .php.

To hunt waterfowl, you are required to have a current hunting license from your state of residence and must be sixteen years of age or older. Anyone can contribute to conservation by buying Duck Stamps. In addition to serving as hunting license and conservation tool, a current Federal Duck Stamp is also a free pass into any national wildlife refuge that charges an entry fee. Because nearly all of the proceeds are used to conserve habitat for birds and other wildlife, birders, nature photographers, and other outdoor enthusiasts buy Duck Stamps to help ensure that they can always see wildlife at their favorite outdoors spots.

Firearms Licenses

Each state has its own requirements regarding licensing gun owners, and some localities impose additional restrictions or requirements. Check the laws in your state. Visit the website of your state police. There you'll find links to information detailing how to apply for a license. You may be able to download the application form directly from the website.

Some states require that the owner of *any* firearm, including shotguns, must be in possession of a firearms license. In Hawaii, Illinois, Massachusetts, and New Jersey, you must have a license to own any kind of firearm. Residents of New York City must have a license to own, and a permit to buy and carry, a shotgun. All firearms in New York City must also be registered with the state (firearms elsewhere in New York State do not need to be registered). One permit covers both possession and purchase of a long gun in New York City. www.nyc.gov/html/nypd/downloads/pdf/permits/rifle_shotgun_permit_application.pdf.

Before You Go Hunting

- As a new hunter, you should review the rules of firearm safety for your own benefit. In time, as hunting becomes a familiar way of life for you, these will become second nature.
- Practice your shooting skills at a range near you.
- Always hunt with a partner. Never go unaccompanied into the woods or a rural area where you plan to hunt, especially if you are

unfamiliar with it. Get a topographical map and acquaint yourself with the area.
- If you hunt on private land, you must first have the *written* permission of the land owner.
- Dress for safety. Always dress in layers—you can always peel off or put on a layer to conform to the weather and temperature.
- If you are hunting in an area where there are snakes, be sure to wear snake chaps or snake boots.
- If you have an allergy to bees, be absolutely sure to have an EpiPen or similar on your person and advise your hunting partner accordingly. Likewise medications such as insulin if you are diabetic, heart medications, and so on.
- Be certain you have the correct size cartridges for your hunt. NEVER mix cartridges in your cartridge bag, coat, or vest pocket.
- Although you may not have cellphone reception in the area in which you are hunting, be sure your cellphone is fully charged and pack a portable charger. Be sure you have downloaded a GPS app on your phone.
- Enjoy a **safe and productive** hunting season.

State Wildlife Agencies

Hunters are the largest contributors to conservation, paying for programs that benefit all Americans and wildlife. According to the US Fish and Wildlife Service, 59 percent of funding, or $3.3 billion, comes from hunting and fishing related activities, of which 35 percent comes from license sales. State websites provide information on where to hunt. You may also find information on the National Shooting Sports foundation's website, "Where to Hunt," www.nssf.org/hunting/where-to-hunt, which provides easy and direct online access to laws and regulations, license and permit information, applications and forms, hunter education classes, shooting ranges, and upland hunting locations for each state. The US Fish and Wildlife Service also maintains a list of state agencies here: www.fws.gov/offices/statelinks.html.

10. Wingshooting in Far-Off Places

I was first introduced to driven shooting more than forty years ago on the Scottish moors and have since returned many times.

By relating some of my own more recent experiences I hope to provide you with good information that goes beyond an understanding of driven shooting and captures something of the experience. Who knows, maybe it will inspire you to go on a driven shoot yourself one day. I have selected two countries, France and Argentina, to give you a sense of the wonderment that is yours when you travel to hunt birds in faraway places.

▲ Chateau de Villette.

Driven Shooting in France

Whenever my thoughts drift back to Chateau de Villette, my first memory is the last drive of the last day, and the wing-beating flurry of birds I saw—not down the rib of a side-by-side shotgun—but as an observer, high on a hillside above the shooting field. It was the end of October and an uncommon wintry chill penetrated the air. A panorama of gently undulating hills and vales unfolded around me as far as the eye could see. My prospect commanded a clear view of the shooting party: seven guns, all seasoned shots, each assisted by a loader. Dog handlers and their dogs waited for their work to begin while in the copse beaters were already doing theirs. Coen Stork who, with his wife, Catherine, owns Chateau de Villette and Villette's head game-keeper, Stephen Beard, had been directing the guns to their assigned pegs when suddenly a flock of ducks streaked across the afternoon sky—too high, too far, too many to count. The guns hastened into position, the loaders loaded cartridges, and in the nearing distance, the strident cries of the beaters whipping the brush with their flags grew louder and

▲ The wingspan of this pheasant is surely as wide as this sturdy field spaniel is long!

▲ Rachel Carrie prepares to take a shot at a high bird. Driven shooting requires the shooter, or gun, to stand at a specific position, or peg. The head gamekeeper or hunt master blows a horn to signal the start of the drive. Wild birds are driven toward the guns by a line of drivers, or beaters, who walk through the woods and fields, beating high grass with flags or sticks to shift birds that then fly toward the guns. This is not an easy feat; the birds fly fast and furious, sometimes too far, too high, or too low, a few sporadically, then in waves. When the hunt master deems the drive to be over, he again blows the hunting horn.

louder. Sturdy English-raised Labs, energetic field spaniels and springers, a true field-bred Irish setter, and a splendid pair of German shorthaired pointers strained at their leads, quivering with excitement, awaiting the command—but not a shot was fired.

The beating line was closing in when suddenly there was the furious cackle of pheasants on the wing—twenty, thirty, more, exploding from the woods. They flew, as fly they must, high above the tree line into a barrage of shot that strafed the sky. The birds that fell were taken at forty yards, no less, but many more dodged the salvo unscathed, and were scooped up by the wind's blustery arms and carried over the bluff. I can still see the surprise in their black-beaded eyes when, without warning, they came upon me! I felt their beating wings against my upturned face . . . why, I could almost reach up and tickle their feathered bellies!

▲ Great flocks of pheasants came in waves across the sky.

Great flocks of pheasants came in waves across the sky like the surf lapping the shore. Sensing peril, they flew like kamikaze pilots breaking formation, zigzagging, accelerating, increasing altitude, challenging the guns on every shot (see page 127 for the basics of driven shooting).

My eyes swept over the sight: the hills of Mâcon rippling like a secret stream in the deep woods, darkening clouds the color of Payne's grey from a watercolor box brushing the impending dusk, the wearying shooters below, the endless bouquet of pheasants soaring above, dogs running so energetically, so tirelessly doing what they had been bred and trained to do—why, their paws barely touched the ground! And in that moment, I understood, to the very depths of my

soul, that this splendor had indeed been rendered by the hand of God.

This is the spectacle I captured in my mind's eye like a Polaroid picture. And whenever I wish, I open the secret compartment in my heart where I store my most treasured memories, take out the one of that last drive at Chateau de Villette, and bask in the warmth of its golden glow.

▲ Catherine Stork in fine shooting form at Chateau de Villette.

Driven shooting generally offers a variety of terrain and game birds, whether in Continental Europe, Great Britain, or, increasingly, in the United States at shoots such as the one my husband John Wiles organizes here, in Pinehurst, North Carolina, through his company, Best Wingshooting (www.bestwingshooting.

▲ Beaters and dog handlers at Chateau de Villette.

com) and notably at Blixt and Company in Idaho. Blixt is operated by Lars and Jennifer Magnusson, who introduced European-style driven shooting to America in 2009 (www.blixtco.com) and theirs is widely considered the premier traditional driven pheasant and partridge shoot in the United States.

At Villette, we had pheasants presented high over dense woodlands, lower over hedgerows, and extremely high when we shot from the valleys as the birds came in over tall treetops. Driven ducks and driven partridges present differently and make for a unique hunting experience.

The Basics of Driven Shooting

Driven shooting technique is learnable, repeatable, and practical on all driven lines. Basically, the shooter is facing the direction from which the birds are anticipated. As a rule, the birds—once they begin to fly—will all be at relatively the same height. That means that if birds start appearing over the woods or over the terrain at thirty or forty yards, the bulk of the birds will be at that height. Similarly, on high-bird shoots the birds appear at fifty to seventy yards or higher, and the bulk of the birds will be at that range. High-bird shooting is indeed a specialist event. Having the right gun, the right choke, and the right shells are critical to high-bird shooting, and you need to be a master of your gun.

On shoots other than high-bird shoots, often the shooter can utilize two modified chokes or even two full chokes to shoot any bird presented and the length of the barrels—twenty-six, twenty-eight, thirty, or thirty-two inches—is strictly the shooter's choice. Since most shoots that we Americans participate in are not high-bird shoots, let's concentrate on those. In a typical driven shoot for pheasants in the United Kingdom and especially in the eastern part of Europe, birds often are presented at distances of twenty to forty yards. Good shooters will concentrate on the birds that challenge, to some extent, their shooting capability. It takes a time or two of this kind of shooting to learn to relax and concentrate singularly on the birds you want to take. As shooting improves, the focus will tend to be on higher birds or more difficult birds, and while the bag number will become smaller, the quality of the shooting will become greater.

▲ Betsy Holden demonstrating proper form for driven shooting.

The shooter stands facing the direction the birds are coming. Once the birds start flying, the gun should be held most of the time in the ready position, at basically a 45-degree angle with the butt of the shotgun tucked slightly under the right armpit (for a right-handed shooter) and the end of the muzzles just below the eyes' line of sight. With a gun held thus, as the bird appears, the shooter focuses on the head of the bird and moves the gun toward the bird's head by pushing it directly away from her body toward the bird. Since the bird is flying toward the shooter, the initial gun mount puts the shooter's weight on her front foot. As the bird approaches, to keep the motion of the shoulders even and symmetrical, the shooter will begin to lean backward, transferring her weight from the front foot to the back foot while gently lifting the heel of her front foot to accomplish this. This takes the strain off the shoulders and arms and allows for a smooth swing. As the shooter continues to focus on the head of the bird, the gun likewise continues to move with the bird in the shooter's peripheral vision until she fires when her subconscious mind says to. There is a lot of unconscious or subconscious work in good shooting, and that only comes from practice and repetition.

Shooting Tips for High Birds

The skill set applied to shooting high birds begins with the basic shooting technique. If you mount your gun properly, nestle the butt firmly in the soft part of your shoulder, and rest the stock confidently against your cheekbone, you have the right start.

Pick your shot. Raise your gun and, with both eyes open, fix your line of sight down the rib of the barrels without fixating on the barrels themselves. Okay, you're on the right track.

When you see the bird's head clearly, swing through, lead the bird, pull the trigger—but here is where things change up. Quite literally, *up*.

Driven shooting is never for the first-time shooter, hardly ever for the beginner, and only for the intermediate shooter who has had sufficient experience in the field to not be caught wholly off guard by the suddenness of a game bird bursting from the brush, a low-slung branch or, even more breath-catching, from underfoot. (Yes, there is always an element of surprise hunting game birds.) Ever employing safety, aware of where others with whom you are shooting are in relation to you and the bird, knowing where your muzzle is pointed at all times, barrels raised, even with, and never pointing down, at an angle in line with the bird's flight pattern—all this must be second nature to you.

▲ Betsy Holden looking over the barrels.

Working in Tandem with Your Loader

A good loader is to a wingshooter what a good caddy is to a proficient golfer. The loaders at Villette are local people with years of knowledge and time in the field. Even though there was a language barrier, you can relate with hand motions, facial expressions, and an occasional French word, such as oui, non, bonjour, and merci. There are no set rules, but my advice to anyone who has the benefit of the assistance of a good loader is to engage in some common understanding: make clear what you expect from him but more important, understand what he expects from you.

For example, never hand the gun to the loader. You break the gun open, out fly the empty hulls, and the loader simply puts two more shells in the gun. You close the gun, take the ready position, safety engaged, and pick your shot. The advantage of having a loader is not to relieve you of loading your gun, it is to allow you to continue to focus in the sky on the birds that are

coming. You don't have to take your eyes away from the landscape to look at the gun. Again, you simply open the gun, the loader pushes the shells into chamber, and you close the action. The gun is now loaded. Safety on or off? Continue to focus on the sky, hold the gun in the ready position. Are you certain no beater or dog handler is in front of you, perhaps half-hidden at the verge of the forest? You wait and a flock bursts from the woods. You raise your gun to your shoulder, focus on one bird in the flock, be absolutely sure it is surrounded entirely by blue sky. See its head? Keeping your eyes on the bird, swing through, and fire. A clean shot! That's what you want to do, every time, and while it won't happen every time, you'll gain proficiency as you acquire consistency in your shooting.

Shooting a matched pair or alternating two guns is more complex. It's not easy, and there's a real rhythm to it that will prove difficult until you get used to it. In a double gun scenario, you would shoot both barrels, usually the right then the left; then, holding the gun at the wrist pointed skyward, you move the gun toward the loader. The loader would have the second gun already loaded and he would hand it to your left hand (providing you are a right-handed shooter) as he takes the spent gun. Now you close the loaded gun, ready to bring to your trigger hand, and make the mount to the birds. Because the guns are changing hands, the safety must always be on. It is the shooter's responsibility to push the safety off in preparation for firing.

The only difference between an over/under and a side-by-side is really down to personal preference. A double gun is favored for driven shooting in Europe—most traditionally, a side-by-side and much of that is because over/unders were rarely seen on the field before World War II and, in fact, did not become popular until sometime after. Semiautomatics are really not acceptable in western Europe except on driven partridges, in lieu of having two guns and that's because you can load up to five shots in a semiauto.

Guns for Driven Shooting

The all-purpose cartridge for ducks, partridges, and pheasants for driven shoots is 2¾-inch, 1 1/16-ounce No. 6 lead shot (lead shot is permitted in France for waterfowl). If you have one gun to shoot, a 12-gauge over/under or side-by-side shotgun with fixed chokes, modified and full, would be a preferred choice. Twelve-gauge shotgun cartridges are readily available anywhere there's shooting in the world. A 12-gauge shotgun with a No. 5 or 6 shell is a good combination for any game bird out from thirty to sixty yards.

Barrel length is a personal preference, and in times past had much to do with the dictate of the day. Back in the days when they made fixed chokes, guns were made in three barrel lengths: twenty-six-inch, imp/mod; twenty-eight-inch, mod/full; and 30-inch, full-and-full and considered more to be waterfowl guns. Most people were shooting upland game—pheasants, partridges, grouse—and the shorter barrels were quicker in brush and in heavy cover, where you had to react quickly. When skeet came along, those guns were used to shoot skeet because the skeet targets were basically twenty-one yards no matter where you were on the field. In trap, longer barrels were used because of the distance of the target, and long barrels provide a better sighting plane. But the twenty-eight-inch barrel is the basic length for wingshooting, and that's what you will mostly find in the gun room at Villette. Now, if you bring your own gun and it has longer barrels, that would be fine. Again, it's up to you.

A gun in the seven-pound category is about right. Straight grip for high birds is traditional and presents the correct attitude for your wrist as you hold the grip. Pistol grip or Prince of Wales grip, which you don't see often these days, will also keep your hand from moving back. But either way, your hand should stay in the same place. Trigger pull should be crisp but again, the poundage of the pull is a personal preference. Somewhere in the four-pound range is good; more than that and there's a tendency of pulling the gun off target.

A borrowed gun, if you don't bring your own, can be very difficult. Length-of-pull, sighting place, straight or pistol grip, cast—any one or more of these things that is not what you're used to may negatively influence your shooting, and makes you think more about the gun than a gun that's fitted to you.

Then there's the safety on an unfamiliar gun. Are you used to an automatic safety or a manual safety? If it's automatic, the safety comes on every time you open the gun. If it's manual, once you push it off it stays off until you push it on again. If it goes on safe every time you open the gun, it means you have to push it off every time you're ready to shoot and so, every time your loader hands you a gun, you have to push the safety off. If a loader is loading just one gun and that gun has a manual safety, he may hand you the gun with the safety on or off. This is the most important thing you have to sort out with him before you take your first shot.

Weather Impacts How Birds Fly

When birds fly in the cold on a raw windy day they use the wind to their advantage, and if the wind is crossing, the birds tend to slide on the wind, meaning they are not only moving toward you, they are also moving to the left or right at the same time and that makes for a much more complex shot. The only reason they say the bird will fly higher in the cold is because by the time it gets really cold, the birds have been driven several times. They have played the game and higher is safer. And they know it—sure they know it! Instinct, preservation. Most driven shooting isn't in really warm weather, except partridges, which tend to fly low anyway.

The birds will fly in rain. They don't like it, but they will. They tend to fly a little lower unless they've been shot at quite a bit, simply because they are trying to seek shelter away from you and trying to find shelter as quickly as possible. On cold, blustery days, birds will have been hunted several times, and they are wary of approaching footsteps; people talking means someone is going to harm them, and they become afraid, and when they are skittish, they will take off fast and furious and likely out of gunshot range. Coen Stork always, as we approached each and every beat, would stop in his tracks, turn, make sure he got the attention of each and every one in the shooting party, and raise his hand to signal quiet—absolute quiet. Though it was the end of October, the birds had already been shot at several weeks and they were cautious. On the first drive I thought Coen's signal of caution was some distance from the pegs, but I soon saw for myself the merit of his caution.

Traveling Abroad with Your Own Gun

Shooting a loaner gun can ruin your hunting trip. An individual can bring up to two shotguns to the countries in the European Union (EU), which includes France, under Directive 91/477/EEC Category C—Subject to Declaration. A child less than eighteen years of age must have parental permission or be under parental guidance or the guidance of an adult with a valid firearms or hunting license or are within a licensed or otherwise approved training center. Hunters are exempted from import authorization for two classified hunting weapons. DO NOT bring shotgun cartridges under any circumstances. You must be able to justify that they are traveling for a hunting purpose. Therefore, contact your outfitter, and he or she will issue you a Letter of Invitation. The applicable customs procedure is that of temporary admission. The owner of the weapon must go to the first customs office at the entrance of the European Union to place his weapons under this regime.

On their return to their own country, hunters are exempt from an export license for firearms re-exported as a result of temporary admission, provided that such weapons remain the property of a person established outside the customs territory of the European Union and that they be re-exported to this person (Article R. 316-46 of the Internal Security Code). Sports shooters holding weapons classified in category C are exempted from import authorization for temporarily imported firearms. Check the website www.diplomatie.gouv.fr/en/the-ministry-and-its-network/protocol/protection-and-security/article/acquisition-possession-and and just call the Embassy of France (or another applicable country) in Washington DC directly so they can help you.

What to Wear

To shoot effectively you must dress efficiently. This means the clothing you wear should not restrict your freedom of movement when you mount your gun. Your clothing should be comfortable, water-resistant, and practical.

There is a centuries-old truth about traditional English shooting attire that lies in the very weft and warp of the wool with which these tweeds are woven. Such glorious fabric in earthy hues will keep the shooting sportswoman dry and warm in rain and snow, yet breathes on those balmy, warmish days of late spring and early autumn. What's more, nothing surpasses tweed in tailored looks, comfort, durability, and practicality. A custom-tailored shooting jacket, vest, breeks,

and slacks has been the uniform of landed gentry, royalty, and gamekeepers for more than two centuries. Estates boast their own family tweed, uniquely created for their clan or family.

The tweed selected by Catherine and Coen for Chateau de Villette was custom-made by Campbell's of Beauly, which holds the royal warrant to Queen Elizabeth II of England as tailors. The warrant that Campbell's held for both the Duke of Windsor and the Queen Mother were as tweed mercers, and the firm has historically been known as "The Guardians of Tweed." Campbell's landmark shop since 1858 is located on High Street in Beauly, Inverness-shire, and it is known as the Highland Tweed House.

▲ Coen Stork and their head gamekeeper.

Never break in a new pair of boots on a driven shoot. You'll regret it. Wear your tried-and-true, field-tested, waterproof field boots with ankle support that allow you to go the distance through marshes, in wet weather, on heather, and through fields and woods.

A brimmed hat, not a visor, is essential for all sorts of reasons—warmth, eyeshade, rain. An English wool cap is ideal; a beret, so common in France and Scotland, is good for warmth.

Many shooters wear gloves not only for weather but because it affords a firm grip on your gun and will protect your hand if the gun gets hot from shooting.

Breeks (the British term for short pants worn during hunting) are practical with Wellingtons or other knee-high boots and a pair of warm wool knee socks. Long pants are awkward to fold and stuff into any knee-high boot.

Physical Condition for a Driven Shoot

You need to be able to walk some distance on a driven shoot and over tricky bits, as well, such as barbed wire fences, cattle grids, wooden footbridges, and occasionally a leap of faith over a narrow stream. I came to Villette with a ruptured Achilles tendon, which I was determined wouldn't keep me down until the last drive on the final day, as I've told you. This said, a Land Rover Discovery was always available for anyone who preferred to get to a beat on four wheels and I confess, I was a regular passenger.

Protective Eyewear, Always

Shooting safety glasses are not an option. If you don't have a pair, don't shoot. It's not worth the risk of injury or potentially losing your sight over some freak accident (and remember, all accidents are unpredictable). You can wear your regular prescription glasses, if you wish, but they must be shatterproof with lenses that are large enough to cover your eyes from brow to cheekbone and the full width of your face. Shooting safety glasses with a set of interchangeable lenses is useful in any shooting scenario but most especially, I think, for driven shooting, where each drive presents a different landscape. The color lens you select is also, of course, determined by the sky, cloud cover, and sunlight. If the day is overcast, red lenses work best. A bright, sunny day requires polarized lenses. Yellow is best in low light conditions and very dark presentations, such as the forest's edge on the last drive of the day with storm-clouds streaming toward you from the horizon. Those three colored lenses cover almost anything.

At a place such as Chateau de Villette, you are treated like a lady or a lord, and while you must not assume airs, you must assume the people you will be among expect you to have manners. How you interact with others will contribute to the success and enjoyment of your shooting party. You may be shy, you may be gregarious; whichever the case, by now you have the skill set needed to interact with others, whether friends or newly met, in a relaxed and easy manner. Have the confidence to engage. Use the opportunity to enhance your relationships with those you know or begin new friendships. As the great American humorist Will Rogers said, "A stranger is just a friend I haven't met yet."

▲ American wingshooting enthusiast Ramon Marks is handsomely outfitted for the field. He is owned by an English setter named Tessa.

There are a variety of socks from which you can choose—thermal, moisture-wicking, neoprene, spandex, insulating, odor-fighting, even battery-heated socks with three heat settings! But nothing bests a heavy wool sock. If wool can keep sheep warm and dry, it will keep you warm, too.

Volume Shooting in Argentina

▲ Pictured from right to left: John, Laurie, Mark Harris and his wife, Marguerite, their friend, Andrew, and Tomas Frontera at La Zaneda, Argentina.

Probably since the 1980s, South America—especially Argentina—has for a long time been the mecca for sportsmen who love to shoot doves. One of the great things about Argentina is that in its diverse landscape, there's an area near Córdoba that is known for its agriculture; corn, soybeans, wheat, sunflowers, and other grain crops are grown in abundance over huge areas of thousands and thousands of acres. Originally, this land was mostly just scrub brush that had grown up. Someone, a long time ago, got the idea of clearing the land and planting crops. It wasn't long before this fertile area had a great reputation among hunters. The scrub areas became home to doves, which found a ready supply of food, a safe place to rest and roost, and a favorable climate that had very few days of frost, mostly warm weather, and lots of water. What started as a few doves became hundreds of doves, and those became millions of doves to the point that they were consuming 20 to 30 percent of the grain crops grown in Córdoba province. The farmers petitioned the government to help them control the bird population, and like all wise governments, the Argentine government decided the best method to control them was to spray the roosts with poison. Not only did this remedy kill most of the doves, it also killed songbirds, raptors, and small wild animals, and it created a terrible human outcry over the destruction.

Someone decided to invite some friends from the United States to come to Argentina to shoot doves.

Americans, especially in the South and in Texas, where dove shooting is a formal event, love shooting doves, but in the United States, there are limits. Here was an opportunity for Americans and other nationalities to participate in hot-barreled action with no prescribed limit. With millions of doves, an unlimited number of shells, and a wonderful environment to stay, dine, and enjoy Argentina's growing wine industry, the sport of volume dove shooting was born. Since that time, tens of thousands of sportsmen and women have traveled to Argentina to go dove shooting. Originally there were only one or two outfitters who catered to foreign sportsmen. Those few outfitters have become many. Everyone is looking for the American dollar.

▲ The sky was dark with doves flying at dawn from the roost.

The Argentine dove is called the eared dove. It looks a great deal like our mourning dove except the eared dove has a shorter, square tail. Like North American doves, they create a flimsy nest, generally in thorny bushes, to protect the young from what few predators there are and will have two eggs per nest and nest sometimes four or five times in a mating season. That season runs from late August through the end of February. Assume that a roost has one million birds on it at the beginning of nesting season. If each pair of birds brings off four successful nests of two chicks each, that's three million birds in the roost at the end of February. And there are many roosts—some are very large where the birds live year-round; some are seasonal roosts, where the birds only gather when it is nesting season. No matter which, the numbers are mind-boggling.

The dove shooting industry is a multi-billion-dollar industry for the Argentine people. In addition to the outfitter, the government, which controls things like powder, shot, licenses, and importation of guns, makes a significant amount of money.

Wild doves were the principle reason sportsmen went to Argentina to go shooting. They also discovered pigeons. These are the wild, spot-winged or picazuro pigeons not unlike the common wood pigeons you find in Europe. They, too, consume the grain crops of the Argentine farmer and, like doves, are considered a pest. They particularly love olives and peanuts and plague the orchards and farms.

Strangely enough, the doves and pigeons generally do not fly together and tend to feed in areas separate from one another. Besides doves and pigeons, the Parana River, which cuts through Argentina, is a mecca for South American ducks. There are several species, but the bread-and-butter duck is the rosy-billed pochard. The rosy-bill to South America is like the mallard to North America. Liberal limits bring many duck hunters from the United States to the rivers and swamps of Argentina every year.

Originally, bringing your own gun to Argentina was no problem. You paid a small import fee at the airport, and the government agency in charge of guns checked your paperwork when you arrived and made sure you left with the guns you brought with you. It was quite simple. Today, that simplicity is gone. There's additional paperwork required to bring guns to Argentina; the cost of bringing your own gun has grown exponentially; there's now the concern of your gun being lost with your luggage, a cancelled flight, or a late arrival; and, in truth, the Argentine outfitters have been able to work with some of the gun manufacturers to have quite a number of quality semiautomatics and over/unders for guests to shoot.

Gun fit for the discerning shooter is one of the most important aspects of good shooting, as we have

▲ Marguerite Harris looking over the barrels of John Wiles's gun as he takes a shot.

discussed repeatedly. To tell you that it is probably easier for you to shoot the guns that an outfitter has in Argentina is better than dealing with the hassle of bringing your own gun depends upon your outfitter and you. A good outfitter or representative of the estancia, and sometimes the estancia owner himself will meet you at the airport, where he is known, and expedite your shotguns. If your gun fits you, and you shoot it well, you risk disappointment if you don't bring your own gun and borrow one from the estancia's gun room. If you do not want to bring your gun, ask your outfitter what makes and models of guns the estancia offers and see if there is a gun with a length-of-pull that conforms with yours. If you have a longer than average length-of-pull, bring a strap-on recoil pad to add some length to the buttstock. If you decide to bring your own guns, be sure you have the necessary paperwork organized well in advance of your departure. Your outfitter will go over this with you. But if you are easy about shooting the outfitter's guns, it simply takes one less worry out of the equation of international air travel, which is hassle enough without bringing a shotgun overseas.

One of the problems with Argentina in the early days, says my husband, who has been going there for over thirty years, was the quality of the shells. Early on, shells were imported from the United States or Europe. These were very expensive. The Argentines wanted to manufacture their own shells, but the government was in control of the powder and shot required to make them. Even though the Argentines built manufacturing facilities, the shotshell standards were nowhere near as good as the ones that were imported. Shells were often dirty, meaning the ignition did not cause all of the powder to be burned and you wound up with powder granules in the automatic shotguns, causing them to clog and cease functioning. The government, however, makes money on the domestically manufactured shells and the quality of the shells has continued to improve until today either companies have come to Argentina and built factories that manufacture cartridges to higher standards or the Argentinian factories have raised their standards and improved greatly as now there are quality cartridges.

Argentina did not change to steel shot, so all the birds are shot with lead shot cartridges. You can readily get 20-gauge shells at any estancia. Twenty-gauge has

become the standard for doves and pigeons. You don't need a 12-gauge, and your body can't take the recoil of a thousand shells a day. The standard 20-gauge semiautomatic, which absorbs quite a bit of recoil, generally functions well, is easy to shoot, and which your bird boy will load, is the gun of choice. It is possible to also get 28-gauge shells and even .410 shells, but most outfitters need to know well in advance that you are bringing guns that require these cartridges.

The standard seven-eighths-ounce load of the shells we shoot here, in the United States, are the same as they shoot there. Ducks are usually shot with 12-gauge, one-ounce loads of No. 5 lead shot, because there is less recoil and 90 percent of ducks are shot over decoys at twenty yards or less. Additionally, ducks have limits, which although liberal compared to US standards, do not require the numbers of shells that you use in volume shooting for doves or pigeons.

Here's a typical volume wingshooting trip to Argentina: You fly from the United States, usually overnight, to Córdoba, Argentina. The more directly you can fly to Córdoba, the better. It is a hassle to have to fly through Buenos Aires, because you have to change airports and go through the city to catch a domestic flight to Córdoba, which means collecting your guns at the airport in Buenos Aires, clearing customs, then rechecking them on the domestic flight. It's time-consuming, plus the airports are on opposite sides of the city—a city of fifteen million people. It's a nightmare, but once you arrive in Córdoba, you are met by your outfitter at the airport and he has all your paperwork ready. You only have to get in the van and enjoy the ride. They will carry your luggage and guns. They'll have water, sometimes beer, and sandwiches or snacks for a drive that's as short as one hour and as long as two and one-half hours.

Córdoba is a city of 1.5 million people, so you have to drive a ways to get outside the city and into the farmlands. You will arrive at the estancia, or lodge, where you will be greeted by the staff, who will help unload all of your luggage and take it to your room. Generally, each room at a quality estancia is en suite, with its own private bath, with the dining area centrally located among all the rooms. Once you've washed off the plane, you will meet at the lodge to discuss your guns, meet your bird boy, and learn the events for the afternoon if you are going hunting then or the following morning if you have arrived late. Depending upon when you arrive, lunch will be served. You'll have a chance to rest, get your gear together—glasses, ear plugs, gloves, pouch or vest, gunning bag, and anything else—and you will head out for your first shoot.

If this is your first trip to Argentina, it is almost a guarantee that you will be overwhelmed with the volume of birds. Nowhere in the United States do we see birds in the tens of thousands flying at us for four hours straight. This only happens in Argentina.

Bird Boys

Dove or pigeon shooting in Argentina is a very formalized affair. When you go to the field, the bird boy will already have built your blind, have a stool there for you to sit on, at least one case of five hundred shells (and often two cases), and will have your gun ready to load so that you can begin shooting. The only thing you do when you are at the blind is shoot. When you empty the gun, the bird boy will load it for you, if you choose. It is good to let him load the gun because, first, it will save your thumb from pushing shells in an automatic, and second, he is much more efficient than you. As a result, you only have to focus on the birds in front of you. He will load the gun while you hold it and simply focus and shoot. This is very different from shooting in the United States, and the first thing you discover is that you can shoot five hundred shells in a very short amount of time—probably an hour or less.

The bird boy is your everything. Besides all the things he does, he also will get you water and when you are finished shooting he will unload your gun, put it in the case, take down the blind after you leave, and pick up all the birds. How, you might say, does he know where all the birds are? Actually, once you have experienced this, it is quite simple. You basically stand in one spot. If you're shooting at a 90-degree swathe from left to right in front of you, then 99 percent of the birds fall in an area thirty-five yards or so in a giant arc around the blind. Your bird boy simply goes out forty yards to the right and walks forty yards to the left, back and forth, and further and further away from the blind, until he's picked up all the birds. He will then also pick up all of your hulls and empty boxes, and when you leave, there will be no footprint that you were ever there.

You may wonder why dogs aren't used to retrieve the birds. This is a simple answer. Dogs are not meant to retrieve five hundred to one thousand birds a drive. The simple but efficient bird boy does it much faster and much better. The only bird dogs you really see are a few retrievers for ducks, because your limit is about twenty-five, and pointing dogs for hunting perdix. Perdix are like a small grouse or hen pheasant. Perdix are generally hunted by the landowners who, like the Southern plantation landowners, enjoy walking behind dogs that are pointing, as in quail. In the cooler months—June, July, and August—hunters often get to do some perdix hunting if they choose either a morning or afternoon hunt as a change from volume shooting.

One of the great things about hunting in Argentina is that their seasons are the opposite of ours. When it's cold here, it's warm there. When it's warm here, it's cold there. If you want to enjoy some excellent duck hunting, leave the heat of the United States in July for the winter in Argentina. If you want to escape the cold weather of the northern states, go to Argentina in February, the heart of summer—long days, millions of birds, wonderful swimming pools at most estancias, and as always, incredible food. As far as clothing, usually the good outfitters have laundry service, so you don't need to overpack. Hunts generally last four days, so a hunter can pack lightly and have the laundry service take care of clothing daily.

If you are hunting in warm weather, you need short-sleeved shirts or lightweight, long-sleeved shirts to protect you from the sun; a ball cap, visor, or brimmed hat in drab colors or even camouflage; khaki cotton pants or even shorts, but be careful not to get sunburned; and short, ankle-high boots or even sneakers. There's no need for brush pants normally because your walk from the truck to your blind is about fifteen feet, usually on the edge of a cornfield that has been harvested or the edge of the woods, near a roost.

How do you shoot volume birds in Argentina? Your technique can be practiced at home. You position yourself based on the flight direction of the birds. Although there are a great many, and Argentina doves and pigeons are fast and furious, you must learn to focus on the beak, head, or eye of only one particular bird a shot. Why is this important? Because your success

▲ Kate Trad picks her shot.

▲ Kate swings on a dove.

depends upon your ability to focus on a small part of the moving target. Focus on the beak, the eye, or the head of the bird and you instinctively are aiming at the bird. The barrel is only seen in the peripheral vision of the shooter, which is why gun fit is so important. Your

forward hand on the shotgun is literally pointing the gun where you want your shot go. Focusing on the head of the bird allows your wonderful mind to calculate, without conscious thought, where the muzzle should be in relationship to the moving target so that when you fire, the charge will intercept the target. This is the "art" in the art and science of shooting.

Harvesting the Birds

I have talked throughout this book about the importance of eating what you kill, and this applies especially in Argentina, where the birds you harvest become incredibly delicious dove pâté, dove nuggets, dove brochettes, pigeon burgers, duck ceviche, and other such dishes. There's some deviation from this practice, though. Two things work against you for the consuming of all the doves taken. First, Argentines consider doves to be a pest. In the United States, it would be as if I shot a number of starlings, which we don't even think of as consumable, and then bring them to your house and say, "Look! Here's a bunch of starlings for you to cook!" You would think that I was crazy. In Argentina, the dove gets the same reaction. "Why would I want those things to eat?" the native Argentinian might ask you.

Second, consider simple numbers. Five hunters each shoot five hundred birds on their first day. You now have twenty-five hundred birds to clean and consume. Doves—beyond what the hunters consume—are going to spoil before any preparation can be made. In almost all cases, the doves are returned to the soil in some form of fertilizer. That's what happens to the bulk of the doves killed. Remember, the overall objective to shooting in Argentina is to reduce the dove population so that the farmers can generate more crops. Eliminating the pest is the only way this happens.

11. Recipes

▲ Preparing a dinner of Argentinean beef and grilled doves—a real specialty!

It's important to use the game you shoot. Here are some of my own recipes for game birds. Pair your dish with a wonderful wine, such as this label from Fowles Wine. Ladies Who Shoot Their Lunch is a selection of fine wines that includes pinot noir, Riesling, Shiraz, chardonnay, and gold award–winning 2018 vintage Shiraz. Fowles Vineyards is located in the Strathbogie region of Australia and distributed in the United States. (www.fowleswine.com)

Stewed Partridges

Serves four. This recipe may also be made with any upland bird.

- Four partridge breasts, boned, trimmed, and halved (yields 8 pieces)
- 8 ounces unsalted butter, plus more for gravy
- 6–8 tomatoes, peeled and seeded, or 16-ounce can crushed tomatoes
- 8 ounces mushrooms, whole if small or halved if large
- 1 tablespoon crushed garlic, to taste
- 1 teaspoon ground black pepper
- A pinch of salt
- A pinch of thyme, oregano or your favorite seasoning for fowl
- 1 teaspoon fresh chopped or dried basil
- A glass of white wine
- 1½ pints chicken stock
- Flour
- Toast, to serve

Remove the membrane and any feathers that may have clung to the meat, and be certain there are no tendons or bones. Pat dry each piece with a paper towel and set aside.

Melt butter in a large pan or Dutch oven on the stovetop, keeping the heat low so the butter bubbles but does not blister and turn brown. Add the meat one piece at a time, browning lightly on each side before removing to a platter with a slotted spoon. You want to seal the juices, not cook them through.

Over low heat, add to the pan juices the crushed garlic, tomatoes, and mushrooms, stirring gently with a wooden spatula, then add the spices. Slowly add the wine and stock and continue to stir.

Add the birds and simmer slowly for 2 hours or until the meat is fork tender.

Thicken the pan juices into gravy. Separate juices from fat, thicken slightly by making a roux with the butter and flour in the usual way, and make very hot. Serve partridges on a dish, heaped up with vegetables, surrounded by the gravy. Place triangles of toast round the dish. Serve very hot with plain boiled potatoes or rice. The birds, when served, will need dividing rather than carving.

These next three recipes are adapted from my mother's well-thumbed *Good Housekeeping Cookbook*, published in 1942, which I had rebound and have used as much as she to the point that it needs to be rebound yet again! The recipes are simple, amazing, and reflect a time when food was precious. Shortly after this book was published, the Japanese bombed Pearl Harbor and the United States entered World War II. With that came rationing. Although these next two recipes seem simple, and they are, they not only are a reflection of the times but also make the point that game birds, prepared simply, can make a delicious and ready meal. Butter, lard, salt pork, and bacon are very often used to provide fat for game birds, which are toned athletes of the field and forest and therefore have little body fat of their own.

Roast Quail

- Quail, 1 bird per serving
- Grape leaves, for wrapping
- Several slices fat salt pork
- Butter or margarine

- 1 tablespoon dry sherry
- ¼ cup seedless grapes
- Salt to taste
- Toast, to serve

Preheat oven to 450°F. Heat shallow open pan in the oven.

Finish cleaning quail; wrap in grape leaves if available.

Cover with slices of fat salt pork; tie in place with string. Place quail, with breast side up, in heated pan; spread with a little butter or margarine. Roast, uncovered, basting often, 15 to 20 minutes, depending on degree of rareness desired. When quail is roasted, remove from pan; remove leaves and place under broiler a few minutes to brown.

Meanwhile, add about ½ cup water to pan; simmer, stirring to loosen all browned bits that cling to pan. If desired, add 1 tablespoon dry sherry, ¼ cup seedless grapes. Taste; add salt if needed.

Serve bird on toast. Top with some of the gravy. Serve with potato chips, cranberry or currant jelly, or bread sauce.

Broiled Quail

- Quail, 1 bird per serving
- Salt, to taste
- Butter or margarine, softened
- Toast, to serve
- Cream sauce or currant jelly, to serve

Preheat broiler, with broiler pan warming in oven.

Finish cleaning quail; split. Sprinkle with salt; spread with soft butter or margarine.

Place, with skin sides up, on heated broiler pan. Broil 5 minutes. Turn; broil 6 to 7 minutes. Remove to heated platter.

Serve with a cream sauce or red currant jelly. Serve birds on toast spread with sauce.

Braised Woodcock

Of all the upland game birds, woodcock is the gamiest, in my opinion. For that reason, many people do not enjoy the flavor and mask it by swaddling the little bird in bacon. This destroys the flavor, even if you don't appreciate it as much as other game birds.

Nonetheless, you eat what you kill. That's the unwritten law of the bird-hunter.

- Woodcock, 1 bird per serving
- Fat salt pork, enough to wrap birds
- Butter or margarine, divided
- Salt and pepper, to taste
- Toast, to serve
- Gravy or red currant jelly, to serve

Start heating oven to 475°F. Heat shallow pan in oven.

Finish cleaning bird; wrap with fat salt pork; tie in place with string. Place in pan with a little butter or margarine. Roast, uncovered, 8 to 15 minutes till done. Do not overcook. Remove bird.

Add about ¼ cup water to pan; simmer liquid until it is reduced by about half. Add 1 tablespoon butter or margarine; heat until just melted. Season to taste with salt and pepper. Serve bird on toast with gravy or red currant jelly.

Paprika Pheasant with Mushroom Sauce

Few cooks have sparked my culinary curiosity and fueled my desire to be a better cook more than English chef, author, and television presenter Mary Berry, the great lady of British cookery, who, in 2012, received a CBE (Most Excellent Order of the British Empire) from Queen Elizabeth II for her numerous contributions. This is her recipe, in my own words, for her paprika pheasant with mushroom sauce, serving six.

The secret is to start out with young pheasant, if possible, rather than an old pheasant and—as with every wild bird—do not overcook. If your pheasant is an old, tough cock pheasant, it seems that every bird-hunter believes you have to cook it wrapped in bacon or beat it to a pulp with a meat tenderizer. My solution, which is much simpler, is to marinate the pheasant breasts in Italian dressing overnight. If the meat is really tough, first cook the pheasant in two or three cups of chicken stock in a pressure cooker and then prepare the recipe as you would with tender pheasant. Although this recipe calls for boned breasts, you can prepare it as well with bone-in. No need to prepare the pheasant legs—these are birds that like to run a lot and as a result, their legs are very sinewy, with little meat.

- 6 pheasant breasts
- Sea salt and coarse ground pepper, to taste
- Butter and olive oil, for searing
- 1 onion, roughly chopped into julienne-like pieces
- 2 tablespoons paprika
- 1 tablespoon muscovado or turbinado sugar
- 1¼ cups heavy cream
- ½ pound sliced chestnut mushrooms
- 1 handful Italian parsley, coarsely chopped
- Mashed potatoes, for serving

Bone six pheasant breasts and season with sea salt and coarse ground pepper. Sear them in butter and olive oil in a heavy frying pan—just enough, and just hot enough, so when you place the breasts in the pan, they turn a golden brown and yet are still raw in the middle. Turn the breasts over and sprinkle with a little of the sea salt and coarse ground pepper. This will only take a little time, but you must stand over the pan all the while to avoid burning or overcooking. Remove the breasts and set them aside on a cookie sheet or plate.

With a wooden spatula, stir the dredges of oil and seasoning in the pan and then add the onion. Sauté until translucent and a light golden brown color, then add paprika, muscovado or turbinado sugar, and heavy cream, stirring constantly until well-blended. Return the pheasant breasts and cover with the sauce, keeping the pan on very low heat and making sure that nothing sticks to the bottom of the pan.

In a separate pan, sauté chestnut mushrooms until they, too, turn a light brown and add them to the pleasant pan. By this time, the pheasant should be thoroughly cooked. Sprinkle parsley and set aside, off the heat, while you plate the pheasant with mashed potatoes served on the side. Mary serves this dish with broad beans, which are more familiarly known to us Americans as fava beans; however, lima beans or green peas would equally offset the delicate flavor of the cream sauce, as well.

Dove Pâté

This recipe is my variation of Partridge Pâté from *Game Cookbook* by Geraldine Steindler, first published in 1965, for which I have substituted doves. (You can use any upland bird. Of course, you can use duck or goose, being sure to cut out the oil gland in the tail at the base of the spine.) Mrs. Steindler married a hunter and became an avid hunter herself. One of the many things that stand out regarding Mrs. Steindler's creativity and diversity as a cook is her knowledge of game, what huntable game eat, and how to best prepare the cuts of meat. She keeps her ingredients to a minimum to celebrate the unique and delectable taste of each animal she prepares. *Game Cookbook* and *The Shooter's Bible Cookbook* remain the definitive books on wild game cooking.

This recipe can be made with any wild game. One of the greatest delights of coming in from the field at the end of the day after shooting doves or pigeons in Argentina or Bolivia was being greeted by a large dish of pâté made from the birds we had taken the day before and scooping the creamy paste on a brown rice tortilla cracker.

- 6 doves
- Fatty bacon, for wrapping birds
- Peppercorns, crushed
- 1 glass white wine
- 1 dry roll, 2–3 pieces of bread, or ½ cup seasoned breadcrumbs
- 4 eggs plus 1 yolk
- 1 pound mushrooms, finely sliced
- Butter and olive oil
- 1 clove garlic, minced
- 1 cup very finely minced chicken liver
  TO SERVE
- ½ cup plus 2 tablespoons port wine
- 2 teaspoons sugar
- A pinch ground allspice
- 1 package (about 1 teaspoon) unflavored gelatin
- Toast, crackers, or watercress sandwiches

Blot the birds with paper towels. Wrap the birds in fatty bacon, sprinkled with crushed peppercorns. Cook in a Dutch oven, either on the cooktop on very low heat or in a 275-degree oven until the birds are tender. Add white wine (I prefer sherry—cooking sherry will do—or you can use brandy or cognac) and give it an additional 10-minutes. Let the birds cool but not to the point of being so cold that you can't remove the meat easily from the bones. Be careful of small bones and shot pellets. (Many a tooth has been broken inadvertently chewing down on a pellet.)

The original recipe calls for a dried roll added to the pot to soak up the liquid. If you do not have a dry roll, trim the crust off 2 or 3 pieces of bread and toast, or use seasoned breadcrumbs, stirring until the "bread sauce" has formed. Put the meat, including the bacon, moistened bread, and every bit of liquid in a food processor and puree until very smooth.

Beat eggs, add to the meat mixture, and puree.

Sauté mushrooms in butter and olive oil, along with garlic, and add minced chicken liver. Set aside.

Generously butter a mold and fill with a quarter of the dove meat mixture, pressing it firmly into the mold. Add a thin layer of the mushroom, garlic, and liver layer. Repeat until you finish the mold with a layer of the dove meat mixture. Leave about an inch between the top of the pâté and the rim of the mold. Cover with a piece of buttered waxed paper, cut to fit the mold, then place a sheet of heavy aluminum foil on top of that, secured snugly with twine to the mold.

Set in a covered Dutch oven on the stovetop, filling the pot about half-way up the mold with water. Too much water will splash over the mold. Put the heat high enough to keep the water at a low, rumbling boil. Check fairly frequently and replenish the water as needed. Steam for an hour and a half. Let the pâté rest.

As an option, I love to finish the pâté with a topping of port wine jelly, which adds both flavor and texture. In a small saucepan, add 2 tablespoons of hot water to port wine. Dissolve 2 teaspoons of sugar, a pinch of allspice, and a package (about 1 teaspoon) of unflavored gelatin. Warm thoroughly until the gelatin is completely dissolved. Then, over the back of a large spoon, slowly drizzle the gelatin mixture over the pâté. This prevents the liquid mixture from forming a hole in the pâté, which is very soft. Cover completely with plastic wrap and aluminum foil and refrigerate overnight. Serve cold with toast, crackers, or watercress sandwiches. Some people like a little pot of marmalade on hand, or pepper jelly, to place first on the toast or cracker and then top with the pâté.

Roast Wild Duck

Duck, as with any game bird, gets tough with overcooking. The secret to good game cookery is to keep it moist, either by cooking it quickly but thoroughly, or adding fat to baste the meat, which is why so many recipes suggest wrapping the breast of the bird in bacon or fat of some kind, such as duck fat. The exception is goose, which tends to be an oily meat.

This recipe is adapted from the 1957 edition of *The Gourmet Cookbook*. My copy is well-thumbed, which goes to show how much I have used, and enjoyed, this marvelous two-volume set all these years.

- 3 wild ducks
- Gin
- 1 apple or crabapple, pared, cored, and diced
- 1 tablespoon butter
- 1 small whole onion, pierced with whole cloves
- 1 small stalk thickly diced celery, including the leaves, diced
- 2 sprigs parsley, stems removed and discarded
- 1 small shallot, diced
- Butter, softened
- Salt and coarsely ground black pepper, to taste
- Red wine or sherry, to baste
- 1 cup cognac
- ¼ cup plus 1 tablespoon wine or cognac, divided
- 1 tablespoon flour,

Pluck and remove the innards from ducks and wipe the meat with a cloth soaked liberally in gin.

Prepare a stuffing of apple or crabapple, butter, onion, celery, parsley, and shallot. Stuff the ducks, close the openings, and rub the birds with butter, then season with salt and pepper.

Roast the birds, basting with the butter and red wine or sherry until the meat is rare—15 or 20 minutes, depending upon the size of the duck. Set aside the birds in a baking dish closely together and pour cognac over them. Ignite the cognac and let the flame die down.

To the pan juices add ¼ cup wine or cognac, and 1 tablespoon already blended into tablespoon of flour. Stir thoroughly so the sauce is smooth. Carve the birds into portions and spoon the sauce. Serve with wild rice, Brussel sprouts, and poached apples.

Roast Young Goose with Potato Stuffing

- 10 medium potatoes
- 1 cup chopped onion
- ½ cup chopped celery
- ¼ pound salt pork, diced
- 4 slices dry bread, crumbled, or 1 cup breadcrumbs
- 2 eggs, beaten
- Salt and pepper
- Poultry seasoning
- 1 young goose
- Cranberry sauce, to serve

Preheat oven to 325°F.

Boil potatoes, and rice or process through the coarse blade of a food processor. Sauté onion and celery with salt pork until lightly browned. Stir the mixture into the potatoes, add crumbled dry bread or breadcrumbs, eggs, a dash of salt and pepper, and poultry seasoning.

Stuff the goose with the potato stuffing and bake for 20 to 25 minutes per pound. Make a gravy from the drippings and serve with cranberry sauce. Conversely, you can make a traditional chestnut stuffing or oyster stuffing, either of which would be delicious as well.

Pheasant Ragù à la Doc

Dr. David Sporcic, a dear friend of mine and my sons, was an avid hunter who prepared and served every game animal he ever harvested. At the end of hunting season, he would invite all of his friends to a game dinner, which he prepared entirely himself. There was elk, moose, caribou, venison, grouse, ducks, and, of course, pheasant. Foolishly, Dave—who my sons and I affectionately called "Doc"—went alone one day to hunt ducks off the coast of Maine. A storm kicked up and his boat capsized. Doc died too young—but just as he would have wished, hunting with his best hunting buddy, his beloved chocolate Lab, News.

- 4 pheasant breasts
- 4 tablespoons olive oil
- 1 stick (4 ounces) butter
- 1 tablespoon garlic, crushed, grated, or sliced
- ¼ pound pancetta, cubed
- 1 large can diced tomatoes
- 1 small can tomato paste
- ¼ cup burgundy wine
- 1 handful chopped basil
- 1 pound penne or rotini pasta
- Romano or Parmesan cheese, for serving
- Italian parsley, chopped

Bone pheasant breasts and cut into fork-sized pieces. In a large Dutch oven or deep-sided cast iron frying pan, warm olive oil and butter. Increase the heat till the oil and butter are bubbling slightly and add garlic. Gently turn cubed pancetta into the pan and add the pheasant until the meats are browned. Stir in diced tomatoes and tomato paste. Combine until mixed thoroughly and add burgundy wine, being careful to maintain a thick consistency and adding a little more wine if the consistency seems too thick. Add basil. Simmer about 20 minutes, adding a little more wine to maintain a nice, rich consistency.

Prepare pasta in boiling water with a little salt. When the pasta is cooked *al dente*, drain in a colander and plate in a large bowl or serving dish. Carefully top the pasta with the ragù, sprinkle a generous handful of Romano or Parmesan cheese, and top with some fresh, chopped Italian parsley. Manga!

Part IV

OUTDOOR LITERATURE

To fully engage in wing and clay shooting, a sportswoman must look beyond the target and aim to learn as much as she can. From the comfort of your own home, with your feet propped up and a cup of steaming tea in hand, you can embark upon a remarkable journey whenever you set out to discover the treasure that lies between two covers: books about shotguns—the makes, makers, models, mechanics, and technique; the games and the game birds, the history, legend, lure, and romance, humor and reminiscences. Men dominate this niche, it is true. And yet, read Mrs. Richard H. Tyacke, Kate Martelli, Nora Beatrice Gardner, Isabel Savory, Lady Florence Dixie, Marguerite Roby, Lady Catherine Minna Jenkins, Mrs. S. L. Baillie, Gabrielle Vassal, Ethel Younghusband, and Agnes Herbert, among many. They chronicled their experiences, which were just as wonderous, challenging, and dangerous as those of their male counterparts. So, read. Outdoor literature is addictive, like morning coffee. It's delicious, like fine wine. And it's blessed with the soul and spirit, wit and wisdom, of writers whose words live in print long after they die.

▲ Twombly English setters are a heritage line dating to Legh Higgins's grandfather. He and his wife, Jen, continue to breed this famous line of New England bird dogs.

12. Stories by Shooting Sportswomen

Authors and Stories: A Table of Contents

Mrs. Walter Lancelot Creyke ("Diane Chasseresse")

▲ Mrs. Walter Lancelot Creyke.

Mrs. Creyke wrote under the pseudonym "Diane Chasseresse" (Diana the Huntress) and hunted the Scottish moors with her father and brothers as a young woman, initially preferring the rifle. This is a chapter from her book, *Sporting Sketches* (published by Macmillan in 1890).

"The scene of the 'Sporting Sketches,'" reviewed the *Graphic* in its Saturday, October 18, 1890, number, "is laid in the Highlands. Diane Chasseresse is a sportswoman in the true sense of the term. She prefers to hunt her game, and not to have it driven for her, and can speak enthusiastically of a day's sport even when the wild game or salmon have proved more than a match for her. But as a rule, she was wonderfully successful, and the bag she made was nearly always a notable one. Stags, hinds, roebucks, does, hares, rabbits, grouse, partridge, woodcock, wild duck, teal, sparrow-hawks, and much else fell to her rifle or shotgun."

"On Dress" (1890)

So many articles have been written in ladies' newspapers about the best dress for the Highlands that I intend to devote a whole chapter to this most important subject.

I ought to be well qualified to offer suggestions on this point, for I am inclined to think that no one has been more *un*comfortably clothed for hard walking and wet weather than myself. Now, however, I think I have arrived at a costume that is as near perfection as possible.

The first thing to be studied in dress for the hills is *color*, so that the wearer may be as invisible as possible when moving, and quite invisible when lying still.

The most conspicuous colors on the moors are *white* and *black*; but a mixture of the two in a small check, called the shepherd's plaid, is not at all a bad color for stony ground. Brown and white are also good in a small check, and brown, and black and white. But better than all these is a warm gray, with a dash of pink in it when the heather is in bloom, or of orange, later in the season, when the grass and ferns have assumed their autumnal tints.

The best material both for a skirt and jacket is a waterproof stuff, that used to be made only by Messrs. Phillips of Shrewsbury. It is close in texture, though porous, and is made in all the heather mixtures. This stuff is quite impervious to the heaviest rain, and so long as there are no holes to let in the water, it will keep waterproof for many seasons. Any pressure, however, will let the wet in at once. For instance, you cannot carry a stick or fishing-rod across the shoulder in the rain without the wet penetrating, nor can you sit, or lean your elbow on the wet moss, without letting in the water. My stalking-dress was made of this material, and consisted of a semi-fitting jacket with sleeves coming below the wrists, and a pocket on either side. The skirt was made to button up the front, and had only sufficient fulness to allow plenty of freedom for running or jumping. It reached the tops of my boots. If a skirt made of this stuff were to be at all full, it would be very inconvenient as all the water runs off it down to the bottom, where it accumulates, making your ankles very wet and uncomfortable. This is especially unpleasant in frosty weather, as the frozen water makes a stiff band all round and cuts your skin through the stocking.

To avoid the discomfort of wearing a wet dress all day, even though the wet was only external, I used in very bad and stormy weather to have in addition one of Cording's light, but completely waterproof, mackintoshes. It was made in shepherd's plaid mixture, was almost down to the ground, and had long sleeves fastened round the wrists with elastic. It was so small and light when folded that the stalker could put it into his pocket, and it was impervious to air and water; in fact, you could sit on it in a bog without getting wet. Of course, for going uphill it was not so good as the stuff my dress was made of, in consequence of its being much hotter, as no air could penetrate it.

Belonging to this cloak, but not attached to it, was a mackintosh hood, the greatest possible comfort. It would fit any hat or cap, by being tied in at the neck by a piece of loose string or tape. It kept one's ears and cheeks warm and prevented the rain from running down one's back. On days when it was not bad enough to take a mackintosh, I always took this hood in my pocket, as it made a waterproof seat when required.

Underneath my waterproof jacket I wore a body cut like a Norfolk frock, in either a warm or thin material, according to the weather, with pockets on each side. This was also made in an invisible color, so that I could wear it without a jacket when I was going uphill. The petticoat under the waterproof dress should be short and light, not coming below the knees, which should

have as much freedom as possible. Any weight of petticoats dragging from the waist is most tiring, and quite useless, as warm, close undergarments can always be worn in cold weather.

Stays are useful for warmth and support, but the lace should be left unfastened at the back to give free play to the lungs when taking very violent exercise.

Boots should be of thick leather, and laced up the front, with plenty of large nails in the soles. The heels must be made broad and flat, but a little higher than the soles so as to catch in the ground and prevent falling when running down a slippery hill-side.

Boots should also be a support to the ankles, but at the same time wide enough round the top to give freedom to the muscles of the leg, otherwise it is not possible to move with ease.

With regard to the fit of the boot, the greatest care should be taken that it is not too tight just above the heel, as the skin there gets easily cut through, and if once it is broken, it may be weeks before you are able to put on a boot again.

When we had to start for a long expedition, the first day of the season in new boots, we used to walk into a burn and get them well soaked; this softened the leather and made it take the shape of the foot. Usually the hills are so wet that it is not necessary to go into a burn to attain this object. There is another great advantage to having wet feet, you never feel the same amount of fatigue at the end of a long day as you would if our feet were hot, dry, and blistered. It is a good plan to sap the inside of the foot of the stocking before starting on a hard day's walking. Stockings should be thick and warm, of any color that does not come off with the wet and they should come well up over the knees, which require to be kept as dry as possible, as they have very hard work to perform, and are very likely to get sprained and rheumatic.

When the knees begin to fail, it will be found useful to carry a pair of silk elastic kneecaps, just tight enough to keep up of themselves. These should be put on when descending a steep hill, but they ought to be taken off on level ground, as they soon cut the skin underneath the knee.

A long stick is also of great assistance when the knees begin to fail, but for the young and strong it is only an incumbrance.

A deer-stalker's hat is preferable to a close cap (though the latter keeps the ears warm), as the round upturned brim keeps the water from running down the face and neck, and also gives a certain amount of shade from the sun.

In cold weather the nicest gloves are those used for hunting—knitted woolen gloves with thick leather inside. There is usually so much crawling on the wet ground to be done, that it is a great comfort to have a pair of dry woolen gloves kept in reserve, to put on after the sport is over. The greatest care should be taken in attempting to pull a trigger with a thick glove on, but it is sometimes almost impossible to endure the cold without it.

—From *Sporting Sketches*, by Diane Chasseresse (Mrs. Walter Creyke). Macmillan and Co., London, 1890. Republished in 2016 by Wentworth Press.

Mrs. Richard Humphrey Tyacke

MY TROPHIES.

▲ Mrs. Richard Humphrey Tyacke.

How I Shot My Bears: Or Two Years' Tent Life in Kullu and Lahoul (Sampson Low Marston & Co., London, 1893) was written by a petite woman who accompanied sporting writer Richard Humphrey Tyacke (who may or may not have been her lawful husband) and killed fourteen bears, eleven deer, and more than five hundred birds her first season hunting alone, hunting in the Kullu Valley in the lush, verdant Himachal Pradesh district of India.

"Mrs. Tyacke is clearly not of the opinion of the Yankee," the *Westminster Gazette* commented in its January 23, 1894, edition, "who, when invited to join in a grisly bear hunt, replied, 'Wal, I a'n't lost no grislies.' On the contrary, she is keen in looking after such creatures of the kind as Kullu and Lahoul afford; not so large and fierce, it is true, as the North American grisly, but quite good enough to give fine sport. Kullu and Lahoul, it may be explained, are in the eastern corner of the Punjab, near the borders of Kashmire and Chinese Tibet, and afford, it seems, fair sport to the hunter."

It is, of course, her bird-hunting adventures that interest us particularly in this book—as in this chapter from *How I Shot My Bears…*

Snipe and Ducks in Kullu (1893)

The variety of game in Kullu—Our bag for one year—Small game scarce—The reasons why—Kullu's reputation as a woodcock ground—Why the cock diminish—How they could be preserved—Few snipe or duck—A suggestion for the Kullu duck-shooters.

As may well be imagined in a country of altitudes varying from two thousand to twenty-two thousand feet above the sea, and uninhabited above nine thousand feet, there is plenty of room for sport. The game to be found in Kullu is as follows: panther, bear (both red and black), ibex, serow, burrhel, barking deer, gooral, ounce or snow-leopard, corial and musk-deer; of pheasants, the cheer, kalij, koklas, argus, manal; of partridge, the black, wood and chikor; also, duck, snipe, and woodcock.

Our bag for one year was as follows: pheasants, 137; chikor, 321; cock, 49; snipe, 9; duck, 3; barking deer, 7; goral, 3; black bears, 6; red bears, 8; and musk-deer, 3; and this might have been considerably increased, had we cared to go in for slaughter.

With regard to some of the head, it is not more than would be shot in good coverts at home in one day. But consider the joy of shooting in these lovely mountains, in a perfect climate, where, for sporting purposes, the whole place belongs to you; where you take out no license, pay no keepers; where the birds are *bona fide* wild ones, and take a lot of shooting; where you generally carry a rifle in addition to a gun, and run the chances of knocking over a bear or a panther, as well as a pheasant. All this can only be really understood and appreciated by those who have tried it.

Much is heard of the scarcity of small game in Kullu at the present time, compared to what it was a few years back, and often the European residents said to us, after we had had a good day, half in jest, and half in earnest: "Why, you'll leave us nothing to shoot!" A moment's consideration, however, will convince anyone, that legitimate shooting, at birds fairly on the wing, and during the season only, would tend rather to improve than to deteriorate the stock, especially in the case of *chikor*, the cock of which, when the coverts are too near together and the birds too thick, fight incessantly and *à outrance*.

But it is not difficult to account for the scarcity of game, when one takes into account the manifold enemies the poor birds have to contend with. In the first place, throughout the valley there are literally thousands of *zemidars* (small farmers) to whom are granted licenses to carry a gun, nominally for the protection of their own crops from bears and birds, and their flocks from bears and panthers; but, actually, for the destruction of small game. Every evening hundreds of pheasants are potted in the trees, and scores of *chikor* are slaughtered as they sit huddled together on a rock in the cold mornings. Immense quantities are destroyed in nets, caught in traps, or shot, as they are feeding along a narrow line of corn carefully laid down in a likely spot, and watched by a concealed sportsman. Then, during the breeding season, numbers of eggs are taken either to be eaten or to be wantonly destroyed. The birds are captured, especially *chikor*, and sold in different bazaars, where they are purchased for fighting purposes, to amuse fat and lazy natives, who delight in watching the poor creatures maim each other, though they would rather give up their dearest relative than fight themselves. Besides this, I regret to say, that there are some European residents in the valley, who either provide the natives with powder and shot to go and shoot for them, or else buy the birds when shot. In addition to all this, there are the birds' natural enemies, which abound—the fox, jackal, stoat, weasel, hawk, and kite. With such a host to contend against, is it surprising that the game of Kullu is diminishing? But, for all those evils, except the last named, which presents difficulties, there are remedies to be found. In the first place, licenses should be granted with a more sparing hand. They are neither required, nor are they used for the ostensible purpose for which they are taken out. The price also of the license, now only fourpence

halfpenny, might be raised. With regard to the employment of natives by residents to shoot for them, the remedy is in the hands of the latter. Finally, practical measures might be taken to suppress poaching in a country more poached, I believe, than any other in India.

Kullu is one of the very few places in India having a reputation for woodcock shooting. But during our first year in Kullu, D., shooting over every likely place, and bagging every bird he saw, only shot forty-nine. This was considered a good bag. But in Albania he had shot many more in one day! In years gone by in Kullu, ten or twelve couple a day was considered a good bag. That would now be thought a fair bag for the whole season. The birds have been getting less and less, and the residents, taking it for granted that the woodcock were birds of passage, have accounted for it by the difference in the severity of the different winters. If they find few birds, they argue that they have not been driven down by the snow. D., however, is strong on a theory to account for the diminution of the cock. Every likely place is walked over almost daily, and every sahib tries to get woodcock, with the result that ninety per cent of the birds which come down the valley are shot. Thus, each year there are fewer left to breed from, and if some of the stringent measures are not taken, Kullu will soon know them no more. Now, as an object for sport, a woodcock can hold his own against any game-bird; for among trees he is a most difficult bird to shoot, and as a table delicacy he is unrivalled. In very few places in India are they to be found at all; and it would be a thousand pities if, in any one of these places, he were to become extinct. In Kullu it would be an easy matter to save them. As they are not exactly the kind of bird to give many chances for a pot shot, and as powder and shot are too expensive articles to be wasted on the risk of shooting a bird on the wing, the cock enjoy immunity at the hands of the natives. Kullu is too far distant from a railway to suffer from an influx of winter sportsmen, and therefore, there remains only, practically, the very few European residents, including the assistant-commissioner, forest officer, etc., to account for the cock. Should these few agree among themselves for a close period, I am convinced that Kullu would, in time, regain its old prestige as a ground for cock, and that the residents would be amply rewarded.

As regards snipe, I may mention that there are none in Kullu, except the solitary snipe. A good bag of these is twenty during the season. Duck are occasionally to be got as they pass up and down the river, to and from India and the Central Asian lakes, where they breed. The river, as it passes through Kullu, is too rapid to permit of their resting, which accounts for their being so seldom shot; but a Mr. D——, one of the residents, has now constructed a couple of ponds close to the river, and between it and his house, and the ducks settle in large quantities, and he is able to keep himself and his friends supplied during the season. If other ponds were made, above and below, there would doubtless soon be good duck shooting in the country. The land in the immediate vicinity of the river is all waste land, so that it is merely a case of flooding. I commend the suggestion to those who live in Kullu.

The sad fate of our dogs

Though there are plenty of pheasants without going more than a couple of miles from the house, we were greatly hampered by a lack of dogs. These are an absolute necessity for getting the pheasant out of the dense jungle.

Now, we had brought two dogs out from England, and two others had been lent us. The lamentable tale of their tragic ends would curdle the blood of "doggie" people at home. Before Christmas Day, ere we had been even a month in the country, two had been killed by panthers. Before we had been two months in the country, a third met with the same horrible fate, and the fourth, a spaniel, "Nell," had a very narrow escape.

Kullu abounds in these spotted beasts—I am almost afraid to give them a name, for the grand old controversy among sportsmen as to the difference between a panther and a leopard will probably last till the gentlemen in question change their spots. Some hold that the difference is in the claws, those of the panther being retractile, like a cat's, and those of the leopards resembling a dog's, or *vice versa*. Others assert that Mr. Spots of the plains is the panther, and him of the hills is the leopard. D. says there's no difference at all! Anyhow, whatever they were, they goaded us to desperation with their depredations on our four-footed allies. Not only to sportsmen, but to the sheep-owners in a pastoral district like Kullu, are they an absolute pest. They offer no fair sport, as it is almost impossible to circumvent them. Whenever opportunity occurs, they attack dogs, and the poor farmers suffer heavy losses all the year round by their constant depredations on their flocks and herds. They are insatiable, and if they get a chance will kill a dozen sheep at a time. We knew of one panther which got into an outhouse where one resident kept his dogs and destroyed the whole pack of five in one night! Bold beyond description, their valor somehow is only apparent when one happens to meet them unarmed. Finally, we got into the way, when carrying only guns[1], of always having with us a couple of cartridges loaded with ball, but they never gave us a chance.

Poor Nell's adventure was as follows: —We were returning from shooting and had sent on our rifles. D. was standing close to the edge of the jungle, lighting a cigar, when he heard a cry. He thought it must be a monkey, as there were some about. But a sudden fear seized me that it was Nell, and rushing up on to a boulder near, I looked about. No sooner had I reached the top, than my worst fears were realized, and I shouted down to Dick that a panther had got Nell, and rushed off in the direction the beast had taken. From below D. could see nothing, but fired, knowing that that is the safest thing to do, as it frightens the animal and often makes him drop his prey. The shot had the desired effect. The panther dropped the dog and sneaked off up the hill, where we could see him plainly; and as there was still plenty of daylight, had we only had our rifles, Spots would certainly have run a good risk of making us a present of his skin. Meanwhile, poor Nell rolled down hill, and brought up in a thorn-bush, after a clear drop of twenty feet. When we reached her, she was more dead than alive, probably from fright; but she had a nasty gash in her throat, the place where the panther always seizes his prey. We got her home, and eventually cured her, which was lucky, as the bite of one of these beasts is poisonous to a degree, owing to the carrion on which they subsist when pressed by hunger. Their claws are

---

1 "Guns," in England, often refer to shotguns, whereas here, in the United States, "guns" is generic to all classes of firearms.

equally venomous, and a scratch from them not unfrequently causes blood-poisoning.

—From *How I Shot My Bears—Or, Two Years' Tent Life in Kullu and Lahoul* Published in 1893 by S. Low, Marston & Company, Limited.

Lady Violet Greville

▲ Lady Violet Greville.

Violet, Lady Greville (1842–1932), daughter of the Duke of Montrose and his wife, Caroline, was a popular novelist and social critic whose column, "Place aux Dames," published in the *Graphic*, a weekly London newspaper, gained her national notoriety for her forthright opinion on British society. The first woman widely recognized as an expert in breeding racehorses, she championed shooting sportswomen, writing numerous columns and at least two books on the subject.

"This is the season of shooting parties," she wrote in the Saturday, October 26, 1895, edition of the *Graphic*.

All the great houses are holding high revel among the pheasants, while the number of victims is eagerly and carefully assessed. The question of ladies shooting has begun to be much discussed. A few ladies, like Lady Tweedmouth, are good rifle shots, but it is only of late years that any of them have handled the (shot)gun. It would certainly seem that either at a hot corner beside the wood, with rocketing pheasants flying over their heads, or on the heath where the rabbits scud in and out, making a quick shot uncommonly difficult, the ladies are out of place; nevertheless, there are women who love shooting as much as men, whose aim is certain, whose hand is steady, and whose eye is keen. To such the skill and excitement of sport appeals irresistibly, and there seems no reason why they should not share in their husbands' and brothers' amusements if the latter do not object. Most men, however, dislike seeing a lady shoot and, at any rate, only a small minority would care for the amusement, the love of killing being a purely masculine attribute. At any rate, the sport lends itself to picturesque shooting costumes and a piquant novelty in clothes such as those worn by the ex-Empress Eugenie in the battue days at Compiegne.

Lady Violet did not suffer fools lightly—much like the fictitious Lady Violet of *Downton Abbey* fame. She, too, was suspicious of wealthy young American brides whose dowries secured them a titled English husband. "This," the real Lady Violet wrote in 1909, "has introduced a new element into the simplicity and dignity of old-fashioned households. The rich American has no traditions; no prejudices in favor of old customs, duties, or responsibilities; she is essentially irresponsible, and measures everything by one standard only—money. The result permeating through all classes has considerably increased luxury and made for independence. It has, far more than any suffragette movement, given liberty to women to do as they like; for the American regards her husband as an inferior being, made to work for her, and to lavish pleasures and gifts as a reward for her beauty and sprightliness." And yet, nine months later, Lady Violet—willingly or otherwise—welcomed her new daughter-in-law, American heiress Olive (née Grace) Kerr, formerly Mrs. Henry Kerr of New York, who had married her son, Charles.

In the announcement published on November 19, 1909, in the *Coventry Herald*, Lady Violet was described as "a prominent figure in literary circles. She is a sister of the present Duke of Montrose, and married Lord Greville nearly six-and-forty years ago. Lady Greville, or, as she is better known to the reading public, Lady Violet Greville, is one of the pioneer women journalists, and besides contributing to various newspapers and magazines she is the author of several plays and novels. Lady Greville is tall and slender, and possesses that potent charm, a musical voice. Her manner is cheery, and she is, or was, a keen cyclist, and at one time used to ride through the traffic of London. Lord Greville, who is the second Baron, was once Liberal M.P. for Westmeath, private secretary to Mr. Gladstone, Groom-in-Waiting to Queen Victoria, and one of the Lords of the Treasury."

Of men she was quoted in the *Bath Chronicle and Weekly Gazette* on 5 November 1903, "Women are different from men. When a woman claims equality with men she loses her right to his protection. Tears are a woman's best weapon. Few men can resist them."

Preface to *Ladies in the Field* (1894)

It is scarcely necessary nowadays to offer an apology for sport, with its entrancing excitement, its infinite variety of joys and interests. Women cheerfully share with men, hardships, toil and endurance, climb mountains, sail on the seas, face wind and rain and the chill gusts of winter, as unconcernedly as they once followed their quiet occupations by their firesides. The feverish life of cities too, with its enervating pleasures, is forgotten and neglected for the witchery of legitimate sport, which need not be slaughter or cruelty. Women who prefer exercise and liberty, who revel in the cool sea breeze, and love to feel the fresh mountain air fanning their cheeks, who are afraid neither of a little fatigue nor of a little exertion, are the better, the truer, and the healthier, and can yet remain essentially feminine in their thoughts and manners. They may even by their presence refine the coarser ways of men and contribute to the gradual disuse of bad language in the hunting field, and to the adoption of a habit of courtesy and kindness. The duties of the wife of the M. F. H. fully bear out this view.

When women prove bright and cheerful companions, they add to the man's enjoyment and to the enlarging of their own practical interests. When, in addition, they endeavor to love Nature in her serenest and grandest moods, to snatch from her mighty bosom some secrets of her being, to study sympathetically the habits of birds, beasts and flowers, and to practice patience, skill, ingenuity and self-reliance, they have learnt valuable lessons of life.

Lastly, in the words of a true lover of art: "The sportsman who walked through the turnip fields, thinking of nothing but his dog and his gun, has been drinking in the love of beauty at every pore of his invigorated frame, as, from each new tint of autumn, from every misty September morning, from each variety of fleeting cloud, each flash of light from distant spire or stream, the unnoticed influence stole over him like a breeze, bringing health from pleasant places, and made him capable of clearer thoughts and happier emotions."

Ladies in the Field: Sketches in Sport, published by D. Appleton and Company, New York, 1894.

Lady Boynton (1854–1941)

▲ Lady Boynton.

Mildred Augusta Paget, the Lady Boynton, daughter of the Rev. T. B. Paget, Vicar of Welton and Canon of York, was married in 1876 to Sir Henry Somerville Boynton (1844–1899), 11th baronet, of Burton Agnes Hall, a celebrated naturalist and sportsman. They had one child, a daughter, Cycely Mabel (1877–1947), who married seven months after her father's death to Thomas Lamplugh Wickham. He assumed his wife's surname in order to retain the baronetcy through the family line, changing the family name to Wickham-Boynton. They had two sons: the eldest, Major Henry Fairfax Wickham-Boynton, died in World War II in active service, in 1942, a year after his mother's death. His younger brother, Marcus, inherited the estate and the title, and Burton Agnes Hall continued to pass through the female line. The family continues to live at this gracious estate, which is opened to the public six months of the year.

▲ Burton Agnes Hall.

Burton Agnes Hall

Sir Henry and Lady Boynton were married twenty-three years when, at age fifty-four, he died, leaving her a widow for forty-two years until her own death in 1941. During that time, she lived through the First World War and the early days of the Second, struggling—and succeeding—to maintain the enormous seventeenth century estate (which took a decade to build) and the hundreds of acres upon which it sat. Clearly, she found joy in field sports:

"Her ladyship is fond of all out-door sport and amusements, but is especially devoted to hunting, and is well known with the Holderness and Lord Middleton's packs. She is a fine horsewoman, possessing good hands, seat, nerve, and judgment, and has the knack of making most horses do what she wishes at once. Having a quick eye to hounds, her ladyship generally contrives to secure the first essential to enjoying a gallop, a good start. Lady Boynton is also a very good shot both with gun and rifle and has killed nearly all kinds of British game. Barton Agnes Hall, the seat of Sir Henry and Lady Boynton, is a very fine specimen of Elizabethan architecture, dating from the year 1600, built of red brick, with stone mullions, and stands on a slight eminence overlooking the vale of Holderness. The house is noted for the quantity of fine oak carving it contains." [*Yorkshire Gazette*, Saturday, March 30, 1889, as published in *The Country Gentleman*]

Knowing something of this fine and courageous noble-woman brings life and color to her contemplations on—

"The Shooting-Lady" (1894)

> "The reason firm, the temperate will,
> Endurance, foresight, strength, and skill."
> —WILLIAM WORDSWORTH

A few years ago, a "shooting-lady" was almost as much a *rara avis* as the Great Auk; if here and there one member of the sex, more venturesome than her fellows, were bold enough to take to the gun in preference to the knitting needle, she was looked upon as most eccentric and fast, and underwent much adverse criticism. Now, however, *nous avons changé tout cela*. Ladies who shoot, and who shoot well, too, are springing up on all sides, and the clamor raised by their appearances is gradually subsiding. There are still dissentient voices here and there, it is true, voices which proclaim aloud that women have no place in the covert and among the turnips, and that the cruelty of the sport should be an insuperable objection to their joining it. A discussion of all these pros and cons is, however, outside the scope of these notes, we have simply to deal with facts as they stand, and, undoubtedly, the "shooting-lady" is now as much an established fact as is her sister the "hunting-woman."

That a woman who is fond of sport need lose nothing in grace, charm, or refinement, we have ample evidence to show. She does not necessarily become masculine either in manner or conversation; but she should, nevertheless, endeavor to master the rudiments of whatever sport she engages in; and it is with the hope of assisting some of my fellow-sportswomen to accomplish this, that I here record some of my experiences, not omitting my mistakes, and adding a few hints to beginners; though I regret that I have no moving accidents by flood or field, nor "hairbreadth 'scapes" to recount!

There is certainly a pleasant amount of excitement about shooting—not perhaps equal to that afforded by "forty minutes without a check," but quite enough to make one willing to brave the elements, even on a raw November morning, and to stand with one's fingers aching with cold behind a fence waiting for the advent of that little brown bird who will flash past you like a meteor—alas! Too frequently only to leave a feather or two floating behind him, and then to continue his course rejoicing!

It is of the *first* and greatest importance on beginning to shoot to learn to be careful, and the golden rule is *always* to handle a gun as though it were loaded and cocked; the habit, once acquired, it is just as easy to carry a gun safely as not.

Coolness and confidence are equally necessary— but practice alone will bring these. A beginner is apt to be flurried when the game gets up; she sees nothing else, thinks of nothing else but killing it, and take no account of the beaters, guns, or dogs surrounding her. She points the gun at the bird or beast, and perchance (horrid thought!) follows it around the compass with her finger on the trigger! Wherefore it is better she should not take the field with other guns (unless she wishes to make enemies of her best friends), until she has full command over the gun and can put it up easily and quickly. If the game gets up too near, she must wait till it has reached the proper distance, *then* raise the gun to her shoulder and fire at once. This is the only way to become a quick and steady shot.

Apropos of following, once when grouse-driving I was placed in a butt between two other guns, both of them strangers to me. They looked *very much* askance at me, and I fancy one of them thanked his stars he'd insured his life the week before! The one in the left-hand butt at once moved both his "guards" on the side of the butt next to me. Soon three birds, the forerunners of an army to follow, came over between my right-hand neighbor and me, two of them making straight for his butt. To my surprise he did not fire. The third bird I hit with my first barrel and seeing as it passed me that it had a leg down, I turned round and killed it going away from me with the left barrel. After the drive was over, I asked him why he hadn't shot. "To tell you the truth," he said, "I was watching you. I was a little anxious to see if you would *follow* that bird, but after, I saw you were *all right!*" My left-hand warrior confessed, later on, that he had been peppered by the gun on the other side of him! Whereat I chuckled!

As to the gun used, everybody must please themselves. I shoot a 20-bore, the left barrel slightly choked, weight 5 lbs., and loaded with 2¼ drachms black powder, ¾-ounce No 6 shot. For covert shooting, E. C. or Schulze[2] is better, it is quicker up to the game and almost smokeless.

A 16-bore makes killing easier, but the extra weight, at the end of a long day, counterbalances this advantage. I shot with a 28-bore belonging to a friend one day last winter, and was perfectly astonished at the way and the distance it killed, but you have to be *very* dead on to make good practice with so small a bore. A gun to fit you should come up to the shoulder quite easily, and, without any adjusting, and you must bring the line of sight straight on to the object. If you see all down the barrel, the stock is too straight; if, on the contrary, you see nothing but the breech, it is too much bent and you will shoot under everything. But I would advise the beginner to go to the "Worth" of London gunmakers (Mr. Purdey), put herself in his hands, and, like the sartorial genius of Paris, he will turn her out fitted to perfection. An India rubber heel-plate[3] is sometimes a wise precaution, to avoid a bruised shoulder and arm, which if you happen to be going to a ball, does not perhaps add to your beauty!

The left hand should be held *well forward*. This gives much more power over the gun; it also looks much better. With regard to the position of the feet, it is well to recollect that elegance *is* compatible with ease!

It is a matter of some difficulty, at first, to judge distance correctly. The novice generally begins by blowing her game to bits, to make sure of killing it, I suppose, though in reality this makes it far harder. The other extreme, firing very long shots, is equally reprehensible, as nine times out of ten the game goes away wounded, even when occasionally it is dropped by a fluke. Any distance between twenty and forty yards is legitimate, though the latter is rather far for a target going away from you.

Never hand the gun cocked to an attendant, and always unload when getting over a fence, and on putting the gun down for luncheon.

---

2   E.C., Schulze, and DuPont Bulk were smokeless powders for shotgun cartridges that were in general use in the 1890s and measured by weight in grams.

3   Hard rubber buttplate.

Now for a few words on aiming; but I must here protest that this does not profess to be a shooting "Bradshaw[4]," but merely, as it were, an A B C guide![5]

For a beginner, no doubt the easiest way, in the case of any ordinary crossing shot, is to put up the gun on the object, then fling it forward as far in front as is thought fit, and fire, but, after a time, I think this kind of double action will no longer be found necessary. The gun will be put up *at once* in front of the game, the eye taking in by instinct and practice the line of the object, and experience telling how far in front of the game to hold the gun. This is certainly true with regard to ground game. Quite high-class aiming is to put the gun up a little before the head of the object, and swing the gun forward with the bird, pulling the trigger *without stopping the gun*. This is beyond doubt the best and most correct method, but not easy to accomplish.

I take it for granted that you shoot with both eyes open.

It is impossible to lay down a rule how far in front to hold the gun for a crossing shot. It depends upon the pace the bird is going, and its distance from you, but roughly speaking, for an ordinary shot at twenty-five yards, the object's own length in front *may* be enough (but I write this with some diffidence). For a driven bird or high pheasant, my experience is, you can't get too far ahead! For a rabbit or hare going away from you aim at the back of his head, coming towards you, at its chest.

One of the greatest charms of shooting is its "infinite variety." Let us take for example, to begin with, a day's covert shooting:

There has been a sharp frost, the cobwebs are all glistening in the sun; the leaves are mostly off the trees, but here and there some few remaining ones shiver gently to the ground: it is music to the ears of the shooting-woman; the bracken is brown and withered, and rustles crisply as the deer brush through it, startled at the sight of you approaching. The wind is keen and biting, but you turn up your collar and defy "rude Boreas."[6]

Arrived at the starting point, you make your way to the first cover. You form a line, a beater or two between each gun across the pasture. Before you have gone ten yards, a rabbit jumps up from underneath a beater's foot, and makes tracks for the nearest hedgerow or plantation, only, however, to fall a victim to the right-hand gun. The report alarms another who, without delay, seeks to follow in the steps of his predecessor, but a charge of No. 5 interferes with his scheme, and he also succumbs to fate.

Soon the fun becomes "fast and furious," four or five partridges at a time, necessitating quick loading and steady shooting. Here one breaks back through the line and comes past you full tilt. You take a rapid look round to see that no unlucky beater lurks in the rear picking up the wounded—bang—ah! You didn't allow for the oblique line of a partridge's course and were half a foot behind him. The second barrel, however, stretches him a corpse on the field of battle.

At the end of the pasture runs a narrow strip of plantation. Here the shooting is more difficult. The brambles are very thick; you have to take snap-shots; you must fire where you think the bird will *go* (not where he is), but even this maneuver is not always successful, as that old man who has been acting as stop at the end of the strip will tell you. "Nobbut eleven!" he says, "there's a bin forty shots fired! Ah conted 'em!" Conscience-stricken, you look at one another, and positively tremble before the scorn depicted in that old man's eye.

Then comes a small outlying covert. Two guns placed back to back command the end—the rest go with the beaters. A wood-pigeon is the first to make a move, which it does with a tremendous bustle and fuss; it affords a pretty shot, coming straight overhead, and falls with a "plop" behind you.

Meanwhile, four rabbits make good their escape. You fire a snap-shot at one as he bobs into the fence. "Mark over," and a pheasant whirrs over the top of the wood. You hastily cram a cartridge into your gun, raise it and pull, only to find that you've forgotten to cock the right barrel; you change on to the left trigger, but this has put you "off," the pheasant goes scatheless, and is handsomely knocked down by your

---

4 Bradshaw's Guides was a series of railway timetables and travel books first published in England in 1839.

5 A B C Rail Guides, first published in Great Britain in 1853, were alphabetically arranged railway timetables that were easier to use than Bradshaw's Guides.

6 Boreas is the god of the north wind, the god of winter, in Greek mythology.

companion-in-arms. Perhaps this is an argument in favor of a hammerless gun!

On reaching the big covert the aspect of things is changed. The guns are placed at intervals down the rides, and the beaters go to the far end to bring it up towards you. It is always well to let the guns on either side of you know your whereabouts, both for your own sake and theirs. Only let us hope you won't meet with the treatment that a friend of ours received. He was placed next to a very deaf old gentleman. Aware that he could not make him hear by calling, or (which is much preferable) by whistling, he took out his hand-kerchief and waved it to attract his attention. The old gentleman caught sight of it, put up his gun and took a steady and deliberate aim at it! You can easily imagine how our friend ducked and bobbed and threw himself prone on the grass round the corner!

After a pause a distant shot is heard, then another, and soon you hear the *tap tap* of the beaters and "Bird up," "Mark over," "Bird to the right," may be continually heard, unless, as in some places, silence is enjoined on the beaters. "Mark cock" is, however, everywhere an exception to this rule, and at the magic words, every gun is on the alert! I never understand why a woodcock should be productive of such wild excitement and reckless shooting as it generally is! The bird flits through the trees a little above the height of a man's head, looking as easy to kill as an owl, but it is a gay deceiver, for barrel after barrel may discharge its deadly contents at it, and still that brown bird flits on as before, turning up and down as it goes. Of course (on paper) *you* are the one to kill it, when you are loaded with congratulations—their very weight testify-ing how unexpected was that feat. Rather a doubtful compliment! Half the wood being shot, the guns move round to the outside. What has hitherto been done, has been chiefly a means to an end. The pheasants have been driven with the object of getting them into this particular corner. Possibly the wood stands on the slope of a hill; this gives the best shooting, as the birds fly over the valley, affording high and difficult shots, especially if coming down-wind. I think there is noth-ing prettier than to see real high birds well killed. They fall like stones, with heads doubled up—not waving down, wings and legs out-stretched.

"Thick and fast they come at last,
And more, and more, and more."

But do not let this tempt you into firing too quick. Pick your bird and kill it, though I grant you this is not an easy thing to do. Many men seem quite to lose their head at a hot corner. They fire almost at random, though, in the case of a few birds coming, they will scarcely miss a shot.

By this time, it is growing dusk. The December after-noon is closing in. There is a mist rising from the river, the air feels damp and chill, and our thoughts turn to a bright fire, a tea-gown, and those delicious two hours before dinner.

To my mind, grouse-shooting is the cream of sport. To begin with, Scotland itself has a charm which no other country possesses. Then it is such a nice clean walking! However much you may curtail your skirt, *mud* will stick to it, but on the heather, there is noth-ing to handicap you—you are almost on a level with MAN!

From the moment you leave the lodge on a shooting morning, your pleasure begins. The dogs and keepers have preceded you. A couple of gillies are waiting with the ponies. You mount, and wend your way over the hill road, ruminating as you go, on the possible bag, and tak-ing in, almost unconsciously, the bewitching feast that nature with such a bountiful hand has spread before you.

On either side a wide expanse of moorland, one mass of bloom, broken here and there by a burnt patch or some grey lichen-covered boulders. The ground gently slopes on the right towards a few scrubby alders or birches, with one or two rowan trees, the fringe of green bracken denoting the little burn[7] which to-day trickles placidly along, but in a spate becomes a roar-ing torrent of brown water[8] and white foam. Beyond is a wide stretch of purple heather, then a strip of yel-low and crimson bents, dotted with the white cotton-flower. The broken, undulating ground, with its little knolls and hollows, tells of nice covert for the grouse when the mid-day sun is high, and the birds are, as an old keeper used to say, "lying deid in the heather."

---

7 In Scotland, a burn means "a running stream," usually in the Highlands.

8 The brown water is colored from peat moss. I have stayed at old hotels around Inverness, Scotland, and run a bath to find, to my amazement, that the water is brown from peat moss.

Further away rise the hills in their stately grandeur, green, and olive, and grey, and purple; how the light changes on them! One behind the other they lie in massive splendor, and, more distant still, the faint blue outline of some giant overtops the rest, with here and there a rugged peak standing out against the sky. And, pervading all, that wonderful, exhilarating, intoxicating air!

Round a bend in the road, you come across three or four hill-sheep, standing in the shade of the overhanging bank. Startled, they lift their heads and gaze at you, then rush away, bounding over the stones and heather with an agility very unlike the "woolly waddle" of our fat Leicesters.

Anon, in the distance, you see Donald and the dogs on the look-out for you, the dogs clustered around the keeper, a most picturesque group.

When you reach them and dismount, a brace of setters is uncoupled and boisterously tear around, till peremptorily called to order. You take your guns, etc., the dogs are told to "hold up," and the sport begins.

In a few moments, Rake pulls up short and stands like a rock; Ruby backs him. You advance slowly, always, when possible, at the side of the dog standing, and pause for your companion to come up. Rake moves forward, a step at a time, his lip twitching and his eyes eager with excitement; another second and the birds get up. Seven of them. (Here let me give the beginner a hint. Take the birds nearest you and furthest from your companion, never shoot across him, don't change your bird, and don't fire too soon.) You re-load and walk up to where they rose, there will probably be a bird left. Up he gets, right under your feet. You let him go a proper distance, then neatly drop him in the heather.

This kind of thing is repeated again and again, varied by an odd "blue hare" or a twisting snipe. The dogs quarter their ground beautifully, it is a pleasure to see them work, for grouse are plentiful, the shooting good, and they are encouraged to do their best. Perhaps there may be a bit of swamp surrounded by rushes in which an occasional duck is to be found. The dogs are taken up, and the guns creep cautiously forward, taking care to keep out of sight till within shot. You then show yourselves simultaneously on the right and left, when the birds will generally spring. Remember to aim *above* a duck—because it is always rising.

Later on, in the season grouse get wilder, and the shooting consequently more amusing. The old cocks grow very wary, but sometimes, coming around the brow of a hill, you light suddenly on a grand old fellow, who, with a *Bak-a-bak-bak*, rises right up into the air, turns, and goes off downwind forty miles an hour. Catch him under the wing just on the turn—a lovely shot. If you miss him, he won't give you another chance that day!

By way of variety you are sometimes bidden to assist at a neighboring "drive" for black game.[9] A grey-hen[10] is not a difficult bird to kill. Heavy and slow, it flops along through the birch trees (though, when driven, and coming from some distance it acquires much greater speed), looking more like a barn-door fowl than a game bird; but the Sultan of the tribe is quite a different thing. Wild, wary, and watchful, he is ever on the *qui vive*. When you do get a shot at him, he is traveling by express, and having, most probably, been put up some distance off, he has considerable "way" on. You see his white feathers gleam in the sun, and the curl of his tail against the sky. Shoot well ahead of him. Ah! Great is the satisfaction of hearing the dull thud as he falls, and of seeing him bounce up with the force of the contact with mother-earth. Truly, an old black-cock is a grand bird! His glossy blue-black plumage, white under-wings and tail, and red eye make such a pleasing contrast.

I remember once, when grouse-driving towards the end of the day, the beaters brought up a small birch wood which stood near the last row of butts. There were two or three ladies with us. One of them, a most bewitching and lovely young woman, accompanied a gallant soldier into his butt, to mark his prowess. As luck would have it, nine old black-cock flew over the brave colonel's butt, but, strange to say, four went away without a shot, and not one of the nine remained as witnesses of his skill! Now, let me point out, had that said charming girl been *shooting*, she would have been stationed in a butt by herself, and, judging by that soldier's usual performance, at least five of those old

9 Black grouse, which is native to Scotland, and roe deer, a small deer that weighs between 22 and 77 lbs.
10 Female black grouse

black-cock would have bitten the dust that day! And "the moral of that is"—give a graceful girl a gun!

Two days later found me keen as mustard to scale the heights of Ben Hope[11] for ptarmigan. It was almost the only game bird, except capercaillie, I had never shot, and I was extremely anxious to seize an opportunity of doing so. Five guns set out. We rode a considerable distance, until the ground became too soft for ponies to travel. Arrived at the foot of the hill I gazed in dismay at its steep, stony height, and felt like the child in the allegory who turns back at its first difficulty! But pluck and ambition prevailed, and I struggled gamely up, though hot and breathless. I was forced to pause more than once ere we got even halfway. We had agreed that, on no account, were we to fire at anything but ptarmigan. When we had ascended about 1300 feet a covey of grouse got up. One of the sportsmen, nay, the very one who had been foremost in suggesting that ptarmigan only should be our prey, turned round, and feebly let fly both barrels, wounding one wretched bird which disappeared into the depths below, never to be seen again! As the report reverberated through the hill, the whole place above us seemed to be alive with the cackling of ptarmigan, and, in a moment, without any exaggeration at least twenty brace were on the wing at once, making their way round the shoulder, over the Green Corrie to the highest part of Ben Hope. I think the specter of that grouse must haunt that sportsman yet!

Of course, there were a few odd birds left, and, before we gained the top, we had each picked up one or two, though, through another contretemps, I missed my best chance. I had unwillingly, over a very steep and rock bit of ground, given up my gun to the keeper. The moment after I had done so, two ptarmigan got up to my left, offering a lovely cross shot, and, before I could seize the gun, they fell, a very pretty double shot, to our host on my right. When we reached the summit, we found ourselves enveloped in a thick fog, although down below it was a brilliant hot day; so dense was it, that, notwithstanding we were walking in line, some of us got separated, and it must have been almost an hour before we joined forces again. Altogether it was a hard day's work, but, having attained my object, I was sublimely indifferent to everything else.

Driving is certainly the form of shooting that requires the most skill, whether it be grouse or partridge, and is most fascinating when you can hit your birds! Grouse-driving appears to me the easier of the two; partly because they come straight, and partly because you can see them much further off, also they are rather bigger, though they may, perhaps, come the quicker of the two. Nothing but experience will show you how soon you can fire at a driven grouse coming towards you. Some people get on to their birds much quicker than others. I have heard it said that as soon as you can distinguish the plumage of the bird, he is within shot. Aim a little above if he is coming towards you—a long way ahead if he is crossing.

If you shoot with two guns, I assume that you have practiced giving and taking with a loader. Otherwise, there will be a fine clashing of barrels and possibly an unintentional explosion. The cap and jacket for driving must be of some neutral tint, any white showing is liable to turn the birds. Of course, you must be most careful never to fire a side shot within range of the next butt. A beginner is more apt to do this, from being naturally a slow shot at first.

The same rules hold good for partridge-driving, only there you usually stand behind a high hedge, consequently you cannot see the birds approaching. You hear "Ma-a-rk" in the distance, and the next moment—whish! They are over, scattering at the sight of you to right or left; take one as he comes over you, and you may get another going away from you—or a side shot, provided there is no gun lower down whom you run the risk of peppering.

Walking up partridges in turnips affords the same kind of shooting as grouse over dogs; not bad fun when they are plentiful, but hardish work for petticoats!

You will occasionally come across snipe in turnips. They are horrid little zig-zagging wretches! If you wait till their first gyrations are over, they do, for a second, fly straight (for them), and even a 20-bore can sometimes lay them low.

I once shot a quail. I mistook it for a "cheaper" minus a tail, and gazed placidly at its retreating form, murmuring to myself, "too small," when I was electrified by a hell—"Shoot, shoot!" Being trained to habits

---

11 The most northerly of the Munros in northern Scotland, it is extremely difficult climbing as it is short and extremely steep.

of obedience, I promptly did as I was told, and brought the "little flutterer" down. A quail in a turnip field! I should as soon have expected to meet one of the children of Israel.

One a winter afternoon, *faute-de-mieux*, shooting woodpigeons coming in to roost, is a pastime not to be despised, but it is very cold work. A windy evening is the best; luckily pigeons always fly in against the wind, so you can get on the leeside of the plantation and shoot them coming in, or you can ensconce yourself under the shelter of some fir-boughs near the trees in which they are accustomed to roost. A pigeon takes a lot of killing, he possesses so many feathers; then he has an eye like a hawk and can turn with incredible speed. If there are several guns in different woods you may easily get one hundred in an hour or two, and often many more.

With regard to dress—I believe, for those who can endure the feel, wearing all wool is a great safeguard against rheumatism, chills, and all evils of that ilk. But, on this subject, every woman will of course please herself. I will therefore merely give an outline of my own get-up. A short plain skirt of Harris tweed, with just enough width to allow of striding or jumping, a half tight-fitting jacket to match, with turn-up collar and strap like a cover-coat, pockets big enough to get the hands in and out easily, a flannel shirt and leather belt, or, for smarter occasions, a stiff shirt and waist-coat. Knickerbockers of thin dark tweed, high laced boots with nails, or brown leather gaiters and shoes. If a petticoat is worn, *silk* is the best material for walking in. I have neither mackintosh nor leather on my dress, I dislike the feel of both. For wet weather, a waterproof cape, with straps over the shoulders so that it can be thrown back, if required, in the act of shooting, is very convenient.

But there is only one essential in a shooting costume. It MUST be loose enough to give the arms *perfect freedom* in every direction—without this, it is impossible to shoot well or quickly.

One last hint. Never go on shooting when you are tired. It will only cause you disappointment, and other vexation of spirit, for you will assuredly shoot under everything. Bird after bird will go away wounded, time after time your mentor (or tormentor) will cry "low and behind, low and behind," until, in angry despair, you long to fling the empty cartridge at his head. Take my advice "give it up and go home!"

That the above notes may not be free from numerous sins of omission and commission, I am well aware. It would be great presumption on my part to suppose that my feeble pen could do what many men have failed to accomplish. But if any hints I have given prove of service to beginners and encourage them to persevere (even though at present, like the old woman's false teeth "they misses as often as they hits"), my pleasant task will not have been in vain.

—From *Ladies in the Field: Sketches of Sport*, edited by Violet, The Lady Greville Published in 1894 by D. Appleton and Company, New York

The Hon. Mrs. Lancelot Lowther
(Gwendoline Sophia Alice Sheffield Lowther)
(1869–1921)

The Hon. Mrs Lowther

▲ Lady Lancelot Lowther.

The Honorable Mrs. Lancelot Lowther was the first wife of an English peer, with whom she had two daughters and a son. She too was the daughter of a peer-of-the-realm, Sir Robert Sheffield, 5th Baronet.

"The Hon. Mrs. Lancelot Lowther at Asfordby Hall," the *Penrith Observer* wrote on 16 March 1897, is "the daughter of a hunting house, and the wife of one of the keenest sportsmen in the Shires. Mrs. Lowther shares to the full the tastes of the men of her family. Not only is she enthusiastic on the subject of hunting, but she is an excellent shot, and takes the greatest interest in the practice, and though she never joins large shooting parties, she always delights in a day after pheasants or partridges with her husband or brother about her old home in Lincolnshire."

On November 18, 1889, the *Yorkshire Gazette* reported, "While hunting with the Quorn Hounds, the Hon. Mrs. Lancelot Lowther met with an unfortunate accident. During the afternoon run she was severely thrown, and broke her arm. Mrs. Lowther was conveyed to her resident, Asfordby Hall, and medical assistance was summoned from Melton Mowbray.

She died in London in 1921 at the age of fifty-two, after a brief illness, predeceasing her husband by thirty-two years.

"Shooting" (1898)

In these few words on Shooting for Women, I must begin by saying that as this is my first attempt to writing, I hope any faults I may make will be lightly treated. It is only within the last few years that the idea of a woman being able to see a gun without screaming, much less fire one off, has even been thought of, but now I venture to say that there are many women who are just as good shots with both gun and rifle as men, and perhaps some better. I do not mean to infer that we can count amongst our number anyone who can take the place which Lord de Gray, Lord Walsingham, and a few others take amongst men, but as shooting becomes more popular, and is more practiced among women, I daresay we shall in years to come see some of the latter just as good even as those I have named.

I am afraid it will take some time for men to ever get over the terror which the sight of a woman with a loaded gun in her hand always give them. The reason of this is that they think we are much too careless to be trusted with such a dangerous weapon, and that we think no more of carrying a loaded gun that if we had a walking-stick in our hands. The first thing, therefore, that a woman who takes up shooting has to remember is, that as an Irishman once said about a gun, "loaded or unloaded, she's dangerous." One cannot be too

careful in handling either a gun or rifle, always to have it at half cock when not actually shooting, and always to take out the cartridges when getting over or through a fence. Accidents happen quite easily enough without Providence being tempted by the neglect of these simple precautions.

A woman requires a light gun if she is to carry it all day. There are, of course, as everyone knows, a variety of different bores. I will mention the ones mostly used, which are the 20-, 16-, 14-[12], and 12-bores. The 20- and 16-bores are mostly made for women, but personally I prefer a 12-bore double-barreled hammerless gun. Of course, it must be made rather lighter than for a man. I have always myself used one of these that was specially made for me, weighing exactly 6 lbs., both barrels medium choke, and a thick India rubber pad[13] at the end of the stock to prevent all recoil. The cartridges I use are made with Schultze powder 35 grains, and seven-eighths of No. 6 shot. I have found this a perfect gun, and one I should always recommend. It is not too heavy, and is first-rate for shooting pheasants, partridges, pigeons, etc.

The great thing in ordering a gun is to have it very well balanced, a thing which is hard to describe but which is easily told apart, as no one who has tried the two can fail to appreciate the well-balanced gun as against the badly-balanced one. It chiefly consists in having the muzzle and stock of the gun to divide their weight, neither one nor the other being a half ounce too heavy. When choosing a gun, it is necessary to put it several times quickly to the shoulder at an object level with the eye, and if the sight taken comes fair on the mark aimed at, the gun will probably suit. Another thing to remember and guard against is having cartridges loaded too heavily for the gun, as it makes the gun "kick," and nothing puts you off shooting so much as expecting every time you fire to have your shoulder bruised. This is beside very dangerous for a woman. If, however, a gun fits you properly, and the charge of the cartridges is proportionate to the size of the gun, a "kick" should never happen.

You must also be particular to have the stock exactly the right length, so that it can be brought up quickly and easily to the shoulder. It must be held firmly

---

12 The 14-bore is long obsolete

13 Hard rubber pad

against the shoulder, with the left arm extended as straight as possible from the shoulder and the right hand behind the trigger guard.

More accidents happen by *following* game with the gun than by any other means. There are very strict rules of etiquette to be observed in shooting, as in hunting or any other sport, and nobody is more hated and feared than a jealous shot. These are indeed a source of danger to everyone, as they are always so anxious to add another bird to their score that they never give any thought to their neighbors or think of other people. For a person, whether a man or woman, who is beginning to shoot, the best thing is to go out with some experienced shot or keeper who will thoroughly explain the art of shooting, and show how to load and unload a gun and how to hold it. To quote from the excellent article on Shooting in the *Badminton Library*: "A beginner should at first start with a small charge of powder and be taught to fire this off at small birds, every attention being paid to his handling his gun with safety as if it were loaded. He may next shoot at small birds with a half-ounce of shot. If he succeed pretty well, and is above all things careful in the way he manages his gun, he can next be permitted to fire at pigeons—with their wings slightly clipped, so as not to fly too fast—from under a flowerpot or out of a trap, at a distance of fifteen yards."

You must remember that accuracy of aim will only come by practice. When you are fairly sure of yourself the next step is to go out to walk birds up, but you must get it carefully explained by an authority what birds you ought to fire at, and what are to be left alone, and on no account should you, if walking in line, fire across a neighbor's gun, or at birds that strictly belong to others from their having got up nearer to them than to you. It is always better to fire a yard too far ahead of flying birds or running game than too far in the rear. In the former case, the shot is more likely to meet the mark, in the latter it never can. In the former if it does count a hit it means one in a vital part, the head, in the latter at most it means a wound in the extremities. It is utterly impossible to measure distances in the air in front of a flying bird or running game; instinct, aided by practical experience, will alone teach the hand and eye to obey the brain in this respect, and to give the correct distance at which to aim in front.

I may say at once that I have a decided preference for the rifle as opposed to the gun, though I should be the last to minimize the pleasures of pheasant and partridge shooting. I am not one of those women who prefer the excitement of a regular "battue"[14] to the more sober joys of a quiet pot-hunt. To begin with, there is no doubt that a woman is a great bore at anything like an organized shooting party. It would do the intending lady-shot good to see the faces of the men on hearing that they are to have the honor of her company during the day. The smothered grumbles of the younger sportsmen are drowned in the more forcible ejaculations of the older generation. But apart from this, and I am not for one moment assuming that it is the duty of women to consider exclusively the whims of the sterner sex, there always seems to me to be some special enjoyment in sallying forth with the object of replenishing an exhausted larder, and with the certainty of having to work one's hardest to accomplish the task. Every shot then becomes of importance, and the comparative scarcity of the prey redoubles one's vigilance and activity. Should the wily partridge elude your aim on these occasions, you feel as if some tremendous disaster had occurred, and your spirits do not recover their normal condition until some special success has rewarded your efforts, and a long and difficult shot has added another victim to the bag. In shooting, as in so many other pursuits, it is quality not quantity that should be sought.

One of the most amusing day's shooting I ever remember was a hare drive in Austria. We left the house at one o'clock and drove about eight miles through a very flat country to the rendezvous, where we found a perfect army of beaters who were chatting volubly in an unknown tongue. I discovered later that they were talking Polish, which is the common language of the peasants in that part of Silesia adjoining the Austrian-Russian frontier. The men were mostly barefooted, but in other respects resembled the average English beater. The keepers were distinguished by their green livery and Austrian conical hats. They carried horns slung from their shoulders, and when a line had been formed some quarter of a mile in length, the signal was given by the head-keeper on his horn and was taken up by his subordinates. An excellent method was observed in allotting a certain number of beaters to the care of

---

14 Flat clay target that is thrown flat and as it starts to lose speed, turns over.

each keeper, who was then responsible for their maintaining a good line and preventing stragglers.

The ten guns were of course distributed at intervals along the line, and we started across level fields of potato and beet-root sugar roots which took the place of our turnips and were much easier to walk through. There were no fences, and the fields were divided by ditches and low banks. Game was plentiful, and although we only shot for about two-and-a-half hours, we succeeded in killing about two hundred hares and several partridges. The beater who carried my cartridges was greatly excited whenever I was fortunate enough to kill a hare and jabbered away in his native tongue. I have never heard anything approaching that language. It is a fearful and wonderful thing, and I wished I could have brought some of it way with me to use on special occasions in England. The only drawback was the weather. It rained cats and dogs, and while I was glad to note that England has not the monopoly of inclement weather, I must confess that the Austrians think no more of a wet jacket than we do. At five o'clock we gave up, and returned home wet to the skin, but none the less my husband and I have the pleasantest recollection of our first day's shooting in Austria.

Before closing this article, I must refer shortly to the subject of dress. The first thing to remember, is always to have a dress of some dark or neutral tinted material that will not be conspicuous on a moor or when birds are being driven, and which will also keep out the rain. A short skirt, breeches, thick boots, and either woolen stockings or gaiters, and a double-breasted loose coat are the most convenient as well as the most sportsman-like. But the coat must be loosely made, so as to allow one to bring the gun up to the shoulder quickly and easily.

—From *The Sportswoman's Library*, Vol. I Edited by Frances E. Slaughter Published in 1898 by Archibald Constable & So., 2, Whitehall Gardens, Westminster.

Hilda Murray of Elibank
(Baroness. Hilda Louisa Janey Woulf Murray)

Hilda Murray of Elibank's *Echoes of Sport* is a wonderful account by a sportswoman who was as proficient with a shotgun and flyrod as she was formidable as a horsewoman and fox hunter. A contributor to *Country Life* magazine, she wrote, "To stalk a stag, to hunt the

▲ Hilda Murray of Elibank.

fox, to shoot driven grouse, whirring partridge, and rocketing pheasant, to tempt a salmon to hook himself on to a glaring fly, or play a fat trout on a gossamer web, each of these things demands a different set of nerve and eye, skill, daring, or patience." Time cannot diminish the strength and power of her words and observations. This was a sportswoman in the truest sense of the word.

"In the passing of Lady Hilda Murray," Lady Elibank wrote of her lifelong friend in the Saturday, August 22, 1931, edition of the *Tamworth Herald*, "the Empire loses a charming and greatly beloved friend. There are thousands of our overseas men and women who were her devoted friends and admirers. Throughout the Great War her creation and brilliant administration of the Beyond Seas Officers' Association was of inestimable value to the world, bringing her into personal contact with, and wise sympathetic understanding of, large numbers of officers of our Dominion troops. It was not only her great powers of organization, but her enchanting sweetness and her crystal-clear mental vision that marked her out for work of high achievement."

"Days in the Stubbles" (1910)
I must own to a love of stalking, hunting, shooting, fishing, and low be it Spoken poaching in any form, for which my gentler sisters may blush for me, though I aver that the pursuit of such tastes has taught me some of the best lessons in life and some small store of natural lore. No one can pursue any Sport satisfactorily without developing an acute sense of observation and a familiarity with some of

Nature's big outposts, such as wind, sky, atmosphere, to say nothing of the myriad smaller details of color, shade, covert, lie of ground and country. But even love of Nature and her ways is not my keynote. What delightful hours these words recall and bring to the mind's vision!

Glorious afternoons in late September or early October, when the corn is partly carried, according to the late or early season; when some of the fields are complete stubble, others are still dotted with stooks[15]; perhaps on the high ground the reaping machines is still at work, cutting a last strip of standing corn; or if it be into October, the plough is snailing up and down the hillside, turning the golden ground to "brown and fruitful earth."

Our fears that the birds of which we have come in search, black game in particular, grouse and partridges thrown in, may be scared by the whirring machine or the plough, but little care they. Their supper to them is of first import, and familiarity breeds contempt; they pay little heed to the silent workers.

There is a certain valley which springs vividly to my eye at the word stubbles, where I would bid you share an afternoon's stoking and stubbling with me. It is at the entrance to a wild sea of moorland among the hills of Tweed; through it a road runs that leads over into the solitudes of Yarrow. A babbling burn scurries down it, curling and purling in haste to lose itself in the larger river, fringed here and there with birch and hoary alder, "the last that is left of the birken shaw."

The trees are still playing at summer this dazzling hot October day, and flaunt their shimmering green finery, though here and there the age of the year has touched them with his tell-tale brush. The heather on the hillside above gives them away, it has ceased to play at make-believe in St. Martin's summer; the royal coat is exchanged for one of ruddy brown, patched here and there with gold of bracken.

Our small party of four leave the roadside down by the burn and climb up the hill of fields. The younger brother of the kind Laird who gives me these treats is my host to-day; he is also my master of shotgun lore;

we two are the guns, and the head keeper and his son are the beaters. They are to post themselves as sentries at the corners of the two stubble fields, one to the southeast, the other to the north-west of the dyke that runs as a center line, dividing the two feeding grounds, up to the moor above us. When a sufficient number of birds collect in the fields, then the sentries will walk slowly across and drive them, as best they can, over us at our respective stands by the said dyke. Such is the plan.

There is a certain gate where four fields meet, two grass and the aforesaid stubbles, which my quondam[16] host declares to be the usual flight of the black game coming in and out to feed.

"I advise you to go there, but please yourself; I am going to stay here"; and he lazily makes his preparations to settle himself down, for hours maybe, to the north side of the wall, about fifty or sixty yards below the gate. Now he and I are on those most delightful terms, long past all the old milestones of politeness and conventional good manners, where the host proffers his best, which the guest accepts for fear of seeming ungrateful or unappreciative. We are on the better ground of true friendship, where one pleases the other best by doing what they each most wish. I know that "Maister Chairles," as the keeper calls him, having spread out his old coat to sit on, lit his pipe, and made his bristly Irish terrier squat beside him, will not take the gate stand were I at the North Pole, and so I too know I may please myself without seeming churlishly to refuse what he in his unselfish kindness chose to offer me as the best place.

He is a sportsman of many years' standing and experience, of infinite patience and powers of silent, immovable waiting, which I, the novice, can abundantly admire but cannot altogether emulate. He comes to the stubbles for only one object—blackcock[17]. I come for two, the call of the moor and as much game as I can get. The gate stand is too tame for my restless spirit, and it is only three o'clock. I explain all this.

---

15 sheaves.

16 sometime.

17 Blackcock, so called because of its distinctive black plumage, is also known as black grouse or blackgame (*Lyrurus tetrix*) is a large game bird and member of the grouse family and whose habitat is primarily moorland. The female, called the grey-hen, is greyish brown and, as is often the case in the avian world, plain in comparison to the colorful, handsome male of the species. The female sits on the nest, raises, and feeds her chicks entirely without the help of her husband, which is why only males are meant to be taken in sport shooting. The female simply is too valuable from the standpoint of propagation.

"Go where you please, and do what you like, and shoot what you can get—except grey-hen." The last command, in a sterner tone, is a standing order. I don't require the rules of the game; I only wish the grey-hen respected their side of it. Neither willingly nor wittingly do I ever shoot at the foolish creatures, but if they *will* come along with their black lords, or mix themselves up in covey of grouse[18] close over my head, right in the line of fire, is it my fault if now and then stray pellets hit the tiresome birds?

So, I leave him with his dog and his pipe and up I go with my black spaniel Glossy towards the moor. It is there where the stubble flanks it that the grouse come in for their supper earlier than the black game, who mostly come from the moor the east side of the burn; and we are on the west.

I am on the south side of the wall; the field below, which my host commands, has still some stooks in it, but the high field to the north is already being ploughed. In its far corner, Lol, the keeper's son, is doing sentry, and no bird ever escapes his wonderful, young, hawk-like eyes, and he and his little water-wagtail spaniel are likely to have a busy afternoon.

His father has gone to the corner of the south field, away below me, and in direct line with the other gun.

The day was so gorgeous and hot that the birds were loath to leave the moor, which gave me ample time to thoroughly enjoy my first quest. I stretched out in the sun and watched the lazy clouds; great white masses lumbering along as if they were too hot and idle to move at all. The hills to the north lost themselves in filmy blue, those to the south stood out in stronger relief, the road winding in and out, a shining thread, through their billowy green and brown. The air was full of quiet sound: far away the voices of children by the burnside at the farm, near at hand the clank of the plough, now and then the grouse's call as they prepare to leave the moor at last, hunger overcoming sentiment. Somewhere near by *cheep, cheep* is twittering in the grass with promise of a partridge for the bag. Away in the valley a heron flaps lazily along, blue-grey against the tawny backgrounds, and now and then pigeons wheel and croon in the trees below.

Other days flit through my memory during the waiting hour. The very sight and touch of my twenty-bore brings my dear old father before me, who gave it me when I was only fourteen. It was his teaching of sport lore that prepared the ground for so much of the pleasure and fun of later days, though the teacher has alas long since passed away. An ardent and keen sportsman himself, one of his chief interests was to give his children every opportunity of becoming the same. He taught me to ride, drive, fish, and shoot, all before I was twelve; and well do I remember my wild excitement and delight at shooting my first rabbit at thirty yards with a pea-rifle out of the drawing-room window.

Many is the time I have had pellets whizzing all round me, and leaves dropping on to me shot off just above my head when out with my father, as it must be confessed he did not add safety to his other shooting virtues; a dangerous shot is however, a very good school for the young idea, and some of our lucky escapes may have made my brothers and me more careful than we might otherwise have been. My father certainly never hurt any one seriously, though he peppered most of his friends and neighbors!

"Mr. Wolfe Murray wud shoot his gran'mither if she war risin' afore him" was the comment of a keeper at some neighbor's covert shoot when the order "no hen pheasants[19]" having been given my father promptly shot three consecutively. His keenness certainly exceeded his caution, but for all that he was a fine type of the old-fashioned sportsman, preferring to go in search of his quarry rather than have it brought to him, as the fashion of to-day has—alas!—become to such a great extent. Mounted on his Russian shooting pony Moscow, who paid no more attention to a shot fired from his back than to a tickling fly, he was a picturesque and handsome figure.

The small gun could tell of proud days also, when it has been honored by kind friends at being counted as a "gun," occasionally in a butt, or at covert-shoots.

---

18 Red grouse, which is also a moor bird, is a smaller cousin of the Blackcock, Capercaillie, and willow ptarmigan. See page 94 for the species of North American grouse.

19 Pheasants likewise are not native to Great Britain but were introduced by the Normans in the eleventh century, however they were largely forgotten, indeed, almost extinct, until the nineteenth century, when the population was revived for sport by gamekeepers on large estates.

If there is one bird that defeats me more often than another, it is the driven grouse. He is on to you faster than any other, and so noiselessly. Most people probably give the palm to the driven partridge for speed and difficulty, but the grouse is to me far the worst of the two. Yet some of the days I look back on and forward to with the greatest zest are those after grouse, whether walking or driven.

What fun too have I and my twenty-bore had with the pheasants, and mostly those belonging to the good Laird on whose land we are stoking to-day. Great rocketing cocks whose flight is miles above my prowess to attain, yet now and then comes one somewhere within range.

There is something so satisfactory about a pheasant, from his guttural *cock-cock* and the splutter of his wings as he rises to the heavy thud when he falls. He is a generous bird, and gives full notice of his approach; if he gets safely past it's all your own stupidity and lack of skill or quickness. He cannot be blamed as a sneak, as the singleton grouse or partridge may be, for whizzing by without any warning.

The sound of the pigeons in the trees by the burn brings back other scenes. An autumn evening high up on wooded hillside, when the setting sun lights up with gorgeous splendor the gold and russet and grey of massive beech trees, the velvet of stately firs, when the cushies[20] come for their supper and their roost. There are myriads of them, and their flight is that of rippling, quiet laughter, that is like nothing else. Listening to it one forgets or forbears to shoot, for fear of breaking the spell and scaring away that wonderful sense of sound as it sweeps to and fro, making the air throb to our listening ears, the music of wings overhead, with the low murmuring accompaniment of a mighty river far below at our feet.

Well would it be for these birds if they knew the magic of their sound, as in it lies their safety from me, for all that it recalls; but when pigeon comes gliding in noiselessly by ones and twos, it is a different affair; then my patience, that has kept me waiting an hour or two on a winter evening, either in keen, frosty air or in a driving sleet or rain-storm, demands its reward, and pigeon has to pay toll.

It is an absorbing occupation to wait and watch for any animal or bird; above all as to do it successfully the watcher must be unobserved by the watched. To come to the stubbles without a small Zeiss glass is to lose half the interest; part of the fun is to watch the birds through it. One learns much of their wonderful instincts and quaint ways, especially their unerring sense of danger at the slightest sound or sight of anything betokening the presence of approach of a foe, human or animal. A blackcock and a wild duck will teach one more of the difficult art of stalking than any birds I know and exercise one's patience and ingenuity sorely before one or other is put in the bag.

And now it is time to get to business, so a truce to further meanderings, though to remain up on the moor tempted me sorely; but the field of the plough was getting black-speckled, so I hied me down to a likely seeming place for the birds' flight both in and out of the field. Luck certainly befriended me, for no sooner had I got into position behind the wall, ranged cartridges in rows on a flat stone in order to reload quickly, than a regular cross fire of birds began to fly near me. Lol of course spied my grey cap keeking over the dyke and managed to drive a good many of the feeding birds straight at my stand.

The first to come was a big covey of grouse, and the fun began by two birds dropping to one shot.[21] Then came a big old blackcock on his way to supper, which alas! For him, he never reached. Soon after from the field quickly flew another to share his comrade's fate, a grand old cock whose deep sapphire breast gleamed in the strong light, and whose piebald tail will make a good cockade for some one's hat. So it went on; birds seemed to fly at me from every side, some within shot and some without (of mine any way), some coming from the low stubble, put up by the keeper, the others coming from Lol's side, and some on their own.

Below me the other gun was busy, booming out, and my twenty-bore kept popping back its echoes. The climax of my luck was reached when a perfect swarm of partridges buzzed high and fast over me, and to my second barrel one fell a good sixty yards or more behind my stand.

---

20 Wood pigeons.

21 This is referred to as a "Scotch double."

All round me lay grouse and black game, the partridge bringing my total up to ten: five grouse, four black game, one partridge, and every one of them driven shots. For once my little gun had not disgraced itself nor displeased me. "Maister Chairles'" bag amounted to seven, mostly blackcock, and fine old birds too, bringing our bag up to seventeen. A mysterious greyhen was picked up also, and though I honestly disclaimed all knowledge of it alive or dead, it being found within shot of my stand marked me as the innocent culprit. As usual I supposed, it had played me one of its silly tricks; mixed itself up with grouse and come in for some stray pellets. However, my master was gracious to be pleased enough with my afternoon's work to pass the greyhen peccadillo gently by.

We wended our way home in the evening light, having added one more delightful memory of stoking hours to life's diary, and with the words of the old song singing to us—

"O where has ye been
This bonnie summer e'en,
And what have ye heard that was worth your heed?
I heard the cushies croon
Through the garden afternoon.
And the Quair burn singing doon the Vale o' Tweed."
—From *Echoes of Sport*
Published by T. N. Foulis, London, in 1910

Paul(ina) Brandreth

▲ Paulina Brandreth.

Paulina Brandreth (1885–1946) was a skilled deer hunter, naturalist, and photographer who published under the name Paul Brandreth, yet she was the first woman outdoor writer in America. Her home hunting grounds were her grandparents' 24,038-acre Adirondack estate. First published in *Forest and Stream* in 1894 when she was only nine years old, *Trails of Enchantment*, published in 1930, is esteemed as one of the first major books written on white-tailed deer hunting.

"The Spirit of the Primitive" (1930)

The spirit of the primitive is in most of us, still strong. If this were not true, why, then, do so many turn to life in the open in preference to more complex forms of relaxation and enjoyment? Why do we take a holiday with our camping kit instead of going to some comfortable and well-appointed resort where we can be served and waited on instead of doing for ourselves? Why do we like to sleep on boughs or in tents, and cook our meals over campfires, and tramp, and fish, and hunt rather than imbibe the saccharine cup of civilized pleasures? If there was not a deep-rooted desire in our beings to get back to the best and most enlivening methods of our primitive forebears, we would rest content and experience no particular urge outside of our self-imposed conventional channels. But although this may be the case with a vast majority. The man of wealth takes his family on a vacation out West, or to the wilds of Canada; the poor man packs his outfit on a Ford and camps nearer home. Both are prompted to do the same thing by the same primitive call. Both wish to enjoy themselves by conforming once again to a simple and expansive mode of life; by tasting the old freedom amid natural beauties and quietude, and by stripping themselves, for the time being, at any rate, of cast-iron responsibilities and needless restraints.

It is essentially a primitive passion which draws men to the mountains, the sea, the desert, and all the wild and lonely places of the earth. It is the spirit of the primitive which makes us willing to undergo actual discomfort and sometimes real hardship, in order to gratify our ancestral longing for an open-air existence. In spirt of civilization, in spite of luxury and money and modern conveniences and mechanical progress, we are products of nature, and to nature we turn for the realization of things that are often infinitely more satisfying and stimulating than the creations of our brains and hands. NO—the cave man is not extinct. He is smoothed off and polished and spiritualized, and he no longer is a savage; but he is not dead, and may it be hoped that he will never die utterly.

Shams and artificialities crowd the highroads constructed by human effort, but nature is always real. She is salutary, she is health-giving, she is profound. Augmented by mental progress, cultural development, and scientific enlightenment, we find in her the well springs that are perennial. While the untutored brain of the savage fails to grasp that which the civilized mind absorbs and is nourished by, the influence of nature on all races of mankind has along certain lines invariably reacted to something higher. Worship and reverence are primitive, and they are both golden inheritances.

I do not wish to be misunderstood in trying to interpret what I mean by the spirit of the primitive. I have no sympathy with "back to Nature cults" and fanatical extremists and people who seek to avoid certain social obligations that are necessary to human advancement. We do not have to be uncouth or crude or weirdly eccentric in order to establish a fundamental and stimulating relationship with the source of all things. What I do wish to make clear is the belief that a complete submerging of the spirit of the primitive, in an over-civilized state, would not be a gain, but a loss. Just as soon as we begin to depend too much on others and become helpless with regard to looking after ourselves then individual self-reliance, purpose, and physical vitality suffer. It has been written in history that nations become effete and perish because of super-civilized conditions and too great prosperity. And this is undoubtedly caused by the weakening of the individual unit. That contact with the rugged forces of nature keeps at bay the decline of those elements which are productive of health, independence, and resourcefulness is an indisputable fact.

A love of outdoor life is the greatest antidote in the world for the strain of modern living. When we are out in camp, we have perforce to look after our own bodily needs. If we want fuel, we have to chop it; if we want a fire, we have to make it; if we wish to eat, we very often have to secure, as well as cook, our food.

Should we find ourselves in a tight place, or in actual physical danger, we must use our wits and muscles to get clear of the predicament. We cannot go to the telephone and call for help. We must learn to depend on ourselves. It is splendid. The beautiful moods and aspects of nature broaden our vision and feed our souls, but her raw relentless side teaches us lessons of incalculable value.

Contrary to much popular belief and the idea that man's innate tendency to the savage is encouraged and fostered by living in a so-called uncivilized environment, there are men who, having lived their lives in such places, are yet more humane and possess a deeper philosophy of life than many who have known only the influence of bustling communities. Nature molds according to character and intelligence. The wilderness is accused of making brutes out of some individuals, but undoubtedly, they would have reverted to the brute under any unfettered condition. Quiet manners, a refinement that is not artificial, a kindness that seeks no reward, are more often the fruits of solitude. And what Conrad says of the men of the sea "who understand each other very well in their view of earthly things, for simplicity is a good counsellor, and isolation not a bad educator" applies also to the men of wild and remote habitation.

May it be hoped, indeed, that our ears shall never grow deaf to the call of the Red Gods. Reassuring, moreover, is the thought that on our own continent alone, there are still thousands of square miles of rugged territory where the thirst of the primitive spirit within us can be assuaged.

I am speaking primarily of the mountains and the forest, for it is these I know best. Majestic and inspiring manifestations of the universe, the sea and the desert are at times vain sanctuaries and show no mercy to the human atoms who invade their dominions. The jungle, too, is often treacherous. But the forest and mountains retain a more beneficent attitude towards man. Food, shelter and water they offer us, and within their boundaries, howsoever desperate the situation, there is always a fighting chance. To know them intimately is to love them. They yield us a sense of security, support and friendliness which in the lure of salt water and desert wastes and jungle mystery can never be realized.

Men like to hunt because of a primitive instinct. Nor does this necessarily mean that they are prompted solely by a desire to kill. Rather it is the fascination of the chase, the pitting of skill and energy and intelligence against the wild creature's power of self-preservation and ingenuity to escape which stirs the blood and lends the excitement and interest which the sportsman is seeking. After the shot is fired, and this is especially true with regard to big game hunting, the best part of the adventure is nearly always finished. Up to that moment we must work and often work hard to attain the end desired. We must use strategy and cultivate ability if we are going to win out. Blundering into an animal and shooting it down is never the same as the trophy brought to bag in a painstaking and thoroughly clean sportsmanlike fashion.

If, as some people believe, the enjoyment we take out of hunting is merely a gratification of the savage instinct to possess and destroy, there would then be no need for us to go into the wilderness. A rifle in the barnyard would furnish us with ample sport according to the above idea. We would be satisfied with knocking over sheep and cattle if our chief desire was to kill something. Such, of course, is not the case. As a matter of fact, I have found good sportsmen to be invariably more gentle and understanding in their treatment of animals than many individuals who have no interest or predilection for the pastime of hunting. When we commence to analyze the cruelty attached to sport and decry it on that count, we must in all sincerity become vegetarians or the argument can have no weight.

The most fundamental part of the spirit of the primitive, as we are trying to understand it, certainly does not lie in pleasure derived from the taking of life. Among a rough type of hunters and uncivilized races the lust to kill is undoubtedly a very potent factor. But this is not so with regard to the sporting instinct of men and women whose mentalities are refined. People of the latter class are prompted to hunt by the lure of the chase, by a love of nature, by a desire to study the habits of wild creatures, and by the clamor and freedom of life in wilderness places.

Yet a word remains to be said of the esthetic value of the spirit of the primitive. Within the magic circle of forested and mountainous solitudes we find inspirations that cannot be found elsewhere. There is much more attached to hunting than the mere pursuit of a game animal. First of all, we learn to be patient and observant. Through experience we become self-reliant and attuned to influences that are strengthening and beneficial. Communication with nature makes it possible to commune with ourselves. In the present age of high tension and hurried endeavors, we are constantly under the pressure of the nerve-racking forces which surround us. But of this atmosphere, the mountains and forests and unreclaimed places of the earth know nothing. Here is peace, here is beauty, here is time.

We cannot live in close touch with beautiful scenes and stimulating environments without being enriched by them. It is likely that we will forget the way the wilderness appeared on a certain autumn morning when every brilliantly hued leaf was encased in glittering snow-crystals and kindled into prismatic fires by the beams of the rising sun? Do we cease to remember the advent of the Hunter's Moon—a blood-red and fabulous lantern as it peered at us across the lonely mazes of a black spruce swamp? Do we fail to recollect the spell-bound mystery of a secluded lake, girdled by virgin timber, and sleeping like a liquid tourmaline in the shadowland of twilight? These are things that time cannot take from us as long as memory lasts. The deerskin on our study floor, the buck's head over the fireplace, what are these after all but the keys which have unlocked enchanted doors, and granted us not only health and vigor, but a fresh and fairer vision of existence?

—From *Trails of Enchantment*, published by G. H. Watt, 1930. Reprinted by Stackpole Books in 2003, with an afterword by Mary Zeiss Stange.

Courtney Borden

(Courtney Letts de Espil)
(1899–1995)

Courtney Louise Letts, daughter of wealthy Midwestern industrialist Frank Crawford Letts and his wife, Cora, was, with Ginevra King, Edith Cummings, and Margaret Carry, Chicago's celebrated "debutante quartet," famously known as Lake Forest's "Big Four." "So legendary [were they] for their beauty that they were

▲ Courtney Borden.

known by that designation for the rest of their lives,"[22] and had identical engraved gold rings made as a binding symbol of their sisterhood.

Ginevra, the daughter of Chicago financier Charles King, was author F. Scott Fitzgerald's first love and the woman he immortalized as Isabelle Borgé in his first novel, *This Side of Paradise*, and Daisy Buchanan in his Jazz Age masterwork, *The Great Gatsby*.

Edith Cummings, daughter of a prosperous banker, soared to fame as a professional golf champion, winning the 1923 US Women's Amateur and becoming the first female athlete to appear on the cover of *Time* magazine. Impersonating life, Fitzgerald formed Daisy's close friend, professional golfer Jordan Baker, after Edith.

Fitzgerald mentions Margaret "Peg" Carry, daughter of the president of the Pullman Company (railroad cars) in his diary. In a letter to a friend, written August 16, 1916, Fitzgerald mentioned that Courtney and Edith went Out West to join Ginevra and her family on a ranch.

The "Big Four" lived in their families' opulent Gold Coast mansions, drove their *own* cars—imagine!—played golf and tennis at the exclusive Onwentsia Club, lunched together before returning to the Club for tea, then home for a quick change into a sheer, bugle-beaded, form-hugging dress with plunging necklines for an evening party where they danced the Charleston, Fox Trot, and waltzed the night away—until the storm clouds of war darkened the world.

This is the life that Courtney Letts was born into; as Courtney Letts Stillwell Borden de Espil Adams, she had followed her own path, leading the most adventurous, independent, exciting, passionate, worthy life of any woman of her—or any other woman's—day.

The first of her four marriages was to Yale graduate and World War I ensign Wellesley Stillwell, which lasted four years. A few months later, she married forty-one-year-old divorced dairy scion John Borden, thirteen years her senior. He gave her a house on Astor Street, a Rolls Royce, priceless jewelry, and a trust fund for the children from her first marriage upon their marriage—but most of all, he exposed her to the sporting life. Though she might "prefer trips to London, Paris, and the Riviera," he instead suggested "I'd like to take you along—just to see how you would like this sort of thing . . . cold . . . getting up at dawn . . . because if you do—I've always led that kind of life, you know."

She proved a keen traveler and hunting partner on an expedition that took five months. Setting sail from San Francisco on the *Northern Light*, a 140-foot yacht Borden had custom-built for the journey, they, the crew, and their group of socialite friends and scientists explored the coast of Alaska, as far north as Wrangel Island in the Arctic Ocean, the last place the woolly mammoth may have survived. They returned with authentic scientific information and harvested 106 plant specimens and Peninsula brown bears for Chicago's Field Museum, of which Borden was a trustee. Courtney kept three notebooks from which she would write *The Cruise of the Northern Lights* (The Macmillan Company, 1928) recounting the events between April and September 1927, and recorded on film by Borden, of Ketchikan, Juneau, Unalaska, Bogosolof, Pribilof, Nome, King Island, Diomede Isle, Point Hope, Cape Serdze-kamen, and Herald Island.

"To look at her you would never suspect that the delicate, lovely creature who is always one of the most

---

22 *Hemingway vs. Fitzgerald: The Rise and Fall of a Literary Friendship*, by Scott Donaldson

beautiful women in any drawing room really has the passion for the outdoors that lures men to the Wilds for solace and soul repair," a reviewer pronounced of Courtney's second book, "but after reading *Adventures in a Man's World* you know that she has, for there is a real joy in its pages unmistakable zest."

▲ Glenwild.

Glenwild

In 1920, John Borden bought Glenwild, a six-thousand-acre Mississippi plantation where Courtney led the sporting life. "Dogs, and guns, and hunting togs had already replaced fur coats and were becoming more important than a closet of dressed-up clothes," she observed. Famous for their hunting parties, Borden built his own airstrip and railway station where the rich and famous would arrive from Chicago, New York, and Washington to join their hosts at Glenwild and hunt quail, play polo, and party. "Perhaps I am leaving a wrong impression," Courtney wrote. "The impression that life, for us, has been one continual merry-go-round of sport—one continual search for this recreation and that adventure. Quite the contrary. These excursions into the refreshing peace of the woods and waters have been our greatest luxury." However, this marriage, too, did not last. The Bordens divorced in 1933 after eight years of marriage and Courtney got Glenwild as part of the divorce settlement (though sadly, the mansion burned to the ground in the early 1940s).

Just three weeks after her second divorce, Courtney married Felipe A. Espil, forty-six, the Argentine Ambassador to the United States, who spurned his infatuated lover, Wallis Simpson, to win Courtney, leaving Wallis to follow her destiny to England. As the wife of an ambassador, Courtney was in her element. Acclaimed by *Time* magazine in 1943 "one of the world's ten best-dressed women, and an able diplomat herself, the couple returned to Buenos Aires during World War II and afterwards, Espil was appointed Argentina's Ambassador to Spain. After a diplomatic tour in Brazil, the couple retired to Buenos Aires in 1959, where Felipe died in 1972. Courtney moved to New York and in 1974, married a fourth and final time, to Foster Adams. Courtney wrote seven books in all, including *La Esposa del Embajador* (The Ambassador's Wife: 10 Years in the Argentinean Embassy in Washington, 1933–1943),[23] and *Noticias Confidenciales de Buenos Aires a USA*[24], about life in Argentina under Juan Perón. She died in 1995 in Washington, D.C. at the age of ninety-six.

"Quail at Glenwild" (1933)

Seldom do we go duck shooting anymore, not, anyway, when Glenwild is our home. For here at our own front door, in the fields beyond our house, lie the prettiest, the gamest, and the most respected of all hunted birds, the Bob White quail.

Glenwild in the Deep South of Mississippi is a cotton plantation and a quail preserve as well, where cotton and quail supplement one another in the necessary balance of existence—economic need and the pleasure of living. There are also to be had squirrels and rabbits and dove, game we do not take. Here we have come from the North to live quietly and calmly and appreciate the richness of each day as it moves inevitably from sun-up to sun-down, in a leisurely fashion so easy to enjoy. At night the balmy Southern skies listening with shining constellations each laid like crystals on a piece of fine jewelry are like clear Tropic heavens seen from the helm of a ship. Only in this Southland of the United States there comes to you at dusk the faint unrespectable order of pine-burning pine logs on some distant cabin hearth, now and then mingled with the green stronger fragrance of tall pines still standing in the rolling woodlands.

In a way it all started on the plantation. It was ours to love. But we never considered making it a home. The place was merely to stop-in while shooting. Those

---

23 *La Esposa del Embajador* was published by Editorial Jorge Alvarez S.A., Buenos Aires, in 1967.

24 *Confidential News from Buenos Aires to the USA*, published in Buenos Aires by Editorial Jorge Alvarez S.A. 1969.

were the days when I was audience, or a stay-at-home relegated to the brick galleries and the courtyard, to the tennis courts, or perhaps left with the colored boys who held the horses. Only the men went quail shooting. Yet in those days, not knowing what I was missing, like a child I was satisfied with little.

Now there are two of us who consider it worthwhile—since we can't live in two places and the season on quail comes at the same time as the season for residing in cities—two of us who consider it worthwhile giving up the attractive and stimulating amusements of a sophisticated urban existence in order to dwell in the depths of the country. Thus it is each winter that we are living on this tract of land in the Deep South, and in adding to its interests are concentrating on encouraging the growth of wildlife which to us particularly means the raising and propagating by natural methods, the Bob White quail. It is indeed a fascinating process well worth all efforts. It is far and away increased the number of coveys on our preserve, has illuminated the necessity and expense each year of turning out birds to live or die, and has not in any way decreased the yield of our crops. But this is something, that to go into here, would take a whole other volume in itself, of such is its importance!

This plantation has offered, as well as sport, a refuge of peace and rest from the industrial cities of the North during the last winter or two of hard times period here, all winter I have stayed, and the children with me. Here on Saturdays—oftentimes Fridays—came the head of the house, or in this case the master of the plantation, from his affairs in the North. Here has been for our guests a temporary release from all worries until the dreaded Sunday night that comes all too soon.

So, thankful I was when we actually changed our winter residence from a Great Northern city we all loved to a plantation in the South, that at last I was no longer considered only an onlooker at a man's sport. At last it had become a recognized part of my own life. Dogs, and guns, and hunting tags had already replaced fur coats and were becoming more important than a closet full of dressed-up clothes. "Mother has gone hunting," my children now smile and say to any casual visitor who might be calling, and to them It seems little different than as though they had said, "Mother is planting tulips."

It was Mac, Pal, Girlie, and the others who aided a former city dweller in finding a substitute for lectures, and museums, concerts, theaters, clubs, movies and shops, all the engrossing panorama of things and people which I had once deemed essential to the joys of living. Mac, Pal, and Girlie, the grouse dog Duke, honest slow old Jake, Major and Peggy, have provided a fund of faithful friendships, a sportsmanship and companionship such as can be offered a human being by only a hunting dog. They have superseded my one-time passion for china and glass, old furniture, old silver, and new possessions. They are worth being interested in. They pay dividends in labor and affection.

Thus it is that I work hard at writing or domestic responsibilities on certain days of the week in order that I can deserve to go afield with those dogs for a part of two days, or the whole of one day, during the beginning of each week of November, December, and January. Four weekends are given over to entertaining friends.

Ill with influenza during the planning of this book, the doctor who came out to call began telling me of the hard cases he had had of late, and the tremendous amount of charity he and his associates had been called upon to do among the "poor whites." He did look tired. Then he crossed his knees, pushed himself farther back in the chair, when a smile broke over his face. "But I'll work all night, every night if necessary," he added, "so long as I can get off every now and then dash with my dogs . . . quail shooting is the greatest pleasure of my life."

Then he glanced toward me. But I had said nothing. "Duck shooting—that's fun too . . . but quail shooting is another matter. Quail fly fast—that's all! And, oh boy, the thrill I get when the birds go—*Burrrr*."

Our own kennel, neither large or small, has served satisfactorily ourselves and guests. The dogs have come from various parts of the United States. Some of them, Victor Kelly and Joe Momoney, were field trial winners; others were sired by really great dogs which we did not own. Peggy, a slender black and white bitch had a mother sired by Mr. Eugene M., who was himself sired by Eugene M. whom some consider the champion of them all. But often our best-bred dogs have been outplayed by humbler ones whose distinguished ancestors may have been several generations behind.

Registered dogs or nonregistered dogs, what difference in the shooting field? If he is faithful, has bird sense and uses keen initiative in his plans and method of search, is strong and eager to please, these are the things that count. No human being would ever work this hard for you and if he is yours—you feed him and handle him—he perhaps thinks more of you than you do of yourself. If he is to be merely a hunting dog, and you do not plan to sell either him or his puppies for large sums, a slip of paper, a fancy name, will not better him except in the eyes of a judge.

Pointer or setter—that is a question. We must appreciate both for their separate qualities. For several years we acquired nothing except English setters. But now things have happened in the kennel. The favorites are two pointers. One of these is Mac, the large orange and white fellow with an inquisitive face and a pair of round friendly eyes the color of tangerines. "Mac would be an elegant looking dog," the handler once said of him, "if he only didn't have that crooked tail." But crooked tail or straight tail he comes to a point with as grand a manner, staunchly holding it for hours if necessary, as you would ever care to see. Mac is, besides, all but human and seems to understand in magical ways your words and gestures. He never gives in, and never potters; he never returns to the horses once he is afield and casts out directly and independently to go about the business of his day. And is absolutely insane about his chosen occupation—as you will see. He is all the more precious to us now because when he first came three years ago, he not only jumped into coveys—when he imagined his handler was not watching—but preceded to devour the first two birds shot over his back. But catch him making a mistake now? Never!

When morning dawns and the dew lies like white frost on the ground it is soon the hour to be off with one of these dogs, and to carry with you no cares in the world other than the correctness of your eye and behavior of the trigger finger. You will feel refreshed, if you came the day before from a city, or exhilarated if you live here every day.

You enter the room where an enormous breakfast before blazing logs awaits you. This large breakfast will add the finishing touch of confidence in yourself and a sense of well-being. For—"Life is pleasant. Life is good. The mere process of life is satisfactory"—says Virginia Woolf, in the process of it holds lovely moments like home-made sausage and fried apples and cakes from buckwheat ground by an old stone mill, and a polite servant who speaks to you in his soft low drawl about stuffed eggs and cold turkey sandwiches that he will "carry out" at noon.

Over wool shirts, for though the day may be warm, the evening will cool suddenly, you will wear a white drill hunting jacket, like the red cap of the deer hunter safer than khaki which fades into the autumn ground. You will carry your own well-cherished gun, and I, the faithful 20-gauge Remington pump using the 26-inch barrel. If it be early in the season, we will bring number nine shot; later in the year when the birds are stronger and wilder, number 8; And always chilled shot. Everything is in readiness, the horse and the stable boy, but as it happens the handler has not yet arrived with the dogs. This is unusual. Ordinarily he stands outside the gun room, waiting. When we reach the kennel, we might learn that Mac has jumped the nine-foot wire enclosure of his runway and is nowhere to be found. . . .

"He's de jumpinest dawg I evah did see," laughed Little Orange one morning when this actually occurred, as he tried to apologize, but you could see that the erring dog who cared so much for this fine sport of hunting was a favorite with the colored boy as well as with us. The handler raised his gun in the air and shot one shell. A few seconds later, from the field where he had stolen off to hunt alone, Mac appeared. He had not been taken out the preceding day, nor the day before, and apparently could not bear it any longer. He had been missing too many golden opportunities to find those feathered beauties whose scent so intrigued him.

Mac came trotting casually towards his handler, looked over the guns and men and horses—having perhaps figured he had better hurry back when he heard the shot but not quite certain the hunt would include him—and ambled off a trifle sheepishly to join his setter companions restlessly awaiting to be off.

"Does this happen often?" someone inquired of the handler.

Leighton smiled, "Well," he drawled, a slow twinkle in his eye, ". . . not so often, but quite often when we don't give him enough huntin'. Sometimes he gets so bad we have to tie a ball and chain on him to keep him home nights."

Through tall fields of broom sedge we went this day, Mac, Major a large and garrulous Llewellyn, Peggy, and Pal who always reminds me of a wise old man. He never gets excited, never displays any unusual emotion—his hazel eyes give the impression of having seen all there is to see—except when the hunters delay too long at their lunch, then he commences to bark and demand that they hurry. Major and Pal were to stay with us during the forenoon while Mac and Peggy were to be tied in a negro's yard till time for the afternoon hunt.

The sun shone warm and delicious. Crimson sumac waved at us from fence rails, and all round us spread the copper yellow of sage, the green of pines, and we breathed that familiar fragrance of burning pine-logs so peculiar to the Southland. Negro cabins dotted here and there, offered us their porches overflowing with laughing children and their yards with chickens, stray dogs, and an occasional hog. Crops were picked so the fields were bare of yield.

The morning proved to be Major's. It had not been often that this bigger dog could outwit Pal. Out of the first nine coveys Major claimed six. On a second find it took him several points to pin the birds that were all this time—so we discovered later—traveling along the ground ahead of his nose. When he froze for the seventh time, we thought him still a bit uncertain and not one of us courted the effort, perhaps again unnecessary, of jumping down off the horses. We were tired of false alarms. So, we chatted a few seconds about what we'd considered the chances of there actually being birds this time. When, to our disgust—and Major's—a large covey of about eighteen rose from under the dog's nose and sailed across the breadth of the cornfield. Words could not describe our feelings. Not one gun even loaded!

Ten minutes later when the same dog pointed once more his handler leaned over his saddle and said: "I'd hate to tell old Major he's prevaricatin' again. I'm going to get off anyway—and mighty quick!"

Major was not prevaricating. A good-sized covey got up between us and the dog who had gone into point in a sideways fashion, his nose turned well around, his warning. And when three birds fell, he stood there,

steady, until he heard the familiar *Daid*, Major, *Daid*, Pal," and off they scurried to retrieve.

I am glad of Major's one day of victory over Pal, whose actions in the field are always experienced and competent, because Major's record, though he was sired by an imported Llewellin, had not been as good. And Major died not long afterward from some strange malady no one could name.

The afternoon was nearly as fruitful of coveys as the morning, twenty-eight birds in all, a good fare for Sunday dinner. The last covey was flushed in a sorghum field. Dusk had fallen before we had rounded up the singles in thickets and briar patches and along the edge of a stream where quicksand detained us from crossing just anywhere we would have wanted. Mac had carried himself in his usual independent manner "running off by himself certain he's going to find the birds" as some one remarked. While Peggy kept up her own end of the day with three or four coveys and several good honorings of her brace mate's finds. Peggy's ancestor, after all, was Eugene M.

As we climbed back on our mounts, tired in every muscle, but pleasantly so, we heard from all about us in the increasing darkness the scatter call of the Bob White quail. *Ka—loi—kee....Ka—loi—kee* came the faint notes from first a plum thicket, then a briar patch. And who could refrain from pulling in his reins and stand still while watching these birds rise out of the ground and fly off to some chosen sanctuary. Before many more minutes the little gang would be together again, all that had not fallen to the gun, and in a solid found formation no larger than the rim of a plate a formation that affords warmth and instant readiness to spring at the approach of danger.

For eight solid hours we had no thoughts other than the fields and woods, the possible whereabouts of birds, the dogs, and even horses who have, after many such seasons, learned to cooperate in an astonishingly intelligent manner.

We turned now, the dogs trudging tiredly by our sides, through lanes of mud between ghostly armies of battered corn and cotton stalks. A three-mile ride lay ahead. Complete darkness came with a star or two in the sky. It was strange and mysterious riding that evening through dark silent cotton fields which had yielded a bumper crop and were now asleep. Yet it was not those wet slumbering fields which were most mysterious. For we are passing tiny, isolated cabins, shadows lying between perhaps two gaunt trees. They were small oases in the desert of last fall's crops. No children stood on the porches now and waved to us, for through the windows shone the fitful pinkish glow of a fire on every hearth. And as we rode by, we glanced within and saw a roomful of black faces, black heads, black forms—all sizes—silhouetted against the walls where a reflection of red flames danced. Close to the fire they sat, munching on their frugal meal.

I thought of the scene in *Porgy* [*and Bess*], inside the house, on the wild night when rang the dreaded hurricane bell. I thought of it more when we caught, in the cool still air, the sound of distant voices singing. The wavering shadows, though, were the only reminder. For those lighted cabins in cotton furrows did not offer a foreboding of tragedy. Instead we witnessed a great peace and contentment. Dogs barked lazily as we trotted by; soft voices called them back; children lay asleep in the arms of women near the crude family hearths where pine logs flickered.

—From *Adventures in A Man's World: The Initiation of a Sportsman's Wife*, published by The Macmillan Company in 1933

Mary Zeiss Stange

▲ Mary Zeiss Stange.

Mary Zeiss Stange is a prominent voice on the topic of women and hunting. A featured speaker at the 2012 inaugural International Conference on Women and Sustainable Hunting, in Bratislava, Slovakia, she was a member of the US Delegation of the International Council for Game and Wildlife Conservation (CIC), which sponsored the conference, and sits on the CIC's Artemis Organizing Committee. A director of Orion The Hunters Institute and the editorial Board of Contributors of *USA Today*, she is published in *Big Sky Journal, High Country News,* and the *Los Angeles Times.* Her essay, "Last Man Out of the Hunting Lodge, Please Turn Out the Lights," received the Izaak Walton League's "Thinking Like a Mountain" award in 1998, and in 2006 she won first prize in Sierra Club's "Why I Hunt" essay contest. A professor of women's studies and religion at Skidmore College and the Edwin R. Mosely Faculty Lecturer, Mary and her husband, Douglas, live in Montana.

"Forest Reflexes" (1997)

The moon, just past full, hangs in an ice-blue early morning sky. It is the third day of a forest hunt for whitetail, something to which I'm fairly unaccustomed, being by experience and by inclination a hunter of wide-open Western spaces. Mostly, I've hunted mule deer and antelope, and the whitetail deer (all does) I have shot have been at reasonably long range. I have, I suppose, a prairie hunter's prejudice against sitting still for too long. The mystique of scents, lures, and rattling-in largely escapes me. When I do take a stand, I prefer one with a long broad view.

Nonetheless, I have been enjoying still-hunting amid brushy Ponderosa pines and cottonwood-cluttered ravines. A mid-November snowstorm has impeded access and kept most hunters home. My partner and I have these woods virtually to ourselves. The snow is fluffy and the wind cooperative, and the rut is in full swing. I am carrying two Montana deer tags: an either-species buck tag, and a B-tag for antlerless whitetail. Our first morning out, as the snow was just starting to fall, we surprised a formidable buck, bedded down with a doe. He was up and gone in a heartbeat and has been a phantom in the back of my mind ever since. Now, we glimpse a solitary whitetail doe a hundred or so yards off in the trees. She senses our presence and bounds toward denser cover. My companion, who grew up deer hunting the woods and field-edges of Wisconsin, remarks, "The thing about a forest stalk is, once you've seen deer, they're *really* there. Up until you see them, they're ghosts."

We only hunt the dawn and morning hours. In the last three days, we have seen several whitetails, mostly does and fawns. None of the bucks we've jumped have measured up to that phantom-buck in my mind, but my failure to take any shots at them owes, in all honesty, as much to awkwardness as to choosiness on my part. I've got to develop better forest reflexes.

We've been following game trails through knee-deep snow for two hours now, and aside from a few wary does and the departing flag of a buck whose morning courting we interrupted, have seen nothing. Birds compare notes high in the trees, and the sun begins its ascent in a clear sky. Looking up at the moon, I think, "Artemis is on the animals' side today." Instantly I make a mental correction: Artemis, of course, does not take sides.

Working downhill, I tread the dormant undergrowth and deadfall carefully, feeling them through the snow. The air is still and impossibly clear. We come upon a rub and a fresh-looking scrape not too far from where we originally jumped that big buck, suggesting he may still be somewhere nearby. Threading along well-traveled deer runs, I cradle my .270 in readiness for a sudden surprise calling for a quick shot. But I'm skeptical, both about my chances and my reflexes. I've read too many hunting stories about monster bucks abruptly crashing through the brush and into the crosshairs to believe the things will actually happen. The whitetail I'm hunting is too smart to be a cliché, and I'm not a fancy enough shot to be one.

That big buck, the reality and nearness of which I am certain, will remain a ghost for the rest of the morning. I know that, and so, I imagine, does he.

The woods occupy a broad bowl-shaped divide, funneling steeply down from the open flats. We are working our way along the hillside, well below the rim. Concentrating so hard on training my attention upwards, where a late-lingering deer might be coming down off the top. I am suddenly startled to spy a deer straight ahead. A hundred yards, no less than that, away—a *big* deer (as big, it appears to me, as a cow), but clearly a whitetail. I can see all of it, except its head.

I creep closer, the snow muffling my steps. I wait, my rifle steadied on a tree limb, the crosshairs behind the deer's shoulder. I wait some more. This is the best

shot I've had in three days; I know it won't happen again, and the opportunity won't last forever. After what seems an interminable time, but is probably more like three minutes, the deer raises her head. A doe. A *big* doe. Does she have company? I wait some more, and I begin to get a cramp in my back from the rather awkward position I've been hunched in. She is still unaware of me, so I slowly lower my rifle and arch my back. This action spooks another deer, one I cannot even see; he (I am convinced it's *him*) is in too-thick cover. The doe wheels around and follows him. I manage to glimpse their tails, zigzagging down through a cottonwood swale. Thinking I was right about the kinds of things that only happen in other people's hunting stories, I rejoin my partner, who had been lingering several yards behind me.

We pace a few steps, and almost immediately notice that we are being watched. A little whitetail doe is poised at the edge of the woods, perhaps seventy yards above us. She seems oddly unruffled by our presence; one would expect her to flee, especially as convection currents are wafting our scent in her direction. She takes a cautious step, then another. "She's injured," my companion—who has a clearer view of her than I—says. "See, she's limping." This situation calls for a hunting reflex that is not so specific to the forest. I move to where I can get a clear shot, take aim, and fire.

When we make our way to the rim, we discover the little doe's left front leg had been broken above the knee, by a bullet that cut to the bone—the result, clearly, of someone's foolish, or careless, shooting earlier in the season. Her wound is partially healed over, but the little deer would likely have been a coyote's meal before winter's end.

The next day's forest stalk is an exercise in futility. The weather had turned temperate yesterday afternoon, with bright sunshine and brisk breezes, glazing everything over. Gone are the loft and quiet of the previous days' snow. Today it sounds like we're crunching through a toppled box of Crispix. There is nothing "still" about this hunting.

We decide to try some rattling-in—to no avail. Nobody's home in the woods. After a couple of hours, we concede defeat and head for more open country.

Now we are well into the final week of deer season, and although I had dedicated myself this year to the quest of the elusive whitetail, I am by no means opposed to the notion of shooting a nice mule deer buck. I do not see this as a question of "compromise," although I realize some would. I respect the animals I hunt too much to ever regard myself as settling for one because I cannot have another. I have healthy admiration for the wily whitetail. But I have little patience with the widespread prejudice (manufactured, I suspect, by the same folks who gave us *eau de* buck-in-rut and doe-in-heat) that mule deer are, by comparison, intellectually challenged. From the vantage point of a still-hunter, mature bucks of either species are a challenge. They get to be mature *because* they are a challenge.

So, I do not mind, or not too much, abandoning the quest for the phantom whitetail as we descend out of the woods into the valley below. This is more familiar country for me, rolling grassland cleft here and there by deep brushing draws and rambling creek beds. Though the snow is crunchy, in these open spaces the sound dissipates, and I feel like I can hear myself think again. That forest was beginning to feel a bit claustrophobic. It's a pleasant change of pace to get back out into the open, where the deer don't behave like ghosts. Back to the essentials.

I am thinking this, walking fifty or so yards behind my partner, along the crest of a rise that overlooks an open pasture. It's midmorning now, so at most I expect to see mule deer fawns whose mothers are in deeper cover with their gentlemen callers, or immature bucks on the make for a stray doe. I let my mind, and attention, wander.

Suddenly, two deer leap into view at the far side of the pasture, about three hundred yards off. *"WHITETAILS!!!"* my companion explodes. I can't quite believe my eyes: a doe, with a buck—yes, my binoculars confirm, he's *that* buck—in ardent pursuit. He is not a ghost anymore. But what on earth is he doing out here? The terrain, and the time of day, are all wrong for a whitetail buck that's smart enough to have gotten this big, even if the rut is in progress. Either he was led astray by one dumb but beautiful doe, or this is the whitetail romance of the century and they both threw caution to the wind.

While I am expending precious seconds trying to work this out, my companion (he of the finely tuned forest reflexes, who knows opportunity when he sees

it, whatever the context) has more sensibly moved a few yards into better shooting position. The deer have discovered us and are on the run. I drop to a sitting position and put my scope on the buck, but cannot steady it enough to get a confident shot off at this distance. I hear myself let out a yelp of frustration.

The whitetails reach a fence line, the doe jumping it and heading for the trees, the buck hesitating for a mere instant. My partner fires, and the buck goes down.

He is a real beauty; a broad, heavy 5 x 5 with long, elegant tines. His body is as big as a mule deer. I would love to have shot him myself, but cannot begrudge my partner's success, or his superior marksmanship. A hunter for more than forty years, who has deferred to me on more than one occasion, he deserves this one.

This does not prevent me, of course, from wishing I had the last several minutes to live over again. It's a long drag back to the pickup.

The next morning, Thanksgiving, dawns overcast and frosty. As I step outside and pause to let my eyes become accustomed to the dark, a round break opens in the clouds, the moon precisely centered, shining through. Taking this as a good omen, I set off for a stretch of sage country where a series of knobs and rocky hills gradually rise into rugged buttes.

I do not have to go very far. By seven o'clock I have killed a good buck, a large robust mule deer in his prime. It was one of those rare "textbook" stalks where conditions are ideal and everything goes right—that is to say, a fine memory, but not the makings of much of a story.

Sitting on the hillside, next to my buck, I watch the sun clear the horizon. Turkeys are calling down in the creek, and a little forked-horn buck is trying to impress a doe on a neighboring hilltop. I am happy with the morning and with my deer. It has been a good season.

I find myself thinking about those days, this past week, in the woods. There are lessons I need to learn there, skills to develop, instincts to train to the altered rhythms of the understory. I notice that the moon has set. Next year I will start earlier in the season, and stay longer each day. I want to spend more time in that forest.

—Prologue to chapter 6. From *Woman the Hunter*, by Mary Zeiss Stange. Published by Beacon Press, 1997.

Other Books by Mary Zeiss Strange

Gun Women: Firearms and Feminism in Contemporary America. With Carol K. Oyster, NYU Press, 2000.

Hard Grass: Life on the Crazy Woman Bison Ranch. University of New Mexico Press, 2011. Gold Medal winner for Best Regional Non-Fiction from the Independent Publisher Book Awards

Heart Shots: Women Write About Hunting. Originally published in 2003, reprinted in 2018 by Stackpole Books. An anthology of contemporary women's outdoor writing includes stories and essays.

Laurie Bogart Wiles

"Lost" (2002)

You gain strength, courage and confidence by every experience in which you really stop to look fear in the face. You are able to say to yourself, "I lived through this horror. I can take the next thing that comes along." You must do the thing you think you cannot do.

—Eleanor Roosevelt, 1960

She knew the tears would come. They didn't come often, and she hated it when they did. But she was lost, really lost in the woods, and she was beginning to get frightened. She had never been frightened before, at least not like this, but it came from the same place, the fear. It came from within, that helpless place in her soul, the dark compartment she kept securely locked. She knew too well what it was to feel helpless.

Helpless, like the day she lost her only daughter.

She didn't want to think about that right now; she couldn't. She had to find her way out of the woods and get home. Home to her family. It was going to be dark in a couple of hours, and she was completely turned around.

They would be getting worried. Even her little springer spaniel seemed concerned as she stood alongside her, looking up expectantly. Her husband knew where she had gone, or at least where she was going. Her sons knew this place well, too. They learned to hunt here. That was . . . what? Ten years ago . . .

"Don't worry," her husband had assured her. "I'll take care of them. No, they're not too young. I was eight when my father took me bird-hunting for the first time . . ."

Now their sons were teenagers, and yet it seemed like only yesterday. She wouldn't have been lost if they were with her; she shouldn't have gotten lost in the first place. After all, she learned to hunt here too, all those years ago. But then she gave it up, had the children, kept the home-fires burning.

Then the baby died.

Afterwards, when she learned to live with the terrible emptiness in her heart and tried to get on with it, she took up hunting again. Bird hunting, and now this fall she was going after deer with her husband and their boys. She loved the woods; it was so peaceful. And the hunting, well, that was a good way to fill the place her daughter was meant to fill, to dull the loss, to understand that expectation always falls short when you want something so very, very much.

No, she shouldn't have gotten lost, but she did.

These woods went on and on for miles, through swamps and hills and valleys and on to nowhere, for all any one knew.

Once, long ago, it had been a thriving New Hampshire village with homesteads and even a meeting house. You could still make out the road that led to it, but now it was only forested trail. Here and there lay foundations of old houses and barns. A stone corral for sheep had tumbled with time, barely an outline, bordered by ancient lilac bushes. Apple trees marked the foundation of an outlying farmhouse, out here, and another there; they were overgrown and gnarled and shouldn't, but did, still bear fruit in the fall.

She picked a ruby red apple from a low-hanging branch and pierced it lightly with her teeth, expecting bitter juice. But the apple was sweet, and she was hungry, and she ate it and picked another. Her dog jumped up, begging, and she tossed her the core and watched the juice run down the corners of her mouth as she chewed. She stopped crying because the apple was comforting, and she felt revived.

The leaves were brilliant, more brilliant against the blanket of darkening gray sky than they ever are on a cloudless, peacock blue day. Good artists never attempted to paint autumn, she thought, because only nature knew how to mix the right palette. She used to paint, but she had given it up. When the baby died, she lost her inspiration. She couldn't deal with joy unrealized after she had been robbed of her only chance to raise a daughter. She wanted her so much. As time passed, it hurt more, and she didn't understand why. Tears again pricked behind her eyes and she tried to fight them back, but the wind had come up and swept across her eyes and the tears coursed down her cheek.

Would she have raised her little girl to hunt? No, probably not. When her sons and husband went hunting, she and her daughter would have gone shopping and done girlish things together. But there was no point thinking about what could have been, not anymore.

How did she get so turned around? She opened her shotgun at the breech, hefted it over her shoulder and headed out of the old orchard, away from the abandoned town. Stupidly, she left her compass in her other jacket, but the sun was setting, and she made that her marker. Her dog became lively again, as if to say, "Good, let's go home." But that wasn't it, she thought, that wasn't it at all. She brought her gun down, loaded a shell in each chamber, and no sooner had she closed the breech than her dog pounced on a fat grouse hen. The bird exploded from the forest floor with a whirr, hell-bent for safe haven. She swung her gun to her shoulder, pointed the barrels, and felled the bird with the second shot.

A sudden gust like a tailwind lifted the spaniel high over a crumbling stone wall as she bounded to retrieve the grouse. So majestic, the ruffed grouse, and she remembered the legend her husband told her of how Indians would say a prayer over their game, thanking their brother of the forest for sacrificing his life to sustain theirs. She whispered a tender prayer. She needed to speak to the silence; and the mighty pines arched overhead like a forest cathedral. The brisk evening wind blew her damp cheeks dry: It was at dusk eight Octobers ago today that her baby died in her arms.

Now she found herself in a fern-covered glen. The forest floor was awash with that golden cast peculiar to autumn sunsets. It reminded her of a happy time— how many years ago?—it must be going on twenty-five, when she and her husband first hunted together here. Here? Yes! She knew this place! She was at the beaver pond. They had brought a picnic and drank wine and then made love in the soft grass there, at the shoulder of the pond. The leaves shivered and shook loose the memory of a long-ago soft summer breeze that caressed their bare bodies, warmed by the sun,

warmed from the love-making. But those days were gone and so was their love. Now all that remained was an abiding respect, an "I'm used to you" mentality that wilts into resignation; that maybe there's no more to life, you play the cards you're dealt, and that's that. . . Sometimes grief and tragedy are just too much for two people to bear and like a wedge, splits in two what should always ever be one. That's when she realized, she wasn't only mourning the death of her daughter; she was mourning the death of her marriage.

She saw the hill beyond the beaver pond and knew that uphill was the forgotten cemetery and beyond that, the road. It was a hard climb, but she was sure about it now, and it gave her renewed strength and hope. Her dog got hung up in some brambles, freed herself, and sailed over fallen branches that choked the dirt road. There was a birch tree that had splintered and fallen into the fork of a giant maple and she remembered seeing it when she had come into the woods. *I know where I am*, she thought, when out of nowhere, a tree limb suddenly slingshot across her face and cut her above the chin. She felt it sting, and a drop of blood trickled onto her red turtleneck, against her black hair, and she grabbed at the branch that dared to injure her and broke it off with a snap.

It was getting darker now. At the top of the road she could see dusk peeking through the pines and maples, and she lunged forward, her arm bent to shield her face as other tree limbs tore at her clothes as if trying to hold her back. Then she saw it, there it was: the little cemetery. Seven ancient headstones, that's all, but they told the whole story.

"Their name was Eldridge," old Fort Fall's voice whispered across the years—dear Fort, who taught her boys to hunt and fish, just as he had taught Corey Ford, who considered him more a brother-under-the-skin than his estate manager. How she missed him. Fort knew Tinkhamtown, every inch of it. He and Corey never missed opening day here either, and Fort knew the stories.

"They owned that farm over there. Look. You can see the foundation." She turned her eyes in the direction he had pointed all those years ago, as if he was standing beside her again, speaking to her. "A father, a mother, and their five children. See this little stone marker with the lamb carved on top?" She was the first. She died shortly after birth. . ."

Just like my daughter, she thought. Just like my own precious baby.

"And next to that," the memory-voice continued, "three children, one after the other, two boys and a girl, ages two, three, and five. All within a week. It was smallpox. The epidemic took the whole village."

She thought, Oh my God. I lost one child. How did that poor mother survive the loss of four?

Then she saw the fifth stone and remembered the mother hadn't lost just four.

"Within a year," Fort's voice whispered in the wind, "the mother died from grief."

"And the sixth stone?"

"The sixth is the tombstone of the last child, a son, killed in the first World War. He had just turned eighteen."

And the last stone, the seventh, less tarnished by years than the others, was the father's. He was helpless, alone. There was nothing he could do as each of his loved ones faded away. . . .

"They say he couldn't take the grief," Fort had said.

Helpless, she thought. Helpless . . .

She didn't know how much time had passed, how long she sat on the crumbled stone wall pondering over the fate of the tragic family, how long she mourned for them, and for herself. Her pup was asleep at her feet and the autumn air was now cold with damp and the sky pitch-dark with no moon to light the way. This was a good place to leave her grief, she thought.

Let it go, get on with it, find the road, find your way home. But she felt the weight of her soul heavy upon her as she stood up.

She left the cemetery, squeezing through the stone posts and a sapling that had grown smack between them. How tremendous, she thought, as she realized it was a Gilead tree. She picked a leaf and rubbed it on her hand, aching for some of the balm to heal her wounded spirit.

A bank of opaque clouds uncovered the moon and she could make out the road ahead. Now she knew her way! Her pace quickened as each step brought her closer to familiar ground, each became lighter, each quicker. It's time to get on with it, she thought. Cast aside sorrow. She had blessings to enjoy, far more blessings than sadnesses.

And then she saw them. Ahead, on the road, were three ruffed grouse. They were dancing, jumping up and down, beating their wings all for joy, dusting the dry dirt road with their tails. Even her dog paused to look at the pageant. The birds continued to whirl and flutter against the shimmer of gold and red and orange leaves kissed by the glint of moonbeams and accompanied by the delicate music of rustling leaves. All she could do was watch with wonder.

The cover of night was gently descending upon the forest when a light shone from the distance, getting brighter and brighter. Headlights!

"Mom? Mom!" voices cried. "Are you all right?" Her sons raced toward her, scattering the grouse, which pirouetted high into the air like fireworks and disappeared into the night.

"Yes! I'm here! I'm all right!" she cried as she ran to her boys. Each step felt lighter. Each step carried her closer to the shelter of her loved ones.

Each step took her further from the burden she carried. Finally, she was able to unlock the closed compartment in her heart, and gently and lovingly parted with her sorrow, and lay it to rest in the sanctity of the woods.

—From *The Hardscrabble Chronicles*
Published by Penguin Putnam, 2002.

Her Grace, the Duchess of Rutland

▲ Her Grace, the Duchess of Rutland.

Emma Manners, Duchess of Rutland, and her family live in a house with 356 rooms and a fifteen-thousand-acre backyard, Belvoir Castle, the Manners family home for over five centuries. Lady Emma is one of Britain's thirty-one duchesses. Her book, *Shooting: A Season of Discovery* (Quiller Publishing, Ltd., 2012, with Jane Pruden), may not, however, be the book you'd expect. And that's because Lady Emma appears a warm, lively, grounded woman who grew up on a farm in Wales flanked by two shooting estates where the pheasants knew no boundaries, and was raised in a family where shooting was a way of life. As a young girl, she helped prepare sausage rolls in the kitchen for elevenses between drives. She trudged through the heather and beat with the beaters. She learned to speak the language of retrievers and setters with the dog handlers and as a young girl, she couldn't wait to be old enough to be taught to shoot. The duchess is the best kind of shooting sportswoman because she developed her knowledge over time and experience, and that's how she raised her five children.

"I have a clear, early memory of being out shooting, when I was about thirteen," she recalls of growing up on her family's 450-acre farm in the southeast corner of Wales and participating in her first driven shoot. "Intensely excited, with my devoted springer spaniel Janie at heel, I was proudly beating [wild birds] for my father and his friend, Peter. I was always encouraged to beat, and I loved it. I ran the line with Janie and three other beaters, and we took it very seriously. To this day, I can still recapture that feeling of exhilaration when my willing dog retrieved her first pheasant from the fast-flowing River Teme."

Born Emma Watkins in Cardiff, Wales, in 1963, she studied opera at the Guildhall School of Music and subsequently worked as a London estate agent and interior designer before marrying David Manners, 11th Duke of Rutland, in 1992. They have three daughters—Lady Violet, Lady Alice, and Lady Eliza—and two sons, Charles, Marquess of Granby and Lord Hugo Manners. Upon the death of the tenth duke in 2001, the family moved into Belvoir (meaning 'beautiful view' and pronounced *BEE-vour*) Castle, Leicestershire, England, the stately home of the Manners family for thirty-six generations. A castle has stood on the site since Norman times and was recorded in the Doomsday Book as the land of Robert de Todeni, a nobleman who claimed, or was bestowed, the land after the Battle of Hastings in 1066.

The fourth incarnation of the castle was designed by English architect James Wyatt in the romantic Gothic Revival style, an architectural movement that began in the late 1740s and dominated western European architecture into the early nineteenth century. Belvoir was nearing completion in 1816 when, on October 25, a devastating fire broke out. Much of the new construction burned to the ground and tragically, priceless paintings by Titian, Rubens, Van Dyck and Joshua Reynolds perished. The rebuild, supervised by the architect Sir James Thornton, took sixteen years to complete, in 1832. Viewers of the British historical drama series *The Crown* will be interested to know that Belvoir was used to portray Windsor Castle, home of HRH Queen Elizabeth.

Impressive from a horticultural standpoint are Belvoir Gardens, designed and landscaped by Elizabeth Howard, 5th Duchess of Rutland, in 1799, when construction began under Wyatt's supervision. Today, "Friends of Belvoir Gardens" are engaged in a largely volunteer program to restore the landscape and gardens to its original design and beauty.

It was at Belvoir that a peckish Anna, Duchess of Bedford, felt the need for some late afternoon refreshment while awaiting dinner at the usual 8:30 p.m. A pot of Darjeeling tea, tea cakes, and finger sandwiches fit the bill, and in that moment, the afternoon tea was born and remains a 5 o'clock ritual in Britain and 'round the world to this day. Tea anyone?

Lady Emma's own influence on Belvoir is evident. She has applied her keen eye and background in interior design to debut a line of traditional, handcrafted furniture with Tetrad Furniture, reproduced from original pieces at Belvoir, and, with Crown Pavillions, traditional garden buildings crafted from Canadian western red cedar. But it is The Rutland Range of English game guns, made by Longhorne Gunmakers, that most closely reflects Lady Emma's own personal story.

The Duke and Duchess have raised all five of their children in the traditions and pleasures of the shooting life at Belvoir. His Grace the Duke of Rutland, himself a noted shot, mentions in the foreword to his wife's book *Shooting: A Season of Discovery* that "I have enjoyed (shooting) most of my life here at Belvoir and around the United Kingdom, and I have encouraged my five children to shoot."

The mark of a true and responsible shooting sportswoman is embodied by Lady Emma herself, when she wrote, "For me, the joy of bagging fifty birds in a day compared to the vertiginous numbers shot at Belvoir was just as intense. Bags of ten birds can, and should, give as much pleasure and be equally as sporting as five hundred."

"The Ladies' Shoot" (2012)

Another new departure is the ladies' shoot. My dear friend, Heather McGregor, who writes a weekly column in the *Financial Times*, loves her shooting, and brought a team of girlfriends to stay with us in September 2011. She and I had first met when she came to shoot with a corporate party in 2006.

I do try to welcome as many visitors as I can personally on shoot days but with five children it isn't always easy to switch from working mum to hostess with the mostest—and on time! Back on that day in 2006 I'd been picking children up from school on a freezing cold winter's afternoon and was wrapped in a fur coat that David had bought me from a great second-hand shop in London. I may just have mentioned, even grumbled, to him once that subzero temperatures on a particularly cold day were penetrating the thick castle walls—and I think he thought the coat would be a good investment and cheaper than extra heating! Anyway, I was late to greet the shoot guests, so I jumped quickly out of the car, ushered the children out of the way and rushed into the Guard Hall to say hello.

"So, you're the Duchess," Heather said, smiling at me. "Don't tell me all duchesses wear mink coats for the school run?"

With that, she took the contact details of the fur coat shop (subsequently buying her own) and we clicked. I love her directness and no messing attitude, and I don't know anyone else who can get so much done in a day.

Heather's guests were no ordinary girls' party. The "girls" turned out to be a serious bunch of high-achieving movers and shakers from the City, P.R., law, recruitment, and media firms. Heather has this amazing ability to put people together and she excelled

herself on this particular trip with twenty of her "top team." She is always telling me that she loves her shooting but is far too often the only woman on the line, particularly on corporate days, and wants to get more women shooting.

At the time, we had a new chef cooking his first dinner, who probably hadn't expected his food to be scrutinized by twenty women—but he needn't have worried. Seasonal and local produce was all cooked well and his pudding was absolutely delicious. Amongst the guests I met Emma Weir, who runs her own financial services headhunter firm, Eban. I discovered that she has a woodcock and snipe shoot on the Isle of Muck and she invited me along to find out as much as I could for my chapter on woodcock.[25] I sat close to Henrietta Royle, a wonderfully colorful and forthright lady, who had shot in Heather's charity clay shoot team at the Royal Berkshire Shooting School, and on the other side was a very glamorous television presenter. I was surprised how tight-knit this little group is and the big subject during dinner wasn't targets, mergers, and acquisitions, but our children. The usual concerns were discussed: teenage hormones, schools, and first boyfriends and girlfriends.

The next morning, a dense mist had descended, hanging thickly in the valley. It looked as if shooting could be delayed at best, cancelled at worse. But "no" won't do, so Phil Burtt decided to escort the ladies to Frog Hollow to shoot duck, in the hope that the weather would improve later. For now, the Guns would be given an opportunity to get their eye in over a relatively straightforward target. Phil had sent out for reinforcements as there were so many Guns who were novices and a team of helpers was very happy to assist. Everyone has to be a "first timer" at some stage and Heather and Phil allocated two novices to each peg and they swapped in and out. Any squeamishness was soon dispelled by the realization that for every duck that fell, hundreds got away. The sun broke through and it didn't take long for several shots to be fired and a few whoops of accomplishment to be heard as birds hit the ground. Everyone relaxed and I left them to it as they departed for a partridge drive. I overheard one of Phil's recruits discussing the euro with one of the Guns and I realized the chemistry of

---

25 Chapter 7, *Shooting: A Season of Discovery*, by The Duchess of Rutland.

the whole party was working just as well as Heather had predicted.

By tea, several Guns had shot their first birds, the mood was electric, and everyone had had a fabulous day. More to the point, as it was late September, everyone had refreshed their knowledge of the difference between a partridge and a hen pheasant!

Heather reminds me that game shooting for those who have never done it before can seem intimidating with all the requirements around safety, tipping, the draw, and many other rituals. Historically, many women have accompanied their menfolk to shoots but in the twenty-first century, more of these career women did not have husbands who shoot, so I hope that we were able to welcome and reassure them all at Belvoir. Before the team left, they had all changed back into their business suits with briefcases and overnight bags at the ready, resuming their corporate identities after a brief, but I sincerely hope enjoyable, respite from their high-pressure lives.

I lose count of the times when I wonder what David's ancestors would make of life in their home today. But when the castle is bulging at the cornerstones with shooting parties, I like to think there would be a nod of approval that so many different people are enjoying their legacy.

—From *Shooting: A Season of Discovery*, by The Duchess of Rutland, with Jane Pruden. Quiller Publishing Ltd., 2012.

13. Books by Shooting Sportswomen: An Index of Authors

he shooting sportswomen on this list wrote about their travels and adventures with a shotgun for company. Were those books written by women on handguns and rifles included, the list would be appreciably longer—but that's not what this book is about. There are, however, some few, carefully selected exceptions included here nonetheless for their insight and importance on the subjects of conservation, social issues, and living well the outdoor life. All, without exception, contribute to the meaning of what it is to be a shooting sportswoman.

APSLEY, LADY, VIOLET EMILY MILDRED BATHURST
(1895–1966)

Lady Violet Apsley was a thoroughly remarkable woman. She earned her pilot's license in 1930, but later that very same year she was thrown from her horse and confined to a wheelchair the rest of her life. *That didn't stop her.* She served in the Auxiliary Territorial Service in World War II and succeeded her husband, Lord Apsley, as member of parliament for Bristol Central upon his death in 1943. Among the four books she wrote were *To Whom the Goddess: Hunting and Riding for Women* (Hutchinson & Co. Publishers, Ltd., 1932) about the history of women as huntresses.

ASH, VICKI and ASH, GIL. *See page 54.*
Coaching Hour Chronicles. OSP Press, 2002–2019.

If It Ain't Broke, Fix It: Lessons in Shotgunning and Life. OSP Press, 2004.

Sporting Clays Consistency: You Gotta Be Out of Your Mind: A Shooter's Guide to the Mental Aspects of Sporting Clays & Life. With Ty Adams. OSP Press, 2006.

Traveling the Inner State. OSP Press, 2009.

Available through the OSP Shooting School, P.O. Box 826, Fulshear, TX 77441 or by email at gm@ospschool.com. The OSP Knowledge Vault, an online teaching classroom, features hundreds of videos, tutorials, and clips at www.ospschool.com/sample-knowledge.

BAILLIE, MRS. W.W.
Mrs. Baillie accompanied her husband, a British Army clergyman, to India. Refusing to stay behind on his hunting expeditions, she, too, hunted tigers, bison, ibex, and panthers with a black powder .500 Express rifle. She wrote her only book, *Days and Nights of Shikar* in 1921, at the age of sixty-five (republished in 2017 by Andesite Press), advising readers that, "if bitten by a scorpion, to kill and mash it up as a poultice to avoid the poison."

BELANGER, DIAN OLSON
Belanger—historian, author, speaker, associate curator and technical editor for engineering exhibits at the National Building Museum in Washington, D.C., docent at the Smithsonian's National Museum of American History and subsequently, at the Smithsonian's National Portrait Gallery—is a remarkable, accomplished woman whose list of academic degrees is as long as your arm. Her volume of work includes extensive research into the lives and work of pioneering scientists who probed the secrets of Antarctica, chronicled in *Deep Freeze: The United States, the International Geophysical Year, and the Origins of Antarctica's Age of Science* (University Press of Colorado, 2006). Her first book is of particular interest to outdoorswomen: *Managing American Wildlife* (University of Massachusetts Press, 1988); it won The Wildlife Society's national book award the year of its publication as the "outstanding publication in wildlife ecology and management."

BORDEN, COURTNEY (1899–1995). *See page 167.*

BOYD, JOYCE
Joyce Boyd decided to make a fresh start after her divorce and set out with her daughters in tow for East Africa. There, in 1925, she married Lionel Boyd and together they established a coffee plantation in Arusha. Their neighbors were Bror and Karen Blixen (Isak Dinesen). *My Farm in Lion Country* (Frederick A. Stokes Company, 1933) recounts her colorful and often dangerous life at home and on safari.

BOYNTON, LADY MILDRED AUGUSTA PAGET
(1854–1941). *See page 151.*

BRANDRETH, PAUL(INA) (1885–1946). *See page 165.*

BROWDER, LAURA
Her Best Shot: Women and Guns in America. University of North Carolina Press, 2008. University of North

Carolina Press, 2008. Browder examines, from past to present, the relationship between women and guns, citing such notables as Annie Oakley, Osa Johnson, and Confederate spy Pauline Cushman, who posed as a man. This is not a sporting book—not by a stretch—but it is a seminal book on armed women and position, and impact, in American culture.

CAPSTICK, FIONA CLAIRE

Born in South Africa, Fiona Capstick is a prolific, award-winning author and the widow of the late African hunting writer, Peter Hathaway Capstick (1940–1996), author of *Death in the Long Grass. The Diana Files: The Huntress-Traveller Through History* (Rowland Ward Publications, 2004) earned her the CIC Literary Award. Mrs. Capstick also wrote *Between Two Fires* (Rowland Ward, 2012), the biography of Margarete Trappe, who settled in German East Africa in 1907 and, for fifty years, was the first full-time professional woman huntress on the continent.

CARSON, RACHEL (1907–1954)

Rachel Louise Carson was born in 1907 on her family's sixty-five-acre farm near Springdale, Pennsylvania, above Pittsburgh on the Allegheny River. Her childhood delight in exploring Nature would build the framework for the rest of her all-too-brief life as one of America's foremost conservationists and proponents of the global environmental movement.

It was Carson who launched the global environmental movement. Carson identified and studied the environment—and set out to do something about it, and make a difference. That difference Rachel made was to identify the effects of synthetic pesticides, as passages in her greatest work, *Silent Spring*, attest.

Silent Spring was originally published in 1962. The title was inspired by John Keats's poem, "La Belle Dame sans Merci": "The sedge is wither'd from the lake, and no birds sing." Her conclusions were in part drawn from the work of two women: environmentalist and Waldorf teacher Marjorie Spock (1904–2008) and Mary Richards, an organic farmer, biodynamic farming advocate of Ehrenfried Pfeiffer (1899–1961), and associate of Rudolf Steiner, whose philosophy is the foundation of the Waldorf School.

In its first year of publication, *Silent Spring* won eight awards, among them the Schweitzer Medal from the Animal Welfare Institute; the Constance Lindsay Skinner Achievement Award from the Women's National Book Association; the Conservation Award for 1962 by the Rod and Gun Editors of Metropolitan Manhattan; the Conservationist of the Year Award by the National Wildlife Federation; the Annual Founders Award by the Izaak Walton League; and a citation by the International and US Councils of Women.

CREYKE, MRS. WALTER (DIANE CHASSERESSE). *See page 145.*

CLARKE, EILEEN

Eileen is the author of *The Venison Cookbook, The Freshwater Fish Cookbook, Classic Freshwater Fish Cooking,* and *The Game Grill.* A celebrated food writer and avid outdoorswoman, she lives in Townsend, Montana, with her husband, outdoor writer John Barsness. Their website is www.riflesandrecipes.com.

Duck & Goose Cookery. Ducks Unlimited, 2002.

Upland Game Bird Cookery. With Sil Strung. Ducks Unlimited, 2003. Over ninety game bird recipes along with chapters on field care, aging, freezing, storing, crockpot dishes, dry rubs and marinades.

COLEGATE, ISABEL (1931–)

Before Downton Abbey or Gosford Park there was another fictitious Edwardian England estate called Nettleby Park. Adapted to film in 1985, *The Shooting Party* (Avon, 1982) was one of Colegate's thirteen books. It takes place during a wingshooting weekend gone foul, at a time when the aristocracy and working classes were distinctive social tiers in a deeply divided caste system.

CRON, GRETCHEN GANS

Gretchen Cron learned to shoot on the hunting estate of her husband, German brewer Herman Cron. In 1925, they embarked upon the first of four safaris to East Africa, inspiring her to write *The Roaring Veldt* (G.P. Putnam's Sons, 1930).

DE QUINTANILLA, ISABEL

Isabel De Quintanilla was the wife of renowned professional hunter, and author of numerous books on African hunting, Tony Sanchez-Arno. She wrote *A Thousand Trails Through Africa* (Rowland Ward, 2005).

DE WATTEVILLE, VIVIENNE (1900–1957)

Vivienne de Watteville was a British writer and adventurer who hunted extensively in Africa with her father to acquire trophies for the Natural History Museum in Berne, Switzerland. Her father was killed by a lion and she continued, alone, to harvest his list of trophy animals for the museum. *Out of the Blue* (Methuen, London, 1927) and *Speak to the Earth: Wanderings and Reflections Among Elephants and Mountains* (Methuen, London 1936) recount her adventures.

DI FRANCIA, DUCHESSA D'AOSTA, ELENA (1871–1951)

Elena, Duchessa D'Aosta (also called Princess Hélène of Orléans) is all but forgotten today and yet, in her time, this English-born noblewoman who married into the Italian royal family of Orléans was universally admired for her courage, fortitude, and grace. She wrote *Viaggi in Africa*, published in 1913, which chronicled her several African hunting safaris. *The Wandering Princess*, by Edward W. Hanson (Fonthill Media, 2017) recounts the dramatic, romantic, turbulent life of this remarkable woman.

EDEN, FANNY (1801–1849)

Tigers, Durbars and Kings: Fanny Eden's Indian Journals, 1837 to 1838, by English aristocrat, Fanny Eden. Born in 1797, she visited her brother, George, when he was governor-general of India and remained for six years, accompanying him on his travels and hunting trips, and recording them in her illustrated journals. They were discovered after one hundred fifty years in the India Office Library and Records, and published for the first time in 1989 by John Murray Publishers, Ltd.

GARDNER, NORA (1866–1944)

Nora Beatrice Blythe, the Honorable Mrs. Col. Alan Coulston Gardner, joined her husband, a British military officer, when he was serving in India. Unwilling to be left alone, she joined him on his hunting trips. Her 1895 account, *Rifle and Spear with the Rajpoots: Being the Narrative of a Winter's Travel and Sport in Northern India* was originally published by Chatto and Windus in London and republished in 2016 by Wentworth Press.

GOLOB, JULIE

Golob, a freelance writer and contributing editor to *SHOT Business* magazine, the trade magazine of the National Shooting Sports Foundation, has written an important book on how parents can teach their children and establish rules for gun safety in the home. *Toys, Tools, Guns & Rules* is a self-published book, written in 2018, and is invaluable, even critical, to the family that owns guns. Illustrated by Nancy Batra. Also:

Shoot: Your Guide to Shooting and Competition. Skyhorse Publishing, 2012.

GREVILLE, LADY VIOLET (1842–1932). *See page 150.*

HAMERSTROM, FRANCES (1907–1998)

Frances Hamerstrom studied under Aldo Leopold at the University of Wisconsin. Frances was Leopold's only female graduate student. In 1949, she became the second woman to work as a wildlife professional in the state of Wisconsin, where her interests centered on the habitat support and restoration of native prairie grouse (prairie chicken) populations, the northern harrier, American kestrels, and peregrine falcons; she also became a licensed falconer. She was an original outdoorswoman and conservationist who lived life the way she wanted and made a difference in her world—and ours.

Adventures of the Stone Man. A children's book, illustrated by William Kimber. Crossing Press, 1977.

An Eagle to the Sky. Iowa State University Press, 1971.

Bird Trapping & Bird Banding: A Handbook for Trapping Methods All Over the World. Cornell University Press, 1996.

Birding with a Purpose: Of Raptors, Gabboons, and Other Creatures. Wiley-Blackwell, 1991.

Birds of Prey of Wisconsin. Department of Natural Resources, 1972.

Fran and Frederick Hamerstrom: Wildlife Conservation Pioneers, by Susan Tupper. A biography by Susan Tupper. Wisconsin Historical Society Press, 2016.

My Double Life: Memoirs of a Naturalist. University of Wisconsin Press, 1994.

Sharptails in the Shadows. Game Management Division, Wisconsin Conservation Dept., 1952.
Strictly for Chickens. Iowa State Press, 1980.
Walk When the Moon is Full. Schneider Publications, 2013.
Wild Food Cookbook. Iowa State Press, 1988.

HOLMES, MADELYN

Madelyn is an author of social and cultural books on women, among which is this biographical account of the lives of prominent women conservationists:

American Women Conservationists: Twelve Profiles. McFarland & Company, 2004.

HOUSTON, PAM

Women on Hunting: Essays, Fiction, and Poetry, was compiled by Houston and published by Ecco Press in 1994 and features award-winning authors, such as Margaret Atwood (*The Handmaid's Tale*) and Joyce Carol Oates.

HOUTMAN, K. J.

Why Women Hunt (Wild River Press, 2019) is an intimate look at eighteen women hunters and how they connected with, and embraced, hunting as an integral part of their lives. www.whywomenhunt.com

HURST, MRS. VICTOR

Mrs. Hurst wrote *Hunting, Shooting and Fishing* (Arthur Barker, 1953), the chronicle of her half-century of fox hunting, game shooting, and trout and salmon fishing throughout her native Britain. A field sportswoman, she published *Ponies and Riders: A Book of Instruction for Young Riders* with Charles Scribner's Sons in 1950.

JAQUES, FLORENCE PAGE (1890–1972)

Florence Jaques was an American nature, travel, and children's poetry writer. Born in Decatur, Illinois, she received her A.B. degree from Millikin University in 1911 and went on to Columbia University for her graduate degree at a time when few women sought higher education. Her husband was Francis Lee Jaques, a wildlife artist and the remarkable painter of the dioramas at the American Museum of Natural History in New York. They collaborated on seven illustrated outdoor books of which one, *Snowshoe Country*,

was awarded the John Burroughs Medal in 1946 for distinguished work in natural history. They retired to Minnesota in the 1950s, where they lived out their years.

As Far as the Yukon. Harper & Brothers, 1951.
Birds Across the Sky. Harper & Brothers, 1942.
Canadian Spring. Harper, 1947.
Canoe Country (1938) and *Snowshoe Country* (1944) were published together in 1999 by University of Minnesota Press.
Francis Lee Jaques: Artist of the Wilderness World. Doubleday, 1973.
The Geese Fly High. The University of Minnesota Pres, 1939.

JENKINS, LADY CATHERINE MINNA

Born and raised on her British father's sugar plantation in Natal (now South Africa), Catherine Jenkins had an inborn love of the outdoors—and an appetite for danger. Antonia Williams, who accompanied her on a hunting trip to Somaliland, recording the experience on film and in watercolor, described the always beautifully dressed huntress as "a most tiresome woman running unnecessary risks and increasing the danger to everyone else very seriously." But the woman had pluck. She embarked upon a fiercely cold, grueling trek to Chinese Tibet, the highest region on earth and site of Mount Everest, which she recounted in *Sport and Travel in Both Tibets*, originally published in 1910 by Blades, East and Blades, and reprinted in 2012 by Ulan Press.

JOHNSON, JULIA C. and D. M.

Guide to Pheasant Hunting, by outdoor photographer Julia Johnson and her husband, writer D. M. Johnson. Stackpole, 2006.
Waterfowling: Beyond the Basics. Stackpole Books, 2008.

JOHNSON, OSA.

Bride in the Solomons. Originally published in 1946.
Four Years in Paradise. Stackpole, 2018.
I Married Adventure. Kodansha, 2020.
Last Adventure: The Martin Johnsons in Borneo. William Morrow, 1966.

Osa Johnson's Jungle Friends. J.B. Lippincott Company, 1939.

Tarnish: The True Story of a Lion Cub. Kessinger Publishing, 2010.

KING, GRACE WATKINS (1877–1975)

Hunting Big Game in Africa was Mrs. King's account of her 1924 safari to Kenya. This book was privately printed in 1926 and is extremely rare.

LACY, ANN TANDY

Perdew, an Illinois River Tradition: The Genius and Artistry of Charles and Edna Perdew (D.A. Galliher, 1993) is Ann's book about the Perdews of Henry, Illinois, among America's most famous decoy carvers, makers of duck calls, and folk artists, producing thousands of pieces over the course of a half-century from their home workshop, between 1902 and his death in 1963. The Charles Perdew Museum Association preserves the Perdews' homestead as a museum.

LOWTHER, THE HON. MRS. LANCELOT (1869–1921). *See page 158.*

LUNDVALL, ASHLEE

When Ashlee was sixteen, she fell out of a hayloft and onto a pitchfork—which did not impale her, but the wooden handle broke her spine and left her permanently paralyzed. She got over her almost insurmountable hurdles with spirit, positive attitude, and sheer determination and today lives a full and wondrous life as a loving wife, mother of a young daughter, accomplished careerwoman, and spokeswoman for people with disabilities—and she's not yet forty. What's more, she is an active hunter and outdoorswoman who spends her leisure time with her family camping, kayaking, fly fishing, and hand-cycling. As a "champion for change," she's made a difference as a Committee Member on the President's Council on Sports, Fitness, and Nutrition, a National Pro Staffer for Mossy Oak, a member of the NRA Disabled Shooting Sports Committee—and that's to name just a few of the many organizations to which she serves as a director, member, volunteer, or columnist. Let Ashlee tell you about her life by logging on to You Tube and search for Ashlee Lundvall. Prepare to be inspired.

MATURIN, MRS. FRED

Born in India of English parents, twice-married, and a staunch suffragette, Mrs. Maturin wrote *Adventures Beyond the Zambesi: Of the O'Flaherty, the Insular Miss, The Soldier Man, and the Rebel Woman* (Brentano's, 1913) and *Petticoat Pilgrims on Trek* (Eveleigh Nash, 1909). Ferociously independent, she moved to South Africa after her divorce from Maturin. "Nov. 30, 1904. I have heard of a dear little cottage in a Dutch dorp," she wrote, "twelve miles out of Johannesburg, where, so far, they have only had one murder, one house blown up by dynamite, another set fire to by a man who had insured it and was on his last legs financially, and four housebreakings by Chinese in four months. There is a scramble for it because it is so safe."

McCAULOU, LILY RAFF

A gun-fearing environmentalist and animal lover leaves New York and her indie film production career and takes up a job in central Oregon, only to realize that if she wants trout *en papillote*, she's going to have to fish for the trout and cook it herself. Inspired to take a hunter's safety course, she soon finds herself hunting for her supper. This isn't a movie script—it's a personal memoir written by a young woman who had the courage to reexamine and question her life; McCaulou ventures out into the wilderness, where she learns to sustain herself, body and soul, in the simplicity and beauty of the great outdoors. To learn about Lily, log onto www.lilyrm.com.

Call of the Mild: Learning to Hunt My Own Dinner. Grand Central Publishing, 2012.

McCONNAUGHEY, LUCILLE HARRIS (1905–1996)

Lucille McConnaughey was a longtime member of the Michigan House of Representatives and is recorded in the *Guinness Book of World Records* for 100 percent voting attendance. Her book *Woman Afield* (Vantage Press, 1987) recounts her hunting trip to Alaska, guided by bush pilot Jay Sterner Hammond (1922–2005), a US Army Air Corps fighter pilot in World War II and member of the Black Sheep Squadron, who was fourth governor of Alaska from 1974 to 1982, during the construction of the Trans-Alaska Pipeline.

MEIKLE, MRS. M.E.

After Big Game: The Story of an African Holiday (T. Werner Laurie, Ltd., London, 1915) was jointly authored by R. S. Meikle and his wife. The book recounts their adventures and observations on safari in British East Africa.

MORDEN, FLORENCE H.

From the Field Notebook of Florence H. Morden was privately published in 1940. It is an autobiographical account of hunting in British East Africa, the Kashmir, and Ladakh.

MURIE, MARGARET THOMAS "MARDY"

(1902–2003)

"Mardy" Murie, "the grandmother of the conservation movement," was raised in Anchorage, Alaska, from the age of nine, when her stepfather assumed a government position and moved the family from Seattle, Washington. In those days, Anchorage was a rough and raw gold rush town, boasting twenty-three saloons, a fenced-in red light district, and little else. Mardy led a very protected life and immersed herself in academics, becoming the first woman to graduate from Alaska Agricultural College and School of Mines (now called the University of Alaska), where she met her Norwegian-born husband, Olaus Murie, a wildlife biologist, today heralded as the "greatest naturalist of the North American continent."

Mardy and Olaus were a team, working together as wilderness advocates, advisors, and consultants to the Wilderness Society, the National Park Service, and the Sierra Club, loving it, and loving one another. Reflecting on the moment they first met, Mardy said, "Our affection increased as each day went by until nothing else mattered." Their shared passion for, and dedication to, the great outdoors had them often living as nomads, moving from one wilderness place to the next, pitching their tent, setting up camp, hunting, fishing, and living off the land in the Grand Tetons and in Alaska, often braving extreme weather and hazardous conditions as far north as eighty miles from the Arctic Circle.

In 1927, they made Jackson, Wyoming, their lifelong home, had three children, and, for the last ten years of her life, housed Olaus's Norwegian mother, taking them all on their camping trips for several weeks at a stretch. Mardy collaborated with Olaus on his research and books until his death in 1963, and their four decades of untiring work led to the establishment of the Arctic National Wildlife Refuge.

Mardy was widowed for forty years. She died, age of 101, in the log cabin she called home for seventy years. The year before her death, the Presidential Medal of Freedom was added to her many awards.

The Alaskan Bird Sketches of Olaus Murie, with his Field Notes. Alaska Northwest Books, 1979.

Island Between. University of Alaska Press, 1977.

Two in the Far North: A Conservation Champion's Story of Life, Love, and Adventure in the Wilderness. Alaska Northwest Books, 2020.

Wapiti Wilderness. University Press of Colorado, 1987.

MURRAY, HILDA (1872–1929). *See page 161.*

PELLEGRINI, GEORGIA

Georgia is among the new generation of outdoorswomen who have embraced the wild and the wilderness and change the way we live, eat, cook, and sustain ourselves body and soul. Her website is www.georgiapellegrini.com.

Food Heroes: 16 Culinary Artisans Preserving Tradition. Stewart, Tabori & Chang, 2014.

Girl Hunter: Revolutionizing the Way We Eat, One Hunt at a Time. Da Capo Lifelong Books, 2011.

Modern Pioneering: More Than 150 Recipes. Clarkson Potter, 2014.

ROBY, MARGUERITE

Roby's autobiographical account of her travels to Central Africa, *My Adventures in the Congo*, was originally published in 1911 by Edward Arnold, London (Palala Press, 2015). She was among the amazingly large number of Victorian and Edwardian Englishwomen who traveled to Africa and India, seeking adventure and putting their courage and skills to the test. "From Cape Town I wrote home for a .303 Enfield sporting rifle, a .22 Winchester, and a 12-bore shotgun, with ammunition," she wrote, "and guns in hand, set out on safari, notably stopping at the tree at Ujiji, where Stanley and Livingstone first met.

RUTLAND, HER GRACE THE DUCHESS OF *See page 178.*

SAMPSON, KAY EVON

Kay Sampson chronicled twenty years of hunting in *The Twilight Zone of a Huntress*. At fifty-four, she married a big game hunter and set out for adventure, hunting Kodiak brown bear and mountain goat on Kodiak Island, big game in Namibia, and traveling to other distant places. She was awarded Safari Club International's Diana Award. "It is much more humane to allow an animal to live out its life in a natural setting and then quickly dispatch it, rather than pen up a cow in what my husband calls a cow concentration camp for the sole purpose of raising it to kill for meat or leather," she wrote.

SCHRODER, PIFFA

Piffa Schroder, the first wife of late British billionaire Bruno Lionel Schroder, penned witty little books on country sports with barbed insights such as, "You must remember that, as far as shooting is concerned, you will be regarded by every male as a member of not the fairer, but the inferior sex." Her potshots at the sporting fraternity were meant to be taken in good humor.

> *Bags and Baggage: A Visitor's Guide*. Gun Room Publishing, 1997.
> *Banging On: A Bird's-Eye View of Country Sport*. Ashford, Buchan and Enright, 1990.
> *Cocks Only*. Swan Hill Press, 2000.
> *Fair Game: A Lady's Guide to Shooting*. Ashford Press Publishing, 1988.

SHOCKEY, EVA

Author of *Taking Aim: Daring to be Different, Happier, and Healthier in the Great Outdoors* (Random House, 2017), self-described "mama, author, and TV host" Eva is known as a bow hunter, not a shotgunner, but she nonetheless deserves mention here. She has over 2 million followers on social media and was voted "Most Admired Prominent Outdoorswoman" by *Field & Stream* magazine in 2016 and with good reason—the pretty, grounded, joyful young woman has helped define what it is to hunt and live the outdoor life as a modern woman. Raised by loving parents, Eva co-hosts her father's long-running show on the Outdoor Channel, *Jim Shockey's Hunting Adventures*. Visit her website at www.evashockey.com.

SMYTHIES, OLIVE

Olive was the wife of E. A. Smythies, chief conservator of the forest of Nepal. The couple hunted together, and with their friend and great hunter, Jim Corbett, who spared thousands of lives from man-eating tigers and leopards and for whom the Jim Corbett National Park in the Nainital District of India is named.

> *Jungle Families*. William Heinemann, 1954.
> *Ten Thousand Miles on Elephants*. Seeley, Service & Co., 1961.
> *Tiger Lady: Adventures in the Indian Jungle*. William Heinemann, 1953.

STANGE, MARY ZEISS. *See page 173.*

SUCKSDORFF, ASTRID BERGMAN (1927–2015)

> Astrid Sucksdorff was a Swedish naturalist and hunter.
> *Chendru, the Boy and the Tiger*, Harcourt, 1960.
> *Tiger in Sight*. Delacorte Press, 1977.
> *Tooni, the Elephant Boy*. Collins, 1971.

TYACKE, MRS. R. H. *See page 147.*

THOMPSON, GRACE GALLATIN SETON
(1872–1959)

The wife of English-born author and wildlife artist Ernest Thompson Seton (1860–1946), a pioneering founder of the Boy Scouts of America, Grace hunted and traveled throughout the American West with her husband in the early days of their marriage. Her first book, *A Woman Tenderfoot*, in 1900, five years after their marriage, recounted their hunting trip on horseback through the Rocky Mountains. *Nimrod's Wife*, published in 1907, had them starting out in Sacramento, California, camping under the stars in a canvas tent she called The Inn of the Silver Moon. "I have camped in a region where bears prowled unceasingly," she wrote, "where the smaller fourfoots, wolves, foxes, lynxes, knew very well of my presence. A mountain lion once walked half way around my bed as I lay peacefully sleeping, his nose not a hand's breadth from mine, as the great padded tracks next morning amply testified."

Grace's life took an abrupt turn in 1910, when she threw herself into the women's suffragist movement as vice president of the Connecticut Woman Suffrage

Association. But in 1916, as the storm clouds of the Great War darkened the horizon, she felt compelled to take a new path and left her husband and daughter for France, where she founded Le Bien-Être du Blessé (Welfare of the Injured), an all-female motor unit that saw action on the front lines transporting the injured and war materiel.

After the war, she returned home to her family and resumed her work with the Connecticut Woman Suffrage Association as president. By now, however, her marriage had all but ended. Grace had become a practicing theosophist, a follower of a new religious sect created by Russian immigrant Helena Blavatsky, a self-proclaimed "enlightened being" who, as a "Master of the Ancient Wisdom" drew upon the occult, Western esotericism, astrology, and Neoplatonism. Again, Grace left her family and for much of the 1920s and 1930s, traveled to such faraway places as China, Egypt, Hawaii, India, Indochina, Japan, and South America, writing three books about her adventures. Grace and Ernest's divorce became final in 1935 and shortly after, he remarried. She never did. For the remainder of her life, she immersed herself in women's organizations, including the International Council of Women, the Society of Woman Geographers, and the Women's National Republican Club. Their only child, a daughter, was Anya Seton (1904–1990), a nationally acclaimed author of historical romances.

> A Woman Tenderfoot. Originally published in 1900. Republished by Wentworth Press in 2016.
>
> A Woman Tenderfoot in Egypt. Dodd, Mead and Company, 1923.
>
> Chinese Lanterns. Dodd, Mead and Company, 1924.
>
> Nimrod's Wife (1907). Republished in 2015 by Palala Press.
>
> Poison Arrows: A Strange Journey with an Opium Dreamer Through Annam, Cambodia, Siam, and the Lotus Isle of Bali. House of Field, Inc., 1940.
>
> Yes, Lady Saheb: A Woman's Adventurings. Harper & Bros., 1925.

WILES, LAURIE BOGART (formerly published as LAURIE BOGART MORROW) is the author of this book.

> Cold Noses and Warm Hearts. Willow Creek Press, 2012.
>
> The Giant Book of Dog Names. Simon & Schuster, 2012.
>
> The Gigantic Book of Hunting Stories (contributor). Skyhorse Publishing, 2008.
>
> The Hardscrabble Chronicles. Berkley, 2002; large print edition, Center Point, 2011.
>
> The Italian Gun. Wilderness Adventures Press, 1997.
>
> The Orvis Guide to Gun Care and Maintenance. Willow Creek Press, 2000.
>
> The Orvis Guide to Shotgunning Technique, Willow Creek Press, 2000.
>
> The Orvis Guide to Sporting Dog First Aid. With Dr. Chuck Divinnie. Willow Creek Press, 2000.
>
> Shooter's Bible Guide to Shotgun Sports for Women: A Comprehensive Guide to the Art and Science of Wing and Clay Shooting. Skyhorse Publishing, 2020.
>
> Shooting Sports for Women. St. Martin's Press, 1996.
>
> Trout Tales and Other Angling Stories: Corey Ford compendium, 1995.
>
> The Trickiest Thing in Feathers: Corey Ford compendium, 1996.
>
> The Woman Angler. St. Martin's Press, 1997.

YOUNGHUSBAND, ETHEL

Mrs. Younghusband accompanied her husband, a captain in the King's African Rifles, on his hunting excursions in East Africa, concluding that Africa was a wondrous place for a woman to visit, but not to live. She recorded their adventures in Glimpses of East Africa and Zanzibar (John Long, Limited, 1910).

Woman the Hunter. Beacon Press, 1998. A cultural history of women and hunting.

ZASTROW, BERDETTE ELAINE

A practical and valuable guide for women who are new to bird hunting written by a former head of the South Dakota Game, Fish and Parks Commission. Berdette discusses how to connect with other women who hunt, state hunting programs that are available to women, and much more.

Woman's Guide to Hunting: Learn to Hunt Pheasant, Turkey, Waterfowl and Deer. Krause Publications, 2000.

SHOOTING ORGANIZATIONS AND CLUBS

Women's Shooting Organizations

These shooting organizations are among an increasing number that offer programs, resources, and activities designed specifically for women seeking the opportunity to receive firearms training by certified instructors, engage in competitions, and share their interest and passion for the outdoors and shooting sports with other like-minded women.

Annie Oakley Shooters

www.annieoakleyshooters.com

The "Annies" were formed from a relationship with a charity shoot in Atlanta, the Atlanta Charity Clays, which raises money for Atlanta's children's charities. Originally, women were volunteers responsible for the cocktail party and the silent auction the night before, as well as volunteering at two days of shooting events. Many Annies are past co-chairs of Atlanta Charity Clays. In 1999, ACC introduced Annie Oakley Day, a Thursday, for women to come out and shoot sporting clays. Since only a few women had ever handled a gun, instruction was offered in the morning and shooting the course in the afternoon. The Annie Oakley Day struggled along for several years but was never as successful as was hoped. To add a third shooting day to Atlanta Charity Clays was a lot of work for the committee and the volunteers.

After one fun afternoon of breaking clays, a group of shooting friends discussed how to establish their own women's tournament. In May 2004, six women met for breakfast and brainstorming. Mary Huntz looked at her good friend Margaret Bosbyshell and said, "I'll chair the first Annie Oakley Tournament if you will be my co-chair and be in charge of the cocktail party." With a big smile Margaret agreed, and the Annies were off and running to produce their women's shooting event: A New Tournament, A New Day, A New Cause.

The Trust for Public Land was their first charity partner, and the Annies proudly donated five hundred thousand dollars to the Trust.

Sixteen tournaments later, the Annies have grown to be a diverse group of women shooters—young, and not so young, professional women and stay-at-home moms, peashooters, and sharpshooters. There is no formal membership and no dues, but they send out an email notice for Annie Monday, the second Monday in every month except July and August, rain or shine, holiday or not. About fifty women come for instruction or to shoot the course; then at noon they gather for lunch and announcements before heading home or to the office. September kicks off the shooting season and the annual Annie Oakley Tournament, which includes women and men shooters, is in November. As the largest group of women shooters in the country, it's wonderful being an Annie!

A Girl & A Gun Women's Shooting League

www.agirlandagun.org

A Girl & A Gun Women's Shooting League (AG & AG) is a shooting club established by women shooters for women shooters. AG & AG events are intended to be fun, social gatherings where women can come together for support and encouragement, ask questions in a safe and nonjudgmental environment, improve on their marksmanship, and bond together in the shooting community. AG & AG Chapters are listed on their website so you can readily find one near you and look into joining.

DIVA Women Outdoors Worldwide
www.divawow.org

▲ Judy Rhodes, founder of DIVA.

Judy Rhodes is a rancher's daughter who grew up shooting and hunting, so it stands to reason that from an early age, she understood what it means to enjoy the outdoors in meaningful ways. In 1999, at the age of fifty, she determined to share her knowledge and passion for the outdoors with like-minded women and founded DIVA Internationals or Women Outdoors Worldwide.

Today Judy is identified as "the voice of women in the outdoors" as she continues to mentor women and youth and promote women in the shooting sports, most recently as co-host for the "Hunting Heritage" episodes of The Sporting Life podcast, hosted by Bob Svetich. With members in forty-nine states and fifteen foreign countries, the DIVAs advocate safe hunting practices and encourage women to take up shooting sports.

DIVA WOW's mission is to help and support women in the outdoors by offering shooting, fly fishing, rifle marksmanship, archery, and hunting classes; pistol leagues and clinics; NRA certification and CHL classes; social events and trips; and sporting dog training, trials, and events. This all-volunteer organization has introduced thousands of women to shooting and the outdoors. DIVA WOW embodies the spirit of sisterhood—teaching women, many for the first time, about the great outdoors and all that it has to offer.

G.R.I.T.S.
www.gritsgobang.org

The GRITS—Girls Really into Shooting—is a women's shotgun shooting group with over a dozen chapters around the country. Founded by Elizabeth Lanier Fennell, a Level III NSCA Shooting Instructor, the GRITS teach all levels of shooters how to improve their shooting and have fun. Elizabeth married PSCA Tour Pro and fourteen-time NSCA Team USA member Will Fennell in 2017. They merged their respective shooting schools and today own and operate the Fennell Shooting School at Blue Branch Farm in Sharon, South Carolina.

NRA Women on Target
wot.nra.org

Women on Target is the perfect place to start if you are interested in learning to shoot. NRA-sanctioned instructional shooting clinics teach firearm safety and the fundamentals of marksmanship, providing the confidence to safely handle and operate a firearm upon completion. Women on Target clinics are available only to women; it's a safe and friendly environment whether you're picking up a gun for the very first time or are just brushing off some dust and need a little refresher.

NRA Women's Leadership Forum
"Ring of Freedom"
www.nrawlf.org

The NRA Women's Leadership Forum began with a vision to form a community just for women within the NRA. Today they are one of the NRA's largest and most influential philanthropic groups, sharing time, resources, energy, and passion to protect Americans' Second Amendment rights.

Shoot Like a Girl

www.shootlikeagirl.com

Shoot Like a Girl is an organization that empowers women in the hunting and shooting industries. Go online to learn more about Shoot Like a Girl's commitment to inspiring women to participate in the shooting sports, watch videos such as "How to Pattern a Shotgun," and download their "Shoot Like a Girl Anthem" on iTunes.

National Shotgun Sports Organizations

Amateur Trapshooting Association

www.shootata.com

The ATA is the largest clay target shooting organization in the world and serves as the governing body for the sport's rules and regulations. Founded in 1900, as the American Trapshooting Association, in 1923 the organization changed its name to the Amateur Trapshooting Association. The national headquarters and home grounds are located in Sparta, Illinois, where the Grand American World Trapshooting Championships

attract over four thousand competitors every August. ATA members participate in more than six thousand registered tournaments and shoot at more than 60 million targets. More than nine hundred gun clubs are affiliated with the ATA.

NSSF/SHOT Show

www.nssf.org

The NSSF's mission is to promote, protect, and preserve hunting and the shooting sports. Formed in 1961, the NSSF has a membership of thousands of manufacturers, distributors, firearms retailers, shooting ranges, sportsmen's organizations, and publishers nationwide. NSSF.org has a comprehensive website that addresses firearms safety, information on where to shoot, where to hunt, where to buy sporting firearms, and more. Through the NSSF's Project ChildSafe, over 37 million free gun locks with accompanying educational materials have been distributed nationwide to family households with guns. As the barometer for the Outdoor Industry, the NSSF closely monitors industry statistics and projections. Every year, the NSSF hosts the SHOT Show (Shooting, Hunting, Outdoor Trade Show, www. shotshow.org), the largest annual tradeshow for the shooting, hunting, and firearms industry in the world.

National Skeet Shooting Association

National Sporting Clays Association

www.nssa-nsca.org

The National Skeet Shooting Association (NSSA) and the National Sporting Clays Association (NSCA) are the official governing and sanctioning bodies for their sports. The NSSA was founded in 1928 and is a nonprofit organization owned and operated by its members. It is the world's largest skeet shooting organization and annually hosts the World Skeet Championships. NSCA was founded in 1989 as a division of NSSA, and it is now the world's largest sporting clays organization. It annually hosts members from all fifty states and many foreign countries at the National Sporting Clays Championship.

USA Shooting
www.usashooting.org

USA Shooting, a 501c3 nonprofit corporation, was chartered by the United States Olympic and Paralympic Committee as the national governing body for the sport of shooting in April 1995. The organization implements and manages development programs and sanctions events at the local, state, regional, and national levels.

Headquartered in Colorado Springs, Colorado, at the US Olympic and Paralympic Training Center, USA Shooting has a full-time staff dedicated to furthering the sport and supporting athletes and members of the organization. The organization has a *USA Shooting News* magazine publication, as well as public and member-specific websites. Partially funded by the US Olympic and Paralympic Committee, USA Shooting relies on donations from supporters of the Olympic Movement, membership dues, event fees, and corporate partners who take a strong interest in the development of the US Shooting Team.

The Shooting Center is the largest indoor shooting facility in the Western Hemisphere and the third largest in the world. It also houses the administration offices, a gunsmith room, and locker rooms for resident and visiting athletes. In addition to the indoor ranges at the USOPTC, the outdoor ranges at the International Shooting Park include four superimposed international-style skeet and bunker trap fields, shade shelters, and a clubhouse for US Shooting Team members.

The USA Shooting Team comprises the top Olympic-style shooters in the country. For those who have dedicated their dreams to the pursuit of the Olympic path, the USA Shooting Team is a stepping stone to the top of the podium. As athletes (both junior and open division shooters) deliver top notch performances, they are named to one of the teams. The first step is the National Junior Team, which is open for athletes under twenty years of age. As a shooter, you can earn a spot on the National Junior Team through National Championships, National Junior Olympic Championships for Shooting, and more.

Shooters over twenty years of age (and talented youth who qualify) are eligible to make the National Development Team. Athletes on this team have shown promise as a future Olympian. The National Development Team is nominated and approved by a committee composed of coaches, the executive director, and athlete representatives.

The National Team includes the top pistol, rifle, and shotgun athletes in the country. These individuals have demonstrated consistent success on a national level. Additionally, athletes on the National Team travel around the world representing the United States at various world cups, world championships, and intercontinental championships.

Youth and College Shooting Programs
As a shooting sportswoman with children (or a youthful sportswoman yourself), it is important to consider the education as future hunters and shooters. The best way to do this is by enrolling children in a youth and college shooting program. Give them the opportunity to learn while they are young, and you are opening the door for them to a lifetime of satisfaction and fulfillment in the great outdoors.

ACUI Clay Target
www.acui.org/claytargets

The ACUI Collegiate Clay Target Championships program provides a quality experience for college students that teaches fair play, concentration, and logic skills while enhancing interpersonal relationships. This is the only collegiate event featuring all six clay target events: international skeet and trap, American skeet and trap, five-stand, and sporting clays.

AIM
www.aim4ata.com

AIM (Academics, Integrity, Marksmanship) is the official youth program of the Amateur Trapshooting Association. The program allows elementary- through college-age shooters the chance to compete in registered competition on a level playing field either as a team or as individuals.

International Hunter Education Association
www.ihea-usa.org

IHEA is the official organization representing the interests of state, provincial, and federal hunter education coordinators and hunter education instructors who teach hunter safety, ethics, and conservation to approximately six hundred fifty thousand students each year.

Every Kid Outdoors
www.everykidoutdoors.gov

Every Kid Outdoors allows fourth graders and family members in the United States free access to over two thousand federal lands and waters so they can discover the wildlife, resources, and history of US public lands and parks, and inspire a future generation of stewards.

Every Kid Outdoors begins each year on September 1 and goes through August 31.

National 4-H Shooting Sports
www.4-hshootingsports.org

The focus of all 4-H programs is the development of youths as individuals and as responsible and productive citizens. Youths learn marksmanship, the safe and responsible use of firearms, the principles of hunting and archery, and much more.

National Rifle Association (NRA) Youth Interests
explore.nra.org/interests/youth-interests

The NRA's interest in promoting the shooting sports among America's youth began in 1903 with the establishment of rifle clubs at all major colleges, universities, and military academies. Today, youth programs are still a cornerstone of the NRA, with more than one million youth participating in NRA shooting sports events and affiliated programs with groups such as 4-H, the Boy Scouts of America, the American Legion, Royal Rangers, National High School Rodeo Association, and others.

Royal Rangers National Shooting Sports Program
www.royalrangers.com/nssp

NSSP is the shooting sports program for the Royal Rangers, a Christian church ministry for boys ages five to eighteen. Their mission is to support youth while promoting a safe and rewarding shooting sports experience. NSSP encourages participation in all shooting sports and archery. Royal Rangers is the second largest scouting group in the United States and internationally with approximately 125,000 members. They are the world's largest mentoring program for boys, with chapters in more than one hundred countries.

Scholastic Clay Target Program

mysctp.com

The Scholastic Clay Target Program (SCTP) provides youths in grades twelve and under an opportunity to compete as a team for state and national championships in trap, skeet, and sporting clays. The ultimate goal is to instill in young participants a commitment to safe firearm handling, teamwork, and leadership. SCTP was developed by the National Shooting Sports Foundation and is managed nationally by the Scholastic Shooting Sports Foundation.

USA Youth Education in Shooting Sports

www.usayess.org

USA Youth Education in Shooting Sports (USAYESS) exists to develop, grow, and support state foundations and associations that use hands-on events, competitive shooting sports, and wildlife habitat and conservation programs to introduce and educate young people and their families about safe firearm handling, competitive shooting, and outdoor conservation activities.

Shooting, Wildlife, and Conservation Organizations

The North American Model of Wildlife Conservation

American hunters have the unique position of being the original conservationists. In the early twentieth century, many wildlife species in the United States were facing an uncertain future due to unregulated over-harvesting of many species and habitat destruction. Sportsmen and women watching this unfold led the call for new approaches for the responsible management and use of these resources. Seasons, game limits, and funds for wildlife conservation programs all originated with the hunting community. These efforts were able to turn the tide and save populations that were once disappearing, including white-tailed deer, pronghorn antelope, elk, wild turkeys, and wood ducks. Part of this effort was a push for legislation to create a funding mechanism to implement the principles of what is known as the North American Model of Wildlife Conservation. Hunters were successful, and in 1937 the landmark Pittman-Robertson Federal Aid in Wildlife Restoration Act was signed into law.

To date, hunters and recreational shooters have contributed nearly $11 billion to wildlife conservation through the excise tax paid by manufacturers of hunting and shooting arms and ammunition. The tax revenue is distributed to state fish and wildlife agencies, which combine the funds with those raised through the sale of hunting licenses to conserve and manage wildlife populations, including non-game species, and to help create opportunities for all Americans to enjoy wildlife recreation. Due to the unparalleled success of the North American Model of Wildlife Conservation, every state today has thriving wildlife populations in natural habitats that sustain hunted as well as non-hunted species. While all Americans benefit from these conservation efforts, most are unaware of the sportsmen-funded mechanisms that sustain and provide public access to these resources.

Association for Conservation Information

www.aci-net.org

The Association for Conservation Information (ACI) is a nonprofit organization of natural resources communicators. They serve to further natural resource conservation and exchange. They are made up of professionals representing US state, US federal, and Canadian wildlife conservation and parks and natural resource agencies as well as private conservation organizations.

Association of Fish and Wildlife Agencies

www.fishwildlife.org

State, provincial, and territorial fish and wildlife agencies in North America have safeguarded fish and wildlife for over one hundred years. The public entrusts these agencies with primary stewardship over vital wildlife resources. The Association of Fish and Wildlife Agencies lends collective voice to its agencies in fulfillment of that responsibility.

Boone and Crockett Club

www.boone-crockett.org

It is the mission of the Boone and Crockett Club to promote the conservation and management of wildlife and its habitat, to preserve and encourage hunting, and to maintain the highest ethical standards of fair chase and sportsmanship in North America. Boone and Crockett Club also offers youth outdoor adventure camps (www.boone-crockett.org/outdoor-adventure-camps) and hunter education courses (www.boone-crockett.org/hunter-education-courses).

The Conservation Alliance

www.conservationalliance.com

The Conservation Alliance is a group of like-minded companies that disburses its collective annual membership dues to grassroots environmental organizations. They direct funding to community-based campaigns to protect threatened wild habitat and outdoor recreation. The Alliance was founded in 1989 by outdoor industry leaders who shared the goal of increasing outdoor

industry support for conservation efforts. They now have more than two hundred fifty member companies.

Delta Waterfowl

www.deltawaterfowl.org

The Delta Waterfowl foundation is North America's oldest waterfowl conservation organization and promotes the restoration and management of all natural resources, especially aquatic areas.

Ducks Unlimited

www.ducks.org

Ducks Unlimited (DU) is dedicated to the betterment of waterfowl and waterfowling in all of North America. DU has helped build and restore millions of acres of prime waterfowl nesting habitat, including thousands of miles of vital protective shoreline, and DU is working toward the development of additional nesting habitat in the United States and Canada.

Izaak Walton League of America

www.iwla.org

There are fifty-four thousand outdoor enthusiasts who are united through a network of local clubs to implement the Izaak Walton League's national program for clean waters and improved hunting and fishing.

National Association of University Fisheries and Wildlife Programs

www.naufwp.org

The NAUFWP represent, strengthen, and advocate for all college and university programs educating fish and wildlife conservation and management professionals. Established in 1991, they have forty members from more than thirty states who represent nine thousand students and four hundred faculty across the United States. They are the only academic association representing the field of fish and wildlife conservation and management. Key attributes include being a forward-looking influencer in fish and wildlife higher education and the primary advocate for research and education funding related to fish and wildlife resources.

National Audubon Society

www.audubon.org

When a birder meets a duck hunter on a trail through a marsh, it might seem they have little in common. This is an unfortunate misperception, because the two often share essential values: a fascination with waterfowl and a commitment to conserving wetlands.

National Wildlife Federation

www.nwf.org

America's experience with cherished landscapes and wildlife has helped define and shape its national character and identity for generations. Protecting these natural resources is a cause that has long united Americans from all walks of life and political stripes. To hunters, anglers, hikers, birders, wildlife watchers, boaters, climbers, campers, cyclists, gardeners, farmers, forest stewards, and other outdoor enthusiasts, this conservation ethic represents a sacred duty and obligation to protect and build upon a conservation heritage for the sake of wildlife, ourselves, our neighbors, and—most of all—for future generations. Being successful in saving wildlife requires sweeping numbers to unite toward a shared vision. The National Wildlife Federation was built on the principle that joint effort and solid cooperation are critical to conservation.

National Wild Turkey Federation

www.nwtf.org

The National Wild Turkey Federation is the nation's largest member-supported conservation group working for wise conservation of all the nation's resources. The NWTF is dedicated to the conservation of the wild turkey and the preservation of a hunting heritage. The NWTF is leading a collaborative effort to solve the problem with the Save the Habitat. Save the Hunt. initiative, and our contribution is our dynamic volunteer base.

The Nature Conservancy

www.nature.org

The Nature Conservancy is a global environmental nonprofit working to create a world where people and nature can thrive. Founded as a grassroots organization in the United States in 1951, the Nature Conservancy has grown to become one of the most effective and wide-reaching environmental organizations in the world. Thanks to more than a million members and the dedicated efforts of a diverse staff and more than four hundred scientists, the Nature Conservancy impacts conservation in seventy-nine countries and territories across six continents. Their mission is to conserve the lands and waters on which all life depends; their vision is a world where the diversity of life thrives, and people act to conserve nature for its own sake and its ability to fulfill our needs and enrich our lives.

North American Grouse Partnership
www.grousepartners.org

The North American Grouse Partnership (NAGP) is the only conservation organization that advocates for all twelve North American grouse species and their habitats with the goal of ensuring that grouse conservation is guided by science, public policies are beneficial to grouse, and on-the-ground management of lands lead to positive outcomes for grouse.

Pheasants Forever and Quail Forever
www.pheasantsforever.org
www.quailforever.org

Since forming in 1982, Pheasants Forever (and its subsequent quail division, Quail Forever, formed in 2005) has created or enhanced wildlife habitat on more than 15.8 million acres across the United States and parts of Canada. With a network of more than seven hundred chapters and 149,000 members, Quail Forever and Pheasants Forever are able to accomplish thousands of wildlife habitat projects annually. Additionally, they participate in land acquisitions to permanently protect critical habitat for upland wildlife while simultaneously opening the areas to public recreation, including hunting.

Ruffed Grouse Society/American Woodcock Society
www.ruffedgrousesociety.org

Established in 1961, the Ruffed Grouse Society is North America's foremost conservation organization dedicated to preserving our sporting traditions by creating healthy forest habitat for ruffed grouse, American woodcock, and other wildlife. RGS works with landowners and government agencies to develop critical habitat utilizing scientific management practices. Members are mainly grouse and woodcock hunters who support national scientific conservation and management efforts to ensure the future of the species.

Safari Club International Foundation/Sables
safariclubfoundation.org

SCI Foundation funds and directs worldwide programs dedicated to wildlife conservation, outdoor education, and wildlife policy and management in the constructive role that hunting and hunters play in biodiversity around the world. Since 2000, SCIF have put over $70 million in hunter dollars to work on over one hundred conservation projects in thirty countries. Among SCI's many offerings is the Disabled Hunters Program, designed to give courage and dignity while enabling the disabled to enjoy hunts locally and worldwide.

Founded in 1984 by the women of SCI, the SCI Foundation Sables is a committee of SCI dedicated to furthering the understanding of our outdoor heritage, including the positive role of hunting, through the creation and support of wildlife and conservation educational programs. Sables women and men help advance outstanding SCI Foundation education programs that instill a love of the outdoors and respect for nature. They also recognize that the future of the shooting sports and hunting rest with today's youth. Their efforts are directed toward educating teachers, youth group leaders, and young people about our outdoor heritage.

SCIF Sables come from all walks of life: stay-at-home moms, teachers, business people, lawyers, nurses, and many others. Using their many talents and skills, they work together to share their joy and enthusiasm for wildlife conservation.

Sportsmen's Alliance
www.sportsmensalliance.org

The collective efforts of Sportsmen's Alliance helps protect and promote our outdoor heritage. Join today to create a powerful and unified voice for sportsmen across the country. Our collective efforts build a legacy for the next generation to carry forward.

Theodore Roosevelt Conservation Partnership
www.trcp.org

In 1912, Roosevelt said, "There can be no greater issue than that of conservation in this country." T. R. had the foresight to address these issues still so significant to sportsmen today, understanding that if we want to safeguard critical habitat, productive hunting grounds, and favorite fishing holes for future generations, we must plan carefully. TRCP helps create federal policy and funding solutions by uniting its partners and amplifying the voices of American sportsmen and women in service of Theodore Roosevelt's conservation legacy.

The Wilderness Society
www.wilderness.org

The Wilderness Society works to secure the preservation of wilderness and the proper management of all federal lands and forge trusted, respectful relationships and lasting collaborations. It is committed to the ideal that wilderness and all public lands can bring people and communities together and that everyone should share equitably in their benefits.

Wildlife Management Institute
www.wildlifemanagement.institute

The Wildlife Management Institute was established in 1911 by sportsmen–businessmen gravely concerned about the dramatic declines of many wildlife populations. Its founders saw a need for a small, independent, and aggressive cadre of people dedicated to restoring and ensuring the well-being of wild populations and their habitats.

The Wildlife Society

THE WILDLIFE SOCIETY
Leaders in Wildlife Science, Management and Conservation

Founded in 1937, its mission is "to inspire, empower, and enable wildlife professionals to sustain wildlife populations and habitats through science-based management and conservation." The Wildlife Society provides numerous ways for its members to get more involved in creating a better future for wildlife and wildlife habitat.

US Fish & Wildlife Service Migratory Bird Program
www.fws.gov/birds/index.php

The Migratory Bird Program works with partners to protect, restore, and conserve bird populations and their habitats for the benefit of future generations by ensuring long-term ecological sustainability of all migratory bird populations, increasing socioeconomic benefits derived from birds, improving hunting and bird watching and other outdoor bird-related experiences, and increasing awareness of the value of migratory birds and their habitats for their aesthetic, ecological, recreational, and economic significance. Among its major roles in bird management and habitat conservation, FWS conducts surveys; coordinates with public-private bird conservation partnerships; provides matching grants for partner-based conservation efforts; administers conservation laws and develops policies and regulations; and issues permits that allow individuals and organizations to participate in migratory bird conservation in a variety of ways. FWS also helps educate and engage the nation's youth in wildlife conservation topics and provide resources for parents and educators who want to help their students explore and appreciate our natural world and our feathered friends.

OUTFITTERS

ALASKA

Alaska Wildfowl Adventures
www.akduckhunts.com
(907) 322–3825

Alaska Wilderness Enterprises
www.wildernessenterprises.com
(907) 488-7517

Aleutian Island Waterfowlers
www.alaskaduckhuntingguides
.com
(877) 359-3003

All Alaska Outdoors Lodge
www.allalaska.com
(907) 953-0186

Alpine Creek Lodge
www.alpinecreeklodge.com
(907) 398-9673

Cold Bay Adventures Lodge
www.coldbayoutfitters.com
(877) 359-3003

Crystal Creek Lodge
www.crystalcreeklodge.com
(907) 357-3153

Fowl Weather
www.alaskaseaduckhunts.com
(907) 399-8753

Izembek Lodge
coldbayalaska.com
(888) 797-5520

Julson Kennel
www.julsonkennel.com
(605) 530-0074

Kodiak Raspberry Island Remote
Lodge
www.kodiakseaducks.com
(701) 526-1677

Kodiak Wilderness Adventures
www.kodiakwilderness.com
(907) 454-2418

Larsen Bay Lodge
www.larsenbaylodge.com
(800) 748-2238

Wilderness Beach Lodge
www.wildernessbeachlodge.com
(877) 710-WILD

Wildman Lodge
Wildmanlodge.com
(830) 522-4947

ARIZONA

Arizona Covey Breaks
www.azquailguide.com
azquailguide@gmail.com
(928) 713-9961

Arizona Pheasant and Chukar
Hunting
(480) 201-2264

Blue Rooster Hunting Ranch
www.azhuntingclub.com
(928) 241-3221

Border to Border Outfitters
www.bordertoborderoutfitters.com
(480) 285-5529

Dave Brown Outfitters
www.davebrownoutfitters.com
(800) 453-3991

Desert Creek Sportsman's Club
dcsportsmansclub.com
(623) 512-8496

Desert Pheasant Recreation
www.pheasantrec.com
(520) 709-1019

LunaRita Outfitters
www.lunaritaoutfitters.com
(520) 235-9095

ARKANSAS

Arkansas County Guide Service
www.arcountyguideservice.com
(870) 830-7430

Belle Gulley Duck Lodge
www.arkansasduckhuntinglodges
.com
(870) 946-5071

Big Creek Waterfowl Club
www.mallardhunter.com
(901) 497-7381

Buckshot Duck Lodge
www.buckshotducklodge.com
(870) 548-3334

Duck Guides Inc.
www.duckguidesinc.com
(800) 260-2993

Dry Lake Hunting Service
www.drylakehuntingservice.com
(870) 830-0299

Duxmen Outfitters
www.duxmenoutfitters.com
(870) 897-3066

Five Oaks Duck Lodge
www.fiveoaksducklodge.com
(870) 873-4444

Heavy Shot Guide Service
www.stuttgartduckhunts.com
(870) 830-7644

Old Post Lodge
www.oldpostducklodge.com
(870) 344-3012

Pluck A Duck Outfitters
www.pluck-a-duck.com
(870) 588-5608

Prairie View Hunting Lodge
www.arkansasducklodge.com
(501) 454-2315

Quail Mountain Enterprises
www.quailmountainenterprises
    .com/services.php
(479) 369-2322

Salt Bayou Hunting Lodge
www.saltbayouhuntinglodge.com
(501) 215-9055

Stan Jones Mallard Lodge
www.stanjonesmallardlodge.com
(870) 886-3000

The Elms Grand Prairie Waterfowl
    Lodge
www.theelmslodge.com
(501) 690-0164

Whispering Oaks Hunting Lodge
www.whisperingoakshunting.com
(901) 373-4868

Wildlife Farms
www.wildlife-farms.com
(972) 446-9000

CALIFORNIA
Antelope Valley Sportsman's Club
www.avschunt.com
(661) 268-9116

Blakes Guide Service
www.blakesguideservice.com
(530) 347-6540

Green Gulch Ranch
www.greengulchranch.com
(530) 993-1129

Guns & Roosters Hunting Preserve
www.gunsandroostershunting.com
(559) 798-1966

Lone Pine Pheasant Club
www.lonepinepheasantclub.com
(760) 876-4590

Oak Stone Outfitters
www.oakstoneoutfitters.com
(805) 622-9485

Red Bank Ale & Quail Outfitters
www.redbankhunting.com
(530) 529-9435

River Valley Outfitters
www.valleywaterfowlhunting.com
(530) 592-9931

Western Wildlife Adventures
www.wildlifeadv.com
(530) 894-1400

Wilderness Unlimited
www.wildernessunlimited.com
(877) 611-4868

COLORADO
A-Plus Game Birds
www.aplusgamebirds.com
(720) 300-7504

Aspen Outfitting Company
www.aspenoutfitting.com
(970) 925-3406

Birds and Bucks Outdoors Sports
    Club
www.birdsandbucksoutdoors.com
(303) 870-3862

Black Canyon Wing & Clay
www.bcwandc.com
(970) 874-7195

Double Barrel Hunting Lodge
www.dbhlodge.com
(720) 936-0678

High Lonesome Ranch
www.thehighlonesomeranch.com
(970) 283-9420

Rocky Mountain Roosters
www.rmroosters.com
(719) 635-3257

Stillwater Outfitters
www.stillwateroutfitters.net
(303) 659-8665

The Bluffs
www.huntthebluffs.com
(303) 822-8479

Valhalla
www.valhallahuntclub.com
(303) 644-4300

Western Waterfowl Outfitters
www.westernwaterfowloutfitters.
    com
(970) 381-7798

CONNECTICUT
Markover Game Farm and Hunting
    Preserve
www.markover.com
(860) 774-4116

Millstream Hunting Preserve
www.millstreampreserve.com
(860) 295-9974

DELAWARE
Blue Horizon Quail Preserve
www.bluehorizonquailpreserve.com
(336) 953-7269

Del-Bay Guide Service
www.delbayguide.com
(302) 383-9902

Kevin Popo Guide Service
www.kevinpopoguideservice.com
(302) 220-9043

Marshtown Hunting Preserve
www.marshtownhuntingpreserve
  .com
(302) 528-1203

Owens Station Shooting Preserve
www.owensstationpreserve.webs
  .com
(302) 275-4917

Pratt Farm Lodge
www.deerandduckhunting.com
(302) 377-3459

FLORIDA
Fox Brown Outfitters
www.foxbrownoutfitters.com
(772) 597-5900

Gilchrist Club
www.gilchristclub.com
ahammond@gilchristclub.com
(888) 535-4868

Hardscrabble Plantation Hunting
  Preserve
www.HardscrabblePlantation.com
(850) 637-4868

Osceola Outdoors
www.osceolaoutdoors.com
(239) 253-5876

Quail Creek Plantation
www.quailcreekplantation.com
(863) 763-2529

Quail Hunting Florida
www.quailhuntingflorida.com
info@quailhunting.com

Roberts Ranch
www.robertsranch.com
(386) 937-1208

Silver Lake Preserve at Lykes
  Ranch
www.silverlakepreserve.com
(863) 273-7712

Sportsmans Preserve
www.sportsmanspreserve.com
(813) 719-6041

GEORGIA
Ashburn Hill Plantation
www.ashburnhillplantation.com
(229) 985-5069

Beaver Creek Plantation
www.beavercreekplantation.com
(478) 763-2920

Boggy Pond Plantation
www.boggypond.com
(229) 985-5395

Burnt Pine Plantation
www.burntpine.com
706-557-0407

Covey Rise Plantation
www.coveyrise.com
(229) 336-8600

Fishing Creek Farms
www.fishingcreekfarms.com
(541) 678-3551

Five Springs Hunting Preserve
www.5springshunting.com
(770) 786-1388

Live Oak Plantation
www.huntliveoak.com
(800) 682-HUNT

McCranie Quail Plantation
www.mccranieplantation.com
(478) 374-3064

Morrison Pines Plantation
www.morrisonpines.com
(229) 985-7272

Myrtle Wood Hunting/Sporting
  Clays
myrtlewoodplantation.com
(229) 228-6232

Noontootla Creek Farms
www.ncfga.net
(706) 838-0585

Partridge Creek Gun Club
www.partridgecreekgunclub.com
(843) 575-8160

Pine Hill Plantation
www.pinehillplantation.com
(229) 758-2464

Pine Ridge Hunting Plantation
www.pineridgehunting.net
(229) 942-0350

Piney Creek Plantation
www.ultimatequailhunting.com
  /business/piney-creek-plantation/
(229) 317-3624

Pope Plantation
www.popeplantation.com
(706) 318-5389

Quail Ridge Plantation
www.quailridgeplantation.com
(229) 891-7679

Quail Run Hunting Preserve
(918) 569-9404

Red Fern Plantation Hunting
  Preserve
redfernplantation.com
(912) 531-2482

Red Pebble Plantation
www.redpebbleplantation.com
(229) 643-1888

Rio Piedra Plantation
www.riopiedraplantation.com
(229) 336-1677

Riverview Plantation
www.riverviewplantation.com
(229) 294-4904

Samara Plantation
www.samaraplantation.com/
  quail-hunting
(229) 776-3994

Sea Island
www.seaisland.com/recreation
  /activities/hunting-shooting
(855) 572-4975

Shadow Oak Plantation
www.shadowoakplantation.com
(866) 228-9162

Silver Shoe Ranch
www.silvershoeranch.com
(770) 548-2200

South Fork Hunting Preserve
www.southforkhuntingpreserve.com
(706) 255-9524

Southern Woods Plantation
www.southernwoodsplantation.
  com
(229) 347-0725

Southwind Plantation
www.huntsouthwind.com
(800) 456-5208

Southwind Sporting Clays and
  Quail Hunting
www.southwindclaysandquail.com
(229) 605-0085

Sundown Farms Plantation
www.sundownfarmsplantation
  .com
(229) 985-0652

Wiley Creek Duck Preserve
www.wileycreek.com
(770) 712-5910

Wynfield Plantation
www.wynfieldplantation.com
(229) 889-0193

HAWAII

The State of Hawaii, Division of Forestry and Wildlife (DOFAW) supervises wild bird hunting on each of the six major islands. This is hunting on public land and a far cry from luaus and leis. The terrain can be challenging, the birds are unused to being hunted, and the Francolin quail are more apt to run than fly, as a result. For high adventure, consider Hawaii.

Island of Kaua'i
3060 Eiwa Street, Room 306
Lihue, HI 96766
(808) 274-3433

Island of O'ahu
1151 Punchbowl Street, Room 325
Honolulu, HI 96813
(808) 587-0166

Island of Maui
685 Haleakala Highway
Kahului, HI 96732
(808) 984-8100

Island of Moloka'i
P. O. Box 347
Kaunakakai, HI 96748
(808) 553-1745

Island of Lana'i
P. O. Box 630661
Lanai City, HI 96763
(808) 565-7916

Island of Hawai'i
19 E. Kawili Street
Hilo, HI 96720
(808) 974-4221

Parker Ranch
www.hunt.parkerranch.com
hunting@parkerranch.com

Pineapple Brothers Lana'i
www.pineapplebrothers.com
(800) 847-0834

IDAHO

2C Pheasant Hunt
www.pheasanthuntidaho.com
(208) 880-0997

Blixt & Co.
www.blixtco.com
(307) 413-5450

Castle Creek Outfitters
www.castlecreekoutfitters.com
(208) 756-2548

Flying B Ranch
www.flyingbranch.com
(800) 472-1945

Lazy Bear Ranch
www.lazybearranch.com
(208) 550-0440

Lazy Triple Creek Ranch
www.lazytriplecreek.com
(917) 821-7210

Mile High Outfitters
www.milehighoutfitters.com
(208) 879-4500

ILLINOIS
Arrowhead Lodge
www.arrowheadlodge.net
(618) 203-1969

Beckridge Hunting Preserve
www.beckridge.com
(563) 687-2985

Briar Knoll Hunting & Fishing
www.briarknoll.org
(815) 857-2320

Coon Creek Hunt Club
www.cooncreekhuntclub.com
(847) 603-4868

Crannie Mack Bird Hunting
www.cranniemackbirdhunting.com
(217) 720-2901

Doctorman's Cache Core Hunting
www.doctorman.freeservers.com
(618) 845-3367

FLC Outfitters
www.ultimatepheasanthunting
    .com/business/flc-outfitters
(217) 248-9999

Green Acres Sportsman's Club
www.huntgreenacres.com
(217) 395-2588

Gumfarm Hunt Club
www.gumfarmhuntclub.com
(815) 739-2351

Harpole's Heartland Lodge
www.heartlandlodge.com
(217) 734-2526

Hilltop Meadows Hunt Club
www.hilltopmeadowshuntclub
    .com
(815) 535-1056

Koeberlein's Hunting Preserve
www.windrivers-gsp.com
(217) 867-2310

Lick Creek Game Preserve
www.lickcreek.com
(309) 347-7191

Little Wabash Shooting Preserve
www.littlewabashshootingpreserve
    .com
(217) 895-2677

Macedonia Game Preserve
macedoniagamepreserve.com
(618) 728-4328

Mazonia Hunt Club
www.mazoniahuntclub.com
(815) 739-9822

Morrison Hunt Club
www.morrisonhuntclub.com
(815) 772-3394

Otter Creek Hunting Club
www.ottercreekhunting.com
(618) 376-7601

Pheasant Valley Farms
www.pheasantvalleyfarms.com
(610) 693-9836

Rack & Wing
rackandwing.com
(815) 493-6443

Richmond Hunting Club
www.richmondhuntclub.com
(815) 678-3271

River Valley Pheasant Hunting
    Club
www.rivervalleypheasanthunting
    .com
(815) 281-2917

Rock Hollow Hunt Club
www.rockhollowhuntclub.com
(815) 232-5428

Rooster Heaven Hunt Club
www.roosterheaven.org
(815) 832-4327

Sandy Run Hunt Co.
www.sandyrunhuntco.com
(618) 292-8680

Seneca Hunt Club
www.senecahuntclub.net
(815) 357-8080

INDIANA
Dawn to Dusk Hunt Club
www.ultimatepheasanthunting
    .com/business/dawn-to
    -dusk-hunt-club
(219) 763-3362

Lost River Game Farm
www.lostrivergamefarm.net
(812) 865-3021

Maier Hunting Farm
www.huntmaier.com
(574) 229-7638

Sugar Creek Sporting Clays and
    Hunting Preserve
www.sugarcreekhunting.com
812-849-5020

IOWA
Bensink Farms
www.bensinkfarms.com
(641) 891-3026

Brush Dale Hunting Preserve &
  Kennel
www.brushdale.com
(563) 672-3291

Chase the Adventure
www.chasetheadventure.com
(563) 532-9821

Doc's Hunt Club
www.docshuntclub.com
(800) 993-3711

Heritage 1865
www.heritage1865.com
(641) 780-2290

Highland Hideaway Hunting
www.highlandhunting.com
(319) 648-5065

Hole N' the Wall Lodge
www.holenthewalllodge.com
(712) 568-1010

Legacy Acres Hunting Club
www.legacyacreshuntingclub.com
(319) 430-8973

Oakview 2 Hunting Club
www.oakview2huntingclub.com
(515) 966-2095

Three Hills Hunting Preserve
www.threehillshunting.com
(563) 879-3182

Winterset Hunt Club and Lodge
www.huntwinterset.com
(515) 462-2310

KANSAS
Cokeley Farms
cokeleyfarms.com
(785) 771-3817

Irish Creek Outfitters
www.irishcreekoutfitters.com
620-960-3894

Prairie Storm Outfitting
www.prairiestormoutfitting.com
(620) 214-1802

Rader Lodge
www.raderlodge.com
(785) 545-8852

Ravenwood Lodge
www.ravenwoodlodge.com
(800) 656-2454

Ringneck Ranch
www.ringneckranch.net
(785) 373-4835

Scattered Acres Outfitting
www.scatteredacresoutfitting.com
(785) 770-7440

Show-me Birds Hunting Resort
showmebirds.com
(620) 674-8863

Upland Bird Guide Service
www.uplandbirdguideservice.com
(337) 940-1869

KENTUCKY
Best Case Farm
bestcasefarm.com
(859) 654-1540

Elk Creek Hunt Club
www.elkcreekhuntclub.com
(502) 484-4569

King's Country
www.kingscountry.com
(859) 608-1177

Moore's Hunting Preserve
www.ultimatepheasanthunting
  .com/business/
  moores-hunting-preserve
(270) 832-2982

Sawbriar Hunting Club
sawbriarhunting.com
(931) 879-6557

Upland Addiction
kentuckywingshooting.com
(270) 869-4867

Wild Wing Lodge
www.wildwinglodge.com
(810) 813-1608

Winghaven Lodge
www.winghavenlodge.com
(270) 836-7998

LOUISIANA
Bel's Hackberry Hunting Lodge
swladuckhunting.com
(337) 274-4213

Big Woods Fish and Game
  Preserve
www.bwfgp.com
(337) 527-8671, ext. 3

Blu's Hunting Lodge
www.blushuntinglodge.com
(337) 207-0992

Cajun Unlimited
www.cajununlimited.com
(504) 234-2573

Covey Rise Lodge
www.coveyriselodge.com
(985) 747-0310

Doug's Hunting Lodge
www.dougshuntinglodge.com
(800) 888-0960

Grand Coteau Plantation
www.grandcoteauplantation.com
(985) 872-1755

Grosse Savanne Waterfowl Wildlife
 Lodge
www.grossesavanne.com
(337) 598-2357

Hackberry Rod & Gun
www.hackberryrodandgun.com
(888) 762-3391

Honey Brake
www.honeybrake.com
(318) 775-1007

Jelk's Bayou Hunting Lodge
www.jelksbayouhunting.com
(478) 972-9321

Knobbhill Hunting Lodge
www.knobbhillhunting.net
(337) 303-7045

Limitless Waterfowl Outfitters
limitless-waterfowl.com
(504) 201-8799

Megabucks Duck Guides
www.johnnywink.com
(318) 669-3757

Oak Grove Hunting Club
www.whog.net
(337) 542-4682

Waterfowl Specialist Guide Service
waterfowlspecialist.com
(504) 258-4431

MAINE
Allagash Guide Service
www.allagashguideservice.com
(207) 398-3418

Bold Coast Outfitters
www.boldcoastoutfitters.com
(207) 263-6527

Bosebuck Mountain Camps
www.bosebuck.com
(207) 670-0013

Bowlin Camps Lodge
www.bowlincamps.com
(207) 267-0884

Bradford Camps
www.bradfordcamps.com
(207) 433-0660

Bulldog Camps on Enchanted
 Pond
www.bulldogcamp.com
(207) 243-2853

Cedar Ridge Pheasants
www.cedarridgepheasants.com
(207) 827-4051

Chandler Lake Camps and Lodge
www.chandlerlakecamps.com
(207) 731-8938

Eagle Lodge
www.eaglelodgemaine.com
(207) 794-2181

Grant's Kennebago Camps
www.grantscamps.com
(800) 633-4815

Great Northern Outfitters
www.mainetrophyoutfitters.com
(207) 398-3330

Grouse Haven Wing-shooting
www.grousehavenwingshooting.
 com
(207) 491-9856

King and Bartlett Fish and Game
 Club
www.kingandbartlett.com
(207) 926-4147

Leen's Lodge
www.leenslodge.com
(800) 995-3367

Libby Sporting Camps
www.libbycamps.com
(207) 435-8274

Libby Outposts
www.libbyoutposts.com
(207) 551-8292

Matagamon Wilderness
www.matagamon.com
(207) 446-4635

North Country Lodge
www.northcountrylodge.com
(207) 528-2320

Oxbow Outfitters
www.oxbowlodge.com
(207) 435-6140

Penobscot Bay Outfitters
www.seaduck.net
(207) 322-7919

Red Dog Guide Service
www.reddogguideservice.com
(207) 737-4029

Rising Sun Outfitters
www.risingsunoutfitters.com
(207) 461-4611

Ross Lake Camps
www.rosslakecamps.com
(207) 227-7766

South Branch Lake Camps
www.southbranchlakecamps.com
(207) 732-3446

Spaulding Lake Outfitters
www.spauldinglakeoutfitters.com
(207) 841-0508

Sturtevant Pond Camps
www.sturtevantpondcamps.com
(802) 487-4854

Thornehead Guide Service
www.thornehead.com
(207) 725-1336

Three Rivers Wing Shoot
www.threeriverswingshooting.com
(207) 943-7943

Tim Pond Wilderness Camps
www.timpond.com
(207) 243-2947

Traditions Guide Service
www.traditionsguideservice.com
(207) 432-7574

Umcolcus Sporting Camps
www.umcolcus.com
(207) 841-0508

Weatherby's Resort
www.weatherbys.com
(877) 796-5558

Wilderness Escape Outfitters
www.wildernessescape.com
(207) 448-3238

Wilsons on Moosehead Lake
www.wilsonsonmooseheadlake.com
(207) 695-2549

MARYLAND
Barneck Outfitters
www.duckhuntingmd.com
(443) 786-6073

Baydogs Waterfowl
www.baydogswaterfowl.com
(443) 223-1290

Black Duck Outfitters
www.blackduckoutfitters.com
(410) 336-7078

Chesapeake Bay Outdoors
www.chesapeake-bay-outdoors.com
(410) 474-9858

Chesapeake Guide Service
www.chesapeakeguideservice.com
(410) 648-5229

Chesapeake Goose & Duck
   Hunting
www.chesapeakehunting.com
(410) 310-6758

Delmarva Outdoor Adventure
www.doaoutfitters.com
(410) 603-1400

Eastern Shore Guide Service
www.guidefitter.com
   /easternshoreguideservice
(410) 603-1400

Ellen-r Charters Sea Duck Hunting
ellenrfishingcharters.com
(410) 490-0817

Grove Point Outfitters
www.grovepointoutfitters.com
(410) 275-9031

Hester's Wild Wings Maryland
www.wildwingsmaryland.com
(252) 394-5171

Hopkins Hunting and Sporting
   Clays
www.hopkinshunting-clays.com
(410) 348-5287

Mid River Guide Service
www.midriverguideservice.com
(301) 399-9374

Muddy Bottom Outfitters
www.muddybottomoutfitters.com
(410) 831-1361

Pitboss Waterfowl
www.pitbosswaterfowl.com
(410) 937-4034

Poseidon Waterfowl
www.marylandseaduckhunting.
   com
(301) 748-8124

Quaker Neck Gun Club
www.quakerneckgunclub.com
(443) 480-2148

Ruin Gun Club
www.ruingunclub.com
(410) 708-4586

Schrader's Outdoors
www.schradersoutdoors.com
(410) 758-1824

Talbot County Outfitters
www.talbotcountyoutfitter.com
(240) 217-3672

Tollers Gun Club
www.tollersgunclub.com
(410) 820-0163

Williamson Outfitters
www.williamsonoutfitters.com
(410) 443-4880

Winterfarms Hunting
www.winterfarmshunting.com
(410) 708-7133

MASSACHUSETTS
East Coast Guide Service
www.seaduckhunt.com
(508) 617-6761

Hedgerow Kennel & Hunt Club
www.hedgerow.com
(978) 249-7115

Ladywoods Game Preserve
www.ladywoods.com
(508) 278-3529

New England Sea Duck Hunting
www.capecodseaduckhunting.com
(508) 237-9796

MICHIGAN
Bear Creek Hunt Club
www.bearcreekhuntclub.com
734-429-7202

Cedar Hollow Lodge & Outfitters
www.guidefitter.com
    /cedarhollowlodgeoutfitters
(989) 348-2333

Cherry Creek Farm
cherrycreekfarm.com
(248) 762-3314

Crooked Foot Upland Bird and
    Game Hunting Club
www.crookedfoothuntclub.com
(989) 723-9823

Deer Creek Hunt Club
deercreekhuntclub.com
(269) 756-6600

Dundee Pheasant Farm
dundeepheasantfarm.com
(734) 735-7271

Elkhorn Lake Hunt Club
elkhornlakehuntclub.com
(419) 562-6131

Falling Feathers Hunting Preserve
fallingfeathershunting.com
(231) 250-3224

Gleasons Farm
www.michigan.org/property
    /gleasons-farm
(231) 757-3515

Grouse Country Guide Service
www.grousecountry.com
(810) 513-6213

Haymarsh Hunt Club
www.haymarsh.com
(989) 352-7050

Hunters Creek Club
www.hunterscreekclub.com
(810) 664-4307

Janks Pheasant Farm
jankspheasantfarm.com
(989) 843-6576

Meemo's Farm
meemosfarm.com
(231) 734-9066

Mongene's Gamebird Hunting
    Preserve
www.uppheasanthunting.com
(906) 632-2974

Muzzy Pheasant Farm
www.muzzypheasantfarm.com
(810) 577-1779

Nettiebay Lodge
www.nettiebay.com
(989) 734-4688

Olive Acres
www.huntoliveacres.com
(616) 895-4868

Pheasant Ridge Hunt Club
www.pheasantridgehuntclub.com
(810) 395-4556

Pine Hill Sportsman's Club
michiganbirdhunter.com
(616) 874-8459

Rapid Wings Farm
rapidwingsfarm.com
(989) 727-8880

Remington Forest Hunt Club
www.ultimatepheasant.com
    /business/
    remington-forest-hunt-club
(269) 561-5700

Rolling Hills Shooting Preserve
rollinghillshunting.com
(269) 646-9164

Rooster Ranch
roosterranchllc.com
(989) 658-2332

Tails-A-Waggin' Acres
www.preservehunt.com
(231) 743-6483

The Pheasant Farm
www.thepheasantfarm.com
(616) 785-2707

The Ringneck Ranch
www.theringneckranch.com
(517) 524-8294

Thundering Aspens
thunderingaspenssportsmanclub.
    com
(231) 885-2420

Walkiewicz Farms
affordablepheasanthunting.com
(989) 683-2749

Willow Lake Sportsmen's Club
www.willowlakesportsmansclub
.net
(269) 279-7124

Wings & Rings Pheasant Hunting
www.wingsringspheasant.com
(616) 896-8553

MINNESOTA
Pineridge Grouse Camp
www.pineridgegrousecamp.com
(218) 301-6083

Pine River Fish and Game Club
www.pineriverfishandgame.
weebly.com
(218) 232-2252

The Grouse Lodge at Little Moran
www.thegrouselodge.com
(218) 894-3852

The Midwest Shooting School
www.midwestshootingschool.com
(218) 384-3670

MISSISSIPPI
BlackHorse Lodge & Plantation
Sykes Place Plantation
Sloan's Run
www.sykesplaceplantation.com
(205) 799-1320

Burnt Oak Lodge
www.burntoaklodge.com
(662) 272-9550

Fitch Farms/Galena Plantation
www.fitchfarms.com
(901) 487-8054

Little "q" Ranch
www.littleqranch.com
(662) 801-5764

Panther Lake Hunting Lodge
www.ultimatewaterfowlhunting
.com/business/
panther-lake-hunting-lodge
(662) 816-6759

Prairie Wildlife Preserve/Orvis
Wingshooting School
www.prairiewildlife.com
(662) 494-5858

Prairie Farms Hunt Club
www.huntperryfarms.net
(662) 571-3672

River Bend Mallards
www.riverbendmallards.com
(662) 571-5942

Tallahatchie Hunts
www.tallahatchiehunts.com
(662) 392-0740

The Running Creek Ranch
Therunningcreekranch.com
(601) 215-4313

Weavers Waterfowl
Weaverswaterfowl.com
(662) 420-1519

MISSOURI
Bird Fever Hunting Preserve
www.birdfeverhunting.com
(816) 776-8023

Bootheel Bottoms Hunting Club
missouriwaterfowl.com
(901) 351-7148

Dirty Rice Outfitters
www.dirtyriceoutfitters.com
(573) 344-0075

Flying Feathers Game Bird Hunting
www.flyingfeathershunting.com
(417) 232-4033

Gateway River Outfitters
www.gatewayriveroutfitters.com
(636) 368-1463

Habitat Flats
www.habitatflats.com
(816) 592-9146

Heggemeier Game Farm
www.heggemeiergame
farmandkennel.com
(660) 676-0776

Hidden Valley Outfitters
www.hvoutfitters.com
(417) 533-5628

Harding Gamebird Preserve
www.hardinggamebirds.com
(660) 872-6746

Iron Duck Hunting
www.ironduckhunting.com
(816) 210-3969

Missouri Mallards Guided Duck
Hunting
www.missourimallards.com
(731) 225-5036

Ozark Wings
www.ozarkwings.com
(417) 284-3332

Ringneck Game Farm
www.ringneckfarm.com
(660) 272-4179

Show Me Snow Geese
www.showmesnowgeese.com
(314) 814-3088

Wil-nor Outdoors
www.wil-nor.com
(636) 285-7416

MONTANA

Cedar Ridge Outfitters
www.cedarridgeoutfitters.com
(207) 668-4169

Double Deuce Outfitters
www.mtrut.com
(406) 342-5475

Eagle Nest Lodge
www.eaglenestlodge.com
(406) 665-3711

Forrester's Bighorn River Resort
www.forrestersbighorn.com
(406) 333-1449

Milk River Outfitters
www.milkriveroutfitters.com
(406) 648-5494

Montana Bird Hunts
www.montanabirdhunts.com
(406) 223-5923

Montana Upland Outfitters
www.montanauplandoutfitters.com
(406) 544-1441

PRO Outfitters' Sharptail Lodge
prooutfitters.com
(406) 442-5489

Twin Creek Ranch
www.tchunting.com
(406) 429-5615

Wild Wings Hunts
www.ultimatepheasanthunting
    .com/business/wild-wings-hunts
(406) 467-2781

NEBRASKA

Angel Wing Outfitters
angelwingoutfitters.com
(308) 641-3528

Black Goose Outfitters
www.blackgooseoutfitters.com
(402) 660-1220

Central Nebraska Outfitters
www.centralnebraskaoutfitters.com
(308) 289-6607

Pheasant Bonanza
www.pheasantbonanza.com
(402) 374-1765

Rackett Grange and Sporting
    Preserve
www.hunttherackett.com
(303) 910-8187

Real Western Hunting
www.realwesternhunting.com
(307) 221-7434

Rooster Junction
www.roosterjunction.com
(308) 762-1640

NEVADA

Bullhead Hunting Club
www.bullheadhuntingclub.com
(775) 623-1325

G & J Outdoors
www.gandjourdoors.com
(530) 263-0492

On Point Guide Service of Nevada
www.onpointnv.net
(702) 565-1109

NEW HAMPSHIRE

Green Mountain Kennels Hunting
    Preserve
www.greenmountainshooting.com
(603) 539-2106

Lopstick
www.lopstick.com
(800) 538-6659

New England Upland
www.newenglandupland.com
(603) 478-0099

The Timberdoodle Club
www.timberdoodleclub.com
(603) 654-9510

NEW JERSEY

Bent Creek Game Farm
www.bentcreekpreserve.net
(609) 259-9501

Buttonwood Game Preserve
www.ultimatepheasanthunting
    .com/business/
    buttonwood-game-preserve
(908) 454-7116

Game Creek Hunting Farms
www.gamecreek.com
(856) 769-0035

Griffin and Howe Shooting
    Grounds at Hudson Farm
griffinhowe.com
(973) 398-2670

Limit Outfitters
www.limitoutfitters.com
(732) 740-3867

M & M Hunting and Sporting
    Clays/The Matarese Family
www.mmhunting.com
(856) 935-1230

Muddy Creek Outfitters
www.muddycreekoutfitters.com
(609) 517-3119

Shore Winds Hunting Farm
www.shorewindshuntingfarm.com
(856) 327-4949

Skyline Rod and Gun Club
www.skylinegunclub.com
(208) 525-8575

NEW MEXICO
Julson Kennel
www.julsonkennel.com
(605) 530-0074

The Santa Fe Guiding Company
newmexicoquailhunting.com
(505) 466-7964

Tinnin Hunt Club
www.tinninhuntclub.com
(505) 342-1106

NEW YORK
Catskill Pheasantry
www.catskillpheasantry.com
(845) 887-4487

DC Outdoor Adventures
huntfishny.com
(631) 786-7871

Fetherquest
www.fetherquest.com
(585) 489-7053

Orvis Sandanona Shooting
  Grounds
www.orvis.com/sandanona
(845) 677-9701

Over & Under Farms
www.overandunderfarms.com
(413) 575-6999

Pheasant Ridge
www.pheasantridge
  huntingpreserve.com
(518) 692-9459

Ringneck Preserve
www.ringneckpreserve.com
(607) 659-3208

Stuyvesant Outdoor Adventures
www.stuyvesantoutdoor.com
(518) 929-0137

T-M-T Hunting Preserve
www.tmthuntingpreserve.com
(845) 266-5108

NORTH CAROLINA
Allen Brothers Outdoors
www.allenbrothersoutdoors.com
(910) 736-5360

Anderson Creek Hunting
www.andersoncreekhunting.com
(910) 578-6613

Best Wingshooting/Simpler Times
bestwingshooting.com
(443) 624-8719

Berkeley Outdoors
www.obxoutdoors.com/hunting
(910) 612-6673

Blue Horizon Quail Preserve
bluehorizonquailpreserve.com
(336) 953-7269

Dare to Hyde
www.daretohyde.com
(252) 926-9453

DeWitts Outdoor Sports
www.dewittsoutdoorsports.com
(910) 652-2926

Fork Farm and Stables
www.forkstables.com
(704) 474-4052

Fourth Generation Outfitters
www.fourthgenerationoutfitters.com
(252) 619-2880

George Hi Plantation
www.georgehi.com
(910) 564-5860

Gull Rock Hunting
www.gullrockhunting.com
(252) 945-8751

Honey Hill Hunting Preserve
www.honeyhillhuntingpreserve.
  com
(910) 640-7806

Ocracoke Sportfishing & Hunting
www.ocracokesportfishing.com
(252) 928-8064 or (252) 921-0396

Orvis North Carolina
  Wingshooting School, Biltmore
  Shooting Grounds
www.legacy.orvis.com/p/ashville-
  north-carolina-wingshooting-
  school/2NJL
(866) 531-6213

Outer Banks Waterfowl
www.outerbankswaterfowl.net
(252) 261-7842

Parkers Waterfowl Guide Service
www.parkerswaterfowl.com
(252) 599-1739

Quail Haven Hunting Preserve and
  Skeet Shooting
www.quailhavennc.com
(704) 507-4331

The Webb Farm
www.thewebbfarm.com
(910) 995-1522

Wintergreen Hunting Preserve
www.wintergreenhuntingpreserve
.net
(910) 648-6171

NORTH DAKOTA

Absolute Gun Dogs Guided
Pheasant and Waterfowl Hunts
www.absolutegundogs.com
(701) 258-5001

Bald Hill Creek Adventures
www.baldhillcreek.net
(701) 840-8409

Dakota Winds Hunting
www.dakotawindshunting.com
(701) 275-8808

Double JJ Outfitters
www.doublejjoutfitters.com
(888) 2HUNT-ND

Northern Flight Guide Service
www.take-em.com
(701) 739-9616

Paul Nelson Farm
www.paulnelsonfarm.com
(605) 765-2469

Rolling Plains Adventures
www.rollingplainsadventures.com
(701) 367-3737

Show Me Birds
www.showmebirds.com
(620) 674-8863

Stone Prairie Outfitters
www.stoneprairieoutfitters.com
(507) 381-5711

Top Gun Guide Service
www.topgunguideservice.com
(507) 696-0208

OHIO

Arrowhead Pheasant Hunting
www.arrowheadpheasantclub.com
(937) 366-6134

BB Waterfowl
www.bbwaterfowl.com
(740) 586-0007

Buckeye Pheasants Hunting
Preserve
www.buckeyepheasant.com
(937) 687-2523

Bullseye Pheasant and Duck
Hunting
www.bullseyepheasant.net
(740) 922-5633

Capt. Ken's Wild Wings
www.captkenswildwings.com
(419) 552-4676

Cherrybend Pheasant Farm
www.cherrybendhunting.com
(937) 584-4269

Elk Ridge Hunt Club
www.elkridgehuntclub.com
(419) 562-9997

Elkhorn Lake Hunt Club
www.elkhornlakehuntclub.com
(419) 562-6131

Federal Valley Hunting Preserve
www.federalvalleyhunting
preservellc.com
(740) 448-7423

Monigold's Upland Bird Hunting
www.monigolds.com
(330) 365-0664

Mulberry Pheasantry
www.mulberrypheasantry.com
(937) 787-3912

Ohio River H2OFOWL Guide
Service
www.ohioriverduckhunting.com
(740) 616-7236

Old Lake Shore Charters
www.oldlakeshorecharters.com
(419) 541-0765

Sea Breeze Charters
www.seabreezecharters.com
(419) 340-0601

OKLAHOMA

Bluestem Hunting
www.huntbluestem.com
(580) 336-4148

Fowl Skies Outfitters
www.fowlskiesoutfitters.com
(580) 467-1627

High Brass Hunting
www.highbrasshunt.com
(208) 358-1124

Quail Run Hunt Club
www.oklahomaagritourism.com
/producer/quail-run-hunt-club
(918) 289-1014

Red Rock Ranch
www.redrockranchok.com
(508) 268-9663

SM Brown Game Bird Ranch
www.boxoutdoors.com/
location/619
(940) 966-3241

OREGON

Flying Double F Ranch
www.flyingdoublef.weebly.com
(541) 473-3055

Highland Hills Ranch
www.highlandhillsranch.com
(866) 478-4868

Horseshoe Curve Hunt Club
www.horseshoecurvehuntclub.
  com
(503) 539-5206

Luckiamute Valley Pheasants
www.lvpheasants.com
(503) 838-4221

Pheasant Valley Hunting Ranch
www.pheasantvalleyranch.com
(541) 473-3867

Ruggs Ranch
www.huntruggs.com
(541) 676-5390

Sage Canyon Outfitters
www.sagecanyonoutfitters.com
(541) 395-2697

PENNSYLVANIA

Big R Bird Ranch
www.bigrbirdranch.com
(717) 266-6324

Blue Ridge Summit, Pennsylvania
  Wingshooting School
www.orvis.com/blue-ridge-summit
  -pennsylvania-wingshooting-
  school/2Y2M-Family.html
(866) 531-6213

Clover Hollow Hunting Preserve
www.ultimatepheasanthunting
  .com/business/
  clover-hollow-hunting-preserve
(610) 767-3319

Four Seasons Game Bird Farm
www.fourseasonsgamebirdfarm
  .com
(724) 898-2316

Gobblers Knob Hunting Preserve
www.gobblers-knob.com
(724) 601-6441

The Nemacolin Field Club
www.nemacolin.com/experiences
  /the-nemacolin-field-club
(866) 344-6957

Orvis Hill Country Shooting
  Grounds
www.orvis.com/s/
  orvis-hill-country/15167
(717) 253-9665

Seven Springs
www.7springs.com
(800) 452-2223

Scattergun Reserve
www.scattergunreserve.com
(814) 587-3597

Spring Lane Hunt Club
www.springlanehuntclub.com
(814) 880-7091

The Lodge at Glendorn
www.glendorn.com
(814) 362-6511

Warriors Mark Wingshooting
  Lodge and Kennels
www.warriorsmark.com
(814) 378-8380

Wood Crest Point
www.woodcrestpoint.com
(724) 840-0836

RHODE ISLAND

Addieville East Farm
www.addieville.com
(401) 568-3185

Big Game Waterfowl
www.biggamewaterfowl.com
(401) 486-7262

European Hunting at The Preserve
www.europeanhuntingrhodeisland.
  com
(401) 539-4653

SOUTH CAROLINA

Blackwater Hunting
www.blackwaterhunting.com
(803) 541-HUNT

Brays Island
www.braysisland.com
(843) 846-3100

Clinton House Plantation
www.clintonhouse.com
(864) 833-0274

Duck Bottom Plantation
www.duckbottomplantation
(803) 499-2332

Moree's Preserve
Moreespreserve.com
(843) 378-4831

River Bend Sportsman's Resort
www.rvrbend.com
(864) 592-1348

Toney Creek Plantation
www.toneycreekplantation.com
(864) 304-7400

Williams Hunting
www.williamshunting.com
(843) 459-8866

Woodside Plantation
www.woodsideplantationsc.com
(803) 625-0744

SOUTH DAKOTA
Bird Down Lodge
www.birddownlodge.com
(605) 281-1231

Century Farm Hunts
centuryfarmhunts.com
(605) 835-8281

Firesteel Creek Lodge
firesteelcreeklodge.com
(605) 850-3899

Flatland Flyways
www.flatlandflyways.com
(605) 216-8424

Grand Ciel Lodge
www.grandciellodge.com
(605) 770-2024

Maple River Pheasant Hunts
www.mapleriverpheasanthunts.
   com
(507) 271-2474

Olsen's Pheasant Phun
www.pheasantphun.com
(605) 450-0501

Paul Nelson Farm
paulnelsonfarm.com
(605) 765-2469

Pheasant City
www.pheasantcity.com
(605) 539-9244

Platte Creek Lodge
www.plattecreek.com
(605) 337-9777

Rooster Ridge
www.roosterridgelodge.com
(763) 595-5936

The Signature Lodge by Cheyenne
   Ridge Outfitters
thesignaturelodge.com
(877) 850-5144

Thunderstik Lodge
www.thunderstik.com
(763) 595-5936

Tinker Kennels, LLC., and The
   Rocking Horses Hunt Club
www.tinkerkennels.com
(605) 295-0439

Tumbleweed Lodge
www.tumbleweedlodge.com
(605) 875-3440

Upland Wings Preserve
www.scquailhunting.com
(864) 876-8327

TENNESSEE
Craig Game Preserve
www.hornandfin.com/guides-and
   -outfitters/craig-game-preserve
(931) 703-4254

Cumberland Fields Sportsman's
   Club
www.cumberlandfields.com
(865) 805-8722

Eagle Nest Resort Duck Hunting
www.eaglenestresort.com
(731) 538-2143

Mallard Estates Outfitter
www.mallardestates.com
(731) 697-6691

Meadow Brook Game Farm
www.meadowbrookgamefarm.com
(615) 888-2411

Sawbriar Hunting
sawbriarhunting.com
(931) 879-6557

Snowstorm Outfitters
www.snowstormoutfitters.com
(270) 627-1876

Waterfowl Outfitters of West
   Tennessee
www.waterfowltennessee.com
(731) 414-9392

Waterfowl Unlimited Guide
   Service
www.floodedtimber.com
(731) 588-4531

Wilderness Hunting Lodge
www.wildernesshuntinglodge.com
(931) 839-2091

Willow Tail Farm
www.willowtailfarm.com
(731) 431-7627

TEXAS
Big Easy Ranch
www.bigeasyranch.com
(979) 733-8635

First Shot Outfitters
www.firstshothunts.com
(325) 280-3676

Flying 5B Ranch
www.flying5b.com
(254) 300-6190

Garwood Hunting Club
www.garwoodhunt.com
(979) 758-3200

Greystone Castle Sporting Club
greystonecastle.com
(800) 399-3006

Hidden Lakes Hunting Resort
www.hiddenlakeshr.com
(903) 335-2200

JD Monte Cruz Ranch and Outfitters
montecruzhunts.com
(830) 275-0157

Joshua Creek Ranch
www.joshuacreek.com
(830) 537-5090

Mathers Ranch
www.texasdovehunt.com
(956) 542-2223

OX Ranch
www.oxhuntingranch.com
(830) 275-4962

Pintail Hunting Club
www.pintailhuntingclub.com
(979) 966-7732

Stanfield Hunting Outfitters
www.stanfieldhunting.com
(940) 658-3172

Tule Creek Outfitters
www.tulecreek.com
(806) 441-4868

UTAH
Castle Valley Outdoors
www.castlevalleyoutdoors.com
(800) 586-6503

Falcon's Ledge
www.falconsledge.com
(435) 253-7306

Pheasant Run Outfitters
www.pheasantrunoutfitters.com
(801) 420-1867

Pheasant Valley Hunting Preserve
www.pvhunting.com
(435) 646-3194

Sportsman's Paradise
www.whitesranch.com
(435) 245-3053

Wasatch Wing & Clay
www.wasatchwingandclay.com
(801) 310-1300

VERMONT
Frost Fire Guide Service
www.frostfireguideservice.com
(603) 331-5251

Orvis Manchester Wingshooting
    School
www.orvis.com/manchester-
    vermont-wingshooting-
    schools/10RC-Family.html
(866) 531-6213

Peaceable Hill Farm
www.peaceablehill.com
(802) 897-5913

Quimby Country
www.quimbycounry.com
(802) 822-5533

Wild Rivers Outfitting
www.wildriversoutfitting.com
(802) 324-4682

VIRGINIA
Green Valley Hunter's Paradise
www.greenvalley
    huntersparadiseva.webs.com
(540) 996-4134

Orapax Hunting Preserve
www.orapax.com
(804) 556-2261

PriestView Hunting Preserve
www.priestview.com
(434) 277-8748

Primland
primland.com
(276) 222-3800

Rasawek Hunting Preserve
www.uplandbirdhunting.org
(804) 467-9000

Rose Hill Game Preserve
www.rosehillgamepreserve.com
(540) 827-7484

Wild Rivers Outfitting
www.wildriversoutfitting.com
(802) 324-4682

Winter Haven Game Farm &
    Hunting Preserve
www.winterhavenpreserve.com
(434) 589-6977

WASHINGTON STATE
Cooke Canyon Hunt Club
www.cookecanyon.com
(509) 933-1372

Double Barrel Ranch
www.uplandbirdranch.com
(509) 270-5518

Eagle Lakes Ranch
www.eaglelakesranch.com
(509) 488-4484

Hidden Ranch Outfitters
www.hiddenranchoutfitters.com
(509) 681-0218

Red's Hunting
www.redshunting.com
(509) 933-2300

WEST VIRGINIA

Greenbrier Sporting Club
greenbrierliving.com
(855) 823-0515

Quail Hollow Hunts
www.quailhollowhunts.com
(304) 258-0584

Shenandoah Valley Sportsmen
www.wvabirdhunt.com
(304) 229-7715

Twin Ridge Upland Bird Farm
www.foggytrail.com/land
   /twin-ridge-upland-bird-farm
(301) 834-7632

WISCONSIN

Cedar Valley Preserve
www.cedarvalleypreserve.com
(608) 583-3570

Hunters Point Hunt Club
www.hunterspointwi.com
(920) 583-3935

Riverside Hunting & Fishing Club
www.riversidehfc.net
(920) 999-5501

Woods and Meadow
www.woodsandmeadow.com
(608) 378-4223

WYOMING

Brush Creek Ranch
www.brushcreekranch.com
(307) 327-5284

Little Creek Lodge
www.littlecreeklodge.net
(920) 826-7382

Maximum Waterfowling
www.maximumwaterfowling.com
(307) 409-8010

Pheasants on Kara Creek
www.wyomingpheasants.com
(307) 761-0106

The Wilderness Reserve
www.thewildernessreserve.com
(715) 545-2700

Three Forks Ranch
threeforksranch.com
(970) 583-7396

INDEX OF GUNMAKERS

NOTE: This listing is not limited only to shotgun manufacturers, nor is it necessarily complete.

Alphabetical Listing

A

A. A. Brown & Sons Gunmakers
Abbiatico & Salvinelli It
Akkar Silah Sanayi ve Tic.
Albert Wilhelm Wolf De
Amerigo Cosmi It
Anderson Wheeler UK
Antonio Zoli It
Arieta Fine Shot Guns Spain
Armas Garbi Spain
Armas Ignacio Zubillaga Spain
Armas Kemen Spain
Armeria Cortesi It
Armi Art It
Armi Salvinelli It
Atkin Grant & Lang UK
AYA Fine Guns Spain

B

Baikal Russia
Benelli Armi, s.p.a. It
Benelli USA Corporation USA
Beretta.it It
Beretta USA
Blaser Jagdwaffen De
Boss & Co Uk
Breda Fucili It
Briley USA
Browning USA
Bruchet Darne, e.u.r.l. Fr

C

Caesar Guerini It
Chapuis Armes Fr
Charles Daly USA
Cogswell & Harrison UK
Cimarron F.A. Co.
Connecticut Shotgun Mfg. Co.
    USA

D

David McKay Brown Gunmakers
    Scotland, UK
Davide Pedersoli & C. It
Demas Fr
Dickson & MacNaughton UK
duPont/Krieghoff Gun Company
    USA

E

Effebi, snc. It (Beretta)
E.J. Churchill Gunmakers UK

F

Fabarm It
Fabbri It
F A I R It
Famars di Abbiatico and Salvinelli
    It
Fanzoj G.m.b.h. Austria
Fausti Stefano, s.r.l. It
F.lli Poli Armi It
Franchi It
FranchiUSA USA
Fratelli Gamba Armi It
Frederick Beesley UK
Fuchs Fine Guns Austria

G

Graham Mackinlay & Co
    Gunmakers Scotland, UK
GRULLA ARMAS, S.L. Spain

H

Hambrusch Jagdwaffen Austria
Holland & Holland Uk
Holloway and Naughton, Ltd. Uk

I

Ithaca Guns USA, LLC USA

J

James Purdey & sons Ltd UK
Jakob Koschat Jagdwaffen Austria
John Rigby & Co UK -USA
Joseph Brazier UK -USA
J.P. Sauer & Sohn De

K

Kolar Arms USA
Kralav Turkey
Krieghoff De
Krieghoff International, Inc. USA
Koschat Jakob

L

Lazzeroni Arms USA
Lebeau Courally Luxembourg
Les Baer USA
Les Paul Gun & Rifle maker
    Canada
London Gun and Rifle Maker Uk
Luciano Bosis It
Ljutic Industries, Inc. USA
Ludwig Borovnik

M

McMillan Bros. USA
Magnum Research USA
Manu Arm Fr
Manufacturas Arrieta, s.l. Spain
Markesbery USA
Marlin Firearms USA
Martini & Hagn, Gunmakers
    Canada
Mathelon Armes Fr
Mauro Battaglia It
Mauser De
Maverickarms USA
Merkel De
Metalstorm USA
Moritz Zapf De
Mossberg Firearms USA

M&U Firearms Turkey

N
Navy Arms USA
NEOSTEAD South Africa
Norica Laurona Spain
North American Arms USA

O
Ohio Ordnance Works, Inc. USA
Olympic Arms USA

P
Para-Ordnance Canada
Para USA, Inc. USA
Pedersoli It
Perazzi Armi, s.r.l. It
Perugini e Visini It
Peter Hofer Jagdwaffen Austria
Philipp Ollendorff Jagdwaffen
   Austria
Piotti Fratelli s.n.c It
P V Nelson Gunmakers, Ltd UK

Q
Quicksilver Manufacturing LLC
   USA

R
Randy's Custom Rifles USA
Remington USA
Renato Gamba It
Rizzini & Tanfoglio, s.r.l. It
Rizzini snc di Rizzini B. & C. It
Robinson Armament USA
Rock River Arms USA
Ronald Wharton Uk
Rossi USA
Ruger Firearm USA

S
Sabatti, s.r.l. It
Safir Silah San Turkey
Sako Finland
Sarsilmaz Turkey
Sauer & Sohn De

Savage Arms, Inc. USA
Sharps Arms USA
Shooters Arms Philippines
Silma It
Sigarms US
Sig Sauer Swiss
Smith & Wesson USA
Springfield-armory USA
SSK Industries USA
Steyr Mannlicher De
STI-guns USA
Strayer Voigt Inc USA
Sturm Ruger USA
Searcy Rifles USA
SKB Arms Company Jp
Skullman Enterprise A.B., Sweden
Springfield Armory USA

T
Tanfoglio It
Taurus USA USA
Thompson Center Arms USA
TISAS-Trabzon Turkey
TJF Jagdwaffen in Suhl, De
Traditions Muzzle USA
Traditions Performance Firearms
   USA
TROMIX USA
Tulsky Oruzheiny Zavod Russia

U
Uberti It
US Fire Arms Mfg. Co., USA

V
Valkyrie Arms, Ltd USA
Vector Arms, Inc. USA
Verney-Carron Fr
Verney-Carron USA
Vincenzo Bernardelli It
Vulcan Group Inc USA
Vyatskie Polyany Russia

W
Walther America USA
Watson Bros. UK

Weatherby USA
Westley Richards UK
Wildeyguns USA
William & Son Uk
William Evans Gun and Rifle
   Makers UK
Wilson Combat USA
Winchester Repeating Arms USA
Wyandot Traditions USA
W.J. Jeffery & Co. UK
W. Richards (Liverpool), Ltd. UK
W. R. Saleri di Saleri William &
   C It
W W Greener UK

Y
Yankee Hill Machine Co, Inc. USA
Yildiz Silah Ltd. Turkey

Z
Zanardini arms It
Ziegenhahn & Sohn De
Z-M Weapons USA

Gunmakers by Country
AMERICAN
Bersa Firearms
Bond Arms
Briley
Browning
Bushmaster
Cavalry Arms Corp.
Charles Daly
Charter Firearms
Christensen Arms
Cimarron-Firearms
Clark Custom Guns, Inc.
Colt
Connecticut Shotgun Mfg. Co.
Cooper Firearms, Inc.
Crawley Custom Guns
Creedmoor Sports
C Sharps Arms
CVA
CZ USA
Daisy Airgun

Dakota Arms
Dan Wesson (CZ USA)
Derringer
Dixie Gun
DPMS Panter Arms
D S Arms, Inc Mil
duPont/Krieghoff Gun Company
EAA Corp
Ed Brown Products, Inc.
Entreprise Arms Mil
FAL Files, Inc. Mil
Feather USA Mil
FN Manufacturing, LLC Mil
Franchi USA
Freedom Arms
Fulton-Armory
Gibbs Rifle
Heckler & Koch
Henry Repeating Arms
Heritage Mfg
High Standard
Hi-Point Firearms
Ithaca Guns USA, LLC
John Rigby & Co
Joseph Brazier
J.P. Rifles
Kahr Pistols
Kel-tec
Kimber America
Knight Rifles USA
Knights Armament
Kolar Arms
Krieghoff International, Inc.
Lazzeroni Arms
Les Baer Pistols
Ljutic Industries, Inc
McMillan Bros.
Magnum Research
Markesbery
Marlin Firearms
Maverick Arms
Metal Storm
Miroku
Mossberg Firearms
Navy Arms
North American Arms

Ohio Ordnance Works, Inc.
Olympic Arms USA
Para USA, Inc.
Quicksilver Manufacturing LLC
Randy's Custom Rifles
Remington
Robinson Armament Mil
Rock River Arms
Ruger Firearm
Rossi USA
Savage Arms, Inc.
Sharps Arms
Sigarms US
Smith & Wesson
Springfield-Armory
SSK Industries
STI-Guns
Strayer Voigt Inc
Sturm Ruger
Taurus USA
Thompson Center Arms
Traditions Performance Firearms
TROMIX
US Fire Arms Mfg. Co.
Valkyrie Arms, Ltd
Vector Arms, Inc.
Vulcan Group Inc Mil
Walther America
Weatherby
Wildey Guns
Wilson Combat
Winchester Repeating Arms
Wyandot Traditions
Searcy Rifles
Springfield Armory
Yankee Hill Machine Co, Inc.
Z-M Weapons

AUSTRIA
Fanzoj G.m.b.h.
Fuchs Fine Guns
Glock Pistol
Hambrusch Jagdwaffen
Jakob Koschat Jagdwaffen
Josef Just
Karl Hauptmann

Peter Hofer Jagdwaffen
Philipp Ollendorff Jagdwaffen
BELGIUM GUNMAKERS
Dumoulin Herstal S A
FN Herstal
Lebeau Courally

CANADA
Diemaco Mil
Les Paul Gun & Rifle Maker
Martini & Hagn, Gunmakers
Para-Ordnance

FINLAND
Sako

FRANCE
Bretton-Gaucher
Bruchet Darne, e.u.r.l.
Chapuis Armes
Demas
G. Granger
Manu Arm
Mathelon Armes
Tony Gicquel
Verney-Carron

DEUTSCH (GERMANY)
Albert Wilhelm Wolf
Blaser Jagdwaffen
Carl-Walther
Gebruder Adamy Jagdwaffen
Heym Waffenfabrik, G.m.b.h.
J.P. Sauer & Sohn
Krieghoff
Mauser ***
Merkel
Moritz Zapf ***
Sauer & Sohn
Steyr Mannlicher
TJF Jagdwaffen in Suhl
Ziegenhahn & Sohn

ITALY
Abbiatico & Salvinelli
Amerigo Cosmi

Antonio Zoli
Armeria Cortesi
Armeria Tucci
Armi Art
Armi Salvinelli
Benelli Armi, s.p.a.
Beretta.it
Breda Fucili
Caesar Guerin
Davide Pedersoli & C.
Effebi, snc.
Fabarm
Fabbri
Fabbrica Armi Val Susa
F A I R
Falco
Famars di Abbiatico and Salvinelli
Fausti Stefano, s.r.l.
Ferlib
F.lli Poli Armi
Franchi
Fratelli Gamba Armi
Investarm, s.p.a.
Luciano Bosis
Mauro Battaglia
Pedersoli
Perazzi Armi, s.r.l.
Perugini e Visini
Piotti Fratelli s.n.c
Redolfi Fratelli, s.n.c.
Renato Gamba
Rizzini & Tanfoglio, s.r.l.
Rizzini snc di Rizzini B. & C.
Sabatti, s.r.l.
Silma
Tanfoglio
Uberti
Vincenzo Bernardelli
W. R. Saleri di Saleri William & C
Zanardini arms

JAPAN
Miroku
SKB Arms Company

PHILIPINES
Armscor

Shooters Arms
RUSSIA
Baikal
Izhevsky Mekhanichesky Zavod
Izhmash, o.j.s.c.
Kalashnikov
KBP Instrument Design Bureau
Tulsky Oruzheiny Zavod
Vyatskie Polyany machine building
    plant "Molot"

SLOVAKIA
Ceská zbrojovka

SOUTH AFRICA
Neostead

SPAIN
Arieta Fine Shot Guns
Armas Aral
Armas Garbi
Armas Ignacio Zubillaga
Armas Kemen
AYA Fine Guns
Comlanber, s.a.
GRULLA ARMAS, S.L.
Pedro Arrizabalaga
Manufacturas Arrieta, s.l.
Norica Laurona

SWEDEN
Skullman Enterprise A.B.

SWITZERLAND
Sig Sauer Swiss

TURKEY
Akkar Silah Sanayi ve Tic.
Hatsan Arms Company
Icten Hunting&Gun Comp
Kralav
M&U Firearms
Safir Silah San
Sarsilmaz
TISAS-Trabzon
Yildiz Silah Ltd.

UNITED KINGDOM
A. A. Brown & Sons
Accuracy International Mil
Anderson Wheeler
Atkin Grant & Lang
Boss & Co
Charles Hellis & Sons
Cogswell & Harrison
David McKay Brown Gunmakers
Dickson & MacNaughton
E.J. Churchill Gunmakers
Frederick Beesley
Graham Mackinlay & Co
    Gunmakers
Holland & Holland
Holloway and Naughton, Ltd.
James Purdey & sons Ltd
John Rigby & Co
Joseph Brazier
London Gun and Rifle Maker
P V Nelson Gunmakers, Ltd
Ronald Wharton
T. R. White & Co.
Watson Bros.
Westley Richards
William & Son
William Evans Gun and Rifle
    Makers
W.J. Jeffery & Co.
W. Richards (Liverpool), Ltd.
W. W. Greener

SHOTGUNS FOR WOMEN

▲ Photo courtesy of the NRA.

SHOTGUNS FOR WOMEN

he standard dimensions for most over-the-counter, mass-produced shotguns are designed for medium-built, right-handed men of average height and weight. As we have already discussed, we of the softer sex generally have longer necks and shorter arms, and our breasts influence gun fit in several significant ways. Below are some shotguns designed for women—but remember, too, there is no such thing as a generic gun made to fit all women equally well. Considering a shotgun made specifically for a woman is a good starting point if you are in the market to buy, but keep in mind your gun must fit *you* properly if you are to shoot effectively and efficiently.

B. Rizzini

▲ B. Rizzini V3.

The B. Rizzini V3 target model shotgun features a raised Monte Carlo comb to accommodate the way a woman mounts a shotgun. This means when you bring the stock up to touch your cheek, you readily acquire a sight line over the barrels without having to bring your head down, as you likely would with a standard factory gun. Available in 12- and 20-gauge with 28-, 30-, or 32-inch barrels and extended choke tubes. MSRP: $2,450. www.rizziniusa.com

Benelli

▲ Benelli Montefeltro.

The action of the Benelli Montefeltro semiautomatic shotgun series consists of only three basic parts: the body bolt, inertia spring, and rotating bolt head. This innovative design, coupled with Benelli's Inertia-Driven System, delivers reliable cycling and consistent shots, whether you're shooting light field loads or 3½-inch magnums. Available in several models, with a black synthetic or satin-finished walnut stock, right-handed or left-handed depending on the model,

in 12- or 20-gauge, with 24-, 26-, or 28-inch barrels. MSRP: $1,129.

Though not specifically made for women, the Montefeltro Silver Featherweight in 20-gauge is a good bet. The satin walnut stock with engraved nickel receiver weighs only 5.3 lb., has a 24-inch barrel with ventilated rib, takes 2¾- and 3-inch loads with a 2+1 magazine capacity, and comes with five extended Crio choke tubes (C, IC, M, IM, F, plus wrench; flush Crio chokes are available as an option). There's little felt recoil to this highly versatile gun. The standard dimensions are as follows: length-of-pull is 14-3/8 inches, drop at heel is 2¼ inches, and drop at comb is 1½ inches. Though a shim kit is available that will allow you to adjust stock drop and cast to customize your sighting plane, you will have to have the stock adjusted by a professional gunsmith because as likely as not, the length-of-pull will be too long for most women. At an MSRP of $1,999, however, this gun is worth the investment.

▲ Benelli M2 Comfortech Compact.

The Benelli M2 Comfortech Compact is a versatile, 12-gauge semiautomatic, inertia-driven shotgun that sports a synthetic Technopolymer GripTight coated pistol grip stock with Air Touch checkering, and an Ergal anodized black matte receiver with a 3-inch chamber that holds three rounds (without limiter), and fast-swinging, 25½-inch ventilated barrels with four interchangeable chokes. The Comfortech System is designed to reduce recoil and features an ergonomic butt pad that fits snugly into the soft part of the shoulder yet spreads the recoil energy over the largest area possible. Designed for women and youth, this compact weighs 6.84 lb. in 12-gauge. Also available in 20-gauge and for left-handed shooters, as well. MSRP: $450. www.benelliusa.com

Beretta

The Beretta A400 Lite Compact semiautomatic is a semimodular, synthetic stocked shotgun; though designed for youth, it can be equally customized for smaller-framed women. The reduced length-of-pull

▲ Beretta A400 Lite Compact.

▲ Blaser F3 Ladies Gun.

factory stock comes with a set of 1- and ½-inch spacers to extend and customize buttstock fit. The A400 features a Microcore recoil pad and the Beretta Kick-Off recoil reducer, a hydraulic dampening reduction system embedded in the stock that works as a shock absorber and softens recoil by an estimated 70 percent. Beretta's GunPod 2, a hunting app that senses and records shots fired, distance covered, and time, allows you to call home, and will send your GPS coordinates (invaluable in an emergency), is inletted in the pistol grip. Available in 20-gauge, the 4+1 (without extension) magazine is chambered for 3-inch loads, the OBHP Steelium, 6x6 ventilated ribbed barrel is available in 26, 28, or 30 inches, and by removing the bead, you can add a barrel extension choke to increase barrel length. At slightly over 6 lb., this shotgun is equally serviceable in the duck blind as it is on the clays course. MSRP: $1,468.

▲ Beretta 691 Vittoria Sporting.

The Vittoria 691 Series is the first range Beretta designed for the shooting sportswoman. Developed on the Beretta 690 platform, the Vittoria Field over/under comes in 20-gauge and is available with 26-, 28-, or 30-inch barrels, a finely checkered (to 1mm) dark walnut stock, and Floral *Rinascimentale* engraving on the receiver.

Also available is the Beretta Vittoria 693 Sporting with 3-inch chambered 26-, 28-, or 30-inch Steelium Optima Bore HP barrels with ventilated rib and single selective trigger. The stock features a Monte Carlo comb, a length-of-pull just shy of 14 inches, a 1.38/1.77/2.17-inch drop-at-comb, and weight of 7.39 lb. www.beretta.com

Blaser

Blaser F3 Ladies Gun

The Blaser F3 Ladies Gun was added in 2014 to the F3 shotgun line after a decade of popularity. At 8 lb. 8 oz.,

this is a somewhat heavy albeit well-balanced shotgun that can easily be customized to the shooter with a length-of-pull that can be modified from 13½ inches to 14-5/8 inches, has an adjustable trigger blade and an adjustable comb, and is cushioned with a shock-absorbent recoil pad. The F3 Ladies also features Blaser's IBS antidoubling system, which prevents fan firing (when two shots are fired in rapid succession) and Blaser's EBS ejecting system, which activates when the gun is fired and cocks the ejecting spring when the gun is opened, keeping resistance to a minimum. a thumb-controlled safety blocks both the trigger and sears. The F3 Ladies comes with Briley Extended Spectrum choke tubes and key. MSRP: $7,995. www.blaser-usa.com

Browning

▲ Browning Golden Clays Ladies Sporting.

The Browning Golden Clays Ladies Sporting was introduced in 1999 as the official gun of the Women's Shooting Sports Foundation. The first gun was made with a painted stock in turquoise blue for the founder and director of WSSF, the late, great Sue King. One morning, around four o'clock, when I was traveling with Sue to hunt waterfowl south of the border, the Mexican border police detained us. They had never seen a blue gun before. After a few tense moments and a strip-search of our car, we convinced them, with two boxes of donuts, not to confiscate the gun. Unfortunately, Browning has ceased production of the Ladies model, but if you are lucky enough to come across one, this is the gun that started it all—a true woman's 2¾-inch, four-shell capacity 12-gauge with ¼-inch rib, 13½-inch length-of-pull, 1¼-inch drop at comb, 1½-inch drop at heel, Turkish walnut stock, with interchangeable chokes (IM, M, Skeet). Originally $1,184 for the standard Sporting and $1,903 for the deluxe, secondhand prices will vary. I see that www.guns.com currently has new, standard model Browning Gold Ladies Sporting Clays for sale for $970.

CZ

▲ CZ 720 G2 Reduced Length 20-gauge semiautomatic.

Built for youth but a fit for smaller-framed women, the gas-operated, 20-gauge, CZ 720 Reduced Length semiautomatic has a 13-inch length-of-pull, 24-inch barrel, and comes with five flush choke tubes (F, IM, M, IC, C). Chambered to accept both 2¾- and 3-inch shells, a black hard-chrome exterior metal finish on the barrel and actions resists corrosion in the field and blind. Stocked in Turkish walnut, the comb measures 1.44 inches, the heel is 2¼ inches, and weighs 6.3 lb. A magazine tube plug installed for waterfowl hunting can easily be removed for a 4+1 shell capacity. Suggested MSRP: $518. www.cz-usa.com

Fausti

▲ Fausti Aphrodite.

▲ The three Fausti sisters, Elena, Giovanna, and Barbara.

Since 1948, the Fausti name has been synonymous with high-quality, affordable trap, skeet and hunting over/unders and side-by-side shotguns. Fausto cav. Stefano e figlie, as Fausti is known, was founded by Stefano Fausti, and his daughters, Elena, Giovanna, and Barbara carry on their father's legacy today. Available from field grade to engraved actions with gold inlays, Fausti boxlocks, with the exception of the Senator and Classic models, are available at a price point that won't bleed your wallet. The Fausti Aphrodite, made especially for women, starts at $6,390. www.faustiusa.com

Franchi

▲ Franchi Catalyst Instinct.

The Franchi Catalyst Instinct was introduced in 2016. This versatile field over/under was designed for women with a raised Monte Carlo comb to put a woman's head higher on the stock and her shooting eye in line with the barrel. As we've discussed already, men tend to bring their shoulder up to the gun, which creates a pocket in their shoulder. We women tend to raise our head. When a woman raises the gun, because of our build, the toe of the gun comes right up against our breast, which usually results in a sore shoulder. That's why the toe of a stock is usually cut down to accommodate a woman. With a raised or Monte Carlo comb, we women bring our face down, away from our breast. Made in 12-gauge with 28-inch barrels and interchangeable chokes, the Franchi Catalyst Instinct is chambered for both 2¾- and 3-inch shells. MSRP: $1,600.

▲ Franchi Catalyst Affinity.

You may also want to take a look at the inertia-operated Franchi Catalyst Affinity semiautomatic, which weighs 6 lb. 12 oz. and is less expensive at $999. Available in 12-gauge with choke tubes.

Ithaca

▲ Ithaca Model 37 Featherlight Pump Shotgun with Ladies' Stock.

Ithaca, one of America's oldest gun manufacturers, has been producing the legendary Model 37 for over seventy years. This classic, with its new Solderless Barrel System, is reliable, and easy to handle and point. This is a bottom-eject pump gun, which is unlike shooting a break-open gun or a semiautomatic and may take some getting used to if you're unfamiliar with this type of action—but once you do, it's seamless. There is no soldering or heat-induced joints in the Ithaca 37, which means the vent rib barrel (the rib is attached with just one screw) can never warp or require corrective straightening, and a lengthened forcing cone reduces recoil and shot deformation. What's more, the Featherlight receiver is machined from a single block of steel (the Ultralight Model 37 action is milled from a single block of aluminum). Stocked in Grade A, AA, or AAA American black walnut for right-handed shooters, the Ithaca 37 is also made for left-handed shooters. The Ladies' stock dimensions are based on a five-foot-five woman, with a 1½-inch drop at comb, 2¼-inch drop at heel, 1/8-inch cast, 3/16-inch toe out, and a 14-inch length-of-pull and if you need a shorter stock, Ithaca will cut the stock to your specifications at no extra cost! When measuring, take into account that the Ithaca 37 has a Pachmayr 752 Decelerator Recoil Pad, which can add as much as an inch to your length-of-pull. The Model 37 is available in 12-, 20-, and 28-gauge, with 24-, 26-, 28-, or 30-inch barrels however the Ladies' stock Model 37 is offered with either 26- or 28-inch barrels in both the Featherlight and Ultralight guns. The action features classic game scene stamped engraving, and the barrels are threaded for Briley chokes. A lot of gun for an MSRP: $1,199.

Krieghoff

▲ Rachel Carrie with her Krieghoff.

H. Krieghoff MmbH was founded in 1886 as a maker of drillings, considered the essential hunting gun in those days, with its combination rifle and shotgun barrels to cover all types of wild game. It was not until 1956, when an American-German alliance married the Remington Model 32 to create the Krieghoff Model 32 clay target gun, that the company entered the shotgun field. The K-32 would spawn the K-80, K-20, and KX-6 Special competition shotgun models.

The elegant Krieghoff K-20 Victoria is built specifically for the shooting sportswoman. Equally effective in the field as it is on the range, the stock has a length-of-pull, pitch, cast, and handswell tailored to fit the average woman and can be precisely customized with an adjustable comb, palm swell, and "Victoria" forearm. The K-20 Victoria's streamline, low-profile receiver, and light, soldered Parcours barrels with 7mm tapered rib allows for a natural swing with either 30- or 32-inch barrels. Available in 20- or 28-gauge, the checkered, full pistol-grip stock can also be ordered for a left-handed shooter.

Dieter Krieghoff is the fourth generation of his family to operate Krieghoff, the 130-year-old German gun manufacturer that produces some of the finest over/under shotguns used in tournament play and in the field today. At his side is his wife, Betty Newman Krieghoff, who grew up in a gun-friendly family in Kinston, North Carolina, and began shooting at the historic Pinehurst Gun Club in Pinehurst, North Carolina, as a young woman and professional nurse. She enjoyed shooting trap and in 1980, joined the ATA, becoming involved with scoring, administration, and association work for the organization. She began to compete and in 1982, shot a 98 in the Maryland State Shoot Handicap Championship, tying for Open winner, and taking the women's trophy in the shoot-off. This would be the first of many tournaments and several state championships Betty would win.

It was soon after that, at the Eastern Zone Shoot in Elysburg, Pennsylvania, that Betty was introduced to Dieter by a mutual friend. He offered her a job at the new Krieghoff USA headquarters and in 1988, the couple married. Now, more than three decades later, they continue to share their passion for shooting and hunting, closely with one another to grow and sustain Krieghoff as one of the world's most respected sporting gun makers.

▲ Father Dave Carrie and his daughter Rachel Carrie.

Dave Carrie is known throughout the world as one of England's most impressive game shots. He did not come into the sport until he was almost forty years old and yet, it was an almost unsurmountable obstacle this amiable Yorkshire gentleman was forced to overcome that distinguishes his many accomplishments and his presence in the world of shooting today as nothing short of miraculous.

"I was eleven years old whilst playing football when I lost my left eye to a sniper shooting an air rifle from his bedroom window," Dave explains. "At that time, I was a decent footballer playing for the school's county league. My football career was over as I could not see balls passing on my left side.

I was about thirty-eight years old when a chap called Jack Hart said he was going clay pigeon shooting. I had never seen or heard of this, and he asked if I would like to come. Jack kindly lent me his Miroku 3800 trap gun. Having to shoot with one eye is a disadvantage! You just have to remember to set up properly for certain types of shots, but your remaining eye does get tired and weakens in vision as the day goes on. Nonetheless, I found that I could easily outshoot the regular Wednesday gang that gathered. I only shot DTL (down the line) and some skeet for a few months and by this time, I had got the bug proper."

Dave then shot Sporting and FITASC and that led him to the field, where he is most at home. Log onto www.DaveCarrieShooting.co.uk to enjoy Dave's incredible high bird and driven bird shooting videos.

Perhaps his greatest accomplishment is his daughter Rachel, age thirty-three. "Early on, when she was seven or eight years old, Rachel kept ferrets," her father explains, "sometimes sneaking them into her bed even though they bit her most of the time. I kept Harris hawks and Rachel would accompany me bushbeating the rabbits into the open for the hawks and sometimes using her ferrets to flush them from their burrows. She has always been 'animal mad' and has reared foxes, lambs, kittens, and young birds. Rachel is very passionate about the countryside and our shooting sports, recognizing at an early age the good that the countryside pastimes do in shaping the beautiful landscapes that we seem to take for granted. Rachel fights passionately for what she believes in and has appeared many times in magazines and mainstream TV fighting in our corner."

She has hunted all over the world for bear, moose, cape buffalo, antelope, deer, "and she fights and wing shoots as good as any man," her proud father says. Rachel often appears in Dave's videos.

Mossberg

▲ Mossberg 500 Youth Super Bantam Waterfowl.

Mossberg 500 Youth Bantam series is designed for the young shooter but also may fit smaller framed women who need a 12- or 13-inch length-of-pull. Also check out the 500 Youth Bantam with wood or synthetic stock in 12- or 20-gauge or .410-caliber. and the Maverick 88 Youth and the Flex 500 Super Bantam All-Purpose and Field/Deer combo. Chambered for 3-inch shells and a 5+1 capacity, these guns are offered with 22- or 24-inch barrel with ventilated rib and Accu-Set choke and weigh anywhere between 5 lb. 4 oz. and 7 lb. 4 oz. Prices vary with model, but any one you look at is going to be affordable and, with care, will last you a lifetime.

Perazzi

▲ Perazzi MX20 SC2.

The Perazzi Ladies Sporter 20-gauge over/under with screw-in chokes was developed by Perazzi USA's Managing Director Al Kondak together with professional shooting instructor Lars Jacob. Built on an MX20 frame, the Ladies Sporter features a forend designed for a woman's hand, a 1-7/16-inch Monte Carlo comb (an adjustable comb is available for a surcharge) to bring the gun properly to the cheek. The stock has a 3/16-inch cast-off, 3/8-inch toecast, and the butt is pitched +7 degrees to accommodate the breast. A 0.87-inch thick, soft rubber recoil pad has rounded edges to fit snuggly in the shoulder. The Perazzi Ladies Sporter comes standard with 30-inch barrels and weighs 7 lb. 4 oz. The half-ventilated side ribs can be removed so barrels ranging from 26- to 34-inches can be interchanged. The MX20 frame accepts 28-gauge and .410-caliber barrels. Available by special order is the Ladies Sporter in 12-gauge, also a left-handed model. www.perazzi.it

Remington

▲ Remington Model 870 Express Trap.

This might as well be an obituary for Remington Arms Company, the largest manufacturer of firearms and ammunition in 2015. Founded in 1816 by Eliphalet Remington in Ilion, New York as E. Remington and Sons, bankruptcy closed its doors for good on July 28, 2020. Go online nonetheless and find a Remington Model 870 Express Compact 20-gauge for women and youth. You won't regret it. (Actually, this would be a good time to buy any new or used Remington shotgun, because you won't see them come down the pike again.) This gun has an adjustable 13-inch length-of-pull that can be extended with 1-, ½-, and ¼-inch buttpad spacers. Available in Realtree Hardwood or pink Mossy Oak synthetic stock, this semiautomatic shotgun weighs 6 lb. and will accept the Rem-Choke system. Original MSRP: $429.

Syren

Syren, a division of Caesar Guerini and Fabarm of Brescia, Italy, is the original leader in designing factory shotguns for women. Their field gun models are the Syren Elos D2, XLR5 Waterfowler, Tempio, and Tempio Light. Syren's line of sporting guns include the Elos N2 Elevate, Elos N2 Sporting, L4S Sporting, and Tempio Sporting. And the amazing Syren Tempio Trap is the only production trap gun made expressly for women. Caesar Guerini was not yet established when I wrote my book, *The Italian Gun*, in 1997. I met brothers Giorgio and Antonio Guerini when they were working for their Uncle Battista (B. Rizzini). Two years later, the brothers founded Caesar Guerini with Giorgio handling business and Antonio, an engineer, the factory. An energetic visionary, Giorgio raised gunmaking to a new level. Of his generation, many would agree he is rising to the stature of Ivo Fabbri and Daniele Perazzi, the greatest innovators of Italian gunmaking and the first to marry CNC technology with the fine art of gunmaking.

▲ Syren N2 Elevate.

The Syren N2 Elevate is the newest entry in Syren's line of women's guns. Fully adjustable and customizable clays gun that will fit every discipline and most women. In 12-gauge and chambered for 3-inch loads, the N2 has 30-inch Tribore HP barrels and a set of two, 10mm to 8mm tapered ventilated, quick release ribs, one at 50/50 P.O.I. (point-of-impact) and the second rib at 65/35 P.O.I. Five EXIS HP competition choke tubes with choke case and choke wrench are included. Stocked in Triwood finished Turkish walnut. The drop at the adjustable comb is 1½ inches and 2 inches at the Monte Carlo, drop at heel is 2½ inches, the 13.9-inch length-of-pull is adjustable, cast at toe is ½ inch, cast at heel is ¼ inch, pitch is 7 degrees, adjustable reach is 3½ inches, and breech to comb measures 7 inches. The gun weighs a solid 7 lb. 10 oz., the top-end range of weight a woman wants in a solid clays gun. MSRP is $3,125 with a surcharge of $155 for a left-handed stock.

▲ Syren Elos Sporting.

The Syren Elos Sporting Over/Under was introduced by Caesar Guerini/Fabarm in 2016, two years after the gunmaker debuted its original women's line of shotguns. Less expensive and less decorative than Syren's debut models, the Elos gun has a rearward-shifting trigger designed for women's fingers and a soft recoil pad. Available only in 12-gauge with 30-inch barrels and interchangeable choke tubes. MSRP: $2,595.

▲ Syren Elos Venti Light 28-gauge over/under.

The Syren Elos Venti Light 28-gauge over/under is stocked in Turkish walnut and features an engraved and inlaid nickel-plated action. Weighing 5 lb. 11 oz. with 28-inch barrels, the Elos Venti is also available in 20-gauge with 28-inch barrels. Available for left-handed shooters, as well. MSRP: $3,275.

▲ Syren Tempio Sporting.

Available in 12- and 20-gauge with 28- or 30-inch barrels and 28-ga (30-inch barrels only) and tapered ventilated rib, the Syren Tempio Sporting over/under has a hand-polished, Invisalloy protective coin-finished, engraved receiver with gold inlay, and a hand-rubbed oil Turkish walnut stock with black rubber recoil pad and 26 lpi engraving at the wrist and rounded forend. With an MSRP of $4,750, left-hand stock option, adjustable stock option, and 32-inch barrels as an option, it behooves you to consider the options and specifications that this classic gun has to offer at https://syrenusa.com. Also consider the Syren Tempio field gun and Syren Tempio Light, the lightest of Syren's models at 5 lb. 5 oz. in the 28-gauge model.

▲ Syren Elos N2 Sporting.

The Syren Elos N2 Sporting is available in 12-gauge and is chambered for 3-inch shells. The 30-inch barrels sport a 10mm ventilated rib that tapers to 8mm and comes with a set of five EXIS HP Competition choke tubes. The trigger is adjustable, and a manual safety is standard (an automatic safety is optional). This gun weighs 7 lb. 9 oz.—somewhat heavy for a woman but in consideration, a relatively heavy gun may have less felt recoil than a lighter gun, depending upon the gun and the load you are shooting. The stock is Turkish walnut with a Triwood finish and features an adjustable comb and Schnabel forend. Drop at comb is 1½ inches, drop at Monte Carlo is 1¾ inches, cast at heal is ¼ inch, and cast at toe is ½ inch, and breech to comb is 7 inches with a 7-degree pitch. The soft black rubber recoil pad is 22mm Microcell. MSRP is $2,895 and an additional $155 for a left-handed gun.

▲ Syren Elos D2.

The Syren Elos D2 is a single selective trigger, over/under shotgun available in 20-gauge (chambered for 3-inch shells) and 28-gauge (chambered for 2¾-inch shells.) The 28-inch Tribore HP barrels have a 6mm ventilated top rib. The action is case colored, the Turkish walnut stock has a 13.9-inch length-of-pull and 12mm soft black rubber Microcell recoil pad.

▲ Syren Elos L4S.

The Syren L4S is a gas-operated semiautomatic 12-gauge is chambered for 2¾-inch loads and is available with a 28- or 30-inch Tribore HP barrel that comes with five EXIS HP competition choke tubes. At 6 lb. 12 oz., this gun—almost a pound less than Syren's Elevate over/under—is a good option for the shooter who wants a lighter gun on the clays field. The drop at comb of this Turkish walnut, Triwood stocked gun is 1½-inch at the Monte Carlo, 2½-inch drop at heel, 13¾-inch length-of-pull, 0.125-inch cast at heel and the same at toe, 7-degree pitch and 4-inch reach from the center of the trigger adjustment. MSRP is $1,990 ($2,185 for a left-handed stock).

▲ Syren Tempio Trap.

Syren Tempio Trap Unsingle and Over/Under is the only factory gun made for the woman competitive shooter. Both sport 12mm tapered ribs with an adjustable rib height of 25mm (the single is adjustable from 50/50 to 120 with no center rib and the over/under adjusts from 50/50 to 90/10 with a ventilated center rib). Both models have a DTS trigger system with two trigger-pull weight options, take up, over travel, and length-of-pull adjustments, and factory selective release triggers available in single or double release with manual safety (automatic is an option.) Chambered for 2¾-inch loads, the unsingle

has 32-inch and the over/under has 30-inch barrels with 5-inch long DuoCon forcing cones and 0.735 Maxis, chrome-lined bores with Maxis competition chokes (M, IM, and Full for the Unsingle and LM, M, IM, LF, and Full for the over/under). The hand-rubbed oil Turkish walnut Monte Carlo stock has a DTS 4-way adjustable comb and 26 lpi checkering at the wrist and on the semi-beavertail, finger-grooved forend. The stock dimensions are the same as the Syren Elevate, and it weighs 8 lb. 6 oz. (the over/under is actually one-ounce lighter). MSRP for the Unsingle and over/under each retail for an MSRP of $7,100, the combo set (over/under and unsingle) is $9,945, and add $255 for a left-handed stock.

▲ Syren XLR5 Waterfowler.

This XLR5 12-gauge waterfowl gun has a synthetic stock in Realtree's MAX-5 Camouflage pattern with soft-touch finish and 13.9-inch length-of-pull. Chambered for 3-inch loads, the 28-inch Tribore HP barrel comes with five Inner HP choke tubes. Weighing only 7 lb. 1 oz., expect little recoil as a result of the Pulse Piston gas operated system.

Weatherby

▲ Weatherby SA-08 Synthetic Compact.

The Weatherby SA-08 Synthetic Compact semiautomatic shotgun is designed for women and at an MSRP of $499, you get a lot of bang for your buck (pardon the pun!). With a short (24-inch) ventilated rib barrel and a 12½-inch stock, this 20-gauge gun is chambered for 3-inch shells and comes with three screw-in chokes (IC, M, F). The CNC machined receiver is made from aircraft-grade aluminum and the drop-out trigger system makes cleaning easy. Synthetic stocked guns sacrifice beauty for functionality—after all, what can be more glorious on a gun than an exhibition grade Turkish walnut stock? However, a gun like this in the duck blind can't be beat.

Editor's Choice

Connecticut Shotgun Manufacturing Company

American gunmaker Tony Galazan set the bar for the finest shotguns made in the United States when he established Connecticut Shotgun Manufacturing Company in 1975. Few in the history of modern gunmaking equal his talent, creative vision, mechanical skills, and engineering genius. CSMC's investment in time and capital to revive and bring new life to the production of the classic Winchester/CSMC Model 21 and CSMC/A.H. Fox sustains this nation's gunmaking heritage and without Tony's dedication, it would be lost.

I first met Tony years ago when he worked out of his garage in New Britain, Connecticut, outside of Hartford. Back then I was an editor of *Shooting Sportsman* magazine and have watched him ever since build his amazing company and expand its range of sporting firearms.

Go online at www.connecticutshotgun.com to see the CSMC line of shotguns, such as the superb Inverness Round Body over/under, the CSMC RBL side-by-side with factory hidden screw-in chokes (at an incredible base price of $3,795), and the CSMC Revelation, also with screw-in chokes, which starts at $2,450—small change for a field gun of such unparalleled quality. CSMC also offers used shotguns, rifles, handguns, and a range of fine products.

Though these are not woman-specific guns, and would in my case require stock-fitting, my personal choice among CSMC's offerings are:

▲ CSMC A10.

The CSMC A10 over/under in 20-gauge with 32-inch barrels with ventilated rib and screw-in choke tubes is a versatile choice. Made in the United States by CSMC's master gunsmiths, the marble-caked, highly figured Turkish walnut stock is hand-rubbed with many coats of Truoil, which is the time-honored, classic finish for fine guns. The long tang trigger guard and single selective trigger of this sidelock shotgun compliments the small frame and slim profile of this 6 lb. 6 oz. gun. This is a highly desirable upland gun, and the longer barrels are ideal as a sporting clays gun. Starting at $6,250, prices vary according to engraving and grade to $28,000 for the Platinum A10; it is available in barrel lengths from 28- to 32-inches and all gauges from 12-gauge to .410-caliber. You can also order a custom gun and "build your own" to your exact specifications.

▲ CSMC Christian Hunter.

The Christian Hunter is an elegant side-by-side, available as a boxlock or full sidelock, with fixed chokes or screw-in chokes in barrel lengths of 26, 28, or 30 inches and available in 12-, 16-, 20-, and 28-gauge or .410-caliber. Personally, I would choose a 16-gauge Christian Hunter with 29-inch barrels. A side-by-side in 16-gauge was long considered the quintessential ruffed grouse gun of the New England woods, and in those days, 26-inch barrels were popular. Longer barrels became more popular, and "fluid" swing and the boxlock, which has fewer parts, was preferred over a sidelock. Sadly, the 16-gauge has significantly lost popularity as loads have increasingly become unavailable these days—except at CSMS, which continues to carry the torch for this most traditional of New England grouse gun gauges.

▲ CSMC Model 21 Baby Frame Grand American.

CSMC's Model 21 Baby Frame Grand American in 28-gauge is a gorgeous gun, with exhibition Turkish walnut stock and delicate beavertail forend with fleur-de-lis checkering and a checkered butt and hand-engraved blued receiver with gold inlays of a Lab, setter, pointer, and rooster pheasants. The ventilated rib 28-inch barrels of this beautifully made side-by-side has fixed chokes (IC/M), automatic ejectors, and an automatic safety. A true Model 21 built on a 28-gauge frame, this gun weighs 5 lb. 12 oz. Gun #31388 is $40,000.

Glossary

▲ Over/under shotgun.

▲ Side-by-side shotgun.

▲ Semiautomatic shotgun.

▲ Pump-action shotgun.

A

ABSORBER, RECOIL Any device that reduces the perceived recoil of a firearm.

ACCELERATOR A device found in some semiautomatic firearms that, through mechanical advantage or spring energy, transfers kinetic energy from one part of the mechanism to another with the resultant speeding up of the action.

ACCIDENTAL DISCHARGE An unexpected and undesirable discharge of a firearm caused by circumstances beyond the control of the shooter, such as a mechanical failure or parts breakage.

ACCURACY (1) The fundamental extent to which a shotgun will consistently shoot "true," meaning the shotgun handles reliably and consistently well. (2) The degree to which a sportswoman takes repeated shots under unchanged conditions and realizes the same results. For example, if she shoots ninety out of one hundred clay targets, she has realized 90 percent shooting accuracy.

ACTION (1) The working mechanism of a firearm involved with presenting the cartridge for firing, and in removing the spent casing and introducing a fresh cartridge. (2) The combination of the receiver or frame and breech bolt together with the other parts of the mechanism by which a firearm is loaded, fired, and unloaded. (3) A firearm that chambers, fires, and ejects cartridges continually as long as the trigger is depressed and there are cartridges available in the feeding system (i.e., magazine or other such mechanism). (4) The mechanism of a breech-loading weapon that handles the ammunition (loads, locks, fires, extracts, and ejects), or the method by which that mechanism works.

ACTION, AUTOMATIC A firearm design that continuously feeds, fires, and ejects cartridge cases as long as the trigger is fully depressed and there are cartridges available in the feed system. Actuation of the mechanism may be from an internal power source, such as gas pressure or recoil, or external power source, such as electricity.

ACTION BAR FLATS Formed or machined surfaces on the action bars that control or actuate, through cams or blocks, the movement of other parts of the firearm as the bars move in a reciprocal motion.

ACTION BAR(S) A member or members used to connect and thus transmit the movement of the forearm or gas system to the breech block. In many designs, the movement of the action bars controls or actuates other parts of the mechanism.

ACTION, BARRELED A combination of barrel and receiver or frame and breech bolt together with the other parts of the mechanism by which a firearm is loaded, fired, and unloaded. Usually a complete firearm less its stock.

ACTION, BLITZ A design in which the moving parts of a break-open gun's action are mounted to the trigger plate instead of integrated into the body of the receiver. The blitz action is common on German and Austrian over/under shotguns and drillings; it is similar to a Dickson round action.

ACTION, BLOWBACK A type of semiautomatic and automatic firearm action where the inertia of some component, usually supplemented with a spring, is the main locking force and no mechanical locking of the breech occurs.

ACTION, BLOW-FORWARD A design for semiautomatic or automatic firearms, wherein the breech block is stationary, and the barrel moves forward by gas pressure to open and eject the cartridge and recycle the action.

ACTION, BOLT An action type, most frequently used on rifles and less so on shotguns, perfected by Peter Paul Mauser in 1898, whereby a cylindrical shaft, controlled by an attached lever, manually feeds a cartridge into the chamber, rotates a partial revolution engaging locking lugs in complementary recesses in the front receiver ring, and allows firing by the fall of an internal spring-loaded pin, opening, extraction, re-cocking, and ejection with the same lever in preparation for the next shot.

ACTION, BOXLOCK A design in which the hammer and hammer springs are located within the frame and the trigger assembly is in the lower tang. A type of action (receiver) for a break-open gun in which the mechanical assembly of the lock is contained within a box-shaped housing. A boxlock requires less wood to be removed from the head of the stock, which is an advantage because wood is more vulnerable than metal. The Anson & Deeley boxlock, patented in 1875, is the simplest, most reliable, and most successful action design. Two pins span the width of the action—one at the bottom rear and one slightly forward and higher—from which the sears and hammers rotate. One of the most successful action designs ever, it has been in continuous production since its invention by countless gunmakers around the world.

ACTION, BREAK-OPEN A firearm that allows loading and unloading by means of opening the action by pivoting the barrel(s) down and away from the breech while activating a release lever. Most commonly used in single-shot and double-barreled shotguns and rifles. This configuration of breech-loading firearm releases the barrels from the action with one of several types of latches. The barrels rotate on a hinge-pin and drop down around 45 degrees, exposing the breech for loading/unloading.

▲ Break-open action.

ACTION, DELAYED BLOWBACK An action that utilizes a mechanical means in conjunction with bolt mass to gain additional delay prior to bolt opening. Also called retarded blowback.

ACTION, DROPPING BLOCK An action in which the breech block moves vertically, or nearly so, inside of the receiver walls. Also called a falling block.

ACTION, FALLING BLOCK An action in which the breech block moves vertically, or nearly so, inside of the receiver walls. Also called a dropping block. This is generally a rifle and military action, and 8-gauge shotguns.

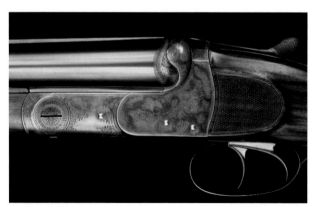
▲ Anson & Deeley boxlock.

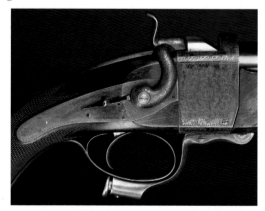
▲ Falling block action.

ACTION, HINGED FRAME A design wherein the barrel(s), one or more being either smooth or rifled, is pivoted on the frame. When the action is open, the barrel may pivot up, down, or sideways for loading or unloading. When the action is closed, the breech of the barrels swings against the standing breech. Opening is normally accomplished by movement of a top lever or sidelever.

ACTION, LOCKED BREECH Any action wherein the breech bolt is locked to the barrel or receiver, through a portion or all of the recoiling motion.

ACTION, OPEN BREECH A type of action wherein the breech bolt is held open until the trigger is pulled.

ACTION, PIVOTING BLOCK An action in which the breech block pivots in an arc to expose or lock the breech.

ACTION, PUMP A firearm that features a movable forearm that is manually actuated to chamber a round, eject the casing, and chamber a subsequent round.

▲ Pump action.

ACTION, SEMIAUTOMATIC A firearm in which each pull of the trigger results in a complete firing cycle, from discharge through reloading of the chamber. It is necessary that the trigger be released and pulled for each cycle. These firearms are also called autoloaders or self-loaders. The discharge and chambering of a round is either blowback operated, recoil operated, or gas operated. Note: An automatic-action firearm loads, discharges, and reloads as long as ammunition is available, and the trigger is depressed. A semiautomatic firearm only discharges one cartridge with each squeeze of the trigger.

ACTION, SIDELOCK A design in which the firing mechanism is attached to a side plate rather than being integral with the frame or trigger plate.

▲ Sidelock action.

ACTION, SINGLE An action requiring the manual cocking of the hammer or striker before sufficient pressure on the trigger releases the firing mechanism. The trigger performs the simple action of holding the hammer in position until pulled.

ACTION, SINGLE-SHOT A firearm with no means in the mechanism for storing or loading more than a single cartridge housed in the chamber of the barrel.

ACTION, SLIDE A firearm which features a moveable forearm which is manually actuated in motion parallel to the barrel. Forearm motion is transmitted to a breech bolt assembly, which performs all the functions of the firing cycle assigned to it by the design. This type of action is prevalent in rimfire rifles and shotguns and to a lesser extent in centerfire rifles. Also known as pump-action or trombone action.

ACTION, SLIDE-LOCK The part of a mechanism, normally found on slide-action firearms, that locks the forearm/slide mechanism in the forward position.

ACTION, STRIPPED A receiver or frame of a firearm from which all parts have been removed.

ACTION, TOP-BREAK A design in which the barrel or barrels are connected to the frame by a hinge-pin below the barrels. Upon release of the locking mechanism, usually by a top lever, sidelever, or underlever, the barrel or barrels rotate around the hinge-pin away from the standing breech.

ACTION, TRAP DOOR This action has a top-hinged breech block that pivots up and forward to open. Locking on this action is accomplished by a cam piece located at the rear of the breech block that fits into a mating recess. Also known as a cam lock.

ACTION, UNDERLEVER The same as a top break mechanism except that the lever that unlocks the firearm, allowing the barrels to pivot and expose the breech, is located below the trigger guard or forms the trigger guard.

ACTUATOR Part of the firing mechanism in certain automatic firearms, such as trigger actuator, which slides forward and back in preparing each round to be fired.

ADJUSTABLE STOCK A stock that can be easily lengthened or shortened to fit the shooter.

ADJUSTABLE TRIGGER A trigger that can be easily adjusted by the user. Adjustable triggers are common on specialized target-shooting firearms but rare on self-defense firearms.

AIM The act of aligning the sights of a firearm on a target.

AIR RESISTANCE The resistance of air to the passage of a projectile in flight.

AIR SPACE The volume in a loaded cartridge or shotshell not occupied by the propellant or the bullet, wads, or shot. Sometimes called ullage.

ALKANET ROOT *Alkanna tinctoria* or *Anchusa officinalis*, related plants of the *Boraginaceae* family, whose root, when steeped in a solution of turpentine and/or linseed oil makes a reddish stain favored by the London gun trade to impart an underlying reddish hue to fine gun stocks. Also called dyers' bugloss or London oil.

AMBIDEXTEROUS SAFETY A manual, external safety that can be accessed easily with either hand.

AMMUNITION ("Ammo") The components in a cartridge case, consisting of a primer (which produces the spark), a charge of propellant (gunpowder), and a projectile (pellets). The cartridge size must match the firearm.

AMMUNITION COLOR CODE A method of distinguishing various gauges of shotshells and types of metallic ammunition by color or plating.

AMMUNITION, FIXED A metallic cartridge or shotshell that is complete and ready to use.

AMMUNITION, MATCH Ammunition made specifically for match target shooting under very precise measures.

ANGLE OF DEPARTURE The angle formed between a horizontal line and the center line of the bore at the moment the projectile leaves the muzzle of the gun.

ANGLE OF ELEVATION The vertical angle formed between the line of sight to the target and the axis of the barrel bore.

ANSON FORE-END RELEASE A catch for securing the fore-end to the barrels of a break-open gun, operated, via a longitudinal rod, by a pushbutton exposed at the very tip of the fore-end. Typically seen on Purdey and Boss guns.

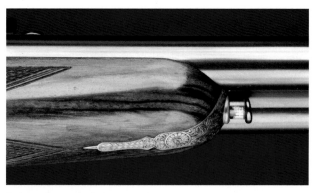

▲ Anson fore-end release.

ANTIQUE FIREARM A federal definition according to Section 921 (a) (16), Title 18, U.S.C. as: A. any firearm (including any firearm with matchlock, flintlock, percussion cap, or similar type of ignition system) manufactured in or before 1898; and B. any replica of any firearm described in subparagraph (A) if such replica (i) is not designed or redesigned for using rimfire or conventional centerfire fixed ammunition, or (ii) uses rimfire or conventional centerfire fixed ammunition which is no longer manufactured in the United States and which is not readily available in the ordinary channels of commercial trade.

APUN (ACTION PATENT USE NUMBER) Under patent law during the period of greatest creativity in the British firearms trade (circa 1860–1910) gunmakers typically numbered each patented component with its own number of use of the patent, not the number of the patent itself as registered with the patent office as in the United States, irrespective of the serial number of the firearm.

ARCADED FENCES A side-by-side gun decorated with a series of engraved crescents; a particular signature of James Woodward guns.

▲ Arcaded fences.

ARM To charge or load a firearm.

ARTICULATED FRONT TRIGGER A spring-loaded hinged front trigger, built to cushion its impact on one's trigger finger as the gun recoils when the rear trigger is pulled.

▲ Articulated front trigger.

ASSEMBLY Any collection of mutually operating parts housed together to form a single unit that may be a subassembly or a principle assembly.

AUTOLOADER A firearm that automatically loads the next cartridge to be fired into the chamber either upon the pull of the trigger in an open-bolt design or upon the firing of the previous round in a close-bolt design. Over time this term has been shortened to just "auto" and sometimes "automatic" thus creating confusion between a fully automatic firearm and a semiautomatic firearm.

AUTOLOADING ACTION A type of firearm which, utilizing some of the recoil or some of the expanding-gas energy from the firing cartridge, cycles the action to eject the spent shell, chamber a fresh one from a magazine, and cock the mainspring in preparation for firing with a manual pull of the trigger. *See also* **Semiautomatic**.

AUTOMATIC SAFETY A safety catch on a break-open gun that resets to the "safe" position each time the gun is opened, usually via a limb attached to the top lever spindle.

B

BACK ACTION A sidelock action where the mainspring is mounted rearward toward the butt. The back action is often used in double rifles where the need for strength requires as little steel as possible be removed from the bar of the action.

BACK BORE A shotgun, chambered for a specified gauge, whose barrel bore diameter is greater than the nominal diameter specified for that gauge, but does not exceed SAAMI maximum.

BACKBORING Enlarging the internal diameter of a shotgun barrel beyond its proper standard (0.729 inch in 12-gauge) by reaming, in an effort to reduce the recoil or to improve the shot pattern. Backboring removes steel and therefore strength from the barrels—possibly making them unsafe. While there is no proof law in the United States, in England to ream out the bore of a shotgun by more than 8 thousandths of an inch would render it out of proof and illegal to sell without passing re-proof.

BACKSTRAP Rear, metal part of a handgun, which together with the frontstrap, provides a mounting frame for the grips.

BACKTHRUST The force exerted on the breech block by the head of the cartridge case during propellant burning.

BAKER EJECTORS A type of mechanism, built into the fore-end of a break-open firearm, utilizing a direct-acting coil spring to kick out a spent shell while only raising an unfired shell far enough to remove manually.

BALANCE The handling characteristic of a break-open gun. Traditionally, the fulcrum of balance should be right at the hinge-pin. If the balance point is ahead of the hinge-pin, the gun would be said to be barrel-heavy with more forward inertia—slower to swing and slower to stop. If the balance point is behind the hinge-pin, the gun would be said to be stock-heavy with less forward inertia—whippier, faster to swing, and faster to stop.

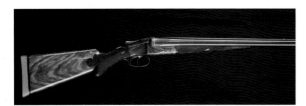

▲ Fulcrum point for a neutrally balanced shotgun.

BALLISTIC COEFFICIENT An index of the manner in which a particular projectile decelerates in free flight expressed mathematically as: $c = w/id^2$ where: c = ballistic coefficient, w = mass, in pounds, i = coefficient of form (a.k.a. form factor), d = bullet diameter, in inches. This represents the bullet's ability to overcome air resistance in flight.

BALLISTICS The science of studying a fired cartridge or bullet and matching it microscopically to a particular firearm. Ballistics can be determined three ways: "interior" (inside the gun), "exterior" (in the air), or "terminal" (at the point of impact).

BALLISTICS, EXTERIOR The branch of applied mechanics that relates to the motion of a projectile from the muzzle of a firearm to the target.

BALLISTICS, INTERIOR The science of ballistics dealing with all aspects of the combustion phenomena occurring within the gun barrel, including pressure development and motion of the projectile along the bore of the firearm.

BALLISTICS, TERMINAL The branch of ballistics that deals with the effects of projectiles at the target.

BALLISTIC TABLE A descriptive and performance data sheet on ammunition. Information usually includes bullet weight and type; muzzle velocity and energy; velocity; energy and trajectory data at various ranges.

BAR The portion of a break-open gun's action extending forward from the bottom of the standing breech, supporting the hinge-pin. In modern side-by-side guns, it is usually machined to accept the cocking limbs and the main locking bolts as well. The top surface of the bar is the watertable.

▲ Bar.

BAR ACTION A sidelock action where the mainspring is mounted forward into the bar of the action. Often more graceful in appearance than the back action and theoretically allowing faster lock times.

BAR-IN-WOOD A configuration style of breech-loading guns, aesthetically vestigial to muzzleloaders, where the hinge-pin and the knuckle of the action is housed as far as possible in wood.

▲ Bar-in-wood action open. Photo courtesy Rock Island Auction Co.

BARREL (BBL) An essential component of a firearm; a tube, sealed at one end (the breech), in which a propellant is ignited, whose rapidly expanding gases create powerful pressure to force a single or multiple projectiles through its bore, out the open end (the muzzle), and down range toward a target.

BARREL ARRANGEMENTS The position, in relationship to each other, in which multiple barrel systems are found in forearms (e.g., over/under, side-by-side).

BARREL ASSEMBLY A barrel of a firearm, either fixed or interchangeable, that has been fitted with necessary parts so that it may be assembled to the remainder of the firearm.

BARREL BLANK An unfinished barrel in any state of completion.

BARREL, BULGED A barrel with an abnormal enlargement in its bore.

BARREL CORROSION Degradation of bore and chamber surface condition due to chemical action.

BARREL, DAMASCUS A barrel formed by twisting or braiding together steel and iron wires or bars. The resulting cable is then wound around a mandrel and forged into a barrel tube. Sometimes called a laminated barrel. There are several qualities of Damascus twist, from standard to finest.

▲ Damascus barrel.

BARREL EROSION The wearing or physical deterioration of the bore or chamber of a firearm caused by hot powder gases or projectile passage.

BARREL, INTERCHANGEABLE Barrels which may be installed on a particular action without factory fitting.

BARREL LENGTH The length of a barrel as measured from the muzzle to the standing breech in a break-open gun or to the bolt face in a closed bolt-action rifle, including the chamber. A revolver barrel measurement, by convention, does not include the cylinder, only the barrel itself.

BARREL LIFE The total number of rounds fired in a barrel before it becomes unserviceable.

BARREL OBSTRUCTION A foreign object or material in the bore of a barrel which prevents unhindered passage of projectile(s) when fired. This is a potentially dangerous situation. *Never look down a barrel or attempt to dislodge an obstruction without making sure the gun is fully unloaded and the barrels are then removed. Never force an obstruction. Take the gun to your gunsmith instead.* Also called bore obstruction.

BARREL PRESSURE The pressure in a barrel developed by propelling gases when a cartridge is fired.

BARREL REFLECTOR A device with a mirror for examining the bore and chamber of a barrel. Also called bore reflector.

BARREL RELINING The replacement of the interior surface of a bore by inserting and fastening a tube. Usually refers to rifled barrels.

BARREL, RINGED A barrel that has been fired while containing an obstruction. The resultant excessive radial pressure causes a circumferential bulge in the barrel.

BARREL SHANK The breech end of the barrel that fits into the action or receiver.

BARREL SLEEVING When the barrels of a gun are damaged or the bore is "shot out," and yet the shotgun itself has life left and real and/or emotional value to the owner, sleeved barrels are a comparatively economical solution. The ribs are removed. The old barrels are cut off three to four inches from the breech end and discarded. The bores of the remaining breech end are reamed out oversize. The sleeve's barrel must be thick enough to provide structural integrity to the barrel and so requires a large enough internal barrel diameter to hold the new barrel and the original method of jointing is preserved. Barrel sleeving must only be done by a professional gunsmith who specializes in this method. Not to be confused with barrel relining.

BARREL TIME Also called ignition barrel time, the elapsed time from the contact of a firing pin with a cartridge primer to the emergence of the projectile(s) from the muzzle of the firearm.

BARREL VENT An opening or series of openings or ports in a barrel, normally near the muzzle, through which gases pass prior to bullet exit. *See also* **Muzzle-brake**.

BARREL VIBRATION The oscillations of a barrel as a result of firing.

BARREL WALL THICKNESS The thickness of the walls of a shotgun barrel tube. It is reasonable to assume that guns built by responsible manufacturers are safe to shoot, when new, with the loads for which they were intended. As the decades go by, however, and barrels are draw-filed or buffed for reblueing and as occasional pits are honed out of the bores, steel is gradually removed from the barrels. The barrel walls, already built thin for lightness, become thinner still. At some point they become too thin for safety. It is important to know the minimum barrel wall thickness of an old, well-used shotgun before shooting it. While no substitute for an actual proof test, a useful rule of thumb states that the minimum barrel wall thickness as measured with a proper barrel wall thickness gauge should be 0.020 inch in a 12-gauge gun.

BARREL WEAR The gradual mechanical deterioration of the bore caused by use, i.e., firing, cleaning, and so on. A barrel that is "shot out" refers to a barrel that has reached the end of its lifetime. *See also* **Barrel Sleeving**.

BARREL WEIGHT A separate weight attached to a regular barrel to change balance.

BARREL WHIP The movement of the muzzle end of a barrel that occurs as the projectile leaves.

BASE, HIGH The term commonly applied to a shotshell with a high metal cup, but properly applies to the height of the internal base wad. Often misused as synonymous with high brass or high cup.

BASE, LOW A term commonly applied to a shotshell with a low metal cup, but properly applies to the height of the internal base wad. Often misused as synonymous with low brass or low cup.

BATTERY A firearm term that indicates when the breech is fully closed, locked, and ready to fire. When the breech is open or unlocked, the gun is out of battery and *no attempt should be made to fire it*. A semiautomatic is out of battery when the slide fails to come all the way forward after the gun has been fired, making it dangerous or impossible to fire the next round. This condition can be created by a misfeed, a dirty gun, weak springs, the shooter's thumbs brushing against the slide, or "riding the slide," among other causes.

BATTERY CUP A component of a shotshell primer; a flanged metallic cup that contains and supports the primer cup and anvil.

BB The designation of spherical shot having a diameter of 0.180 inch used in shotshell loads. The term BB is also used to designate steel or lead air rifle shot of 0.175 inch diameter. Although the two definitions cause some confusion, they have coexisted for many years.

BEESLEY ACTION An inherently assisted-opening action, designed by Frederick Beesley in 1880, the patent sold to Purdey who have used it for every side-by-side sidelock firearm they have built since that year. The Beesley action is most readily recognized by the cams at the front of the action bar, which upon the closing of the barrels, force sliding rods rearwards through the bar of the action to cock the tumblers.

BEND British term for **Drop**.

BENT (British) A notch in a hammer or firing pin housing. The sear rests in this notch when the firearm is cocked. When the trigger is pulled, the sear moves out of the bent, allowing the firing pin to fall under the tension of the mainspring and fire the gun.

BEST GUN A deluxe shotgun made by a London gunmaker. It is a sidelock action with intercepting sears, chopper lump barrels, stocked to the fences with deluxe wood, and has its lumps concealed by the floorplate. A best gun is built to meet the highest standard of quality.

BIFURCATED LUMPS A locking system for over/under shotguns whereby the barrels are mounted to the receiver via trunnions on either side of the lower barrel and where a pair of bolts move forward into recesses on either side of the barrel-set when the gun is closed. This system makes it possible to build an over/under gun with a sleeker, lower profile than possible when mounting the lumps, hook, and locking bites to the underside of the bottom barrel. Boss and Woodward over/under guns are built with bifurcated lumps. Browning and Merkel over/under shotguns are built with traditional lumps under the bottom barrel.

BILLIARD BALL EFFECT The divergence of shot pellets caused by collisions of pellets in the shot string as it comes into contact with the target.

BIRDSHOT Small pellets, usually lead or steel, used in shotshells ranging in size from #12 (less than the diameter of a pencil point) to #4 (about 0.10 inch in diameter). The size of the shot is given as a number or letter—with the larger number the smaller the shot size. It is so named because it is most often used for hunting birds.

BISSELL RISING BITE A lockup design for break-open guns, usually serving as a third fastener to strengthen the lockup of a gun with double Purdey underbolts. A loop-shaped rearward extension of the rib drops into a mating female recess in the top of the standing breech, surrounds a fixed central buttress, and is secured by a rising post at the rear. Often seen on Rigby double rifles of the period from around 1880 to 1920; after which even Rigby discontinued it in favor of the Doll's Head, because it had been exceedingly expensive to build.

BITE A notch cut into a barrel's lump(s) into which a bolt slides to lock the barrels in battery.

BLACKING British word for blueing. *See* **Blueing**

BLACK POWDER The earliest type of firearms propellant that has generally been replaced by smokeless powder except for use in muzzleloaders and older breech-loading guns that demand its lower pressure levels. Composed generally of three-parts potassium nitrate, two-parts powdered charcoal, and one-part sulfur. Black powder explodes, expending its energy in a fraction of a second, producing volumes of dense smoke. The resultant residue promotes rust in gun bores, and it is unpredictable and therefore dangerous to handle. Black powder was replaced in the marketplace by nitro-glycerin-based powders around the turn of the last century, because they burned more slowly; maintained pressure on the projectile longer during its travel through the bore, allowing higher velocities; did not blind shooters with the smoke; did not promote rust in bores; and were much safer to store and to handle. For these reasons, it is dangerous to shoot modern nitro powders in vintage guns, especially guns with Damascus barrels, which were originally designed and contoured for the pressure curve of black powder.

BLANK, CARTRIDGE A cartridge without a projectile designed to make noise.

BLANK, STOCK A rough block of wood from which a gunstock and fore-end are shaped.

BLOWBACK A semiautomatic firearm whose breechblock and barrel are not mechanically locked together when fired. In such a case the breechblock immediately begins to separate from the barrel upon firing. Blowback is used in comparatively low-powered weapons, in which inertia of the breechblock, and cartridge wall adhesion against the chamber, are sufficient enough to retard opening until breech gas pressures have fallen to a safe level.

BLOW, LIGHT Insufficient firing pin energy or protrusion. The result is erratic ignition or failure to ignite the primer.

BLUEING The chemical oxidation to color ferrous metal parts various shades of blue or black. Blueing is a thin surface coloring, induced either by heat or by polishing and the repeated application of an acid solution to form a type of blue-black rust. It reduces the reflectivity of polished steel parts and helps inhibit further rust. The percentage of original blue finish remaining is a quick indicator of the condition of a gun. Blueing provides a measure of corrosion resistance and also helps to maintain the metal finish by resisting superficial scratching and to reduce glare to the shooter's eyes when looking down the barrel of the gun. All blued parts need to be properly oiled to prevent rust. Blueing, being a chemical conversion coating, is not as robust against wear and corrosion resistance as plated coatings, and is typically no thicker than 2.5 micrometers (0.0001 inch). For this reason, it is not considered to add any appreciable thickness to precisely-machined gun parts. Also called hot blueing, rust blueing, fume blueing (no longer used because of long drying time), col building, niter blueing, color case hardening, and browning.

BOLSTERED FRAME A firearms action, most commonly on a heavily recoiling break-open weapon, in which the action forging has been enlarged with extra steel at its weakest point—the line extending downwards from the standing breech, at the beginning of the watertable. Also called a reinforced frame.

▲ Bolstered frame.

BOOT (1) A protective device used on the buttstock of a firearm during test firing. (2) A soft leather or rubber removable recoil pad that can be slipped on or laced up to decrease the recoil of a shotgun and sometimes lengthen the buttstock.

BORE The hollow portion of a barrel through which the bullet travels during its acceleration phase. A smoothbore shotgun, unlike a rifle, does not have rifling on the barrel's internal surface. Also, the British word for gauge.

BORE BRUSH A brush used to clean the interior surface of the barrel of a firearm.

BORE CONSTRICTION A reduction in the internal diameter of a firearm bore.

BORE DIAMETER In shotguns, the interior dimension of the barrel forward of the chamber but before any restrictive choke or expanded muzzle.

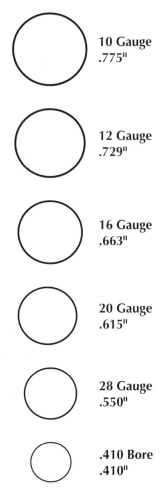

10 Gauge
.775"

12 Gauge
.729"

16 Gauge
.663"

20 Gauge
.615"

28 Gauge
.550"

.410 Bore
.410"

▲ Standard bore diameters.

BRASS, HIGH and LOW Common terminology referring to the length of the external metal cup on a shotshell. The brass of a shotgun shell for more powerful loads extends further up the sides of the shell, while light loads use "low brass" shells. The brass does not provide significantly more strength, but the difference in appearance helps shooters quickly differentiate between high and low powered ammunition. Properly called high or low cup, respectively.

BREAK Also called trigger break. The point at which the trigger allows the hammer to fall, or releases the striker, so that the shot fires. The ideal trigger break is sudden and definite. "Like a glass rod" is the cliché term shooters use to describe the ideal crisp, clean break.

BREECH That portion of the gun that contains the rear chamber portion of the barrel. The rearmost end of a barrel, closest to the shooter.

BREECH BLOCK The part of the weapon that seals the rear of the chamber (the breech) while the gun is firing, preventing the rearward escape of gases.

BREECH BOLT The locking and cartridge head supporting mechanism of a firearm that operates in line with the axis of the bore.

BREECH FACE That portion of the breech block that touches the cartridge when the breech is closed.

BREECHING SYSTEMS
1. **BELT**: A type of chamber design in which the cartridge seats in the chamber on an enlarged band ahead of the extractor groove of the cartridge body.
2. **MOUTH**: A type of chamber design in which the cartridge seats in the chamber on the mouth of the cartridge case.
3. **RIMLESS**: A type of chamber design in which the cartridge seats in the chamber on the shoulder of the cartridge case.
4. **RIMMED**: A type of chamber design in which the cartridge seats in the chamber on the rim or flange of the cartridge case.

BREECHLOADER A firearm that is loaded from the breech end of the barrel, usually with a cartridge (as opposed to a muzzleloader).

BREECH OPENING The open rear of the barrel through which cartridges are inserted into the chamber.

BREECH STANDING The part of the frame of a revolver or break-open firearm that supports the head of the cartridge when it is fired.

BRIDLE A small secondary plate mounted behind and parallel to a sidelock gun's lockplate that supports the inside ends of the pins about which the moving parts rotate.

BROWNING An oxidation process applied to the surface of raw steel, undertaken with acids, to produce a finish that resists further rusting, providing as you might expect, a brownish color, allowing the pattern of Damascus barrels to show through.

BROWNING, JOHN MOSES The world's greatest firearms inventor. Born in Ogden, Utah. While he made some guns himself, normally he licensed his designs to prominent manufacturers such as Colt, Fabrique National, and Winchester. While Samuel Colt and Paul Mauser achieved fame basically as a result of one idea, John M. Browning produced dozens of the most successful rifle, handgun, machine gun, and military gun designs. In shotguns, he designed the Stevens/Savage Model 520/620 pump-action repeating shotgun; the Savage Model 720 long-recoil semiautomatic shotgun; Winchester Model 1887 lever-action repeating shotgun; the Winchester Model 1893 pump-action repeating shotgun; the Winchester Model 1897 pump-action repeating shotgun; the Winchester Model 1912 pump-action repeating shotgun; the Ithaca Model 37 pump-action repeating shotgun; the Browning A5 long-recoil semiautomatic shotgun; the Remington Model 17 pump-action repeating shotgun; and the Browning Superposed over/under shotgun, which was among the last guns Browning was designing at the time of his death on November 26, 1926, in Liège, Belgium, at the age of seventy-one.

▲ John M. Browning.

BRUSH LOAD Lead pellets ranging in size from 0.20 inch to 0.36 inch diameter normally loaded in shotshells.

BUCKSHOT Shotgun ammunition that uses medium- to large-sized pellets measuring 0.24 inch in diameter or greater to be discharged in quantity from a shotgun. Generally, the larger the pellets, the fewer of them there are in casing. Buckshot loads are used in deer hunting with shotguns.

BUFFER In a firearm, any part intended to absorb shock, reduce impact, or check recoil.

BULINO ENGRAVING Shallow, pictorial engraving designs, often of photographic quality, executed directly by hand onto the steel with a fine-pointed scribe called a burin, without the use of a chasing hammer. Also called banknote engraving. Often seen on high-grade, contemporary Italian shotguns.

▲ Bulino engraving.

BUSHED FIRING PINS Circular steel fittings, about ½ inch in diameter, screwed into the breech face of a gun and through which the firing pins pass. Firing pin bushings allow the convenient replacement of broken firing pins. They also allow the renewal of an older gun where, over the decades, leakage of high-pressure gas from corrosive primers has eroded the breech face around the firing pins. In Britain: disk-set strikers.

BUTT (1) The end of a gun stock; the part that rests on the shoulder when the gun is mounted. (2) A fixed-position shooting station for British-style driven bird shooting, often rock-lined and partially underground, providing some effect of a blind for the shooter (the Gun) and his loader.

BUTTPLATE A plate made of some material harder than the wood of the buttstock, fitted to the end of same to protect it. It may be made of hard rubber, horn, plastic, or steel. It may be shaped relatively flat or with projections, such as a Schuetzen buttplate. It may be finished smooth, checkered, striated, or engraved.

BUTT STOCK The structural support of a long gun to which the barrel and action are inletted into the stock and bedded. A buttstock is usually made of wood but also available in synthetic or composite material. Also referred to as shoulder stock.

C

CALIBER (Ca., Cal., Calibre) A term used to designate the specific cartridge(s) for which a firearm is chambered. It is the approximate diameter of the circle formed by the tops of the lands of a rifled barrel. It is the numerical term included in the cartridge name to indicate a rough approximation of the bullet diameter, expressed in either fractions of an inch (.30 cal.) or millimeters (7mm). Unlike all other gauges, the .410-cal. is a numerical term included in a cartridge name to indicate a rough approximation of the bullet diameter.

CAM LOCKING An incline, either helical or straight, to assist in closing the action on a chambered cartridge.

CANNELURE A circumferential groove generally of corrugated appearance cut or impressed into a bullet or cartridge case. Sometimes used in reference to an extraction groove.

CANT/CANTING Tilting the firearm slightly to one side, so the grip is no longer vertical in relation to the ground. Canting the firearm can make precision shooting more difficult but may be necessary in some circumstances.

CAPPER/DE-CAPPER A hand tool used in the field for inserting live, and removing spent, primers from cartridges.

CARRIER A lifting mechanism in some repeating firearms that raises and positions the cartridge for feeding into the chamber. Sometimes called the lifter.

CARRYING STRAP A simplified version of a sling, used for carrying purposes only.

CARTRIDGE Often called a shotshell, a single round of ammunition made up of a case, primer, and propellant. The cartridge is placed into the breech of a firearm.

CARTRIDGE, BLANK A cartridge loaded without a projectile and designed to produce a loud noise. Often sealed at the mouth with a cardboard, plastic, or fiber wad that is propelled from the muzzle with a dangerous force for a short distance when fired.

CARTRIDGE BLOCK A flat container having blind holes into which cartridges can be inserted in an upright position to be readily available to the shooter.

CARTRIDGE CASE The main body of a single round into which other components are inserted to form a cartridge. Usually refers to centerfire and rimfire cartridges. Serves as a gas seal during firing of the cartridge. Usually made of brass, steel, copper, aluminum, or plastic Also referred to as a shell case.

CARTRIDGE CASE LENGTH The dimensions from face of the head to the mouth.

CARTRIDGE, CENTERFIRE Most cartridges, including shotshells, are centerfire. Exceptions include .17- and .22-caliber rimfire ammunition. The rear end of a centerfire cartridge has a primer in its center, hence "centerfire."

CARTRIDGE GUIDE A firearm component that acts as a guide for the cartridge while it is being fed from the magazine to the chamber.

CARTRIDGE, MAGNUM A term commonly used to describe a rimfire or centerfire cartridge (or shotshell), that is larger, contains more shot, or produces higher velocity than standard cartridges or shells of a given caliber or gauge. Shotguns designed to fire magnum cartridges or shells may also be described with the term magnum.

CARTRIDGE RAMP Surface in the receiver or barrel of a repeating action firearm along which the cartridge rides in feeding from magazine to chamber.

CARTRIDGE, RIMFIRE A cartridge containing the priming mixture in the rim of the base.

CASE, BELTED A cartridge case design having an enlarged band ahead of the extractor groove. This type of construction is generally used on large capacity magnum-type cartridges.

CASE/CASING The envelope (container) of a cartridge. For shotguns it is usually of paper or plastic with a metal head and is more often called a shell.

CASEHARDENING Mottled blue/green/brown colors on a shotgun receiver. The colors are the by-product of a heat-treating process that incorporates carbon into the surface molecular structure of the steel, providing a hard-wearing surface without making the entire receiver brittle. The parts to be casehardened are packed in a crucible with carbon-rich media such as bone meal and charcoal, heated to bright orange, about 1800°F, then quenched in bubbling oil. Also called carbonizing. The colors themselves are fairly perishable both from wear and from sunlight. The percentage of original case colors remaining is therefore a quick proxy for the cosmetic condition of the gun.

CASE, SPLIT A longitudinal rupture in the wall of a cartridge case or shotshell.

CAST-OFF An offset of a gun stock to the right, so that the line of sight aligns comfortably with the right eye while the butt of the stock rests comfortably on the right shoulder. Almost all right-handed shooters benefit from a little castoff and most custom-built guns are made this way. To what degree depends upon the measurements of a professional gun fitter. The castoff is correct when the front bead lines up to one's eye with the center of the standing breech when the gun is comfortably and properly mounted. Production guns are normally manufactured with no cast either way.

▲ Cast-off.

CAST-ON An offset of a gun stock to the left, so that the line of sight aligns comfortably with the left eye while the butt of the stock rests comfortably on the left shoulder. Almost all left-handed shooters benefit from a little cast-on and most guns custom built for left-handed shooters are made this way. The only question is how much. The cast-on of a gun is about correct when the front bead lines up to the shooter's eye with the center of the standing breech when the gun is comfortably and properly mounted.

▲ Cast-on.

CENTER OF IMPACT The center of a shot pattern or bullet impacts on a target made by a series of rounds fired at the same aiming point.

CENTRAL VISION A form of stock design, particularly for shotguns, having considerable cast, perhaps an inch and a half, to bring the line of sight centrally between the shooter's two eyes.

C-FASTENER Westley Richards's proprietary top lever actuated bolting system for break-open guns and rifles. The top lever, when pushed to the right, cams against a facet on the top of the action body and withdraws the locking bolts rearward from their respective bites.

CHAMBER The breech (rear) end of a barrel that measures the diameter of the cartridge for which the gun is manufactured in which the cartridge is inserted. The length of a shotgun chamber will accommodate the unfired cartridge allowing for its crimp to open fully when the cartridge is fired. It is possible, but definitely not advisable, to load a longer cartridge than specified for the gun because when the gun is fired, the crimp will open into the forcing cone. The taper of the forcing cone will not enable the crimp to open fully and the gun will develop far greater pressure than it was designed to handle. This could result in a barrel bulge. Although most modern 12-gauge shotguns have 2¾-inch chambers, many pre-World War II American guns and even modern British-made shotguns may have shorter chambers, perhaps 2½ inches. Again, it is extremely important to know the length of a gun's chambers and to use the ammunition for which it was intended.

CHAMBER BULGE A chamber with an abnormal enlargement.

CHAMBER DEPTH GAUGE A cylindrical steel plug of hardened steel engraved with the dimensions and circumferential lines demarking the different typical lengths of cartridges available for that bore. Inserting the plug-gauge into the chamber will indicate the maximum length of cartridge that can be safely shot from that gun.

CHAMBER THROAT This is the area in the barrel that is directly forward of the chamber, which tapers to the bore diameter.

CHARGE (1) The amount, by weight, of a component of a cartridge. (2) To load a firearm.

CHARGE, MAXIMUM The greatest charge weight, in grains, of a particular propellant that may be used with other specified ammunition components without exceeding the safe maximum allowable pressure limit for the specific cartridge or shell being loaded.

CHARGE, NOMINAL A typical charge weight of a specific powder for a specific combination of components.

CHARGE, POWDER The amount of powder by weight in a cartridge case.

CHARGE, REDUCED A less than nominal powder charge.

CHECKERING A diamond-like crosshatch pattern inscribed in the gunstock grip, fore-end, and sometimes the butt of a gunstock (in lieu of a buttplate) to improve gripping the gun and secondarily, for ornamentation. Originally done for utility only, checkering is an art form that requires the expertise of a craftsmen. The pattern can be plain to very ornate. The amount of coverage and the number of lines per inch indicate the quality of the work. Too-fine checkering, however, defeats the purpose of the work altogether.

CHECKERING CRADLE A frame having vertical end supports between which a gun stock may be held while its gripping surfaces are being checkered.

CHECKERING, CUT Checkering which is cut with a tool into the surface, either by hand or machine, rather than impressed.

CHECKERING, FRENCH A type of gunstock line engraving where lines are omitted at regular intervals. Also called skip-line checkering. One of the more ornate checkering patterns is the fleur-de-lis.

CHECKERING, HAND A process of wood carving gun stocks by hand rather than machine.

CHECKERING, IMPRESSED A heated die process which produces a carved effect in the gun stock or forearm.

CHECKERING LINE COUNT A method of expressing the size of the diamonds in a checkering pattern, expressed in lines per inch. The higher the number, the finer the pattern; the lower the number, the fewer lines per inch.

CHECKERING, MACHINE A process of wood carving gun stocks by machine rather than by hand.

CHECKERING, RUNOVER A wood cutting condition which occurs when any line goes beyond the border.

CHECKERING TOOLS The tools used for cutting a checkering pattern in wooden stocks. May be hand or machine powered.

CHEEK/CHEEKPIECE A broad, raised, flat area carved on the side of a gunstock against which the shooter rests his face (on the left side of the stock for the right-handed shooter, and on the right side for a left-handed shooter). It is often associated with a Monte Carlo type stock.

CHOKE The constriction at the end of a shotgun barrel that controls shot dispersion. Chokes typically are cylinder, improved cylinder, modified, improved modified, and full. A cylinder choke produces a very wide shot dispersion, whereas a full choke is the tightest dispersion of shot. Choke is designed to control the spread of the shot as it leaves the barrel. Measurements of muzzle constriction by micrometer predict the pattern thrown by a shotgun barrel and are approximate. Patterns can vary depending on atmospheric pressure, humidity, length of cartridge, type of wad, size of shot, etc. The only way to determine the actual pattern thrown by a shotgun barrel is to shoot that gun at forty yards and count the percentage of pellets falling within a 30-inch circle placed around the visual center of the pattern. Repeat this procedure four or five times and determine the average.

CHOKE CUT A choke formed by a reamer during manufacture of the barrel of a shotgun.

CHOKE, CYLINDER BORE The lack of a uniform constriction at or near the muzzle of a shotgun barrel.

CHOKE, JUG A type of shotgun barrel choke, wherein a slight recess is formed in the bore approximately one inch behind the muzzle. The recess causes the shot to gather before leaving the muzzle resulting in a denser pattern.

CHOKE MARGIN That portion of the choke forward of the greatest constriction.

CHOKE MARKINGS, EUROPEAN	
Full Choke	*
Improved-Modified	**
Modified	***
Improved Cylinder	****
Cylinder	CL
CHOKE MARKINGS, UNITED STATES	
Full	FC
Improved-Modified	Imp. Mod.
Modified	Mod.
Improved-Cylinder	IC, Imp. Cyl.
Skeet	Sk
Cylinder Bore	Cyl.

CHOKE, SWAGED A shotgun barrel constriction that has been formed at or near the muzzle by the use of dies or hammers.

CHOKE TUBE Replaceable, interchangeable, threaded cylinders having different choke diameters (e.g. modified, full) that screw into the muzzle of a shotgun to allow for different shot patterns. (See choke, above) Guns fitted for choke tubes should never be fired without tubes in place.

CHOKE, VARIABLE An adjustable device attached to the muzzle of a shotgun in order to control the shot patterns.

CHOKE, VENTILATED A shotgun choke which is slotted for the release of powder gases.

CHOPPER-LUMP BARRELS *See* **Demi-bloc barrels**

CHURCHILL RIB A relatively tall, narrow, matted, solid top rib on a pair of side-by-side barrels, developed by Robert Churchill.

CLAY PIGEON Originally, live pigeons were used as targets, but they were gradually replaced with clay disks; live pigeons were ultimately banned. Later clay has been replaced with more suitable raw materials.

CLEARING Unloading a gun and double checking that it is unloaded, or fixing a malfunction so that the gun is ready to fire again.

COCK To put tension on the shotgun's mainspring by pulling back the external hammer or opening and closing the barrels of a break-open gun, which places the hammer, firing pin, or striker in position for firing. Some external hammers, and all internal hammers, may be cocked simply by pulling the trigger.

COCKED A state of readiness of a firearm. The hammer (or similar mechanism if there is no hammer) only needs to be released by the trigger to cause the gun to fire.

COCKING INDICATOR Any device to indicate that a firearm hammer or striker is cocked. The cocking indicator is attached to the internal hammers of a break-open gun and visible from the exterior of the gun to show when each lock is cocked and when it has been fired. These are usually in the form of protruding pins on a boxlock gun or in the form of engraved or gold inlaid lines on the tumbler pins of a sidelock gun.

COIN-FINISH A high-polish finish on the receiver of a break-open gun. Coin-finish shows off delicate engraving better than other finishes.

▲ Coin finish.

COMB The top of a gun's stock where a shooter rests his cheek when mounting a gun. The comb of the stock determines the position of the shooter's eye, which is why it is important that a gun fits properly.

COMBUSTION The chemical reaction of a fuel and oxygen, usually initiated by a heat source. When the fuel is oxidized there is an evolution of heat and often light.

COMPENSATOR A device attached to the muzzle end of the barrel that utilizes propelling gases to reduce recoil. They generally increase muzzle blast. They may also, but not necessarily, diminish muzzle flash. Also called a muzzle brake.

CONCEALED THIRD FASTENER An extension protruding rearward from the breech end of a pair of side-by-side barrels. The top of the extension is locked down by a cam attached to the top-lever spindle. When the gun is closed this extra fastener is not visible from the exterior of the gun.

CONE, FORCING The tapered lead from the shotgun chamber diameter to the bore diameter.

COVER Where wild birds hide to escape from predators.

COVERT A wild place, thicket, commonly used in the American Northeast to describe wild bird habitat, specifically woodcock and grouse.

COVEY A flock of wild birds.

CREEP When the trigger is sluggish at the actual point of release.

CRIMP, ROLLED The closure of the mouth of a shotshell by inverting the mouth of the tube over a top wad or slug. The length of the cartridge is measured with the crimp open. The chamber must be long enough to accommodate the crimp.

CRIMP, STAR A type of closure of the mouth of a metallic case or shotshell in which the sidewalls are folded in a star-shaped pattern. Also called rose crimp or pie crimp.

CROSSBOLT A transverse operating type of lock used in some break-open type firearms, sometimes called a Greener crossbolt. A device intended to prevent stock splitting due to recoil. A form of manual safety which operates transversely to prevent or permit firing of a gun.

CROSS-DOMINANT A shooter who is right-handed but left-eyed, or left-handed and right-eyed.

CROSSOVER STOCK A custom made or fitted gunstock with extreme cast, whether cast-off or cast-on, for use by persons with a disability, allowing the shooter to shoot from the right shoulder using the left eye, or from the left shoulder using the right eye. A crossover stock can also be for a right-handed shooter with a severely dominant left master eye.

▲ Crossover stock.

CROSS PIN FASTENER A horizontal wedge that fits through the fore-end of a vintage gun through which a lump is attached to the underside of the barrel and out the other side of the fore-end. Also called a key fastener.

CROTCH FIGURE The generally irregular grain pattern common to a stock blank cut from the crotch of a tree.

CROWN The area inside the bore nearest the muzzle. Damage to the crown can severely and adversely affect the firearm's accuracy.

CROWNING The act of forming the radius on the muzzle end of a barrel.

CUT OFF (1) A mechanical device that is employed in firearms so that only one shell will feed into the carrier (or lifter) with each cycle of the breech mechanism. Also called cartridge stop and shell stop. (2) A manually operated device to prevent the feeding of cartridges from a magazine.

CUTTS COMPENSATOR A cylindrical muzzle extension with slots on the top designed to push the muzzle down when a gun is fired in order to help reduce the recoil and muzzle jump. It does, however, increase noise from the muzzle blast—which shooters in your proximity will not appreciate.

D

DAMASCUS STEEL Barrel tubes built up by twisting alternate strips of iron and steel around a fixed rod (mandrel) and forge-welding them together in varying combinations according to the intended quality and the skill of the maker. The rod is withdrawn, the interior reamed, and the exterior filed until the finished tube is achieved. Damascus barrels may be recognized by any of a variety of twist or spiral patterns visible in the surface of the steel. Before the twentieth century, barrels were typically built in this manner because gunmakers did not have the technology to drill a deep hole the full length of a bar of steel without coming out the side. Damascus barrels were usually intended for use with black powder, then the standard of the day. The contour of the barrel wall thickness, intended for the fast explosion of black powder, was quite thick at the breech and tapered thinner toward the muzzle. It is not advisable to shoot modern smokeless powder in a Damascus barrel. Apart from giving due deference to the age of such barrels and to the method of their construction, smokeless powder burns more slowly, lowering the pressure at the breech end, but considerably raising it further down the barrel to a level such barrels were rarely designed to handle.

▲ Damascus steel.

DECAPPER A tool used to remove primers from cartridge cases or shells.

DE-COCKER A type of action, usually of the break-open type, which readily allows the release of mainspring tension, rendering the gun safe. Normally such a gun is carried in the field loaded, but with the action not cocked as its safety position. Then, when ready to fire, instead of pushing a safety tab forward, the shooter pushes this larger tab forward, cocking the mainspring, making the gun ready to fire. If the shot is not taken, she may simply slide this tab rearwards again, de-cocking the gun and returning it to the still-loaded, but very safe position. In German, it is called a handspanner.

DEELEY FORE-END RELEASE A latch for securing the fore-end to the barrels of a break-open gun, operated by a short pull-down lever mounted to the center of the fore-end. Typically seen on Parker and Prussian Charles Daly guns. More properly known as a Deeley & Edge Fastener.

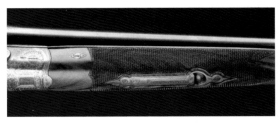

▲ Deeley fore-end release.

DEFLECTION The variation in the normal flight path of a projectile caused by wind or other external influences.

DEFLECTOR A device mounted on the receiver or frame of a firearm to change the direction of fired-case ejection.

DEMI-BLOC BARRELS Called Chopper-lump barrels by the British, a method of joining the two separate tubes of a set of barrels where the right-hand half of the pair of lumps under the barrels are forged integrally with the right barrel and the left-hand half of the pair of lumps under the barrels are forged integrally with the left barrel. Chopper-lump barrels can be recognized by the fine joint-line running longitudinally down the center of each lump. This method of jointing barrels is the best because it is the strongest in relation to its weight, and it allows the two barrels to be mounted closest to each other at the breech end, reducing problems regulating the points of aim of the two separate barrels.

DENT Damage to a shotgun barrel from having taken a hit from a hard object or if the shooter falls and her unloaded gun strikes a stone or hard object.

Thinner-walled barrels are more subject to the risk than thicker ones. While dents a few thousandths of an inch deep may not appear to be dangerous, deeper ones ought to be raised by a skilled gunsmith before firing the gun, best done using a hydraulic dent-raising tool. Never shoot a gun with a dented barrel. The cartridge can get stuck and rupture the barrel. This is extremely dangerous. Exercise caution and take the gun to a gunsmith!

DENT REMOVER A gunsmithing tool used to remove dents from shotgun barrels. Also called dent raiser.

DETONATION An extremely rapid exothermic decomposition reaction which proceeds at a rate greater than the speed of sound within the reacting material. The normal mode of initiation is shock or from initial combustion which accelerates to such a degree that a shock wave is formed. Behind the shock wave is a reaction zone where material is converted to gaseous products at high temperature and pressure. Detonating is a gunmaker's term originally referring to the fitting of percussion hammers. Purdey uses it today to refer to the shaping of the action, particularly the fences.

DIAMOND GRIP The cross-sectional shape at the wrist of a shotgun with diamond checkering.

DISASSEMBLY The act of taking apart a firearm.

DISCHARGE To cause a firearm to fire.

DISCONNECTOR A device intended to disengage the sear from the trigger. In a manually operated firearm, it is intended to prevent firing without pulling the trigger. In a semiautomatic firearm, it is intended to prevent fully automatic firing.

DISC, PAPER Small circular piece of treated paper cut and pressed into the primer cup in contact with the priming mixture. Also called foil.

DISC-SET STRIKERS Circular steel fittings, about ½ inch in diameter, screwed into the breech face of a gun through which the firing pins pass.

DOLL'S HEAD A rib extension on a break-open gun, ending in a circular or semi-circular shape, mating into a similarly-shaped recess in the top of the receiver. A doll's head is designed to resist the tendency of the barrels to pull away from the standing breech when firing. Because an action's center point of flexing when firing is at the base of the standing breech, not at the hinge-pin, a passive doll's head extension makes an effective extra fastener, even without additional mechanical locks operated by the opening lever.

▲ Doll's head.

DOUBLE-BARREL(ED) Two barrels in a firearm mounted to one frame. Can be vertically (over-under) or horizontally (side-by-side) aligned.

DOUBLE FEED A malfunction in which the spent case fails to eject from a semiautomatic firearm and blocks the chamber. As the fresh round is brought forward it cannot enter the chamber. It is cleared by stripping the magazine from the gun, racking the slide several times to eject the spent case, and then reloading.

DOUBLE GUN A two-barrel firearm, usually side-by-side. Also known as double-barrel or simply a double.

DOUBLE TRIGGERS One trigger for each of two barrels of a side-by-side or over/under shotgun. If, for example, the double gun is choked modified and full, the modified barrel (usually the right barrel in a side-by-side or bottom barrel in an over/under) throws a more open pattern, while the full-choked barrel will throw a tighter pattern.

▲ Double triggers.

DOUBLING The unwanted tendency for a double-barreled gun to fire both barrels simultaneously when the recoil from the first barrel's discharge jars the sear for the second barrel, causing it, too, to fire. Doubling results from worn parts, coagulated old oil, or inefficient or no regular maintenance.

DOWN RANGE The area of a gun range where firearms are pointed when they are fired. The area of the range forward of the firing line.

DRAM A black powder or smokeless powder weight measure.

DRAM EQUIVALENT The accepted method of correlating relative velocities of shotshells loaded with smokeless propellant to shotshells loaded with black powder. The reference black powder load chosen was a 3-dram charge of black powder, with 1 1/8 ounces of shot and a velocity of 1200 fps. Therefore, a 3-dram equivalent load using smokeless powder would be with 1 1/8 ounces of shot having a velocity of 1200 fps or 1¼ ounces of shot and a velocity of 1165 fps. A 3¼-dram equivalent load might have 1 1/8 ounces of shot and a velocity of 1255 fps. (Abbreviated as dram equiv.)

DRILLING A three-barrel shoulder-fired gun, primarily built in Germany and Austria, with two identical side-by-side shotgun barrels mounted above one rifle barrel. If with two rifled barrels above a single rifled barrel, it is called a bockdrilling.

DROP The distance from an imaginary straight line of sight extended along the rib of a shotgun rearward toward the butt to the top of the stock at the comb or the heel. The amount of drop determines how high or how low a gun will naturally point. Factory guns usually have a 2 3/8-inch drop at the heel and will best fit the broadest range of shooters for field use. A gun with less drop will shoot higher, while a gun with more drop will shoot lower depending upon the individual. When the gun is comfortably mounted with the cheek snugly on the comb, the drop is about right when you can see the front bead and just a little rib over the standing breech. Trap guns usually have less drop because they are supposed to shoot a little high in order to hit an almost universally rising target. The British refer to drop as bend.

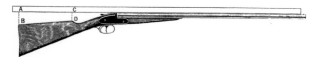

▲ Drop.

DROPLOCK A variation in the nineteenth century by London gunmaker Westley Richards on the Anson & Deeley boxlock design, whereby the locks themselves are removable, without tools, from the action body for cleaning or repair through a hinged or detachable floorplate.

DROP POINTS Raised, carved tear-drop shaped detail behind the lockplates of a sidelock or flat side panels of a boxlock.

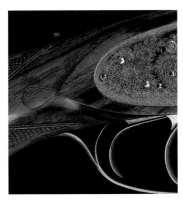

▲ Drop points.

DRY FIRING The operation of a firearm without the use of ammunition as a means of gaining familiarity with the shotgun. Dry firing must be done very carefully with a verified unloaded gun. However, dry firing a gun can shatter the action's internal mechanical parts. Be sure to use snap caps when you dry fire a gun.

DUD A round of ammunition that does not fire.

E

EAR PROTECTION Ear muffs cover both ears and are usually attached to a headband. Ear plugs fit inside the ear canal. Ear muff hearing protection with internal electronics amplify human voices while excluding all noises louder than a given decibel rating. Ear muffs (sometimes called "ears") and ear plugs reduce the intensity of the sound reaching the ears. Shooting causes permanent damage to unprotected ears. Whether you use simple foam plugs you get for free at any shooting range, or expensive custom-made ear plugs or electronic ear muffs, losing your hearing is preventable—and safeguarding your hearing is priceless.

EJECTION The removal of a cartridge (fired or unfired) from the breech of a firearm by means of a mechanical ejector.

EJECTION PORT The opening through which the empty, spent cartridge case is ejected from a shotgun.

EJECTOR Fittings inset into the breech end of a pair of barrels of a break-open gun, operated by a spring mechanism, that kick out fired shells while only raising unfired shells enough to be removed by hand. Recognizable at a glance on the breech end of a double gun because the fitting is split in two, one ejector for each barrel.

▲ Barrel with ejectors and barrel with extractors.

EJECTOR, AUTOMATIC A device in double guns that expels fired cases when the action is opened. Abbreviated AE.

EJECTOR ROD That component that actuates the extractor and/or ejector. Can be manual or automatic. Also called extractor rod.

ENERGY FORMULA The following formula is used to obtain kinetic energy of a projectile: $E = WV^2/14,000gc$ where: W = weight of projectile, in grains V = velocity, in feet per second, gc = gravitational constant, 32.16 feet/second^2

ENGINE TURNING A geometric design of abrasively formed overlapping circles on the metallic surfaces of a firearm. Also called jeweling.

ENGRAVING The precise process by which an engraver inscribes a design into the flat metal surface of the action, screwheads, trigger guard, metal buttplate, fore-end latch, and/to the breech of the barrels. Designs can vary from simple scrollwork to elaborate hunting scenes inlaid with gold.

ESCUTCHEON A plate, often an oval or shield, typically of sterling silver or gold inlaid into a gunstock upon which is engraved the initials, monogram, or coat of arms of the owner.

EXTERNAL SAFETY A safety lever found on the outer surfaces of the firearm and accessible to the user.

EXTRACTION The withdrawal of a cartridge (fired or unfired) from the chamber of a firearm by means of a mechanical extractor.

EXTRACTION GROOVE A groove turned in the side wall of a cartridge case just forward of the face of the head for the purpose of extraction. Also called cannelure.

EXTRACTOR A fitting inset into the breech end of a pair of barrels of a break-open gun. When the gun is opened, the extractor lifts the cartridges (whether fired or not) so they may be removed by hand. Recognizable at a glance on the breech end of a double gun because the fitting is solid—one extractor taking care of both barrels together. Sometimes called lifters. The ejector mechanism itself is normally fitted inside the fore-end. Two common forms are the Southgate (or Holland & Holland system) and the Baker.

EXTRACTOR CUT Usually a recess in the barrel of a firearm to accommodate an extractor.

▲ Your shooting glasses should fit properly and snuggly. Photo courtesy of the NRA.

EYE PROTECTION A recommended safety practice utilizing approved safety glasses. "Eye" is slang for safety glasses or other protection for the eyes. All shooters and spotters are required to wear eye protection while shooting is in progress.

F

FACILE PRINCEPS A proprietary boxlock action design by W.W. Greener, similar to the Anson & Deeley but more easily cocked with the fall of the barrels; the fore-end iron presses on a rod passing through the front barrel lump and acts upon cocking bars just below and behind the front Purdey underbolt.

FACTORY AMMO Ammunition that has been assembled by a commercial vendor of ammunition and sold in retail stores, as opposed to handloads that have been assembled by individuals and are not typically sold.

FAILURE TO EXTRACT A semiautomatic firearm malfunction in which the extractor fails to move the empty case out of the way as the slide travels back. A failure to extract often causes double-feed malfunction.

FAILURE TO FEED A semiautomatic firearm malfunction in which the slide passes entirely over the fresh round, failing to pick it up to insert into the chamber as the slide returns to battery.

FAIL TO FIRE A failure of the firearm to discharge after the trigger has been pulled. It can be one of two types: 1) a complete misfire, or 2) a delayed fire.

FANCY BACK Any one of a number of different contour variations to the rear of a boxlock action abutting the head of the stock to improve the look of a plain gun.

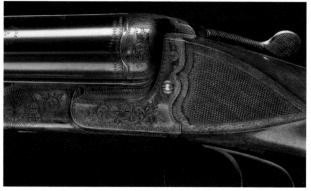

▲ Fancy back.

FEED MECHANISM, AUTOMATIC A system for reloading a firearm utilizing some of the energy realized from firing a cartridge.

FEED RAMP An inclined, polished area on a repeating firearm, just behind the chamber, that helps guide a cartridge into the chamber when pushed forward by the closing bolt.

FEED THROAT A component that guides a cartridge from the magazine to the chamber.

FENCES Hemispherical outgrowths of the receiver of a double gun that mate with the breech ends of the barrels. The term derives from the flanges (or fences) in this position on a muzzle-loading gun that were designed to protect the eyes of the shooter from sparks and escaping gases.

▲ Fences.

FERLACH A city in south-central Austria that, since the 1500s, has been the center of guild makers of fine sporting guns and rifles. Even if no maker's name be found on a Ferlach-built gun, his identity should be revealed by the first two digits of the serial number.

FFL (FEDERAL FIREARMS LICENSE) Under federal law, to ship a firearm a selling dealer must have in his possession a copy of the receiving dealer's license.

FIELD GRADE A generic term for a plain, functional firearm used to hunt in rough terrain where one wouldn't want to subject an expensive, deluxe grade gun to a greater risk of damage.

FIELD GUN A shotgun of relatively light weight for carrying over great distances for upland birds. Recoil is not an important factor in a field gun because shots are generally few and far between.

FIGURED WALNUT Every piece of walnut is different in color and in figure. Some are fancy, streaked, fiddle-backed, burled, or have a flame pattern. You must be very careful when you choose a gunstock blank. It is important to be sure the grain flows through the area where the grip, the narrowest part of the stock, is carved out. Otherwise, it will be more susceptible to breakage as a result of the stress of firing. A blank of walnut is determined by Roman numerals, with I being the plainest grade and IV the fanciest, followed by the finest of all, Exhibition Grade:

Grade I	Plain, with limited or no grain. A Grade I walnut stock makes for a strong field gun.
Grade II	Some grain and color
Grade III	Very good grain and color
Grade IV	Beautiful, tight grain and swirls and excellent color
Exhibition Grade	The highest grade walnut stock, rich in color and full of dramatic grain.

FINGERS The forward-most part of a sidelock gun's stock; the slender flutes of wood extending along the lockplates, heading up to the receiver body. Also known as horns.

FIREARM An assembly of a barrel and action from which a projectile is propelled through a deflagration of propellant as a result of combustion. A rifle, shotgun, or handgun using gunpowder as a propellant is a firearm according to the federal definition under the 1968 Gun Control Act. Air guns are not, by definition, firearms.

FIRING LINE A line, either imaginary or marked, from which people shoot their firearms down range.

FIRING PIN The narrowly rounded, pointed component of a shotgun that strikes the primer or the rim of a cartridge to initiate ignition in order to fire the cartridge.

FIRING PIN, FLOATING A type of firing pin that is unrestrained by a spring or other mechanical means.

FIRING PIN INDENT (1) The impression made by the firing pin in the primer cup of the centerfire primer or the rim of rimfire cartridges. (2) A measure of the kinetic energy delivered by the firing pin.

FIRING PIN, INERTIA A type of firing pin in which the forward movement is restrained until it receives the energy from a hammer blow. It is slightly recessed in the breech face before being struck by the hammer and is shorter in length than the housing in which it is contained. Upon hammer impact, it flies forward using only its own kinetic energy to fire the primer.

FIRING PIN PROTRUSION The distance the firing pin protrudes from the breech face when it is in its most forward position.

FLAKING The tendency for bluing to deteriorate into rust.

FLASH HOLE The hole in the end of a battery cup primer used in shotshells.

FLASH SUPPRESSANT A material that is added to propellant for the purpose of reducing muzzle flash.

FLASH SUPPRESSOR A muzzle attachment designed to reduce muzzle flash. Also called Flash Hider. A flash suppressor is not a silencer.

FLAT-POINT CHECKERING A traditional English style of checkering gunstocks whereby the diamonds are not brought to sharp points. While not offering as firm a grip as standard sharp point-pattern checkering, it is both more durable and allows the grain structure of the wood to show through better.

FLINCH (v) To jerk unconsciously at the instant of firing a shotgun in anticipation of felt recoil.

FLOOR PLATE The bottom of a box magazine. May be hinged, sliding or immovable.

FLUID STEEL BARRELS Stronger than Damascus steel and used for gun barrels since the early 1860s, fluid steel barrels can be credited to two men. Whitworth fluid-compressed steel was invented in 1865 by British engineer Sir Joseph Whitworth (1803–1887) in Birmingham, England. Alfred Krupp (1812–1887), son of Friedrich Krupp, who founded the cast-steel factory *Krupp'sche Gusstahifabrik* (Cast Steel Works) in Essen, Germany, invented a slightly different homogeneous steel and introduced the Bessemer process to mass-produce gun barrels. The process involves casting a solid piece of steel that is then bored.

FLUTED COMB A carved, concave groove at the point of the comb that affords a comfortable position for the thumb as it wraps over the wrist.

FLYER (1) A shot considerably outside the normal group on a target. (2) A shot considerably outside the normal range with regards to velocity or pressure.

FOLLOWER A smooth plate across which cartridges slide when loaded into a chamber.

FORCING CONE The tapered breech of a shotgun barrel between the chamber and the bore that provides the transition between the exterior and the interior diameters of the cartridge. Older shotguns that shot thick-walled paper cartridges with fiber wads will usually have more abrupt forcing cones. Modern shotguns have more gradual, longer forcing cones that are designed to accommodate modern plastic shells with obturating plastic shot-cup wads, which have thinner walls than paper cartridges.

FORE-END Also called the forearm. The forward part of a one-piece stock. The fore-end, barrel set, and action/buttstock are the three major dismountable components of a break-open gun. The fore-end secures the barrels to the receiver, often houses the ejector mechanism, and protects the non-shooting hand from hot barrels.

FORE-END, ANSON FASTENING A fastening method of the fore-end of double-barreled shotguns that utilizes a spring-loaded bolt extending beyond the tip of the fore-end.

▲ Fore-end with Anson fastening.

FORE-END, BEAVERTAIL A broad fore-end, wrapping partially around the barrel(s) to give a more positive grip and to better protect the hand from hot barrels than does a splinter fore-end.

FORE-END IRON The steel skeleton of the fore-end into which any moving parts are fitted and which mates to and revolves about the action knuckle when the gun is opened.

FORE-END, SPLINTER A slender English-style fore-end on a break-open gun, designed to retain the barrels on the receiver when the gun is opened and to house the ejectors—not necessarily to provide a hand-hold. Splinter fore-end guns are more properly grasped by the barrels just ahead of the fore-end. The closer one's hand is to the line of the bore and to the line of sight, the better one's hand-to-eye coordination. Many people consider the splinter fore-end more graceful than a beavertail fore-end on a classic double gun.

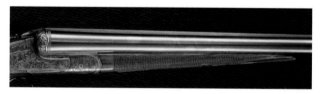
▲ Fore-end splinter.

FOULING The gritty residue removed from the barrel and all areas of the firearm in order to clean it.

FOUR RULES, THE The four universal rules of firearms safety, which apply every single time a firearm is handled in any way or for any reason.

- Rule 1: Always assume a gun is loaded.
- Rule 2: Never point your gun at anything other than your target.
- Rule 3: Never put your finger on the trigger unless you are focused on the target and ready to fire.
- Rule 4: Be sure of your target and what is behind, in front of, and around it before you pull the trigger.

FRENCH GRAY An acid-etched or phosphate finish, applied typically to shotgun actions, forming a gray-colored, nonreflecting matte finish that also provides some protection from rust. Also called gray-etched.

FRICTION RING A metallic ring surrounding the magazine tube to retard the opening velocity of a recoil-operated shotgun.

FULL COCK On an exposed-hammer firearm, the position of the hammer when the firearm is ready to fire.

FURNITURE British term for the visible small steel parts of a double gun: top lever, trigger guard, safety tab, fore-end release lever, etc. These parts are normally blued.

G

GAPE The degree to which the barrel(s) of a break-open gun drop down; the size of the opening space—which should be sufficient to allow for ease of loading, unloading, and properly functioning ejection. A good gape is easier to achieve on a side-by-side than an over/under, where the bottom barrel is well-enclosed by the action body.

▲ Gape.

GAS-OPERATED An automatic or semiautomatic firearm in which the propellant gases are used to unlock the breech bolt and then to complete the cycle of extraction and ejection. This is accomplished usually in conjunction with a spring that returns the operating parts to battery.

GAS VENT A passage built into a firearm to allow the safe conduct of unexpected gas, as from a pierced primer, to minimize damage both to the gun and to the shooter.

GATE, LOADING A spring-loaded cover for the loading port.

GAUGE Frequently abbreviated "ga.," the system of measurement for the internal bore diameter of a smooth-bore firearm based on the diameter of each of that number of spherical lead balls whose total weight equals one pound. The internal diameter of a 12-gauge shotgun barrel equals the diameter of a lead ball weighing 1/12 pound. The British use the word *bore*. The .410-caliber shotgun barrel is measured by caliber.

GLASS BEDDING The application of a mixture of fiberglass and resin between the action and/or barrel and stock.

GRAINS A unit of weight measurement used for bullets and gunpowder. The more grains, the heavier the bullet. Powder is also measured by grains, but this is generally of interest only to reloaders. There are seven thousand grains to a pound.

GREENER CROSSBOLT A tapered round bar, operated by the top lever of a shotgun, passing transversely behind the standing breech of a side-by-side gun and through a matching hole in a rib extension to strengthen the lock-up. Scott's crossbolt operates similarly but is square in cross-section.

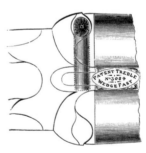
▲ Greener crossbolt.

GREENER SAFETY A safety catch mounted to the left side of a gun, just behind the receiver, that swivels fore and aft on a transverse rod. Often seen on drillings as well as on Greener's own shotguns.

GRIP The narrow part of the gunstock directly behind the action and trigger that is gripped by the shooting hand.

Types of Grips

FULL PISTOL GRIP Preferred grip for target shooting and guns where more control for the hand is preferred.

▲ Full pistol grip.

HALF-PISTOL GRIP Found on some Browning A-5 shotguns and Browning Superposed shotguns. There are two types for the Superposed: round knob, long tang (RKLT) and round knob, short tang (RKST). Also stocked on older Parker Brothers shotguns.

▲ Half pistol grip.

PRINCE OF WALES A grip commonly used on shotguns made for the field.

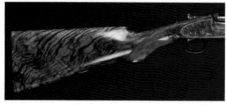

▲ Prince of Wales grip.

STRAIGHT ENGLISH GRIP, or STRAIGHT GRIP Preferred for driven shooting on double guns.

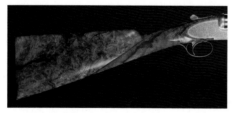

▲ Straight English grip.

GUARD SCREW A screw that extends from the trigger guard into and through the stock.

GUILD GUN A gun whose parts are crafted by individuals who specialize in making specific gun parts,

such as a barrel maker, and then assembled and finished by a gunmaker, who may or may not stamp his name on the gun but will, in any event, stamp an identifying number. Guild gunmakers were a major industry in Germany; however World War II destroyed the factories and workshops. Guilds continue to operate as they have since the 1500s in Italy, Spain, and Germany, among other countries, which require each parts maker to achieve a certain high standard.

GUN A gun refers to any firearm in the United States. In the United Kingdom, a gun is a shotgun. It also refers to a person shooting a shotgun from a butt at a formal driven shoot.

GUNPOWDER Chemical substances of various compositions, particle sizes, shapes, and colors that, on ignition, serve as a propellant. Ignited smokeless powder emits minimal quantities of smoke from a gun's muzzle; the older black powder emits relatively large quantities of whitish smoke.

GUN ROOM A room that is maintained for the purpose of keeping guns in storage, on display, or for repair.

GUN, SKEET A shotgun designed for use in the game of Skeet. Usually made with a cylinder bore or similar type choke.

GUN, SPORTING A firearm intended primarily for sport and recreation.

GUN, TRAP A shotgun specifically designed for the game of trapshooting.

GUNSTOCK The wooden part of the gun to which the barrel and action are attached. A gunstock may also be made of synthetic material and fiberglass.

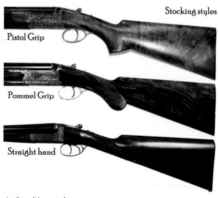

▲ Stocking styles.

H

HAIR TRIGGER A trigger that breaks from an extremely light touch.

HALF-COCK A middle position for an external hammer that effectively provides a safety function. With a firearm with non-rebounding hammers, when on half-cock, the firing pin will not rest on the firing pin. And, whether rebounding or non-rebounding, an inadvertent pull of the trigger should not release the hammer and fire the gun.

HALF GRIP Round knob, semi pistol grip. Also known as the Prince of Wales grip.

HAMMER The part of a gun lock, which driven by a spring and released by a pull of the trigger, falls and (usually via an intervening firing pin) strikes the detonating primer of the load and discharges the gun. Hammers may be external or internal.

HAMMERLESS A firearm with a coil-spring-actuated firing pin, or with its hammer enclosed inside the action body.

HAMMER SPUR The thumb-piece on the top rear of the hammer that enables it to be manually drawn back to full cock.

HAND The British word for the wrist, or grip, of a shotgun or rifle.

HAND-DETACHABLE LOCKS The firing mechanism of a break-open gun that may be removed for inspection or cleaning without the use of tools. The release latch may be plainly visible or concealed. A feature typically seen on sidelock guns but also on the Westley Richards droplock boxlock action.

HANDLOADING The process of assembling cartridge case, shot, wads, and primer to produce a complete cartridge with the use of hand tools in the interest of loading for firearms for which cartridges are not available, experimenting with loads to achieve better performance, or to save money. *Not to be attempted without knowledgeable instruction and careful study of the process.*

HEAD The forward end of a buttstock where it meets the receiver. The bulk of the shotgun's recoil when fired is absorbed by the head.

HEAD CLEARANCE The distance between the head of a fully seated cartridge and the face of the breech bolt when the action is in the closed position.

HEADSPACE The distance from the face of the closed breech of a firearm to the surface in the chamber on which the cartridge case seats.

HEADSTAMP Markings stamped into the base of a brass cartridge case, normally identifying the maker's name and caliber.

▲ Headstamp. Photo: Ashton Drake (CC BY-SA 2.0).

HEEL Of a gun stock, the top of the butt, when the gun is in position on the shoulder to be fired, is called the heel.

HEEL AND TOE PLATES Protective plates made of steel or horn that cover the top and bottom of a gunstock butt only leaving wood exposed in the center.

HIGH BRASS Powerfully loaded shotgun cartridges for hunting with longer than standard brass end-caps.

HINGE-PIN A short cylindrical rod of hardened steel running laterally near the front of the bar of a break-open gun's action around which the barrel hook revolves when the gun is opened. Over time and heavy use, the hinge-pin can wear down and a gun may shoot loose or "come off the face." The proper cure for this condition is to replace the hinge-pin with a new one, slightly oversized, to compensate for wear on both itself and on the barrel hook.

HOLD-OPEN TOP LEVER A catch built into the receiver of a break-open gun to keep the top lever in its extreme right position when the barrels are removed. As the barrels are mounted and the breech closed, the barrels contact some kind of release pin and the top lever automatically returns to the center locked position. Because, however, it requires a separate act to find and to depress this tiny tab to re-center the top lever on a broken-down gun, this feature may be irritating when trying to put a gun away in its case.

HOOK A concave, semi-cylindrical surface cut into the forward lump of a barrel set of a break-open firearm that revolves about the hinge-pin when the gun is opened.

HORNS The forward-most part of a sidelock gun's stock; the slender flutes of wood extending along the lockplates, heading up to the receiver body. Also called fingers.

HULL The outer container of a shotgun shell, typically made of plastic or paper with a metal base.

I

INLAY A form of decoration performed on firearms whereby precious metal, usually gold or sterling silver, is hammered into recesses in the steel surface that have been undercut at the edges so that the soft gold flows under the overlapping steel and is locked securely in place. The inlay is then engraved, carved, and chased into the image of a game animal, linework, or lettering.

▲ Inlay.

INLETTING The process of precisely carving out recesses in wooden stocks with gouges, chisels, and scrapers to accept the steel components of a firearm.

▲ Inletting.

INTERCEPTING SEAR A second sear poised just behind a second notch in the hammer. It is possible that when a cocked firearm is dropped or sharply jarred, a single sear could jump out of its notch and the hammer could fall, firing the gun accidentally. In this event, an intercepting sear would engage before the hammer could fall completely, preventing an accidental discharge.

INVOLUNTARY PULL When a gun is fired and it recoils, the shooter grips the gun tighter, inadvertently pulling the trigger again. The first reliable single trigger, accommodating the involuntary pull, was patented by John Robertson of Boss.

J

JAM A malfunction that prevents the action from operating. Jams may be caused by faulty or altered parts, defective ammunition, poor maintenance, or improper use of the firearm.

JOINT A place where two or more parts come together so as to permit motion. The term is sometimes used in reference to the pivot point of a hinged action.

JONES UNDERLEVER A lever mounted to the underside of the receiver of a break-open gun that extends halfway around the trigger guard to a knob. It is one of the strongest and most durable shotgun levers.

▲ Jones underlever.

JUMP The upward and rearward recoiling movement of a firearm when it is fired.

K

KEEL A spacer used to maintain center distance of double barrels during manufacture.

KEEPER'S GUN A gamekeeper's field-grade, everyday gun.

KERSTEN LOCK A type of crossbolt behind the breech face. Double Kersten locks are two, one on either side of the barrel set. This system is found on Merkel and Simson over/under shotguns.

◀ Kersten lock.

KEY FASTENER A horizontal wedge that secures the fore-end of a vintage gun. Also called a cross-pin or a wedge fastener.

KICK Slang for recoil.

KICKER Draws back a rod that forces home a cartridge on some recoil-operated firearms. Also refers to some break-open shotgun ejectors.

KIPPLAUF German term for a break-open gun derived from *kippen* (tilt) and *lauf* (barrel).

KNUCKLE The curved, forward end of the bar of a break-open action. It should be greased lightly and regularly to avoid wear on the bearing surfaces.

KRUPP Germany's pre-eminent, family-owned steel-making company, established in 1587 in Essen, Germany. Known for firearms barrel-making and cannon production.

L

LAP/LAPPING To polish the bore of a shotgun barrel with a fine abrasive paste in order to remove and minimize fouling.

LEAD To aim at a spot just in front of a moving target so the target moves into the line of fire as the trigger is pulled.

LEFAUCHEUX, CASIMIR (1802–1852) French gunsmith who patented the first efficient, self-contained cartridge system.

LENGTH-OF-PULL (1) The distance between the face of the trigger and the rearmost surface of the gun. (2) The distance the trigger must travel before it fires the gun.

LENGTH, OVERALL Of a firearm, the dimension measured parallel to the axis of the bore from the muzzle to a line at a right angle to the axis, and tangent to the rearmost point of the buttplate. Relating to ammunition, the greatest dimension of a loaded cartridge, i.e., from face of the head to the crimp of the shotshells.

LIFTERS Extractors.

LIMB An internal moving part of the action, such as a transfer bar, plunger, sear, cam, lever, and hammer.

LINE ENGRAVING A form of engraving in which the entire pattern or design consists of shallow line cuts as opposed to engraving done in bas-relief. This type of engraving is often found on the metal parts of firearms.

LINE OF DEPARTURE The direction in which a projectile is moving when it leaves the muzzle of a firearm.

Also defined as the tangent to the trajectory at the muzzle. *See also* **Trajectory**

LOAD (1) A shotgun cartridge. (2) Inserting a cartridge into the chamber of a shotgun in anticipation of firing a shot.

LOAD, BRUSH A shotshell load specifically designed to provide a widely spread pattern at a close range in a choked gun. Also called spreader load, scatterload, bush load, thicket load.

LOAD, FIELD A shotshell loaded for hunting small game animals and birds.

LOAD, SQUIB A cartridge that creates projectile velocity and sound that is lower than normal.

LOCK The mechanism by which a pull of the trigger causes a blow to be struck to the detonating primer.

LOCK ENERGY The amount of energy delivered to the primer from the firing pin blow.

LOCK FRAME Absorbs the shock of the recoiling parts prior to the bolt unlocking and opening.

LOCKPLATE The plate on the side of a sidelock that covers, and attaches, the components of the lock mechanism.

LOCK, REBOUNDING A type of firing mechanism, wherein the hammer or striker after forward movement retracts slightly to a rest position.

LONG GUN A firearm with an extended barrel, designed to be fired while in contact with the shoulder of the shooter. Long guns include rifles and shotguns.

LOW BRASS Cartridges used primarily for target shooting with shorter brass end-caps than powerfully loaded shotgun cartridges intended for hunting.

LUG The fore-end fastener fitted to the underside of a set of shotgun barrels.

LUG, RECOIL A block or plate on the bottom of a receiver and/or barrel to transfer the recoil to the stock.

LUMP, CHOPPER A type of lump which is integral with the barrel.

LUMPS The projections in the breech of a side-by-side action. Also known as bifurcated lumps and chopper lumps. The lumps of a best gun are concealed by the floorplate.

LUMPS, BIFURCATED Divided lumps mainly on over/under shotguns that mount on each side of the lower barrel to reduce the height of the receiver-barrel assembly.

M

MAGAZINE A receptacle that can accommodate and feed more than one cartridge into the chamber utilizing spring-loaded pressure. Types of magazines include box, drum, rotary, and tubular, and may be fixed or removable.

MAGAZINE BOX A receptacle that holds stacked cartridges before they are fed into the chamber one at a time.

MAGAZINE CATCH Releases the magazine. Also known as a magazine latch or magazine release.

MAGAZINE FOLLOWER A spring-activated device that moves cartridges in a magazine into the feeding position.

MAGAZINE PLUG (1) A part inserted in a magazine to reduce its capacity. (2) A part in the end of a tubular magazine that closes the end and retains the spring.

MAGAZINE SPRING The spring in a magazine that exerts its thrust against the follower.

MAGAZINE, TUBULAR A metal tube in which cartridges are loaded end-to-end.

MAGNUM A term indicating a relatively heavily loaded shotshell and a gun safely constructed to fire it. It generally indicates a round which cannot be interchanged with other loadings of the same caliber.

MAINSPRING Also known as a hammer spring. The spring that drives energy to the hammer of a shotgun.

MALFUNCTION Failure of a firearm to perform properly or at all.

MANTON, JOSEPH Inventor, founder of the London gun trade, father of the modern shotgun, and mentor to famous gunmakers who followed, including Thomas Boss, William Greener, Charles William Lancaster, Joseph Lang, and James Purdey.

MANUAL SAFETY A safety the shooter must deliberately disengage in order to fire the gun. The most common form of safety mechanism is a switch that, when set to the safe position, prevents a pull of the trigger from firing the firearm.

MARKINGS Words or symbols, stamped, rolled, cast, or engraved, on a firearm designating the manufacturer, model, origin, caliber or gauge, choke, material, and so on.

MARKSMANSHIP Consistently shooting the target accurately.

MASTER EYE The dominant eye that takes over when pointing the shotgun at the target.

MATTE/MATTE FINISH A dull nonreflecting metallic surface.

METAL FOULING Metallic material left in the bore after firing.

MIRAGE Heated air that deflects light rays and compromises the shooter's vision when looking over a hot barrel.

MISFEED A failure of the next round to completely enter the chamber. Misfeeds and failures to feed are very similar. A failure to feed is when a round never leaves the top of the magazine. A misfeed is a round that leaves the magazine but does not enter the chamber.

MISFIRE A dangerous condition as a result of a cartridge that fails to fire when an attempt to fire it is made. It can be caused by either a defective cartridge or defective firearm. The term is frequently misused to indicate a negligent discharge of a firearm. Hangfire is when there is a delay between pulling the trigger and firing the cartridge. *Always count to thirty before opening the breech of a gun that misfires.*

MONOBLOCK BARRELS A pair of barrels that are machined from one solid piece of steel, fitted with barrel tubes, after which the ribs are attached.

MONOGRAM A personalized marking consisting of initials, often artistically engraved or inlaid, in which the letter for the surname is central and prominent.

MONTE CARLO COMB An elevated comb that lifts the cheek higher while keeping the heel of the stock low. Also known as a hogback comb.

MOUTH The open end of a cartridge case from which the shot charge is expelled when fired.

MULLERED BORDER A borderline at the edge of a checkered area on a gun stock. Typical of fine guns. A mullering tool is used to make a mullered border.

▲ Mullered border as well as a teardrop.

MUZZLE The end of a barrel from which the shot is discharged.

MUZZLE BLAST The noise that results when a cartridge is fired from a shotgun.

MUZZLE BRAKE A perforated fitting attached to the muzzle of a shotgun barrel that is designed to deflect some of the forward-rushing gases; this reduces recoil at the expense of increased muzzle blast. A ported barrel is a barrel with a built-in muzzle brake.

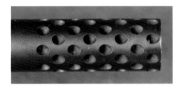
▲ Muzzle brake.

MUZZLE CONTROL Being aware of and responsible for which direction your firearm is pointed at all times and always keeping it pointed in a safe direction.

MUZZLE ENERGY The power of a projectile or a load of shot at the point it exits the muzzle of a firearm. Muzzle energy is measured in foot-pounds.

MUZZLE FLASH The visible light of a muzzle blast, which expels high temperature, high pressure gases from the muzzle of a firearm. The blast and flash are caused by the combustion of the gunpowder and any remaining unburned gunpowder mixing with the ambient air. The size and shape of the muzzle flash is dependent on the type of ammunition being used, individual characteristics of the firearm, and any devices attached to the muzzle (such as a muzzle brake or flash suppressor).

MUZZLE JUMP The generally upward motion of the muzzle of a firearm that occurs upon firing.

MUZZLE VELOCITY The speed of a projectile or a load of shot at the point that it exits the muzzle of a firearm, normally expressed in feet per second.

N

NATIONAL FIREARMS ACT OF 1934 (NFA 34) The set of federal regulations that govern the sale and possession of certain classes of firearms. The act:

- Requires the registration of all fully automatic firearms.
- Requires the registration of all sawed-off rifles and shotguns.
- Requires the registration of firearm silencers.
- Imposes a $200 transfer tax on the above items.
- Regulates the sale, manufacture, transfer, and transportation of the above items, among other things.

THE NATIONAL RIFLE ASSOCIATION (NRA) Organization that coordinates shooting events on a national level, provides firearms training to civilians and law enforcement, fights restrictive firearms legislation, and supports the constitutional right of law-abiding citizens to bear arms.

NEGLIGENT DISCHARGE (ND) The unplanned discharge of a firearm caused by a failure to observe the basic safety rules, not a mechanical failure of the gun. *See* **The Four Rules**

NIB (NEW IN BOX) A new gun that has never been fired in/with its factory box.

NITRO POWDER An explosive powder made from nitrated organic materials, such as nitroglycerine and guncotton.

NITRO PROOF A gun that is tested at an official proof house and marked on the barrels as safe for use.

NON-CORROSIVE A term applied to primers that contain no chemical compounds that could produce corrosion or rust in gun barrels.

NON-REBOUNDING LOCK In the lock of a hammer gun, the lowered hammer rests on the firing pin, which then rests on the primer of the chambered cartridge. When the hammer is pulled back and released, it strikes the firing pin and sets off the cartridge.

▲ Non-rebounding lock.

NSSF National Shooting Sports Foundation

O

OFF-FACE A break-open gun that has been well-used and not well-cared for loosens up at the breech end of the barrels. Easy to determine by shaking the unloaded gun.

OIL BOTTLE A small, screw-top brass vessel fitted with a dipper used to apply a drop of oil to lubricate a metal surface.

OVER-BORE A shotgun whose barrel bore diameter is greater than the SAAMI maximum for that gauge.

OVER-BORE CAPACITY A firearm chambered for a cartridge that contains more powder than normally burned in that bore diameter and volume.

OVER/UNDER (OVER AND UNDER, O/U) A shotgun with two barrels of equal size stacked one above the other. An over/under is casually referred to as a stacked gun.

P

PAIR OF SHOTGUNS Two identically built shotguns that make up a MATCHED PAIR. Both guns have the same barrel lengths, are choked the same, stocked from the same piece of wood, and weigh the same. They are numbered "1" and "2" and fitted together in a custom English-style leather gun case. A matched pair is specifically made for driven shooting. As birds come in high and fast, a loader works in tandem with the shooter to reload one gun and hand it to him from slightly behind after he has fired both barrels. This permits uninterrupted shooting.

PANCAKE CHEEKPIECE A cheekpiece confined completely to the side of a buttstock as opposed to one in which the forward borderline flows into the wrist or up and over the comb.

▲ Pancake cheekpiece.

PARKERIZING A nonreflecting, rust-resistant finish used on metal surfaces of some shotguns. Also referred to as phosphatizing or phosphate coating.

PATTERN The distribution of shot fired from a shotgun. Generally measured as a percentage of pellets striking in a thirty-inch circle at forty yards. Some skeet guns are measured with a thirty-inch circle at twenty-five yards.

PELLETS (PROJECTILE) Small, spherical lead, steel, or bismuth balls loaded into a cartridge. The number and weight of the pellets determine the size of the charge.

PENETRATION The depth that shot pellets impact the target.

PIGEON GUN A double-barreled shotgun choked full and full. Pigeon guns are usually deluxe grade guns with highly figured walnut stocks and fine engraving in keeping with the upper class sport of *columbaire* and *zurito*, live pigeon shooting tournaments famously held in Monaco and Havana that command large purses. Once—and only once—was pigeon shooting an Olympic sport at the 1900 Paris Summer Olympic Games.

PIN British word for a gun screw.

PIN, HINGE A cylindrical hinge in the front of the action upon which the barrel(s) of a break-open shotgun pivot.

PISTOL GRIP CAP A decorative disk of metal, contrasting wood, horn, plastic or other material applied to the flat of a pistol grip to finish off that part of the gunstock.

PISTON, GAS The component in a gas-operated shotgun that enables the release of gas to operate the action.

PIT/PITTING Occurs on the metal surfaces of guns and in the barrel bore, caused by oxidation which results in rust, forming tiny holes, abrasions, and dents. Pitting, found generally on older guns or guns that have been overused and abused, may be removed by reaming, or lapping, the barrel bore provided the barrel walls have not been thinned by previous lapping. It is almost impossible to resurrect the original condition of a pitted receiver.

PITCH The angle of the butt of a gun in relation to the line of sight.

POINT SHOOTING Shooting without using the sights. Point shooters use body position or other cues to provide a sense of where the shots will land.

PORT (1) The opening in the barrel wall that allows gas to operate the action and reduce recoil. (2) The opening in a receiver in which cartridges are loaded and ejected.

PORTED BARREL A barrel with a series of holes or slots drilled near the muzzle. When a cartridge is discharged, the force of the gas down the barrel encounters the holes and pulls the gun forward, off the shoulder, thus reducing felt recoil and counteracting muzzle jump.

PORT, LOADING The opening in a receiver where a cartridge is loaded directly into the chamber or the magazine.

POWDER (PROPELLANT) Common term for the propellant in a cartridge or shotshell. Gunpowder situated in front of the primer where it will be ignited by flames caused by the detonation of the primer compound. The chemical composition that, when ignited by a primer, generates gas. The gas propels the projectile.

POWDER, BLACK The earliest type of propellant that may have been invented by the Chinese and first used in firearms in the thirteenth century. A mixture of potassium or sodium nitrate, charcoal, and sulfur, a large cloud of smoke emits from the muzzle when the gun is fired.

POWDER BURN A pinhole that results from hot powder gases burning through the shotshell case.

POWDER CHARGE The amount of powder in a cartridge case.

POWDER FOULING Powder residue in the barrels of a shotgun. Pitting will result from barrels that are not cleaned after use.

POWDER, SMOKELESS A modern propellant containing mainly nitrocellulose or both nitrocellulose and nitroglycerin. Relatively little smoke is created when fired. Improper storage will result in the chemical decomposition of smokeless powder.

PREMATURE FIRING A cartridge that is accidentally fired before the breech or action of the shotgun is fully closed.

PRESSURE The force developed by the expanding gases generated by the combustion of the propellant.

PREWAR Before World War II.

PRIMER A small metal cup containing a detonating compound fitted into the head of a cartridge. When the primer is struck by the firing pin, the charge explodes, touching off the main powder charge inside the cartridge, thereby launching the shot charge.

PROOF Test-firing a gun at an official establishment in which an extra-heavy load is shot through the barrels to verify the safety of a gun. If the gun passes inspection, it is stamped on the barrel with a proof mark and the accepted load for which the gun was made.

PULL 1) The entire process of making the trigger complete its journey past the trigger break. 2) What a shotgun shooter yells when she wants a target (typically a clay pigeon) to be thrown into the air to shoot.

PULL, LENGTH-OF- The measurement on the stock from the center of the trigger to the center of the butt.

PULL-THROUGH A simple bore cleaning implement consisting of a string with a weight on one end and a small mop on the other that is pulled through the bore.

Q

QUARTERSAWN When a gun stock blank is cut from tree trunk, the annual rings should be oriented horizontally to maximize the grain, figure, and color in when the stock is finished. Also known as slab-sawn.

R

RAILS The metal surfaces upon which the slide of a semiautomatic shotgun travels forward and back as each shot is fired.

RANGE The horizontal distance between the shotgun and the target.

RANGE, EFFECTIVE The maximum distance at which a projectile can be expected to travel.

RANGE, MAXIMUM The greatest distance shot pellets can travel when fired at the optimum angle of elevation of the gun barrel.

REBARREL Replacing a barrel with another barrel.

REBOUNDING LOCK Designed by John Stanton in 1867, this system places the hammer at rest rearward and out of contact with the firing pin.

RECEIVER (1) The frame or action body of a shotgun. (2) The housing that contains the mechanism that fires the gun. A serial number must be stamped on the receiver in order for the gun to be legal.

RECESSED CHOKE The process of reaming the bore to a larger internal diameter a few inches back from the muzzle so that the existing diameter at the muzzle is constricted.

RECOIL The backwards movement of a gun when fired as a reaction to the force of the projectile moving down the barrel. Recoil is generally absorbed at the shoulder. The heavier the gun, the lighter the recoil. The more powerful the cartridge, the heavier the recoil. Sometimes called kick.

RECOIL-OPERATED A semiautomatic shotgun is operated by the force of recoil, which unlocks the breech bolt and completes the cycle of extracting, ejecting, and reloading the cartridge.

RECOIL PAD A pad made of leather, rubber, or nylon fitted to the butt of a shotgun to reduce the felt recoil or kick when the gun is fired. A checkered butt, horn, metal, or plastic buttplate does not absorb recoil. Slip-on recoil sleeves and pads are another option but will add length to the gunstock.

RECOIL SPRING A powerful spring that cushions the slide in its rearward travel and then sends the slide forward again with enough force to drive the fresh round firmly into the chamber. The strength of the recoil spring is calibrated to run the slide without any outside assistance.

REINFORCED FRAME Also known as a bolstered frame, is a double gun action that has been bolstered against heavy recoil with extra steel to strengthen it at its weakest point.

▲ Reinforced frame.

RELEASE TRIGGER Invented for American competition trapshooters who flinched when pulling the trigger in anticipation of recoil, gun noise, or, if the gun was not fitted to the shooter, a production shotgun that kicked painfully into the shoulder. This trigger is designed to fire the gun when you release it instead of when you pull it.

RELOAD A handloaded cartridge. Reloading is popular among recreational target shooters, competitive shooters, and bird hunters. In addition to being cost-effective, reloading enables shooters to develop ammunition specifically designed for her particular shooting discipline or game. Reloading is the process

of manually adding a new primer, propellant and wad to a fired cartridge case.

REPEATER A shotgun equipped with a magazine that holds more than one cartridge, thereby allowing the shooter to discharge the cartridges repeatedly without reloading.

RESTOCK Replacing the original gunstock with another.

RIB A steel strip soldered or fitted down the top center-line of a shotgun barrel or between the two barrels of a side-by-side gun. A rib aids in pointing the gun and can be solid or ventilated, swamped, polished, matted, broad, tall, narrow, etc., depending upon the design of the gun and, if a custom gun, the shooter's preference.

RIB, SOLID A solid raised surface above a barrel or barrels that functions as a sighting plane.

▲ Solid rib.

RIB, SWAMPED A rib with a concave sighting surface.

▲ Swamped rib.

RIB, VENTILATED A raised sighting surface separated from the barrel by means of posts that allow air to circulate to minimize heat waves in the line of sight. Also called a bridge rib.

▲ Ventilated rib.

RIGHT TO BEAR ARMS The unalienable right of all people in the United States, as stated in the Second Amendment to the US Constitution, to possess and use personally owned firearms for sport, recreation, personal protection, and the defense of the nation.

RIM A flange at the base of a cartridge case that allows easy removal of a spent case.

RISING BITE A lockup design for break-open guns, usually serving as a third fastener to strengthen the lockup of a gun with double Purdey underbolts. Designed by J. Rigby and T. Bissell, patent number 1141 of 1879. A loop-shaped rearward extension of the rib drops into a mating female recess in the top of the standing breech, surrounds a fixed central buttress, and is secured by a rising post at the rear. Often seen on Rigby double rifles of the period circa 1880–1920, after which even Rigby discontinued it in favor of the doll's head because it was exceedingly expensive to build. A marvelous feat of gunmaking.

▲ Rising bite.

RIVELLED A damaged shotgun barrel that has sustained slight ring-bulges or wrinkles from heavy loads or a minor obstruction in the bore. Difficult to repair and only in the hands of a professional gunsmith.

ROLLED TRIGGER GUARD A thickened, beaded edge on the side of a trigger guard bow with softened edges helps prevent finger injury when the gun recoils, as is more often the case with a sharp-edged trigger guard.

ROSE AND SCROLL ENGRAVING Traditional English engraving pattern consisting of tight scrollwork surrounding bouquets of roses.

ROUGH SHOOTING British term for hunting upland birds in the field with gun and dog for company.

ROUND Synonym for a cartridge, shell, and shotshell. Typical quantities are twenty and fifty rounds per box.

ROUND ACTION/ROUNDED BODY A unique trigger plate mechanism originated by Scottish gunmaker James MacNaughton (the MacNaughton round action bar-in-wood, also known as a triggerplate action) and adopted by gunmakers such as John Dickson & Son, David McKay Brown, and in Italy, the Ferlib round-action by Libero Ferraglio, a great gunsmith who did not receive in his lifetime the recognition he so justly deserved.

S

SAFETY A device on a firearm designed to provide protection against accidental or unintentional discharge when properly engaged. *Never, under any circumstances, assume a shotgun is safe even though the safety is on!*

SCALLOPED RECEIVER An embellished back edge of the receiver of a boxlock shotgun. Rather than being straight where it joins the wrist, it is scallop-shaped.

SCATTERGUN A casual term for a shotgun.

SEAR A sharp bar resting in the notch of a hammer that holds the hammer back under the tension of the mainspring. When the trigger is pulled, the sear moves from the notch, releases the hammer, and fires the gun.

SECOND AMENDMENT, THE The Second Amendment to the US Constitution that states, "A well-regulated Militia, being necessary to the security of a free State, the right of the people to keep and bear Arms, shall not be infringed."

SELF-OPENING ACTION Sometimes called a Beesley self-opening action, this applies to a break-open shotgun, where the barrels drop down by pressing the top lever of the action rather than manually breaking open the gun. This is desirable in a driven bird gun or in the cornfield where many birds are flying as it enables the wingshooter to load her gun more quickly.

SEMIAUTOMATIC Also called an autoloader, a firearm that cycles the action by utilizing recoil to fire, extract, eject, and reload once for each pull and release of the trigger. It is incorrect to refer to a semiautomatic as an automatic. A machine gun is an automatic weapon.

SHOOTING SPORTS There are a lot of different competitions and games that involve firearms. These are all referred to collectively as the shooting sports.

SHORT-STROKING On a pump-action firearm, being too gentle with the fore-end and either not pulling it all the way back at the beginning of the stroke or not shoving it all the way forward at the end of the stroke. This may result in a misfeed caused by the old case (or shell) failing to eject, or the gun will not fire when the trigger is pulled. The term is used most often to refer to pump-action shotguns; however, it is possible to short-stroke any type of firearm that requires the user to manually cycle the action (lever-action shotguns and rifles, for example).

SHOT Round projectiles, usually of lead or steel. Depending on shot size and load, a shell can contain from 45 to 1,170 shot.

SHOTGUN A smooth-bore long gun that shoots a group of pellets called shot instead of bullets. Depending on the bore size and the size of the pellets, the number of pellets range from less than ten to two hundred or more in a single shotgun cartridge. Shotguns are designed for shooting moving targets, such as flying birds or running rabbits, at close range.

SHOTSHELL Also known as a cartridge or shell. A round of ammunition containing multiple pellets for use in a shotgun.

SHOULDER To bring the butt of a long gun's stock to the shooter's shoulder, preparatory to firing the gun.

SIDE-BY-SIDE A double gun whose two barrels are juxtaposed side by side. A side-by-side shotgun is favored by many wingshooters for its broader sighting plane. Side-by-side guns preceded the commercial availability of over/under shotguns by more than a century.

SIDELOCK The action of a break-open shotgun in which the moving parts—the hammer, sear, mainspring—are mounted to, and covered by, the inside of a plate. A sidelock is considered superior, and is appreciably more expensive, than a boxlock. Less steel needs be removed from the bar of the action, which makes the action stronger.

SIDEPLATES Decorative steel plates mounted to a boxlock to give the gun the appearance of a sidelock.

SIGHT PICTURE What the shooter sees when looking through the sight at the target.

SILVER'S PAD A traditional red rubber English recoil pad with two matching flush-fitted rubber plugs covering the mounting screws.

SINGLE SET TRIGGER A single trigger set between four to six pounds pull that, when pushed forward, converts to a hair trigger. This trigger is usually fitted with a small set screw to adjust the weight of the hair trigger.

SKEET A shotgun shooting sport in which competitors attempt to break aerial targets directed toward them or crossing in front of them from different angles and elevations. Skeet is an Olympic shooting sport.

SKEET GUN A shotgun with an open choke specifically designed for clay target skeet shooting.

SLE Sidelock ejector.

SLEEVED BARRELS Bringing back an older or damaged gun whose barrels are dented, pitted, and no longer functional or safe. A sleeved gun should always be inscribed accordingly next to the proof marks. In England, a sleeved gun must be reproofed. *See also* **Barrel Sleeving**

SLUG More correctly a rifled slug or shotgun slug. An individual cylindrical projectile designed to be discharged from a shotgun. The term is often incorrectly used interchangeably with bullet.

SMOKELESS POWDER The propellant powder used in modern ammunition. It is not an explosive, but rather a flammable solid that burns extremely rapidly releasing a large volume of gas. Commonly called gunpowder and usually made from nitrocellulose, or nitrocellulose and nitroglycerin. It is classified as a flammable solid by the Department of Transportation.

SMOOTHBORE BARREL All shotguns have a smooth bore. A rifle bore, unlike a shotgun's, has interior grooves called rifling. Therefore, shotguns may be known as smoothbores.

SNAP CAPS Dummy cartridges usually made of brass that allow a shotgun to be dry-fired by cushioning the blow of the hammer without breaking the firing pin.

SOLID RIB A solid, sometimes hollow, matte- or smooth-finished strip of steel fitted from the muzzle to the breech of the top barrel of an over/under shotgun, and between the barrels of a side-by-side shotgun.

SPINDLE The vertical rod that connects the top lever to the underbolt in the action of a break-open shotgun.

SPORTING CLAYS A shotgun sport in which clay targets are shot from different stations that simulate upland birds, waterfowl, and rabbit hunting on a course over varying terrain.

SPORTING FIREARM Any firearm that can be used in a sport.

SQUIB LOAD An underpowered powder charge, an old deteriorated cartridge, or a cartridge with primer fitted but no powder at all, caused by a fault in cartridge loading, often insufficient to expel a projectile from the muzzle of a firearm. If such a blockage is not noticed (because of the greatly reduced recoil) and then cleared, the bullet from the next attempted shot could be blocked, the extreme pressure causing the barrel at least to bulge, and very possibly to burst.

SST/SINGLE SELECTIVE TRIGGER A single selective trigger allows the shooter to choose which barrel in a double gun she wishes to discharge first by the push of the bar or switch.

ST/SINGLE TRIGGER. A single, nonselective trigger that discharges a cartridge with one pull of the trigger. In a double gun, the trigger will discharge the first barrel and when pulled again, the second barrel.

STANCE The position in which the shooter stands as she prepares to take a shot.

STANDING BREECH The face of the action of a break-open firearm that houses the firing pins and receives the direct recoil of the fired round.

STEEL SHOT pellets made of steel designed as a non-toxic substitute for traditional lead shot. Unlike lead, steel pellets do not deform as they pass through the choke of a shotgun barrel. Steel shot should not, therefore, be fired through a tight choke (anything more than 0.015 inch constriction in a 12-gauge) or greater pressure will be generated than the gun was designed to handle. The result will be a ring bulge near the barrel's muzzle.

STOCK That part of a shotgun the shooter holds when shooting. A stock may be made of wood, fiberglass, wood laminate, or plastic. The barrel(s) and receiver of a shotgun are attached to, or inletted into, the stock.

STRIKE To draw-file and polish a barrel, or a pair of barrels, lengthwise, in preparation for blueing.

T

TAKEDOWN A firearm that can be separated into at least two subassemblies, primarily to accommodate the shotgun more conveniently for traveling in a half-length gun case, such as an English gun case or leg o'mutton gun case, rather than a full-length case.

TANG An extension of metal from behind the receiver that attaches to, and secures, the receiver to the gunstock. A tang may be short or long depending upon the gunstock wrist and grip. Also called a topstrap.

TARGET The object at which the shooter is aiming.

TARGET, CLAY A circular, domed disc made of pitch and limestone that shatters when it comes in contact with pellets of a shotshell after the gun is fired. Dimensions and weights of clays are regulated by trap and skeet shooting associations. They are often called clay pigeons.

TEARDROPS Carved detail in the shape of a teardrop that is located on either side of the wooden stock of a double gun directly behind the lockplates. Also called drop points.

THROUGH BOLT A simple method of attaching a buttstock to a break-open gun's receiver. Rather than using the traditional English method of upper and lower tang screws, augmented by positioned triggerplates, action screws, and trigger guard screws, a through bolt uses one long bolt only that extends from a longitudinal hole in the end of the butt through the wrist to the rear of the receiver. The steel bolt has the advantage of reinforcing the weak wrist area as well as snugging the stock tightly against the receiver, even in the case of less than totally perfect inletting. It has the disadvantage of making it more difficult for a gunsmith to bend a stock for better fit to the shooter. Common on Browning Superposed and Perazzi shotguns. Normally built with a short trigger guard tang for ease of disassembly.

THUMB SAFETY An external, manual safety typically disengaged with the firing hand thumb.

TIMING The proper adjustment of the various interrelated moving parts of a gun so that every operation works in proper sequence. For example, the spent cases in a double-barreled ejector shotgun will be ejected at the same instant, and with the same force, when the breech is opened.

TOE (OF A GUNSTOCK) The bottom of the butt when the gun is in position on the shoulder to be fired.

TOP LEVER A lever at the top of the receiver on a break-open gun. The shooter pushes the top lever to the right with her thumb to open the gun.

TRAJECTORY The path followed by the spread of shot pellets as it is subjected to given forces after a cartridge is fired from a shotgun.

TRAP (1) The machine used to throw clay targets for trap, skeet, sporting clays, and other shotgun games. (2) A game of competitive clay pigeon shooting on a trap field in which one trap machine is located sixteen yards in front of a straight line, firing rising targets perpendicular to and away from that line. Five competitors shoot five individual targets at each of five stations along that line. Each target is presented at slightly random vectors throwing outgoing and rising. Typically, targets are broken at about thirty-one to thirty-six yards and handicap targets may be broken as far as forty-five to fifty yards from the shooter. A trap gun usually has a single barrel that measures 30, 32, or 34 inches long and, for the competitive or advanced shooter, is generally choked full. A trap gun usually has a higher comb and is heavier than a field gun—heavier to better absorb recoil.

TRIGGER The release device that initiates cartridge discharge. Usually a curved, grooved, or serrated piece that is pulled rearward by the shooter's finger and activates the hammer or striker and fires the gun. Typically, pulling the trigger releases the striker or allows the hammer to fall, causing the firing pin to strike the primer. The primer then ignites the powder within the round. Burning gases from the powder force the bullet out of its case and through the barrel, causing the bullet to exit the muzzle end of the gun and strike the target. In addition to releasing the hammer or striker, some triggers may cock the hammer or striker, rotate a revolver's cylinder, deactivate passive safeties, or perform other functions.

TRIGGER GROUP The entire collection of moving parts that work together to fire the gun when the trigger is pulled. It may include trigger springs, return springs, the trigger itself, the sear, disconnectors, and other parts.

TRIGGER GUARD A bow-shaped flange, normally made of steel but sometimes of horn or other material, designed to cover the trigger well enough to reduce the possibility of accidental discharge while not being so obtrusive as to prevent the firing of a quick shot. Beaded or rolled trigger guards have a thickened, rolled edge on the side of a trigger guard bow. This extra detail allows the trigger guard to be made light, thin, and graceful while at the same time thick enough to avoid finger injury when the gun recoils.

TRIGGER LOCK A locking device put on a firearm to incapacitate the firing mechanism. This is a necessity in any home that has small children. *See the "Children and Guns" section of this book, page 15.*

TRIGGER PULL The process of pulling the trigger back from its forward-most position to its rearward-most position, causing the hammer to fall and the shot to fire.

TRY GUN A shotgun built with multiple adjustments for length-of-pull, drop at comb and heel, and cast-off used by custom gunmakers to establish the proper stock dimensions for a client ordering a custom gun or a gun fitter making adjustments on a gunstock.

U

UNDERBOLTS A sliding bar in a double-barreled shotgun that runs longitudinally through the watertable with openings through which the lumps of the barrels pass when the gun is closed. Patented by the London gunmaker James Purdey in 1883, most modern side-by-side shotguns are designed to lock closed using the Purdey Underbolt.

UNLOAD To remove all unfired ammunition from a firearm.

V

VC CASE A Very Compact trunk case with a wood frame, covered in leather or cloth, typically for a takendown double shotgun to save space. The toe of the stock slides under the muzzle end of the barrels. Also called a toe-under case and more commonly known as a leg o' mutton case.

VELOCITY The speed of a projectile at any point along its trajectory, designated in feet per second.

W

WAD The felt, paper, cardboard, or plastic disk component of a shotgun cartridge.

WAITING PERIOD A legally mandated delay between the purchase of a firearm and its delivery to the customer enforced in some jurisdictions.

WALNUT The type of wood most commonly used for gunstocks. Walnut is light, strong, and resilient to shock compared to other hardwoods due to its close grain, which gives the gunstock stability. Heavily grained walnut is extremely handsome in appearance with wonderful deep color and contrast. Several types of walnut are English, French, Circassian (*Juglans regia*), American Black (*Juglans nigra*), Turkish, Bastogne, and Claro. English walnut and Circassia forests, however, have been depleted since Edwardian times.

WATERTABLE The flat projection on the action of a side-by-side gun. The cocking arms, hinge-pin, and locking bolts are typically mounted inside the bar, below the watertable. The gun's serial number is always struck on the flat surface of the watertable.

▲ Watertable.

WEAPON A firearm or any instrument used in combat. The term should *never* be used in reference to sporting firearms.

WHIP The tendency of a barrel to rise at the muzzle under the pressure of recoil after the gun is fired.

WRIST The thinnest section of the shotgun stock, located between the receiver and the butt and gripped by the trigger-hand. Because it is the slimmest part of a gunstock, it is also the frailest and most vulnerable to breakage and the constant force of recoil when a gun is fired. A 4X or exhibition piece of walnut can be the most beautiful in the world, but if the grain fails to flow through that part of the blank apportioned to the wrist in just the right way, for strength, then the gunstock defeats its practical purpose because invariably, it will break under pressure or if the gun is dropped carelessly or by accident. The British call the wrist of a gunstock the hand.

Y

YOUTH STOCK A short stock, often ideally sized for teenagers, average-sized adult women, and small-statured adult men.